THE BEST BUSINESS STORIES
OF THE YEAR: 2002 *Edition*

Andrew Leckey, nationally syndicated investment columnist for the Chicago Tribune Company, is also contributing editor of the Quicken.com financial Web site. He is director of the Business Reporting Program of the Graduate School of Journalism at the University of California at Berkeley. Leckey was previously a financial anchor on the CNBC cable television network and TV reporter for the syndicated *Quicken.com Money Reports*. He received the National Association of Investors Corporation's Distinguished Service Award in Investment Education. His seven books include *The Morningstar Approach to Investing*, *Global Investing 2000*, and *The Lack of Money Is the Root of All Evil: Mark Twain's Timeless Wisdom on Money and Wealth for Today's Investor*.

Ken Auletta, guest editor, The Annals of Communications columnist for *The New Yorker*, has written four national best-sellers (two being national business best-sellers) among his eight books. Titles include *Three Blind Mice: How the TV Networks Lost Their Way*; *Greed and Glory on Wall Street: The Fall of the House of Lehman*; *The Highwaymen: Warriors of the Information Superhighway*; and *World War 3.0: Microsoft and Its Enemies*. In ranking him America's premier media critic, *The Columbia Journalism Review* concluded "no other reporter has covered the new communications revolution as thoroughly as has Auletta." He was named a Literary Lion by the New York Public Library and one of the twentieth century's top 100 business journalists by a national panel of peers.

THE BEST BUSINESS STORIES

OF THE YEAR: *2002 Edition*

THE BEST
BUSINESS STORIES
OF THE YEAR

2002 Edition

Edited by *Andrew Leckey*

with guest editor *Ken Auletta*

VINTAGE BOOKS
A DIVISION OF RANDOM HOUSE, INC.
NEW YORK

Library of Congress Cataloging-in-Publication Data

The best business stories of the year : 2002 edition / edited by Andrew Leckey,
with guest editor Ken Auletta.
    p.   cm.
  "A Vintage original"—t.p. verso.
  Vintage ISBN 0-375-72501-6
  Pantheon ISBN 0-375-42075-4
   1. Business. 2. Businesspeople. I. Leckey, Andrew. II. Auletta, Ken.
HF1008.B47 2002
070.4'49650—dc21   2001046569

CONTENTS

FOREWORD

THE ONGOING TECHNOLOGY meltdown, the troubled stock market and world economy, and the horrific terrorist attacks of September 11 made 2001 one of the most difficult and painful years in memory. It was a critical time when business journalists were depended upon more than ever before to report effectively on events, and investigate, explain, and ponder the future. These increased demands were being made amid staff cuts and constant second-guessing about whether previous coverage of the tech boom had been too naive. Yet the profession kept its collective head and overcame obstacles as it confronted both the enormous and the small issues. Business journalists maintained a sense of perspective and compassion throughout a year in which they provided some of the best coverage ever.

The Best Business Stories of the Year: 2002 Edition is abundant proof of the high quality of the writing in this field. It touches many topics. The focus moves from tragedy to scurrilous scams, from whimsical observations to defrocked analysts, from inside views of corporate power to ethics of genetics. This anthology underscores the importance of carefully crafted, well-researched stories about the concepts and personalities that matter. Young journalists entering the field definitely get the picture. As I began to write this foreword, I received a phone call from a student of mine at the Graduate School of Journalism at the University of California at Berkeley, who was enthusiastic about her business reporting internship at the *Financial Times*. "There are so many possibilities for the future," she said. "There's the whole world to cover, and business touches on almost everything."

This anthology's stories drive home several truths about the world that business journalists cover:

1. A business journalist can never be complacent, for unforeseen events can quickly and dramatically change what had been commonly accepted as fact.
2. Nothing is ever totally a "brand-new ball game," a term often bandied about during the tech rise, for business basics still require that a company have a viable product and make some money.
3. Journalists must use their sources judiciously, keeping in mind that those providing information could well be profiting from it.
4. Speculation about what the future will bring is a flawed, riveting, and neverending process.

A couple of years ago, reporters and editors were being snatched up by dot-coms offering outrageous salaries and stock options; later many of those same journalists were laid off. Magazines about the Internet, thick as phone books, with hundreds of pages of advertisements during the boom, shrunk to the size of church bulletins when the ad spigot was turned off. Some print publications were forced to merge or close and many of their on-line counterparts suffered the same fate. Whether it was despite the neverending tumult or because of it, business journalism is now the strongest it has ever been and topics covered by publications and Web sites are more diverse than ever before. No publication, whatever its charge, can overlook business coverage anymore. A sophisticated readership is demanding and receiving the solid writing that it deserves. Business journalism is important.

These are primarily longer stories of substance, though we have also included some noteworthy columns and shorter pieces. They merit attention whether the reader is sophisticated in finance or a novice. Few readers regularly see all the business and general publications whose stories are included here. Besides looking through hundreds of articles in print and on Web sites, we consulted editors, writers, and contest officials to seek additional recommendations. We hope that with the publication of this second edition of the anthology, even more people will become aware of our intentions and give us further suggestions so that we can continue to present as diverse a mix as possible each year. We like the stories in this edition and look forward to many more in the future. They reflect positively upon not only their authors but upon their editors and the overall organizations behind them. Everyone can take pride in them.

Many thanks to Ken Auletta, a gifted writer and media critic who as guest editor of this edition was both creative and thorough in making recommendations and assessing articles. I'm delighted that he accepted this challenge with enthusiasm, and our discussions over final selections were invigorating. Also appreciated were recommendations from Marshall Loeb, guest editor of the inaugural 2001 edition, and Bill Barnhart, president of the Society of American Business Editors and Writers (SABEW). Special thanks to my literary agent, Nat Sobel, with whom the initial idea for this series was hatched, and Edward Kastenmeier, the editor at Vintage Books who has capably turned each of the first two editions into reality.

Most of the stories in *The Best Business Stories of the Year: 2002 Edition* were originally published between July 1, 2000, and June 30, 2001. Selections for next year's anthology will be made on that same "fiscal year" basis. However, due to the compelling nature of events on September 11, 2001, we extended our usual timeline for this edition to include two pieces relating to the World Trade Center and Pentagon tragedies. Editors or writers who wish published or on-line business stories to be considered for next year's edition should send copies to Andrew Leckey, c/o *The Best Business Stories of the Year*, Vintage Books, 299 Park Avenue, New York, NY 10171.

—Andrew Leckey

INTRODUCTION

BUSINESS JOURNALISM AIN'T what it used to be. In the last century, it was the rare business leader—think Rockefeller or Ford, Carnegie or Morgan—who achieved celebrity status. Rarely did these moguls, or even those less well known, deign to speak with reporters. Business leaders were mysterious, remote figures. And they remained so because business profiles tended to be superficial. There were the one-dimensional hagiographies. Or there were the one-dimensional evil-empire exposés. (Each inflated the intelligence and control exerted by business leaders.) And there were the paint-by-number accounts of the profits and returns on investment and stock value and cash-on-hand and all those other indices that tell about financial health but not about why decisions are made and who makes them.

Missing from all three journalistic approaches was granularity, the vital human dimension one finds in a good biography or novel, where figures come alive because they are complex and real, not cartoonish. Business writing usually ignored the truths Shakespeare mined when he exhumed the rich complexity of human motives and behavior. Let's stick to business, they seemed to say, as if business were not populated by flesh-and-blood people. Then, as now, there were business crooks and louts and, luckily, investigative muckrakers like Ida Tarbell and Upton Sinclair and Thomas Nast to expose them. But the best business profiles were often to be found in the novels of Sinclair Lewis and Theodore Dreiser.

Today business more often comes alive in the pages of our magazines and newspapers. There are varied reasons for the surfeit of business coverage: the *People*ization of the media has expanded our appetite for celebrities; as the importance of business has grown, the centrality of government has receded; the democratization of the stock market—half the population now owns stock—has aroused more interest in business, as do twenty-four-hour all-business cable channels like CNBC and news shows devoted to commerce; and our culture, with a boost from those 100-richest lists, has come to equate business success with real success. Over the past decade or so we have placed business leaders on magazine covers and probed their personalities and explored their decisions and organizations. A CEO and his or her spouse are as likely to be glimpsed in the gossip columns as Sharon Stone. Business leaders hire platoons of media consultants and make themselves more available. This has resulted in a fair amount of congratulatory journalism—of the ten best companies, or the fifty best managers, or what-a-genius what's-his-name is—but also some very good, penetrating reporting. There is a danger when granted access that journalists will dwell too much on the human qualities of their subjects and not enough on what business bastards they are. But it is false journalistic machismo, not to say ignorant, to keep business executives at a safe distance, to assume they are all alike. The journalists' task is to convey reality, not stereotype. What usually separates the flaccid, celebratory profile from the revelatory one is a sense that the author writes for the reader, not the subject.

In each of the selections in this volume of the finest business reporting to appear in magazines and newspapers since July 1, 2000, we can tell that the author had his or her eye glued to the reader. We also spot a common theme knitting many of these pieces together: the human factor. As business leaders have become more accessible, we better understand that business decisions are not always based on objective dollars-and-cents logic. Sometimes a decision is swayed by vanity, or panic, or greed, anger, hubris, hope, pessimism, loyalty, pride, a corporate culture—in short, by the stuff that separates us from machines. We have little trouble understanding this when we cover politics. It has taken us longer to apply these lessons to business coverage, partly because we believed "the bottom line" made business decisions more rational.

It does, but only in part. We see in many of the pieces in this volume the role played by the softer stuff. James B. Stewart reminds us that Michael Milken's good deeds are overwhelmed by his continuing greed, and this *New Yorker* piece surely played a role in aborting a campaign to award a presidential pardon to the convicted insider trader. If only Stewart had written about Marc Rich! A more blatant exhibition of greed is laid out in Susan Harrigan's *Newsday* series on two Long Island brokers who were friends and stole millions from their clients. Joseph Nocera's *Fortune* profile of Idealab's founder, Bill Gross, captures both his hubris and that of the folks whose mindless exuberance contributed to the dot-com bubble. In related fashion, Peter Elkind's portrait of Mary Meeker and the role played by Wall Street analysts exposes her hubristic zealotry, as well as the greed of investment banks that create rewards for analysts to join the team by writing reports that serve to boost business. As the *Fortune* entries touched on the business environment that transformed the unacceptable into the acceptable, so Kara Swisher's early *Wall Street Journal* piercing of the corporate culture of Yahoo! shows how the business virtues of the team that led that company to success became the insularity that weakened it.

Paranoia and ignorance and misunderstandings—and missed opportunities—haunt a story with more momentous consequences—Alix M. Freedman and Steve Stecklow's account in *The Wall Street Journal* of African children dying because of Unicef and African leaders' banishment of the makers of baby formula. Mark Leibovich's profile of Oracle's Larry Ellison in *The Washington Post* shows how this CEO's vanity and childlike competition with Bill Gates can cloud his judgment. Vanity's cousin, pride, is the ingredient we observe in the *Bloomberg Markets* account by Stephanie Baker-Said and Jacqueline Simmons of Lazard's faltering, emperor-like chairman. Tommy Hilfiger manufactured a successful house of fashion, but as Rene Chun demonstrates in *New York* magazine, the fashion business—like everything else—is based on guess-work, and Hilfiger made some bad guesses. Kris Hundley of the *St. Petersburg Times* offers an astonishing picture of trying to farm shrimp in Nicaragua and running into a buzz saw of ignorance, politics, and cultural differences too vast to easily bridge. And David Brooks's exploration of student values in *The Atlantic* isn't, strictly speaking, a business story, but it is a potent picture of the value system of a college generation that often yearns to conform and aspires to business success.

The human factor is not the only theme explored in this collection. I don't believe that all or even most business decisions are swayed by non-bottom-line reasons, any more than I believe all governmental decisions are swayed by politics. There is a fresh look by Randall Lane in *Worth* magazine at financial powerhouse Charles Schwab refashioning himself as a formidable media mogul and, in the process, further blurring the line between news and marketing. Steve Silberman in *Wired* shows how an old medium—paper—may allow, with a special pen, a digital link to the world. Malcolm Gladwell, who has invented a new beat in *The New Yorker* that is a cross between science, anthropology, and common sense, explores the success of a quirky infomercial salesman who really has something to sell. A tiresome business buzzword—*brands*—is dissected by Kerry A. Dolan and Robyn Meredith in *Forbes.* They show that despite corporate-speak that invests the brand with almost mystical power, increasingly parent companies farm out work to suppliers, meaning that the brand name you often pay extra for was manufactured elsewhere. Samuel Fromartz gives us a rare peek in *Inc.* magazine at the restaurant as a business, how a new CEO figured out why his chain was near bankruptcy, and how he turned the restaurant's business around.

Of course, business values such as maximizing shareholder value are not always consonant with other prized values. Like safety. Keith Bradsher of *The New York Times,* who has owned this particular franchise, exposes the auto-industry thinking that led to unsafe SUVs and exploding Firestone tires on the Ford Explorer. Charles Fishman in *Fast Company* magazine explores an issue that increasingly sabotages public confidence in companies: miserable customer service. Despite dutiful bows to improving customer service, such service is expensive and too often the first victim of cost cutting. Americans have historically had an aversion to bigness, and the *BusinessWeek* cover story by Aaron Bernstein, with assists from Michael Arndt, Wendy Zellner, and Peter Coy, demonstrates that even in flush times the public is uneasy about big business and knows that the values of business sometimes clash with public values. Few business writers have so consistently punctured press-release fables as has Allan Sloan of *Newsweek,* a reason we include a selection of several of his provocative—and still timely—columns. Davan Maharaj in the *Los Angeles Times* reveals how the managers of superstores like Wal-Mart believe customer safety is too expensive, and stacks of goods that fall on customers are like hurricanes or natural disasters, to be blamed on no one, certainly not the profit-conscious management of these stores.

Finally, we include a set of stories that compels us to ponder the future. We begin the book with the aftermath of September 11. This event, as Bruce Nussbaum posits in *BusinessWeek,* will alter not just the New York skyline but the American zeitgeist. And although the collateral damage from the terrorist strike of September 11 dents the American economy, *The New York Times'* Paul Krugman offers a cold-eyed dissection of America's economic travails, awarding the terrorists less credit than they'd like to claim. Lisa Belkin recounts in *Mother Jones* how pharmaceutical companies, now free of government advertising restrictions, are pumping out television ads and inducing consumers to spend for drugs they may not need and can't afford. Wil S. Hylton of *Esquire* alarmingly shows how science, in the service of business, is in the name of genetic research claiming ownership of our DNA. Which, as Hylton cautions, may mean we will not own our own cells and bodies. Toby Lester in *The Atlantic* frets about what happens to privacy in the hands of business, and so should you. And William

Hamilton in *Harper's* gracefully frets about the fate of California wine.

There are pieces we wished to include in this roster but had to excise for reasons of space or because we had a rule that no publication would have more than two entries. However different the selected pieces may be, one characteristic unites them: an outstanding journalist is usually a good storyteller—like the young Moss Hart, who did not play sports and was shunned by his teen friends until they learned that he read voraciously, and so they gathered on a Bronx stoop each night as he held them spellbound by telling stories of places they had never been. The journalists in this volume do more than report facts. They tell vivid stories.

—Ken Auletta

THE BEST BUSINESS STORIES
OF THE YEAR: *2002 Edition*

A job is not just a job, and money isn't everything. The terrorist attacks of September 11, 2001, made us step back and look at everyone and everything around us differently. This essay by *BusinessWeek* editorial page editor Bruce Nussbaum recognizes the brave new stars of our American drama and helps us focus on the nation's true values.

Bruce Nussbaum

Real Masters of the Universe

A SUBTLE SHIFT in the American zeitgeist took place on September 11. It's hard to define, and it may not last. But on the day of the World Trade Center cataclysm, the country changed. Big, beefy working-class guys became heroes once again, replacing the telegenic financial analysts and techno-billionaires who once had held the nation in thrall. Uniforms and public service became "in." Real sacrifice and real courage were on graphic display.

Maybe it was the class reversals that were so revealing. Men and women making forty grand a year working for the city responding—risking their own lives—to save investment bankers and traders making ten times that amount. And dying by the hundreds for the effort. The image of self-sacrifice by civil servants in uniform was simply breathtaking.

For Americans conditioned in the nineties to think of themselves first, to be rich above all else, to accumulate all the good material things, to take safety and security for granted, this was a new reality. So was the contrast of genuine bravery to the faux values of reality TV shows such as *Survivor*.

SEA OF FLAGS

Noteworthy, too, was America's quick return to family, community, church, and patriotism in the aftermath of the tragedy. People became polite and generous to one another without prodding. On that day and the days that followed, they told their wives and husbands and children and parents and significant others they loved them. And the flags, the sea of flags that appeared out of nowhere and spready everywhere, worn by business-suited managers and eyebrow-pierced, tattooed teenagers. As if by magic, city taxicabs, building canopies, and nearly every truck in sight were flying flags.

The offerings of food, money, and blood were overwhelming. The generosity was unsurpassed in our memories. But the manner in which perfect strangers went out of their way to help one another in all kinds of situations was most amazing. To the surprise of its residents, New York became a small-town community. The day-to-day antagonisms among the citizenry melted away.

The rush to church, synagogue, and, yes, mosque was equally unusual. People returned to their religious ceremonies and congregations in huge numbers for support and guidance. The overflow at the doors demonstrated that many who had not visited in years showed up to participate in the familiar and comforting liturgies of their childhoods. They joined with their neighbors in mourning.

LESSONS TAUGHT

It was, for a moment, an old America peeking out from behind the new, me-now America. We saw a glimpse of a country of shared values, not competing interest groups; of common cause, not hateful opposition. There were a few exceptions: Jerry Falwell declaring we brought the death and destruction down on ourselves because of homosexuality, abortion, and the American Civil Liberties Union. A silly, stupid comment to be dismissed in light of the comity of the day—but an extremist remark nonetheless made in the name of God. How sad.

Tragedy has the power to transform us. But rarely is the transformation permanent. People and societies revert back to the norm. But what is the "norm" for America? Where are this nation's true values? Have we stripped too much away in recent years in order to make us lean and mean for the race to riches? It is hard to look at the images of the World Trade Center rescue again and again. At least once, however, we should look at what the rescuers are teaching us, about what matters—and who.

Devastation, anger, and fear were immediate results of the World Trade Center disaster. That tragedy could also have a more long-term psychological impact on a national economy that was already in a precarious condition. Paul Krugman's carefully researched cautionary story in *The New York Times Magazine* urges that the United States avoid the mistakes of history. Prosperity is at risk.

Paul Krugman

The Fear Economy

THE AMERICAN ECONOMY is usually quick to shrug off the effects of disaster. When Hurricane Andrew swept through south Florida in 1992, and again when the Northridge earthquake struck southern California in 1994, the property damage was immense and the lives of millions of people were disrupted for months thereafter. Yet few economists thought of either event as a threat to national prosperity, and if you look at a chart showing the growth of gross domestic product, it's quite hard to see any effects.

Will it be different this time?

Although September 11 was a human tragedy on a scale far greater than any of America's recent natural disasters, in monetary terms the immediate loss was not much more than one might have expected from a severe hurricane or earthquake. Yet many people fear that the terror attack, unlike a hurricane or an earthquake, will have dire consequences for the economy—indeed, that it may even tip the world into recession. And though they are probably wrong, they could be right.

The reason they might be right has little to do with the nature of the calamity. It's true that there is something especially horrific about a disaster that was an act of man rather than an act of God. And the after-effects were unsettling: airlines losing hundreds of millions of dollars a day; empty airports, hotels, and theaters; conventions canceled; Wall Street spiraling downward. It's also true that the story isn't over, that unknown perils—another attack? a full-scale war in central Asia?—lie ahead. And of course the terrorists struck right at the nerve center of global capitalism.

But the economic repercussions from the World Trade Center disaster, unnerving as they are, would soon fade out if the economy had been strong to begin with. The main reason to worry about the economic fallout from the attack is not the attack itself, but the timing. Suppose the terrorists had struck five years ago, while the economy was in the midst of a healthy, investment-led expansion and before the rise and fall of the stock market. Would we have been as worried as we are? I doubt it.

The point is that even before the attack, our economic condition was looking unusually precarious. We weren't in a severe recession; technically, we may not have been in a recession at all. But there was an alarming sense that things were out of control, that our economy's ailments weren't responding to the usual medicine. In another time we might mourn the dead and move on; but this economy was already fragile.

To understand the economic risks we may now be facing, in other words, we need to understand why we were in trouble even before terror struck. It's a story that takes us far afield in time and space—to the Great Depression of the 1930s and to the difficulties of modern Japan. These stories of other times and places give ample reason to be concerned. For they remind us that even highly advanced economies like our own have sometimes stumbled badly. But the stories also give us reason to be optimistic, even if things go badly over the next few months. The terrorists may have taken

us into uncharted territory in many ways, but the economic landscape is fairly familiar, and we have some pretty good ideas about
how to deal with the risks ahead.

But first things first: Although the atrocity was an immense
human tragedy, it was limited to a small part of one city. How
could destroying a few buildings, however large, even possibly
threaten an economy as huge as ours?

THE PSYCHOLOGICAL IMPACT

A disaster can hurt the economy in one of two ways. It can reduce
supply—that is, it can interfere with the economy's ability to produce. Or it can reduce demand—that is, it can make people
unwilling to buy the economy's products. What are we worried
about right now?

The answer is that for all the damage in Lower Manhattan, the
terrorist attack's impact on the supply will be minor compared
with the awesome scale of the United States economy. Perhaps 15
million square feet of office space were lost. While that may sound
like a lot, it's less than half of 1 percent of the office space in the
nation. The cost of clearing the rubble and rebuilding will run
into the tens of billions of dollars—less than 0.1 percent of our
national wealth. While airlines were grounded for the better part
of a week, they are flying again. Yes, the airlines are in financial
trouble, and they have cut back flights and laid off tens of thousands of employees, and Boeing is scaling back in anticipation of
canceled aircraft orders. But the basic ability of the American
economy to move people and products around the country has not
been seriously impaired.

This story might change if a military confrontation leads to a
disruption of oil supplies from the Middle East. For now, though,
the ability of the economy to supply whatever people want to buy
seems to be almost completely intact.

But how much will they want to buy? That is the question.

In the long upward march of American prosperity, there have been occasional setbacks. In the worst of these, from 1929 to 1932, GDP fell by a third. Yet America was no less productive, no less technologically advanced in 1932 than it had been three years before. What happened was that people stopped spending, and the factories that could have been producing found no buyers for their products. It was, in short, a failure of demand rather than supply.

And the thing about demand is that, to a far greater extent than supply, it's a matter of psychology. If you ask how much the United States economy is capable of producing over the next few months, the answer is mainly determined by the physical realities—the capacity of the factories, the bandwidth of the fiber-optic cables, the size of the work force. If you ask how much consumers will consume and investors invest over the next few months, the answer is determined largely by feelings—what John Maynard Keynes called "animal spirits." If frightened people decide not to spend, their nervousness can translate into a depressed economy.

So could the terror attack—a very small thing in terms of its physical impact on the economy—have a disproportionately large psychological impact? Could a small cause have large effects? Yes, it could. After all, the Great Depression had no obvious cause at all.

So the reason to be concerned about the economic effects of terrorism is not the actual damage but the possibility that nervous consumers and investors will stop spending. Truly, the only thing we have to fear is fear itself.

But isn't that always true? Why should we be any more vulnerable to fear now than we would have been five years ago? To answer that question we need to ask why in normal times it would be easy for economic policy to offset the psychological impact of tragedy on overall demand—and why right now that may not be so easy.

When economists discuss the Great Depression, their general sentiment is "never again." This is partly a matter of resolve, but it is also a boast. We think, or we thought until recently, that we have learned enough about fighting economic slumps to prevent a recurrence on that scale. Modern economies, after all, have powerful defenses against economic slowdown and both the will and the knowledge to use them.

The first line of defense against an economic slump is monetary policy: the ability of the central banks—the Federal Reserve, the European Central Bank, the Bank of Japan—to cut interest rates. Lower interest rates are supposed to persuade businesses and consumers to borrow and spend, which creates new jobs, which encourages people to spend even more, and so on. And since the 1930s, this strategy has consistently worked. Specifically, interest-rate cuts have pulled the United States out of each of its big recessions over the past thirty years—in 1975, 1982, and 1991.

In fact, for most of the past forty years the only serious problem with interest-rate cuts as a policy has been that they work too well, tempting countries to pursue overly ambitious targets for growth and employment. When they do that, the result is inflation. That is, when an expansion goes too far, companies take advantage of the good times to raise prices, workers demand higher wages, and a wage-price spiral threatens to develop.

As a result, one preoccupation of economic and political thinkers these past few decades has been how to ensure that governments *not* cut interest rates too readily—to rein in the temptation to seek short-term political gain by revving up the economy at the longer-term expense of price stability. That concern is one of the main reasons that all advanced countries now have independent central banks that are largely insulated from the influence of other branches of government.

Behind the first line of defense is a second line, fiscal policy. If cutting interest rates isn't enough to support the economy, the government can pump up demand by cutting taxes or increasing its own spending. The conventional wisdom among economic analysts is that fiscal policy is not necessary to deal with most recessions, that interest-rate policy is enough. In other words, they believe that stabilizing the economy is properly the job of the Fed, not the Treasury Department. But the possibility of fiscal action always stands in reserve.

Does the existence of these two lines of defense mean that the economy is no longer at risk of recessions? Obviously not: the United States has experienced three major downturns in the last three decades. But in a way there was less to those downturns than met the eye.

For one, they were partly intentional. In each case, the recession started when the Fed deliberately tried to slow the economy in order to cool off inflation. Each went further than the Fed intended, because monetary policy is a blunt instrument. But each recession did end after the Fed reversed policy and cut interest rates. So the overall track record has actually been reassuring. Recent history seems to suggest that recessions may happen, but also that we can deal with them.

So should we be relaxed about the economic picture in the aftermath of the terror attack? Maybe not.

JAPAN'S SLOW-MOTION DEPRESSION

The history of the United States economy since World War II inspires at least a mild sense of complacency about the risks of economic downturn. The defenses in place against any repeat of the Great Depression have held very well. And if our own history were the only evidence at hand, I and many others would probably feel quite at ease about the current situation.

But we are not the only advanced economy that has had to face economic stress, and others have not fared so well. Three years ago I wrote a paper for the Brookings Institution titled "It's Baaack: Japan's Slump and the Return of the Liquidity Trap." The rather flip title was meant to convey the message that events in Japan—a faraway country of which many Americans know little—should trouble us, because they suggested that Japan's economic woes may not be unique. In fact, they seemed to show that we might not be as well defended against depression-style problems as we imagined.

In the 1980s Japan had the most dynamic economy in the advanced world; indeed, many Americans viewed it as a dangerous competitor. But then came a recession in the early 1990s, and Japan has never really recovered. There have been ups and downs over the decade, but each slump has been deeper than the last, each recovery more anemic. The period as a whole amounts to a sort of slow-motion depression.

Still, why should that dismal record trouble us here? Because Japan's troubles show that the usual defenses against economic slowdown can fail. In Japan, the first line of defense, interest-rate cuts, has in effect been overrun by the enemy: short-term interest rates have been reduced all the way to zero, yet the economy remains depressed. Fiscal policy has fared somewhat better: huge deficit spending has kept the economy from experiencing a full replay of the 1930s, at least so far. But the results look more like a holding action than a truly effective defense. And now, with debt piling up alarmingly, there is reason to worry about whether even that holding action can long continue.

But let's look a bit more deeply at Japan's experience and why it should worry us.

Over the past decade Japan's economy has come to look more and more like a 1930s model. However, the Japanese haven't suffered a year like 1931 in the United States, when everything collapsed at once. Instead, depression has crept up gradually.

Averaging the ups and downs, an economy that grew almost 4 percent per year in the 1980s has grown only about 1 percent annually since 1991. Unemployment has risen almost without a break, from 2.1 percent in 1991 to 5 percent today. That still doesn't sound that bad, but Japanese statistics seriously understate the truth: nearly a million Japanese workers have lost their jobs in the last few months, yet only 120,000 of those displaced workers are registered as unemployed. You should probably think of

Japan's labor market as being comparable to what ours looks like at the bottom of a deep recession, with unemployment approaching 10 percent.

The psychological impact of these job losses—and the closely associated surge in bankruptcies, which were rare in the 1980s but have reached epidemic proportions—is particularly severe in a society that usually tries to avoid such stark outcomes. Japan is, after all, the land of lifetime employment and the "convoy system," in which strong companies help weaker companies to stay in business. So perhaps it isn't too surprising that the grimmest indicator of Japan's troubles is a sharp rise in suicides, especially among those who have lost their jobs or their businesses.

So why hasn't Japan tried to get its sluggish economy moving again? The worrying answer is that it has tried, over and over—and failed.

Remember that the first line of defense against recession is monetary policy, the ability of the central bank to cut interest rates. Well, in Japan monetary policy has hit the wall. Interest rates came down and down, falling below 1 percent in 1996. In early 1999, the Bank of Japan, the counterpart of the Federal Reserve, reduced the overnight rate to zero. Yet, there has been no sign of inflation—or of recovery. And you can't push interest rates below zero.

Economists refer to Japan's situation, in which a zero interest rate just isn't low enough to restart growth, as a "liquidity trap." The point is that, other things being equal, "liquid" assets— cash—are better than bonds: you can't use a bond in a vending machine. The only reason people are willing to invest in bonds is that unlike cash, they offer interest. When the interest rate gets very low, this incentive disappears, and people just hoard cash instead. So if even a zero interest rate isn't low enough to get consumers and businesses to spend, there's nothing more you can do with interest-rate policy; you're trapped.

To find another case of a liquidity trap, you have to go back to the United States in the 1930s. In 1939 the interest rate on treasury bills was effectively zero (strictly speaking, it was 0.02 percent), yet the economy was still stuck in a depression. But that was a long time ago. By the 1990s, hardly anybody even thought about the possibility of a liquidity trap, and those who did usually dismissed it as something that probably couldn't happen in real life.

But Japan's example showed, ominously, that it could. The liquidity trap is back.

What about the second line of defense, fiscal policy? Japan has tried that, and it has worked—sort of. Let me explain.

If you have visited Japan recently you know that it does not look like a country in the midst of a depression. There are strong similarities between Japan in the 1990s and the United States in the 1930s, but there is also a big difference. America descended rapidly into depression. Japan's crisis has unfolded far more gradually. What has Japan's depression, if that's what it is, been so low-key?

One important answer—which is, by the way, a reason not to panic in the current situation—is that, being a modern country, Japan has not allowed its banks to fail. Economic historians will tell you that the Great Depression didn't begin with the stock market crash of 1929. Although there was a recession following the crash, it was nothing out of the ordinary. Things didn't really fall apart until late in 1930, when a wave of bank runs swept across America, driving a third of the nation's banks out of business.

Today, no government would allow anything similar to happen. In Japan, furthermore, the government has stepped in repeatedly to prop up the banks, merging weak banks with stronger ones and occasionally putting in big infusions of cash to cover the bank's losses. There is much to criticize about this process, which has kept the banks alive but not restored them to health. But by averting a banking crisis, Japan has helped protect the economy from any sudden collapse.

The other reason that Japan does not look like a country in the midst of a depression is that the government has found a concrete solution to the problem of mass unemployment. By "concrete," I don't mean serious, hardheaded, substantial. I mean concrete, as in roads, dams, and bridges.

Think of it as the WPA on steroids. Over the past decade Japan has used enormous public works projects as a way to create jobs and pump money into the economy. The statistics are awesome. In 1996 Japan's public works spending, as a share of GDP, was more than four times that of the United States. Japan poured as much concrete as we did, though it has a little less than half our population and 4 percent of our land area. One Japanese worker in ten was employed in the construction industry, far more than in other advanced countries.

Without those public works programs, things might have been much worse. For there is no question that enormous public spending has helped keep the economy from sliding into a true, unambiguous depression. As one Japan expert, Adam Posen of the Institute for International Economics, points out, the record of the 1990s is unmistakable. Every time the government tries to scale back its spending, as it did under Prime Minister Ryutaro Hashimoto back in 1997, the economy goes into a recession. Every time the government goes back to its free-spending ways, as it did after Hashimoto resigned in disgrace, the economy perks up a bit.

Now for the bad news: deficit spending has slowed the Japanese economy's slide, but it has not reversed it. That is, the public works programs provide only temporary, symptomatic economic relief. The favorable effects last only as long as the spending itself. They don't seem to lay the basis for a permanent turnaround.

And meanwhile, though Japan has thus far avoided mass unemployment, its policy of massive public works spending has produced many nasty side effects. One is the vast environmental damage that has been inflicted in the name of job creation. Another is pervasive corruption, as rake-offs and kickbacks have become a way of life, distorting the whole economic and political system.

Furthermore, a decade of huge deficit spending has left Japan with an enormous public debt. Japan last ran a budget surplus in 1992. In that year, the nation's public debt was about 60 percent of GDP, about the average for advanced countries and slightly less than the figure for the United States. The years of deficit spending since then have pushed Japan's debt above 130 percent of GDP. That's the highest ratio among advanced nations, considerably worse than either Belgium or Italy, the traditional champions. It's almost twice the advanced-country average and 2.5 times the figure for the United States.

So far, thanks to the extraordinarily low interest rates on its debt, the Japanese government has been able to continue borrowing despite this burden. But how much longer can it go on? And what will happen to the economy when creditors begin to balk? (That may already have started. Just before the terror attack, Moody's, the bond-rating agency, reported that it was considering a downgrade of Japanese debt, which would have the effect of raising interest rates.)

Japan's experience, in other words, should puncture our complacency. It shows that an advanced country with all the advantages that status brings can still fail to cope effectively with economic slowdown.

But does any of this have any relevance to us? Does America look anything like Japan?

IT COULD HAPPEN HERE

I wish I could say with confidence that Japan's dismal experience is of no relevance to the United States. And certainly our nations are very different in many ways. But there is a distinct resemblance between what happened to Japan a decade ago and what was happening to the United States economy just a few weeks ago. Indeed, Japan's story reads all too much like a morality play designed for our edification.

At the most general level, Japan offers an object lesson of pride going before a fall. It has only been a few years since every other cover in the business section of the airport bookstore showed a samurai warrior or a rising sun, when Japanese businessmen and bureaucrats were both admired and feared. Now, to the extent that Americans think at all about Japanese managers and government planners, it is with contempt. These days we're the ones who think we have all the answers.

More specifically, the rise and fall of Japan's financial bubble sounds all too recognizable to post-millennial Americans. An already advanced nation pulls ahead of its first-world peers, taking the lead in all the hot new technologies. Stock prices soar to levels that look insane using conventional criteria, but everyone agrees that in such a dynamic economy old rules no longer apply. And then the bubble bursts, leaving behind a mountain of bad debts and an economic engine that refuses to turn over. Name two countries whose experiences in the last twenty years fit that description.

That similarity between Japan and the United States was causing sleepless nights for many economic analysts, myself included, even before the world revealed itself to be a more dangerous place than any of us imagined.

What did I think when tossing and turning? That we keep saying that we are nothing like Japan, but more and more it looks as if the language may be different but the song remains the same.

When Wall Street first began to show signs of irrational exuberance back in the middle of the 1990s, a few lonely voices warned that we might be about to develop a Japanese-style bubble. But conventional wisdom said that this was nonsense, that our mature financial markets would never get that out of touch with reality. When stock prices reached multiples of earnings that were way above historical norms, some warned that it was indeed a Japanese-style bubble. But conventional wisdom said that this was nonsense, that the New Economy justified those higher multiples.

When our bubble finally burst, some warned that we might have a Japanese-style recession. But conventional wisdom said that this was nonsense, that the economy was more resilient than that. And when the slowdown came, some warned that we might find it as hard as the Japanese did to turn it around. But conventional wisdom said that this was nonsense, that the great Greenspan would soon set things right.

By September 10, however, the Fed had already cut rates seven times, and it was still hard to see where a recovery would come from. Indeed, some business economists had started referring privately to the Fed chairman as "Greenspan-san." Business investment was still falling, because corporations clearly invested way too much back when optimism was the rage. Housing was doing better, thanks to low interest rates, but some analysts were warning about a housing bubble—and even if they were wrong, how solid a recovery could we have from housing alone?

So things were already looking fairly dicey before the terrorists struck. In fact, if we do have a recession now we will never be quite sure whether it was the result of the attack or something that was going to happen anyway.

Still, as they say, everything is different now. What does the economic picture look like after the horror?

THE FEAR ECONOMY

As I've pointed out, the terrorist attack inflicted only minor damage on the American economy's supply side. Its initial effects on demand were much more pronounced. Vacations were canceled, at first because there were no planes and later because people were afraid to fly. Consumers quickly returned to purchasing necessities, but many were in no mood to indulge themselves in luxuries. And businesses, worried about the economic effects of the crisis, scaled back their investment plans, introducing the risk that their concerns could become a self-fulfilling prophecy.

Looking out a bit further, the picture may be better. Life will go on, and people will eventually want their consumer goods—and even their vacations. This return to normalcy will, of course, be delayed if there is another terrorist incident or a large-scale shooting war. At the time of writing, though, military analysts seemed to expect a prolonged but low-intensity campaign—bombs and commandos, not tanks and heavy infantry divisions. If they're right, it will look like the sort of campaign Israel has waged more or less continuously for decades—and Israelis have not lost their taste for life's small luxuries.

Meanwhile, the crisis has led to changes in policy that will offset some of the slump in private demand. In fact, I'd say that the odds are at least even that a year from now it will be clear that the terrorists indirectly gave the economy a boost. That's because the events of September 11 have led to more expansionary policies, on both the monetary and the fiscal side.

First, the Federal Reserve cut interest rates by half a percentage point on the first day the markets opened, just six days after the attack. The case for another rate cut had been building in any event, but the Fed was reluctant to move before its next meeting, which wasn't until October—among other reasons because Greenspan and company didn't want to look as if they were panicking. Distasteful as it is to say this, the atrocity gave the Fed an opportunity to move earlier and more forcefully than it might otherwise have dared.

Second, the attack opened the door to a large but temporary increase in government spending—precisely the kind of fiscal policy some economists had wanted but that had seemed politically impossible before. In early September, discussions of fiscal policy had been mired in bitter partisan politics. Democrats were reluctant to endorse fiscal stumulus because it might let Republicans off the hook on the consequences of their earlier tax cuts. Republicans wanted to use the economy's weak state as justification for further tax cuts. Those debates are still out there, but Congress, meanwhile, quickly agreed on a large spending package for the military and another large package for rebuilding New York. This spending package could quickly get much larger—and provide an even bigger stimulus—if, contrary to expectations, this does turn into a full-scale conventional war.

Finally, the terror attack also seems to have led to some favorable policy changes elsewhere in the world. Until this September, many economists had been gnashing their teeth over the obduracy of the European Central Bank, which refused to cut interest rates in the face of gathering storm clouds over the world economy. And we had begun to suspect that the E.C.B.'s refusal to act was increasingly based on pride and stubbornness—it wouldn't cut precisely because everyone was so critical of its actions. The terrorists changed all that. Just hours after the Fed's action, the E.C.B. matched it.

It's worth remembering that wars usually stimulate rather than depress economies; the main economic danger from war is inflation, not deflation. True, we are not at war in the traditional sense; the analogy with Pearl Harbor is a very bad one in many ways. Still, it wouldn't be that strange if the terror attack turns out to be a short-run plus for the economy.

Yet one can't dismiss the possibility that this time will be different, that the terror attack will have a persistent negative effect. Or, alternatively, that the positive effects will be too weak to offset the bad things that were already in train. How bad could it get?

STOPPING A SLUMP

Before the terrorist attack, my great concern was that Alan Greenspan would run out of ammunition. Having seen him reduce the overnight interest rate from 6.5 percent to 3.5 percent since January without stopping the economy's slide, I envisioned him completing the process by reducing the rate all the way to zero without doing any better.

After the attack my great concern is exactly the same. The overnight rate is now down to 3 percent, which leaves only another 3 percent to go. Will it be enough? How much are we like Japan, anyway?

Here one can offer some slightly reassuring comparisons. Both Japan and the United States had stock market bubbles, and they were of roughly equal size: between 1985 and 1989 the Nikkei, Japan's main stock index, tripled; between 1995 and 2000 the S&P 500 did the same. But Japan also had an equally large bubble in real estate and land prices. I've never known whether to believe the famous factoid that the land under the Imperial Palace in Tokyo was worth more than all of California, but Japanese land prices certainly reached ridiculous levels. And much of the bad debt that still troubles Japan was run up to support real estate speculation. We had nothing comparable in this country.

Moreover, the United States has a marked advantage when it comes to demography. Japan's persistent economic problem is that consumers want to save more than businesses want to invest. One important reason for that, many analysts agree, is the combination of a low birth rate and a refusal to allow large-scale immigration. An aging population tends to save a lot in preparation for retirement, and it's hard to get businesses to invest all those savings when they know that the working-age population will be shrinking for decades to come. We have problems with an aging population here, too. But they are nowhere near as severe, and our working-age population is still growing steadily.

In one way, however, our situation is actually worse than Japan's. For the past decade, Japan has been an island of depression in a sea of prosperity, its economy stagnating even as other major economies—ours in particular—boomed. That was, you might say, quite an achievement. Our current problems, on the other hand, are shared by much of the world—not least by Japan itself.

In fact, Japan, which remains, despite all its problems, the world's second-largest economy and one of our biggest trading partners, has lately seemed to be on the verge of even deeper trouble: its slow-motion depression seems to be going into fast forward.

In the second quarter of 2001, Japan's economy shrank at an

annual rate of more than 3 percent. Indeed, almost all observers believe that Japan was in a severe recession even before the terrorists struck. Aggravating the problem is accelerating deflation: the best measure of Japanese prices, the GDP deflator, has been falling at an annual rate of 2 percent. Deflation adds to the economy's problems, because it gives people an incentive to hoard cash instead of spending.

If you think about this a bit, the story gets even worse. After all, prices are falling because the economy is depressed; now we've just learned that the economy is depressed because prices are falling. That sets the stage for the return of another monster we haven't seen since the 1930s, a "deflationary spiral," in which falling prices and a slumping economy feed on each other, plunging the economy into the abyss. It's pretty scary stuff, not just for Japan but for the rest of us. If Japan slides into the abyss, that will have a direct adverse effect on our economy dwarfing anything the terrorists did.

Yet lately we seem to be living in a world full of dark clouds with potential silver linings—and this one is no exception. The upside to Japan's troubles is that they leave us forewarned and to some extent forearmed. Think of it this way: without Japan's dismal example, economic officials in the United States might blithely dismiss the risks in our current situation, cheerfully proclaiming that prosperity is just around the corner. That, after all, is what Japanese officials did in the early stages of their slump. They didn't know that what did happen, could happen. We do.

And Japan's woes have not only made us aware that depression-type economic problems can occur in the modern world, they have also led to a much better understanding about how to fight them. Without the example of Japan, economic thinking in the 1990s might have been entirely focused on the problems of prosperity. Questions like the causes of slumps and the options for dealing with them would have been a musty field, attracting the attention of only a few economic historians. Instead these questions have been a subject of intense debate, attracting the attention of some of the world's leading economists. (Full disclosure: I've been working on the Japan problem for several years. But the economists I actually have in mind are people like Lars E.O. Svensson, the Swedish macroeconomist, who has produced the most fully worked-out proposal for Japanese recovery.) And this debate has offered some fresh approaches to the problem.

Not long ago, the two lines of defense against slump that I described earlier—interest-rate cuts and deficit spending—were pretty much it as far as economists were concerned. They seemed to be enough: interest cuts had ended every postwar recession, and deficit spending on a grand scale—that is, World War II—had ended the Great Depression. On the other hand, if they should turn out *not* to be enough, economists had few ideas about what might come next.

Now, however, it is widely understood that even if both conventional lines of defense fail, there is still a lot that you can do—as long as you are willing to abandon conventional notions of prudence. For example, normal practice forbids central banks to invest in anything other than short-term government debt, for fear that decisions about what to invest in will become politicized. And since the short-term interest rate in Japan is already zero, there is nothing more that the Bank of Japan can do within the limits of normal practice. But given the economy's grave state, why not go beyond those limits?

For example, why not buy long-term government debt, which does not yet have a zero interest rate and therefore offers some additional traction? Or the Bank of Japan could print yen and use them to buy dollars; this would push the yen down, making Japanese exports more competitive on world markets.

Some economists have also suggested that an economy in Japan's situation can bootstrap itself back to prosperity through "inflation targeting." This means announcing publicly that you intend to push the economy into a state of persistent mild inflation, say at 2.5 percent per year, and that you will do whatever is necessary to achieve that end. If the announcement is credible, potential borrowers will be more likely to take a chance, believing that they will be able to repay their loans more easily, and consumers will have second thoughts about hoarding cash.

Such radical ideas were branded as irresponsible when they first came out but have since become respectable, almost mainstream. And that means that if the worst comes to pass, if the United States economy starts to show signs of the Japan syndrome, we won't be at a loss for ideas about what to do. Admittedly, it would be nice if Japan had actually tried any of these proposals and reassuring if they had been tried and worked. Alas, despite growing support within Japan, they have not been tried. The reason, I think, is fear—fear of the unknown, fear of trying anything that might fail.

Fear of the unknown was presumably behind a bizarre recent outburst from Japan's finance minister. Earlier this year Junichiro Koizumi, a maverick and reformer who is intensely disliked by political insiders, was nonetheless chosen as prime minister by the ruling party in response to public pressure. Koizumi has promised that he will fix the economy. Koizumi is pushing "structural reform"—measures like forcing banks to own up to their bad loans—that will be good for Japan in the long run but will actually depress the economy in the near future.

But there was hope that he would also press for unconventional monetary actions—and some of his advisers have expressed support for such policies. They have been undercut, however, by the finance minister, Masajuro Shiokawa, who declared that this would "cause runaway inflation and send the economy spinning out of control." This at a time when the economy is already spinning out of control and is threatened with runaway deflation. Perhaps Shiokawa is still traumatized by the wartime inflation of his youth.

Meanwhile, the Bank of Japan, which directly controls monetary policy, has refused to do anything unconventional; incredibly, it refused to make any major changes in policy even after the terrorist attacks. This refusal, I believe, is rooted in a pettier kind of fear. After all, if the Bank of Japan were to engage in unconventional monetary policy, it might fail. It would be very embarrassing. It's far safer to declare that your institution has done all it can and that it's up to somebody else to find a way to make the economy recover.

Let's hope that in a similar situation, our policy makers would be bolder and more responsible.

THE NIGHTMARE SCENARIO

Let me be clear: I don't think that the United States is at any imminent risk of following Japan into deep slump. What I do fear is that a combination of factors—the legacy of our bubble economy, the trouble in Japan, and maybe the psychological impact of the terrorist action—will drag us into a prolonged period of stagnation.

Here's my nightmare: America's recovery from its current slump, whenever it comes, is tentative and short-lived, because the business investment that drove our boom in the 1990s remains stagnant. Eventually the housing bubble bursts and we have another slump; then we have another weak recovery, this time driven by deficit spending, but that, too, fades out. Eventually we look around and realize that it's 2009, and the economy still hasn't fully recovered from the slowdown that began at the end of the previous decade.

And we also realize that while the government's subsequent attempts to sustain the economy, mainly through tax cuts and subsidies to energy companies, have arguably staved off depression—the unemployment rate has risen, but only to 8 percent—they have also devastated the environment and left a huge government debt. The fiscal 2010 budget deficit is projected at $800 billion, and nobody has any idea how we will manage in a couple of years, when millions of baby boomers start collecting their Social Security checks.

Is this outlined situation an actual forecast? No, it's only a possibility. And the terrorist attack doesn't make it any more likely—if anything, the fiscal response to terror should help give the economy a boost now, when there is a good chance of heading off the chance that we will slip into a Japanese-style trap.

And even if this possible outcome starts to look a more likely one, we should not give up hope. For although Japan may have failed to come to grips with its long stagnation, that failure was not preordained. Many of us think that if Tokyo would show a bit more courage and imagination it could still turn its economy around. And if the worst happens and we find ourselves in a similar situation, so can we.

A truly worst-case scenario would be if the United States not only fell into a Japanese-style economic trap but also exhibited a Japanese-style unwillingness to do whatever it takes to get out of that trap. But I think, or at least hope, that our economic leaders would be bolder and more imaginative. The Fed, in particular, is a smarter institution than the Bank of Japan, with a lot more talent on hand, and historically has shown a willingness to take responsibility for the economy rather than interpret its job narrowly.

So should we be worried about the world economy in the aftermath of the terrorist attack? Yes, we should—but not because of the attack. In fact, I've been worried about the world economy for several years, ever since I realized that depression-style economic problems could happen in the modern world, and even here in America.

It has become a cliche to say that everything is different now. What worries me is the prospect that some things may be the same—the same as they were here in the 1930s, the same as they have been in Japan for the last ten years.

What would make things really different, in a good way, would be effective leadership that recognizes the gravity of the situation, does not fail to act for fear of political repercussions or, worse yet, try to exploit the crisis for political ends—leadership that is prepared to try unorthodox remedies if conventional solutions fail. Do we have that kind of leadership? We may find out.

Dealmaking can overshadow basic stock analysis on Wall Street and obscure the big picture. The failure to predict the bursting of the Internet bubble was shared by many, but the unbridled enthusiasm of star analyst Mary Meeker clearly stands out. Peter Elkind of *Fortune* puts Meeker's actions under the microscope in a scathing indictment of a Wall Street that values its own profits over all else. It won't be viewed quite the same way again.

Peter Elkind

Where Mary Meeker Went Wrong

ONE DAY IN DECEMBER 1999—near the top of what we now know as the Internet bubble—a couple of East Coast business types with a few hours to kill were cruising Silicon Valley in a chauffeured car. "Yeah, I know 'em all," announced their driver, as they meandered through the streets of Woodside, an exclusive enclave near Palo Alto. Neil Young, for instance—he lives up in the mountains, the driver said. Why, he boasted, his customers even included Mary Meeker. Would they like to see her new California digs?

Within moments the sedan had pulled up to a wooded four-acre estate, marked with white pillars and protected by a wrought-iron gate. As his wide-eyed passengers watched, the driver stepped out and punched a security code into the keypad. The gate swung open, the driver pulled the car onto the property, and the gleeful pair scampered about the grounds, checking out the backyard pool and peeking into ground-floor windows like teenage boys granted admission to Britney Spears's bedroom.

It was a sign of those strange times that a Wall Street analyst could excite such fascination. Then again, Morgan Stanley's Mary Meeker was no ordinary analyst. Anointed by *Barron's* as "Queen of the Net," lovingly profiled by *The New Yorker,* equated with Alan Greenspan and Warren Buffett as a market mover by *The Wall Street Journal,* Meeker was the unquestioned diva of the Internet Age. Tech companies begged her to cover them. Morgan Stanley paid her an eye-popping $15 million in 1999. Ordinary investors hounded her for autographs. During the dot-com craze, Mary Meeker was by far the most important voice for the Internet—and the notion that companies without earnings could transform the world and climb to the moon.

That was then. Today Meeker, forty-one, has become something else entirely: the single most powerful symbol of how Wall Street can lead investors astray. For the past year, as Internet stocks have crumbled and entire companies have vaporized, Meeker has maintained the same upbeat ratings on her companies that characterized her research reports in the glory days. For instance, of the fifteen stocks Meeker currently covers, she has a strong buy or an outperform rating on all but two. Among the stocks she has never downgraded are Priceline, Amazon, Yahoo!, and FreeMarkets—all of which have declined between 85 percent and 97 percent from their peak. For this she has been duly pummeled in the press, accused of cheerleading for Morgan Stanley's investment banking clients.

But Meeker's refusal to downgrade her stocks is only a small piece of a bigger story. This larger story is about how a smart, hardworking analyst became a big part of the world she covered. Meeker came to see herself not merely as an analyst but as a *player*—a power broker, a dealmaker, a force to be reckoned with. She was a true Internet insider—and other Internet insiders, most of whom were her friends, shared this exalted view of her. "I don't think of Mary as an analyst," says venture capitalist John Doerr. "I think of her as a service provider for investors, entrepreneurs, and management teams." As a result Meeker did things that utterly compromised her as a stock picker.

In responding now to criticism that she let investors down, Meeker refuses to admit—or even see—how compromised she is. She defends herself in part by saying she feels protective toward the phenomenon she helped launch—and especially toward the dozens of companies she helped Morgan Stanley take public: "There is something compelling about . . . playing an important role in something that will never happen again. . . . I feel a— 'stewardship' is a strong word—but I feel a keen sense of responsibility." She adds, "If you take a company public and you are really aggressive on the downside, it can be devastating." Of course, if you're *not* aggressive on the downside, it can be devastating for investors. But that was never a Meeker priority.

Though she was Queen of the Bubble, Meeker hardly reigned alone. The stories that follow explore the many ways investment banks now abuse the trust of their core customers—investors trying to build capital and companies trying to raise it. "Betrayal on Wall Street" explains how the IPO market became a racket in which banks consistently shortchange the start-up clients they're advising in order to create quick profits for institutional traders. In "Hear No Risk, See No Risk, Speak No Risk" we learn how a chorus of telecom analysts overlooked warning signs at a company called Winstar and kept croaking "buy" right up until this broadband wanna-be choked on its own debt. And in his confessional essay "Diary of a Financial Pornographer," Nelson Schwartz takes a hit for all of us at *Fortune* and in the media who got caught up in the bubble madness. But first, there's Mary Meeker.

"It's a cool thing to take a great company public," Mary Meeker is saying. "You have to go up to the plate and swing for the fences." We're sitting in a corner conference room at Morgan Stanley's Times Square headquarters, a half hour into the first of several long interviews. I've come to ask Meeker about her record as a research analyst. But it becomes clear almost immediately that her real passion is the investment banking side of her job.

Though it's hardly news anymore that the Chinese Wall once separating investment banking from Wall Street research has eroded, what you realize in talking to Meeker is the extent to which these two supposedly conflicting functions—keeping companies happy and giving investors honest stock advice—are now organically intertwined. She talks unashamedly, for instance, about how she has used her research to help land banking deals for Morgan Stanley. And she describes how upset she became when Morgan Stanley lost a hotly contested deal to archrival Goldman Sachs. "I had never lost an IPO mandate in my life for a company that I wanted to take public," she says, sounding like, well, an investment banker. "I flipped into overdrive."

A notorious workaholic, Meeker left the office at 4 A.M. the day she first spoke to *Fortune*. She seems none the worse for wear; overdrive, in fact, appears to be her perpetual state. She launches into lengthy, digressive answers that hop self-consciously—and often humorously—from one subject to the next. That's typical Meeker. "Mary will just go off on those tangents," says a friend. "It's like trying to catch a meteor. That's how her mind works. It's a complicated place." It's also part of her charm. While she can be brutally high-handed with colleagues and subordinates—she's a diva, remember—she is also quick-witted, fun, and, when the occasion calls for it, self-deprecating. Being an analyst, she says, "is like being a Gumby. You're pulled in a lot of different directions."

Meeker got her first taste of the life fifteen years ago, when she entered the analyst training program at Salomon Brothers. Growing up in a small Indiana farm town, she had been fascinated with Wall Street since high school, when she entered a stock-picking contest and watched her stocks promptly double. By the time she joined Salomon Brothers, she had spent two years as a broker with Merrill Lynch, had earned her MBA from Cornell, and had a clear goal: she wanted to be a portfolio manager. She viewed the Salomon job as a useful stepping-stone.

Instead, she got hooked. Playing second banana to the firm's respected computer analyst, Michele Preston, Meeker covered the likes of Pitney Bowes and Eastman Kodak as well as the computer industry. When Preston jumped to S.G. Cowen in 1990, Meeker followed. A year after that investment banker Frank Quattrone, the legendary leader of Morgan Stanley's technology-banking team—it had taken Cisco and Apple public—offered Meeker a job as a senior analyst covering PCs and computer software. Though Morgan (along with Goldman Sachs) is the most prestigious investment-banking firm, Meeker turned Quattrone down the first time. "I didn't think I was ready to be a stand-alone analyst at a firm like Morgan Stanley," she explains now. But finally she succumbed.

For the next four years, Meeker labored in the lengthy shadow of Quattrone, a swashbuckling character who ran Morgan's tech group like a personal fiefdom. Although Meeker was involved in some IPOs—no underwriting can take place unless the firm's analyst "signs off" on it—her primary responsibility was covering such established companies as Microsoft and Compaq for Morgan Stanley's institutional clients. Soon after arriving at Morgan in 1991, she issued a massive report initiating coverage on ten software and computer stocks. She rated eight of them as buys. The following year most of them plummeted, giving her, as she puts it now, one of her "two shitty years as a stock picker." (The other "shitty year," of course, was 2000.)

That first Morgan Stanley report was more than just a stock-picking document, though. It also sent out what Meeker called her "Ten Commandments for Investing in Technology Stocks"— and it offered remarkably sound advice. "Technology stocks are volatile . . ." she warned. "But when no one is interested in them . . . sell when everyone is interested in technology (or when attendance at technology conferences reaches record levels or when your grandmother wants to buy a hot technology IPO)." Investors should buy "when fundamentals are intact"; they should sell when stocks "begin to trade down after large rises." And the tenth commandment: "Don't fall in love with technology companies. Remember to view them as investments." Sadly, these were rules that Meeker herself would abandon in the coming years.

Two things happened in the mid-1990s that changed everything for Meeker. First, on August 9, 1995, Morgan Stanley underwrote the initial public offering of a tiny software company called Netscape. To this day people in Silicon Valley mark the Netscape IPO as ground zero for the Internet era. Netscape set the pattern for all the hot dot-com IPOs to come: it had incredible buzz and no profits (it gave away its popular Web browser), and it enjoyed a huge pop in the market on its first day of trading. Perhaps most important, it alerted the investing public to the promise of this new thing called the Internet.

Later Meeker would claim to have brought Netscape to Quattrone's attention, telling him, "This is a really big idea." Though Quattrone loyalists scoff at her account, citing his close ties to Netscape cofounder Jim Clark, what's clear is that Netscape was huge for Meeker. For one, she was associated with a big winner in an exciting new industry, something every analyst craves. For another, as the analyst who brought Netscape public, she was suddenly in a position to become the authority on the Internet.

She quickly set out to make the most of this opportunity. Four months after the Netscape IPO, Meeker published a 300-page research report called simply "The Internet Report." Crammed with charts, primers, tables, and stock recommendations, it quickly became the bible for investors interested in the Web. No less a personage than Intel's Andy Grove read it while on vacation in Hawaii—and suddenly realized that Intel needed to embrace the Net. Demand for the report was so high that Morgan Stanley even arranged for it to be commercially published—a first for a piece of Street research. Meeker was becoming a star.

There's one other thing about Meeker's role in the Netscape deal that seems important in retrospect. In covering the newly public company, Meeker displayed the protectiveness that would come to characterize her work. Referring privately to Netscape as "my baby," she aggressively defended the stock, even after Microsoft took dead aim at the company with its competing browser. In January 1997, Deutsche Morgan Grenfell analyst Bill Gurley, citing execution risks, downgraded Netscape from buy to accumulate. The stock dropped nearly 20 percent. Meeker responded two days later by upgrading her own rating to a strong buy—and angrily told another analyst, "If this company dies, it's Bill Gurley's fault." The shares continued their tumble, recovering only after AOL announced it was buying the beleaguered Netscape—almost two years later.

And the second critical mid-1990s event? That was the sudden departure of Frank Quattrone and his top deputies from Morgan Stanley on Easter Sunday, 1996. In what became known inside the firm as "the Easter massacre," Quattrone decamped for Deutsche Morgan Grenfell, which had agreed to give him unheard-of autonomy and pay. In an earlier age a move like that would have been unthinkable. But the world had changed. Though an old-line firm like Morgan still had plenty of prestige, it could no longer expect bankers to stay for life—or business to fall in its lap. Quattrone's departure was just another signal that Morgan had to get in the trenches and work for deals like everyone else.

Though none of Morgan's tech analysts had known of Quattrone's plans, he belatedly made a bid to steal the top three: Meeker, George Kelly, who covered data-networking, and Chuck Phillips, who covered business software. But after Morgan Stanley made them generous counteroffers, they all stayed put.

For Meeker, at least, there was another calculation at play. "Morgan had just lost the people who had built their tech practice," explains a friend. "Mary opted to stay, knowing Morgan needed a new star." With Quattrone gone—replaced by blander souls who lacked his stature—Mary Meeker soon became the new Quattrone.

We need to stop a moment to absorb the implications of this. Plenty of publications, including this one, have pointed out that analysts have become far more involved in the process of landing banking business than they once were. The modern analyst helps the banking team smoke out promising companies, sits in on strategy sessions, and promises—implicitly at least—to "support" the company once it has gone public with favorable research. That this makes tough-minded, independent stock research difficult, if not impossible, is no longer even an issue at most firms; investment banking brings in far more money than, say, brokerage commissions from grateful investors, thankful for unbiased research. Indeed, these days most analysts' pay is directly linked to the number of banking deals they're involved in.

What Meeker did once Quattrone left, however, went far beyond the usual analyst's accommodation. Rather than supporting Morgan's Internet banking effort, she began driving it. She became the firm's Internet rainmaker and its key dealmaker. "When I was at Deutsche Morgan Grenfell," says Gurley, now a venture capitalist (and *Fortune* columnist), "we talked about Mary being one of the best investment bankers on the planet." She developed close ties to VCs like John Doerr, who gave her early peeks at promising companies. She visited all the top start-ups to decide which were Morgan Stanley material. "Mary started to be the primary relationship person," says a high-profile banker at a competing firm (who, like most people *Fortune* spoke to about Meeker, would talk only if promised anonymity). "She'd almost bring her bankers in as a sort of execution team." Replies Meeker: "Our bankers were great. I was part of a team."

There was another dynamic at play: because the Internet was so new, investors wanted a credible source to explain it to them—and tell them which companies to invest in. And who was more credible than Meeker? She became the gold standard, the person who gave a company instant stature merely by her association with it. Thus, even as she was chasing companies for Morgan Stanley, companies were chasing her. "The bankers were superfluous," says Todd Wagner, former CEO of Broadcast.com, recalling his company's decision to go with Morgan when it went public in 1998. "Our rationale was, if we went with Morgan Stanley, we'd get Mary Meeker and we'd get a lot of attention."

"We were not competing with Morgan at all," adds a rival banker. "We were competing with Mary Meeker. The clients made that very clear." Over time, competing firms cooked up strategies to combat the Meeker factor. One favorite was to spread rumors that Meeker was about to leave Morgan Stanley—which the Morgan people would have to quell.

Which is not to say that Meeker chased every deal. On the contrary: in the early years of Internet mania, she was highly selective, choosing only those companies she thought would be huge winners—and that she could support with a clear conscience. Meeker points out today that Morgan Stanley did only about 8 percent of all Internet IPOs—and that she turned down a tremendous number of deals. During due diligence, recalls former Morgan tech banker Andre de Baubigny, Meeker would "torture" companies as she probed management teams. Sometimes she passed on companies she should have grabbed—most notably Yahoo!, which she blew off when it wanted to talk to Morgan Stanley about going public.

What almost never happened was that Meeker lost an Internet deal she really wanted. By Meeker's count, it happened only three times. As she describes the first, she starkly illustrates just how caught up she had become in the competition to win banking business. And the lengths to which she would go to win.

It was May 1998, and Morgan Stanley was in a "bake-off" to land eBay's upcoming IPO. During Morgan's presentation, Meeker and her bankers acted as if the business were already theirs, according to an eBay director. "She was on her pager a lot and getting calls from the CEO of Hewlett-Packard," he says. "The fact that she was a rock star showed itself a little at the meeting. Our concern was that we might not get enough of her attention." The eBay board chose Goldman instead.

Shocked by the rejection, Meeker "flipped into overdrive," as she later put it to *Fortune.* She offered her personal apology to eBay CEO Meg Whitman for failing to convey her full appreciation of eBay's business. Then she held out a carrot no other firm could proffer: a Mary Meeker research report. In July she met Whitman at Boston's Logan Airport for dinner and presented her with a draft of a glowing report on the company. Whitman told Meeker that she felt honor-bound to stick with Goldman. Then, when eBay went public a few months later—and with the Goldman analyst forbidden from issuing any eBay research during the post-IPO quiet period—Meeker took the unprecedented step of publishing her completed eBay report on the very first day of trading. She instantly became the most visible analyst on the stock. "eBay's market opportunity is huge," she proclaimed—and gave the stock an outperform rating. Seven months later, when the company did a $1.1 billion secondary stock offering, eBay forced Goldman to split the business with Morgan.

In 1996, *Institutional Investor* magazine, which has been ranking Wall Street analysts for some thirty years, created a new category: Internet analysts. Mary Meeker, of course, grabbed the top spot.

And deservedly so. Without question, she was way ahead of most analysts in seeing how big the Internet could be—and how profoundly it would touch every aspect of American life and commerce. Major institutional investors devoured her "big picture" reports, which she rolled out regularly on such subjects as Internet advertising, retailing, and infrastructure.

Meeker was also important in helping popularize the notion that the Internet was a giant "land grab," in which companies had to sacrifice profits for rapid growth. And she was a leader in using new metrics to assess Internet companies. How could it be otherwise? These were companies, after all, that were going public with great hopes but no clear path to profits—and yet the analysts needed to be able to justify the stocks to investors. With the original Internet IPO—Netscape—Meeker used a metric she called "discounted terminal valuation," a novel calculation based on anticipated margins and growth rates five years down the road.

As the Internet exploded, Meeker became bolder about relying on nonfinancial metrics such as "eyeballs" and "page views." Here she is, for instance, in a July 1998 report on Yahoo! (entitled

"Yahoo!, Yippee, Cowabunga . . ."): "Forty million unique sets of eyeballs and growing in time should be worth nicely more than Yahoo!'s current market value of $10 billion." Four months later, when she revisited the company, which had just reported its third quarter, she wrote that there were "five key financial highlights." First on her list—even before revenues or operating margins—was the fact that Yahoo!'s page views had risen 25 percent.

She also became amazingly flippant about valuation. On launching coverage, in the fall of 1997, of Amazon—which quickly became one of her flagship stocks (and later used Morgan for three big bond deals)—Meeker wrote that the company's valuation "gives us heartburn of a gargantuan proportion." But she quickly dismissed the concern: "We have one general response to the word 'valuation' these days: 'Bull market.' . . . We believe we have entered a new valuation zone." "She moved out her horizon on fundamentals," says CSFB tech analyst Mark Wolfenberger. "It's like some of those parties you went to in college—man, until the police showed up, it was wonderful."

Did Meeker ever show concern that it might all blow up someday? In fact, she did—repeatedly. In her "overview" reports, she often expressed nervousness at how fast dot-com stocks were rising. One of her mantras throughout the Internet boom was that only 30 percent of Internet companies would wind up being long-term winners, while the other 70 percent would ultimately fall below their IPO price. But which companies were included in that 70 percent? That she never said—except that they weren't any of the companies *she* covered. With rare exceptions, she kept an outperform rating on all her stocks.

To be sure, Morgan Stanley clients who bought Internet stocks that Meeker recommended were making a boatload of money—crazy valuations be damned. Yahoo!, Amazon, eBay—not to mention Priceline, FreeMarkets, and CNET—it seemed like all the Net stocks she covered were doubling and tripling. And whenever one of them hit a bump in the road, she was quick to reassure one and all that it would turn out all right in the end.

Was Meeker's unwillingness to downgrade stocks a function

of her desire to protect banking business? She insists that was not the case. She acknowledges, however, that she was protective of the companies she helped take public: "I am hard-pressed to downgrade a stock of a company I fundamentally believe in over the long term," she says.

But consider the case of America Online (now AOL Time Warner, the owner of *Fortune*'s publisher), a company Meeker began covering way back in 1993—shortly after Morgan Stanley did a follow-on stock offering for the company. She awarded AOL a strong buy and has kept either that rating or an outperform on the company ever since—including the dark days of 1996, when the company was faced with huge losses, service screwups, and questionable accounting.

Today Meeker describes her willingness to stick by AOL during the tough times as one of her best calls ever. But at least one Morgan Stanley client has a dimmer view of her stance during that period. In the fall of 1996, a Denver fund manager heard from a Morgan Stanley salesperson that Meeker had declared during the morning meeting that maintaining her strong buy on AOL was "the worst mistake of her career."

Troubled by the call, the fund manager, who held millions of dollars' worth of AOL stock, spent two weeks trying to reach Meeker. When she finally called back, he recalls, "she waved me off the stock. She basically said, 'Look, I don't think I would mess around with AOL here. There are too many big issues.'" He adds, "She was talking out of both sides of her mouth: 'Look, I've got a strong buy on the stock, but I don't have any conviction.' And when the stock recovered, she took a victory lap!"

Meeker insists she wouldn't have made the "worst mistake" remark at the morning meeting. She acknowledges, however, that her confidence in AOL had evaporated. "The number of people who truly believed in that company at that time was very small. That was pretty lonely. . . . I was basically ready to throw in the towel on the company. The pressure got to me." Meeker also admits that these sentiments were known to members of the Morgan sales force. In fact, she says that it was a couple of institutional salesmen who talked her out of dropping her strong buy rating on the stock.

By 1999, Internet mania was in full swing—and Meeker was its reigning celebrity. Just before the year began, *Barron's* pasted that "Queen of the Net" label on her; in April, *The New Yorker* published its glowing profile, making her, in effect, a crossover hit. By midyear, fielding Meeker's media calls—two dozen or more a day—had become a full-time job for a Morgan PR staffer. When Meeker arrived at a SoHo loft for a *Vanity Fair* photo shoot, the photo team grew hushed—"It's *Mary!*"—and rushed to offer her a cappuccino.

Everyone, it seemed, wanted a piece of Meeker. Dot-com entrepreneurs tried to figure out what red-eye she was taking so they could buttonhole her during the flight. Barbra Streisand, Reggie Jackson, and Saudi prince Alwaleed tapped her personal investing counsel. Morgan's nontech clients wanted her advice on how to bring out their inner Internet. Viacom was so insistent on having Meeker at a meeting of division heads that the company dispatched a corporate jet to ferry her to Bermuda and back for a ninety-minute presentation. "I'd go to China," says a former Morgan executive, "and the bankers would say, 'You gotta get Mary Meeker out here.'"

Did this take a toll? Of course it did. Meeker's hours, always brutal, became death defying. She had assistants working around the clock. She also became stretched incredibly thin, with junior analysts doing much of her research and fund managers and companies alike complaining that it was impossible to get through to her. Although the firm had steadily expanded its Internet research team—ultimately attaching the word "Internet" to the titles of twenty-six analysts—there was only one Morgan Stanley Internet analyst anyone wanted to hear from: Meeker. For her part, she was intent on keeping her finger in everything. Says de Baubigny: "It became hard to scale the business because there was such a reliance on one person."

In time Meeker began signing her name to research reports that were largely written by others. For instance, the business-to-business software company Ariba fell naturally to Meeker's colleague Chuck Phillips, a top-ranked analyst in his own right. But Ariba told Morgan Stanley that it would not get its IPO business unless Meeker's name was on the research reports. Though Phillips did most of the work, Meeker coauthored Morgan's Ariba research. Ditto Martha Stewart Living Omnimedia, a traditional media company that wanted to be perceived—and valued—as a dot-com. That meant that it needed Meeker. To get its IPO business, Meeker signed on as coanalyst.

At the peak, Meeker was following thirty companies—twice the normal research load. "My name ended up on things where I was not the point person," she says now—now that many of those stocks have tanked. "It's the way corporations work. You gotta be a team player." She adds, "I did what I was asked to do."

Trying to cope with the craziness of 1999, Meeker began to feel new pressures both as an analyst and as an investment banker. And, she concedes today, she succumbed.

Let's take investment banking first. Meeker had long prided herself on Morgan Stanley's taking public only the very best prospects—the premier company in every "space," as they used to say. But in 1999 the number of Internet IPOs exploded from 42 the year before to 294, making it virtually impossible for Morgan Stanley to stay on the high road and not fall in the closely watched market-share rankings. With Credit Suisse First Boston—whose tech group was then being run by none other than Frank Quattrone—and Goldman Sachs aggressively pursuing Internet IPOs, Meeker was suddenly under intense pressure to maintain Morgan's share of the business.

For instance: in 1999, Meeker had decided not to pursue the IPO of the Internet grocer Webvan because she didn't have faith in its business model. Similarly, she passed on the women's-content site iVillage. But both companies had spectacular IPOs and were soon sporting monster market caps—$8 billion in the case of Webvan, and $2.6 billion for iVillage. With iVillage now at $1.42 a share and Webvan at thirteen cents, she was clearly right to stay away—from an analyst's standpoint. But from a banking perspective, the initial success of those IPOs meant that Meeker had egg on her face.

How did she react? By lowering her standards. Abandoning her "only the best" dictum, she took public a raft of second-tier companies that have now become embarrassments to Morgan Stanley: HomeGrocer, Women.com, AskJeeves, tickets.com, Last-minute.com.

Meeker could see that deal quality was deteriorating. But, she says, "we had to take risks. . . . We couldn't not be in that game." Thus, in 1999, Morgan Stanley did twenty-seven Internet IPOs. Though that was still less than 10 percent of all Web IPOs, it was more Internet underwritings than the firm had done the previous four years combined. One result: Meeker's salary jumped from a reported $6 million to $15 million.

As an analyst, she was also feeling pressure. Forced to support companies that weren't all that good, at valuations that were increasingly difficult to justify, she was boxed in. In May 1999, Morgan Stanley took a company called Scient public at $20. By the time the quiet period had ended—and Morgan, with Meeker as coanalyst, could initiate coverage—the stock had jumped to almost $40 a share. Because of the run-up, the Morgan analysts gave the stock a rare "neutral" rating, citing valuation concerns. Three months later they upgraded to "outperform"—even though the stock had climbed to $63. "The market was saying, 'You're an idiot, you're an idiot, you're an idiot,'" Meeker says now. "This is the reality of the world we lived in."

"The hardest call to make is to be negative and wrong," says CSFB analyst Wolfenberger. "You had analysts going negative on Amazon and having the stock triple from that point. Those analysts aren't in business anymore."

And then it all fell apart. NASDAQ collapsed, dot-coms imploded, and the valuation bubble burst. Mary Meeker went from hero to goat.

The essential charge that has been hurled at her this past year centers on her refusal to downgrade her stocks, even as they dropped 70 percent, 80 percent, more than 90 percent in some cases. In effect she's being accused of selling out investors to keep Morgan Stanley's banking clients happy. In *The New York Times* last December, Gretchen Morgenson noted that Meeker had an out-perform rating on all of her Internet stocks—down an average of 83 percent—and pointedly asked a Morgan Stanley PR official whether "her nonstop optimism had anything to do with the fact that most of the companies had engaged Morgan Stanley as an investment bank."

Meeker, for her part, feels unfairly maligned. "I'm tired of the witch-hunt punching-bag stuff," she says in frustration. "The other side of the story never seems to get told." The "other side," as Meeker sees it, goes like this. Last year, admittedly, was an awful year for her stock picks—but only the second bad year of her career. ("Do you judge Ted Williams on one bad year?") If you look at the totality of her record, she says, you'll see that in the time she's been at Morgan Stanley, her picks have created nearly $700 billion in wealth. But 88 percent of that figure comes from three computer stocks—Microsoft, Dell, and Compaq, where she hasn't been an important voice in years—plus AOL Time Warner. The dot-com stocks she is most closely associated with—such as Priceline, Yahoo!, and Amazon—have been disasters in the past year.

Yet even now Meeker is not ready to concede that these stocks are disasters, even with Priceline at $4 (from $162), Yahoo! at $19.50 (from $237), and Amazon at $15 (from $106). On the contrary, she insists that they still deserve their "outperform" rat-ing. After the "nuclear winter," she says, we'll see "the spring bloom" for her favorite stocks. Sometime within the next two to three years, the "aggregate" valuation of the "leading names" that make up her recommended list will exceed even the heights they reached during the dot-com bubble. Says Meeker: "Our bet is that the winners that come out of this, the market value of the leaders, are going to make all the things that came before them look like chump change."

As for disgruntled individual investors who feel misled by her recommendations, she offers little sympathy. As she told *The Wall Street Journal,* "Every individual has got to be accountable for how they're allocating their investments." Her "real" constituency, she added, is professional money managers and other institutional investors.

To *Fortune* she said, "Did we do some deals we shouldn't have done? Yes. Did we recommend some stocks we shouldn't have? Yes." But, she added, "it's difficult to get hit and hit and hit when we did a better job than any other firm."

She's right, of course, that individuals who have lost money in this market need to look themselves in the mirror before they begin blaming Wall Street analysts. But the plain implication of her statement is that institutions are sophisticated enough to see through her ratings. And, indeed, some of them are. Former hedge-fund manager Jim Cramer says that it's been clear since last summer that "no one [on Morgan's sales staff] was pushing her stuff, because she wasn't enthusiastic. She has a buy because she's gotta have a buy. I thought she distinguished herself by not pushing the stuff. You might call that duplicitous. I was happy because it made me money."

The most critical point is this: Mary Meeker got so caught up in the allure of the Internet—the celebrity, the money, the thrill of dealmaking—that she forgot that she was supposed to be analyzing companies. "She was flying at 50,000 feet, talking about trends," says a rival banker. "She had no idea what the fundamentals were." Thus, when a company like Priceline turned out to have serious problems, including its disastrous foray into gasoline and groceries, Meeker didn't have a clue. Instead, here's what she says about Priceline, a company (it almost goes without saying) that Morgan took public in 1999: "It wasn't troubled until it was troubled. It was fine on Wednesday, bad on Thursday. . . . You can say, 'Why didn't the idiot analyst figure it out?' [But] you have to have some degree of trust in the concepts and the management team. With Priceline, that was a mistake." Even so, she maintains her outperform rating on the stock.

Then again, why wouldn't she? "It's one thing if you've got a disciplined valuation criteria," says a banker who worked with Meeker. "But if you don't and you're outperform for no good reason, what's the reason for turning it to an underperform?"

In that first interview with *Fortune,* Meeker said that her approach has always been to find the big idea and latch on to it. "If the approach that worked for me in the past doesn't work in the future, I'll make the wrong call," she said. Well, that's one way of looking at it. Here's another: "If you're going to say 'Buy, buy, buy,'" says a former Morgan Stanley executive, "at some point, you gotta say 'Sell.'"

Have you experienced a few worrisome symptoms as you clicked the TV remote? A powerful side effect of the easing of federal restrictions on prescription drug advertising has been a flood of television commercials that tout prescriptions for our well-being. Lisa Belkin in *Mother Jones* presents the implications of marketing sophisticated medicine as you would soap. If we were a nation of hypochondriacs before, we haven't seen anything yet.

Lisa Belkin

Prime-Time Pushers

WHEREVER YOU FLIP on the TV dial nowadays you will find commercials for medications that you cannot actually buy. Not without the permission of your doctor (or the aid of the Internet, but we'll talk more about that later). These are serious drugs, with potentially dangerous consequences, but the mood of the ads is upbeat and cheery. Cholesterol busters battle for market share. Antidepressants come with handy checklists of symptoms. Joan Lunden hawks Claritin. Newman from *Seinfeld* pitches an influenza drug. Pfizer spokesman Bob Dole promotes cures for erectile dysfunction.

No, you are not simply getting old and noticing this more. Television ads for prescription drugs, which were all but outlawed as recently as four years ago, are now taking over your TV set. To wit: pharmaceutical companies spent an estimated $1.7 billion on TV advertising in 2000, 50 percent more than what they spent in 1999, more than double the 1998 amount. In 1991, only one brand of prescription medication was marketed on network television by the route the industry calls "direct to consumer," or DTC. By the end of 1997, there were twelve drugs on that list, and by 2000, there were at least fifty.

The rush to the airwaves was triggered by the U.S. Food and Drug Administration, which, until four years ago, had required that manufacturers include nearly all of the consumer warning label in any pitch—something possible in a magazine advertisement but prohibitive in a thirty-second television spot. The sole exceptions were for so-called reminder and help-seeking ads— ones that named either the product or the condition being treated, but not both. The result was some very confusing ads.

For the better part of a decade, advertising agencies, pharmaceutical companies, and the major television networks lobbied for less restrictive rules, and, in August 1997, the FDA issued a "clarification" of its thirty-year-old regulations. Television commercials may now name both the product and the disease, as long as viewers are given information about "major" risks of the drug and directed to other sources of information—Web sites, magazine ads, toll-free numbers—for more detail. (And you thought those phone numbers were simply there to be helpful.)

Thus the United States became one of only two countries in the world (New Zealand being the other) where prescription drugs are hawked in prime time. Proponents of the FDA's policy shift say it creates a more informed patient because viewers see the ads, then have an intelligent give-and-take with a doctor. Critics say the shift creates more business for pharmaceutical companies by encouraging patients to seek out expensive, potentially dangerous drugs that they—and too often their doctors—know little about. "It was a sellout," says Larry D. Sasich, a pharmacist with Public Citizen's Health Research Group in Washington, D.C. "It's nothing more than a response to pressure from Madison Avenue."

Whatever the motivation, the shift has resulted in a quiet but dramatic transformation of the whole of our health care system. Gone is the time when doctors held complete power and prescription medicines were treated as a sacred and separate world. These ads mark the full dawning of an age when our very health is sold to us like soap. So turn on your TV set, relax, and take a pill. It's Prilosec time.

Before we talk about what is wrong (and unseemly and potentially dangerous about all of this), let's look at what's right. Seen through a certain lens, the explosion of DTC drug advertising is a continuation of the patients'-rights movement that began in force thirty years ago. Allowing such ads, says Nancy Ostrove, a branch chief within the FDA's Division of Drug Marketing, Advertising, and Communication, is not only a recognition of the unstoppable power of television but also the best way to inform consumers about available drugs. "There are certain real health benefits that can be achieved," she says.

Talk to any pharmaceutical company and they will tell you how thrilled they are to be educating the public. "From our point of view, one of the main purposes of direct-to-consumer advertising is education," says Emily Denney, a program manager in public affairs at AstraZeneca. Her company makes Prilosec, a drug that treats gastroesophageal reflux disease, a painful condition in which acid leaks from the stomach, causing chronic heartburn and even ulceration of the esophagus. Because of the $79.5 million the company spent on Prilosec ads in 1999, Denney says, "patients have been more easily able to diagnose symptoms that went ignored for many years. Our whole goal is just to encourage a conversation with your health care provider."

It is, to be sure, a self-interested, image-polishing argument, but the fact is that millions of us are sick and do not know it. According to the American Diabetes Association, more than 5 million diabetics in this country are unaware that they have the disease; one-third of Americans with major depression seek no treatment; and millions of Americans are ignorant of the fact that they have high blood pressure. Now consider this: in the two years since ads for Viagra first began to air, millions of men have visited their doctors specifically to get that drug—and thousands of them were diagnosed with serious underlying conditions. The Pharmaceutical Research and Manufacturers of America (PHRMA) estimates that for every million men who asked for the medicine, it was discovered that 30,000 had untreated diabetes, 140,000 had untreated high blood pressure, and 50,000 had untreated heart disease.

Let's face it, though; even the drug companies would agree that they are not spending all this money just to be helpful. They are spending all this money to sell their products. "We don't invest in things we don't find valuable to the business," says AstraZeneca's Denney.

Direct-to-consumer advertising has paid off handsomely for the pharmaceutical companies—often turning solid earners into blockbuster drugs. After spending nearly $80 million on Prilosec advertising in 1999 (up from $50 million in 1998), AstraZeneca saw sales rise 27 percent, to $3.8 billion. Pfizer, in turn, upped consumer advertising for its cholesterol drug, Lipitor, by more than $45 million in 1999, and sales of the drug jumped too—56 percent, to $2.7 billion.

Some of the most dramatic ad-and-effect can be seen in the category of allergy drugs. Claritin maker Schering-Plough launched the televised assault against sneezing in 1998 when it spent $185 million on advertising and saw sales more than double to $2.1 billion. Following the leader, Pfizer spent $57 million to promote its drug Zyrtec in 1999 and saw a 32 percent increase in sales; that same year, Aventis spent $43 million to promote Allegra, and sales increased by 50 percent.

There is no reason to believe, however, that there was any increase in the number of allergy sufferers in the United States during this time, and no sudden outpouring of pollen either. There was just an increase in the sale of prescription allergy medications. According to Scott-Levin, a pharmaceutical consulting company in Pennsylvania, doctor visits by patients complaining of allergy symptoms were relatively stable between 1990 and 1998, at a rate of 13 to 14 million per year. In 1999, there were 18 million allergy visits. The cause of the spike, critics point out, is clearly the advertising.

The purpose of allergy ads in particular and pharmaceutical ads in general "is to drive patients into doctors' offices and ask for drugs by brand name," says Sasich, of Public Citizen. And once they are in that office, patients often get what they want. "Physicians are more interested in pleasing their patients than you might think," says Steven D. Findlay, an analyst who is director of research and policy at the National Institute for Health Care Management. "It's a subtle interchange and exchange that happens between patient and doctor."

"Patients can be difficult to dissuade," says Dr. Jack Berger, an internist and rheumatologist in private practice in White Plains, New York, and sometimes it is easier for doctors to give in. "It adds an extra source of confusion and frustration to the doctor/patient relationship when the patient starts directing the treatment based on what they learned on TV," he says.

Studies have shown that patients requesting specific drugs often get just what they ask for. A survey by the FDA of people who had recently been to their doctors, for instance, found that 72 percent had seen or heard an ad for prescription drugs in the previous three months, mostly on TV. Close to 25 percent of those respondents had also asked their doctors for the first time about a condition or illness. Of those who asked for a specific drug by name, nearly half were given a prescription for it; 21 percent were recommended a different drug.

"These ads have had a very large impact on a somewhat hypochondriacal public," says Findlay. The ads do, in fact, educate consumers, he says, but what they often teach is how to describe your symptoms so you will be given a certain medication. "The purpose of advertising is not to inform people," Findlay continues. "It never has been and it never will be. The purpose of advertising, as we all know, is to make people buy more product so the company can make more money. It makes you desire that new product, just like that new car or that new gizmo."

Yes, doctors still hold the prescription pad, but parents have long held the credit cards, and toys are advertised directly to kids. At a dinner recently, Findlay listened as two other guests "kept going on and on about Celebrex," a new arthritis drug from Pfizer/Pharmacia. "They were talking about it like you talk about PCs," he says, "and there was a pride in the fact that they both were taking Celebrex, because it's advertised, it's on TV."

Evolution in advertising favors the slick and jazzy, and so it is with DTC television spots. In the old days, when the ads could not mention both the disease and the cure, the industry argued that such rules led to confusion. In the words of the PHRMA, the restrictions "prompted companies to advertise on television in more oblique ways, which, while meeting legal requirements, may have been less helpful to consumers. Consumers were often left to guess what the medicine was for."

Now the rules have changed. What, then, are we to make of new ads like those for Prilosec that feature a lithe woman in a flowing purple gown against the background of a clock with the uninformative slogan "It's Prilosec Time"? Is this a cure for depression? Irregularity? The ad itself gives no clue.

The original Prilosec ads, AstraZeneca's Denney says, described gastroesophageal reflux disease, or GERD, in some detail, showing cartoons of people in obvious distress and quizzing viewers about how often they experience heartburn. But GERD "is not the most pleasing-sounding word," Denney explains, and "you can't describe it perfectly in sixty seconds"—which may be why the company shifted to these more free-form reminder ads, which play up the fact that the pill itself is purple. And it's not just on television. The woman in the purple dress also appears in print ads, on the Web, and in subway stations plastered with purple pills. "The purpleness is a form of branding," Denney says. "People know Prilosec as 'the little purple pill.'"

One can't help but wonder, however, if such branding is having a far more troubling effect—whether occasional heartburn sufferers looking for a silver (or, in this case, purple) bullet might not be pressing their doctors for a powerful drug they don't really need. Americans tend to prefer the easy fix, and the ubiquitousness of direct-to-consumer ads, which dress medicine up in the same telegenic tinsel as perfume or sports cars, make our health seem as simple as we would like it to be. "The ads send a strong signal," says a report from the National Institute for Health Care Management, "that prescription drugs are just like any consumer product—soap, cereal, cars, snack food, et cetera."

Look more closely at a category of drugs known as statins—sold under such brand names as Lipitor, Pravachol, and Zocor—which have proved so effective at lowering cholesterol that some doctors see advertising them as a public service. "There are countless people who would be better served if they knew these drugs were available," says Dr. Ira S. Nash, associate director of the cardiovascular institute at the Mount Sinai School of Medicine in New York City. Yet other doctors worry about the side effect of those same ads. Statins can cause dangerous liver complications and their use needs to be carefully monitored by a doctor. In most cases, statins should be prescribed only to patients who have tried the lines of first defense—namely, diet and exercise—and who have failed to lower their cholesterol in spite of these lifestyle changes. If the ads make fighting cholesterol look too easy, patients may insist on skipping the hard part and going straight for the pill. "It takes time to speak to a patient about exercise, weight control, and diet. It takes less time to just write a prescription," says Dr. Berger, the private practitioner, and there is a danger that doctors will choose the easier course.

Cholesterol, at least, is a problem that can be measured. What about conditions whose symptoms are far more difficult to evaluate? Last year's ads for Paxil fall into this category. Paxil is an antidepressant approved by the FDA for the secondary purpose of treating social anxiety disorder, which Glaxo-SmithKline's ads describe as "an intense, persistent fear and avoidance of social situations." In its true, clinical form, it is a real and debilitating condition, but by reducing it to an ad—in which the subject experiences dread while giving an office presentation—Paxil can too easily sound like a pill for shyness.

One television ad that I find particularly egregious, bordering on offensive, is for a relatively new drug called Sarafem. The chemical composition of the pill is identical to that of Prozac, but last summer manufacturer Eli Lilly and Company received FDA permission to market it simultaneously for treatment of premenstrual disphoric disorder, or PMDD. The condition differs from PMS in that its symptoms are more emotional than physical and include depression, anxiety, and bursts of anger. And yet a television spot for the drug shows a frustrated woman struggling with a shopping cart in front of a supermarket, and makes Sarafem look like an easy fix for your average bad day.

"They're making everything into a disease," adds Dr. Nash, "and not only is it a disease, but it's a disease that society has a pill for."

Because more is at stake, viewers should bring a higher level of skepticism to pharmaceutical ads. Instead, there is reason to believe they are bringing less. A recent study in the *Journal of General Internal Medicine* found that nearly half of respondents believed that drug ads are prescreened and somehow sanctioned by the FDA. In fact, quite the opposite is true. The FDA's Ostrove explains that the agency is "forbidden by law from requiring preclearance." Although some pharmaceutical companies choose to submit their ads in advance, she says, they do so at their own discretion. All the FDA can require is that a copy of an ad be sent to its office when the ad begins to air.

Once the commercial arrives at the agency's Rockville, Maryland, headquarters, it is reviewed by one of the fourteen employees who screen 30,000 pieces of promotional material each year. "We allow a certain degree of puffery," Ostrove says, "but we don't allow overstatement of effectiveness or minimization of the risks." Even with such allowances, the FDA found that for the first thirty-seven drugs marketed directly to consumers on television, twenty ads failed to comply with federal regulations, including those requiring "fair balance" and the disclosure of side effects.

Of the estimated 200 television drug spots aired since the 1997 FDA rule change, the agency has cited thirty-two for non-compliance and has asked the companies to change all or part of the ads. The FDA told Pfizer/Pharmacia, for instance, that an advertisement for the arthritis drug Celebrex was misleading because "various multiple physical activities portrayed by arthritis patients (such as rowing a boat and riding a scooter)," along with "the audio statement 'Powerful twenty-four-hour relief from osteo-arthritis pain and stiffness,' collectively suggest that Celebrex is more effective than has been demonstrated by substantial evidence." In other words, the product does not work as advertised. Judith Glova, a spokeswoman for the company, says the ad was pulled and modified slightly—a statement was added, for example, noting that "individual results may vary"—and put back on television.

Similarly, Eli Lilly and Company was told that an ad for the osteoporosis drug Evista was misleading because "it mischaracterizes the nature of osteoporosis, resulting in an overstatement of Evista's benefits." Specifically, the agency said, the ad's description of osteoporosis as "a disease of thin, weak bones that can fracture and take away your independence" exaggerated both the risk and the consequence of a fracture. Eli Lilly spokesman David Marbaugh says the ad has been "suspended" while the company works with the FDA to revise it.

Most recently, I was pleased to learn, the FDA sent a letter to Eli Lilly about the ads for Sarafem—the very spots showing a woman struggling with a shopping cart. The ad does not define the condition it is designed to treat, the agency said, and as a result "trivializes the seriousness of PMDD." The company was asked to "immediately cease using this broadcast advertisement."

Eli Lilly decided to honor the agency's request, but, legally, the company could have kept running the ads indefinitely. As Findlay, the health care analyst, notes, "Everybody thinks the agency [the FDA] is this big nine-hundred-pound gorilla, but their actual power is limited." Essentially, all the agency can do is request compliance. If a company refuses, the FDA cannot impose fines or other punishments but must instead go through the courts for an injunction. "As a matter of course, most companies do change their ads," Findlay says, "but that is because they are concerned about the public relations implications. The heaviest hammer the FDA has in this department is embarrassing manufacturers."

The guiding rule of medicine is, "First, do no harm." What, then is the harm of pharmaceutical ads? Yes, they may be misleading, but it can be argued that most consumer ads are misleading. Why should we care? Who is this hurting? The most measurable harm is economic. "There is very strong circumstantial evidence," says Public Citizen's Sasich, "that some patients are getting drugs that may be stronger than they need. A less expensive, more easily obtained drug may be more appropriate."

Celebrex, says Findlay, is one example of potential pharmaceutical overkill. With first-year sales of $1.3 billion in 1999, it was the most successful drug launch in history. Celebrex and similar new arthritis drugs, such as Vioxx, represent an advance because they do not cause the level of gastrointestinal distress that alternative treatments, such as over-the-counter ibuprofen tablets, can. However, Findlay says that "the proportion of people with arthritis at high risk for that side effect is between 10 and 20 percent." But if you extrapolate from the number of prescriptions written for the drug, he says, then Celebrex and similar medications are "being taken by potentially 40 percent of arthritis patients. These medicines are going to people who have no clinically defined need."

A one-year dosage of Celebrex costs $900, says William Pierce, a spokesman for the Blue Cross and Blue Shield Association (BCBSA), while a one-year dosage of generic ibuprofen costs $24. Numbers like these are the major reason why BCBSA expects prescription drug costs to rise at least 15 percent each year through 2004.

"In some plans we are spending more on prescription drugs than on in-patient hospitalization, and one of the major reasons is direct-to-consumer advertising," says Christine Simmon, also of BCBSA, who notes that another reason is the aging of the population. Last year alone, BCBSA saw an estimated "25 percent increase in the cost of prescription drugs compared with 6 to 8 percent for physician and hospital services," she says.

In an effort to curb demand for expensive prescriptions, BCBSA has gone so far as to launch a new corporation, called RxIntelligence, which will attempt to inform the public about why they may not need the newest, flashiest drugs on the market. RxIntelligence, says Simmon, will study such things as the "cost benefit and risk of the drug and whether the existing treatment is just as good"—the sort of information that does not appear in pharmaceutical ads.

The PHRMA argues that the increase in prescription drug use "reflects the extraordinary value that medicines provide, to patients and the health care system. Increased utilization of medicines is a good thing—it helps many patients get well quicker." But Findlay reminds us that what we allocate to one slice of the health care pie must be taken from another. "Is this how we want to be spending our money?" he asks. "Do we want to be spending 25 percent of health care dollars on medication at the expense of home care or PET scans?"

A second harm of rampant pharmaceutical advertising, a harm that is harder to quantify but far more frightening, is to our health. The entire system of direct-to-consumer advertising relies on the assumption that there is an intermediary between the patient and the potentially harmful drug. "While DTC ads prompt patients to consult their doctors about available medicines," says a recent PHRMA report, "the doctor still holds the prescribing pen. Patients cannot get prescription medicines unless their physicians find that the medicines are necessary and appropriate."

But the world is changing in ways that make this statement untrue. Patients are increasingly hearing about new drugs before their doctors do. A recent poll by the American Association of Retired Persons found that 21 percent of consumers had asked their doctors for prescription drugs that the doctors knew little or nothing about. Dr. Berger tells me he knows of doctors who began to prescribe Celebrex before the clinical trials were even published, because patients were asking for it and because initial reports in the press indicated it was effective. Indeed, sales of Celebrex reached $1 billion before the final clinical-trial results were published in a peer-reviewed journal. Many doctors apparently didn't read Celebrex's package insert either. The drug contains sulfa, which can cause an allergic reaction in some patients. "People came in itching with hives," says Berger.

Even when all the known facts about a drug are published, there is no guarantee that new facts might not emerge, especially when the drug is new. One example is the ongoing controversy over the GlaxoSK drug Relenza. Approved in 1999, Relenza is an inhalable powder designed to treat common flu symptoms, reducing the illness's length by about a day. It was introduced with a cheeky television campaign featuring the character Newman from *Seinfeld.* The campaign received awards within the advertising industry, but the FDA was not amused. It described the ads as "misleading because they . . . suggest that Relenza is more effective" than has been "demonstrated by substantial evidence."

Soon after Relenza hit the market in October 1999, seven patients using it died. In part because Relenza had been so heavily promoted, the FDA then issued a "public health advisory" saying that while the exact involvement of the drug was unclear, there had been "several reports of deterioration of respiratory function following inhalation of Relenza" in patients with underlying breathing problems. By June 2000, use of Relenza had been linked to twenty-two deaths; in July, GlaxoSK announced a strengthened warning label for the drug. The FDA has since re-affirmed the safety of Relenza, when it is used as directed, and attributes many of the deaths to its use by patients to whom it should never have been prescribed. Relenza remains on the market, says GlaxoSK spokeswoman Laura Sutton, but the ads are no longer on the air.

It is still possible to buy Relenza over the Internet, however, which adds another variable to consumer access to prescription drugs. In March 1999, fifty-two-year-old Robert McCutcheon, of Lisle, Illinois, died of a heart attack that may have been triggered by Viagra, although there is no definitive way to know. Despite a family history of heart problems, which would have meant he was a poor candidate for the drug, McCutcheon had ordered Viagra online, at one of the growing number of Web sites that sell prescription medications without a doctor visit.

Viagra is hardly the only drug being sold this way. As part of my research for this article, I spent less than five minutes on-line and purchased a month's supply of Xenical, the Hoffmann–La Roche product for weight loss. It is intended only for patients who are clinically obese, but since no doctor ever saw me, I lied and said I weighed 300 pounds. The site even provided a handy chart telling me the exact weight cutoff for any given height in order to qualify. The pills arrived, as promised, within five business days, charged to my credit card.

Pharmaceutical companies, it should be said, are distressed by this phenomenon. Pfizer, which manufactures Viagra, recently reminded physicians that it is "improper" (though not actually illegal) to prescribe the drug without first examining the patient. And Ostrove calls the availability of drugs on-line "a separate but serious issue." When the FDA announced in 1997 that it was "clarifying" its regulations to favor television ads, it also announced that it would review the new approach this coming summer. "If we have reason to believe that our policies are creating a public health problem," Ostrove says, "we will reevaluate."

In the meantime, I have this bottle of Xenical sitting on my desk. While I'm not obese, there are those "few extra pounds" I put on over the holidays. What could be the harm? After all, the ads say that this stuff really works.

This article chronicles with painstaking accuracy the many millions of dollars paid to securities felon Michael Milken by big business since he left prison. Written by James B. Stewart in *The New Yorker*, it probably helped sway departing president Clinton from granting Milken a pardon. Stewart separates good works from big deals to present us with two decidedly different sides of Milken. Yet rest assured that the former junk-bond king retains his legendary ability to move mountains of money.

James B. Stewart

The Milken File: Neither Prison nor a Consent Decree Could Stop History's Greatest Dealmaker

I—THE GOOD WORKS

On May 6, 1995, two years after being released from prison, the securities felon Michael Milken, on behalf of the Milken Family Foundation, welcomed participants to a National Educator Awards ceremony and three-day conference at the Century Plaza Hotel, in Los Angeles. The honorees, educators from thirty states, received $25,000 each; a photograph on the foundation's Web site showed a group of excited teachers waving their checks in the air. Milken and his brother Lowell, who once worked with him at the now defunct securities firm of Drexel Burnham Lambert, launched the awards presentations in 1987, during the government's investigation into Milken's junk-bond empire. Although critics initially derided the awards event as a self-serving effort to gain public sympathy, no one can question the foundation's good works today. Thanks to Milken, more than 1,600 teachers and administrators have received awards totaling more than $40 million.

Each winner also received an all-expenses-paid trip to Los Angeles for the ceremony and the conference. "We were treated like royalty," Patricia Brooks, an elementary-school principal from Maryland who was honored at the 1995 conference, told me recently. "It was one of the most magnificent experiences I have ever had. Every detail was carefully and thoughtfully attended to. It made me feel so valued as a professional—as someone making a contribution not just to my students but to the future." She recalled meeting Milken, who she says was "very personable," and she admired his helpfulness and concern as he conducted a math demonstration with students from Mike's Math Club, a project that involved teaching math to inner-city children, and which began as part of Milken's court-ordered community service. Brooks has been invited back to the conference every year since, with all her expenses paid by the Milkens. Last year, conference participants attended the premiere of a Mel Gibson movie, with the actor himself present.

Brooks and some of her fellow educators were aware of Milken's past activities, and his prison sentence. "We focused on the fact that the family foundation provides this opportunity for teachers—that it had something to do with giving back and making us better at what we are doing," she said. "But it takes money, and he has money. I think the Milken family is taking a bold step, for whatever reason, to try to touch the future in a very different way."

Milken has poured a staggering amount of money and energy into the foundation. In 1993, soon after he was released from a minimum-security prison in Pleasanton, California, having served almost two years of a ten-year sentence, he received a diagnosis of prostate cancer. With the stamina that once had him at his famous X-shaped trading desk by 4:30 A.M., and with the assistance of many veterans of the public relations and legal teams that had fought government prosecutors on his behalf, he set out to rehabilitate both his health and his image. He embraced an array of mental, physical, and spiritual techniques, from meditation to holistic diets. (His cancer is now said to be in remission.) He put more than $50 million into a charitable organization called Cap Cure, which funds prostate-cancer research. He established the Milken Scholars Program, to provide college scholarships to needy students, and Dare Plus, an outgrowth of his community service. He has also started a scholarly nonprofit think tank, the Milken Institute; it publishes a magazine and sponsors the Milken Institute Global Conference, which is modeled on the Davos conference.

Milken finds time for other projects as well, including an educational outreach program at his alma mater, the University of Pennsylvania's Wharton School; the National Coalition for Cancer Survivorship; and the Stephen S. Wise Temple, in Los Angeles, where he has served on the board. These various good works have helped him win back the trust and confidence of a number of powerful public officials. At a fund-raising luncheon for Senate Democrats at the Beverly Hills home of Haim Saban, the creator of the Power Rangers and a generous contributor to the presidential campaigns of both Bill Clinton and Al Gore, Milken was seated at the table of the Senate majority leader, Tom Daschle. Mayor Rudolph Giuliani, who as a U.S. Attorney prosecuted Milken for securities fraud, recently consulted him on the subject of his own prostate cancer. Even President Clinton has called, to wish Milken well with his Cap Cure efforts. Last month, the *Times* reported that Clinton was considering pardoning Milken. Milken has the support of Ron Burkle, a prominent Democratic party contributor, and Giuliani recently told *The Wall Street Journal* that he, too, now supports a pardon for Milken.

Milken was a principal subject of my 1991 book, *Den of Thieves,* which chronicled the rise and fall of his junk-bond empire. (As a result of the book, a libel suit, financed largely by Lowell Milken, was brought against me and my publisher, and continued until last year, when a judge dismissed it. It is now on appeal.) During the corporate-buyout frenzy of the 1980s, Milken was the most dynamic—and the most highly paid—figure in American finance. In 1987, he received a bonus of $550 million from Drexel Burnham Lambert. By then, his annual conference of Drexel clients and potential clients had evolved into the notorious Predators' Ball in Beverly Hills, where corporate raiders like Carl Icahn and arbitrageurs like Ivan Boesky plotted hostile takeovers as Milken lectured on job formation and the scarcity of human capital. There were surprise appearances by Frank Sinatra and Diana Ross, followed by private parties in bungalows at the Beverly Hills Hotel. It was all part of Milken's phenomenally successful promotion of high-yield, high-risk bonds, which provided capital for companies that had been deemed too risky by conventional banks and bond underwriters. Today, junk bonds have become an integral part of American finance. Some Milken clients, such as the long-distance telephone service provider MCI, and Turner Broadcasting, did extremely well. But other entities, including many savings and loans, went bankrupt under the weight of the high-interest debt burden.

Most controversial among Milken's activities was the use of his bonds by corporate raiders. In deals fueled by his financing schemes, entire corporations changed hands, often at a pace that had never been seen before. Profits were sacrificed to pay interest costs on the deals, and many companies were forced into bankruptcy and restructurings; others survived but were nearly crippled. Bondholders and shareholders lost millions of dollars, and thousands of workers lost their jobs. Milken's supporters argued that, ultimately, these upheavals strengthened the nation's economy, produced new jobs, and helped create the boom of the nineties. Whether or not that is true, on September 7, 1988, the Securities and Exchange Commission filed a complaint against Milken alleging that he had conspired with Ivan Boesky and the corporate raider Victor Posner to engage in securities fraud and other violations in connection with more than eighteen separate transactions involving billions of dollars. The crimes and illegal conduct included market manipulation, defrauding Milken's own customers, insider trading, concealing the ownership of securities, and filing false information about the purpose of securities purchases. In 1990, Milken pleaded guilty to six felonies, including conspiracy with Boesky, who testified against him; concealing the true ownership of large stock positions; and aiding and abetting the evasion of net-capital rules. The S.E.C. estimated that the cost of his crimes to investors was more than $1 billion.

In sentencing Milken, Judge Kimba Wood, of the Southern District of New York, emphasized that financial markets must be "free of secret manipulation" and told him, "When a man of your power in the financial world, at the head of the most important department of one of the most important investment banking houses in this country, repeatedly conspires to violate, and violates, securities and tax laws in order to achieve more power and wealth . . . a significant prison term is required in order to deter others." She then sentenced him to ten years.

At the time of Milken's sentencing, he was ordered to pay more than $1 billion. Still, upon his parole, in 1993, he possessed a fortune estimated to be $1 billion. Under the terms of a March 1991 consent agreement that he made with the S.E.C., he was free to embark on any moneymaking activity he liked save one: he was barred for life from the securities business and, specifically, "association with any broker, dealer, investment adviser, investment company, or municipal securities dealer." Milken chose, instead, to devote himself to charitable endeavors. "I have never been motivated by money in my entire life," he told *Fortune* in 1996. He appeared to be a parole officer's dream.

Thus it would have taken an unusually cynical observer at Milken's 1995 National Educator Awards gala to question the presence of a number of well-known corporate executives and former Milken investment-banking clients. These included Bert Roberts, Jr., the chairman of MCI, who addressed the conference; Rupert Murdoch, the chairman of the media conglomerate News Corporation, who had delivered the conference's opening speech the previous year; and Lawrence Ellison, the chairman of the software company Oracle. These men had, in fact, become ubiquitous in the Milken charitable universe. Roberts had joined the Cap

Cure board, and he spoke at Milken Institute programs and at a program cosponsored by News Corporation.

Milken, who introduced Roberts and Murdoch to each other at the previous year's awards, had been guiding them toward a major business deal. He later told S.E.C. investigators that he had suggested that "they would be good partners . . . I tried to encourage them to talk to one another or spend time with one another over time and visit."

By the time of the 1995 conference, however, these visits were not going well. So at the conference luncheon, Milken seated Murdoch and Roberts at a table with him. Later, one of Milken's employees, Steven Fink, drove Roberts to Murdoch's offices, down the street from the hotel, and remained there while the two men hammered out a deal.

Fink had been Milken's next-door neighbor, in Encino, for more than a decade, and had gone to work for him just before he pleaded guilty and went to prison. Fink now worked for a Milken business entity called MC Group. Fink later recalled telling Roberts and Murdoch, "If you guys are going to enter into a joint venture, this is it." Fink took notes of the two sides' demands, then typed them into a proposed agreement. As the terms of the deal evolved, he typed new versions, preparing three drafts in all. After nearly four hours of negotiations, Murdoch and Roberts signed an agreement. The deal committed MCI to an investment of as much as $2 billion in News Corporation.

After shredding all but the two signed copies of the final agreement, Fink returned to the Century Plaza, where Patricia Brooks and her fellow educators were enjoying that evening's awards dinner. Fink reported back to Milken, "Rupert and Bert resolved their differences."

"Great," Milken replied.

Four days later, MCI announced that it was buying a $1 billion stake in News Corporation, with the option to invest an additional $1 billion, and embarking on several joint ventures, including a satellite-broadcasting deal. News Corporation paid Milken $27 million for his "consulting" services in the transaction and agreed to pay another $20 million if MCI exercised its option to invest the second billion. Milken also asked MCI for a payment.

On September 29, 1995, before Milken and MCI could agree on a fee, an article appeared in *The Wall Street Journal* about a separate deal that he was involved in, between Time Warner and the Turner Broadcasting System. The article revealed that Milken had received a fee of $50 million for "counseling" Ted Turner. The S.E.C. responded by opening an informal investigation into whether Milken was violating the consent decree.

The precise definition of what constitutes working as an investment adviser or broker in a case like Milken's had rarely been tested in court. Merely accepting a fee for introducing two people who subsequently forge a transaction does not in itself constitute forbidden activity. But more overt investment-banking activities, such as negotiating transactions, either directly or indirectly, or helping to structure such transactions, would generally be prohibited. The investigation into whether Milken had crossed that line eventually expanded to cover possible criminal activity.

The S.E.C. issued subpoenas calling for Milken and others to produce records, and for Milken to disclose the full extent of his business activity. Lawyers for Milken and for most of the witnesses who were subpoenaed demanded that the investigation be conducted confidentially, and so its substance has never been made public. In July 1999, after the S.E.C. completed its investigation, I made a formal request for access to deposition testimony and exhibits under the Freedom of Information Act. Milken and the other witnesses were given an opportunity to contest the public release of the materials and to request certain redactions, but nearly a year and a half later, in November 2000, thousands of pages of transcripts and additional pages of exhibits were made available to me.

This written record of the government's investigation provides a portrait of Milken's activities from 1993, when he was released from prison, until 1996, when he again came under scrutiny. It is sharply at odds with Milken's image as someone engaged almost exclusively in charitable endeavors, for during that period he earned some $92 million in fees for "facilitating" deals. The S.E.C. investigated Milken's involvement in many major transactions or proposed transactions, some of which have never been revealed, including News Corporation's 1994 acquisition of a dozen television affiliates from New World Communications Group; MCI's deal with News Corporation in 1995; a proposed $1 billion investment in Turner Broadcasting by Microsoft in 1995; and Time Warner's acquisition of Turner Broadcasting in 1996. The transcripts also mention a number of other proposed deals in which Milken was involved; the principals' identities were deleted on the grounds that they constitute proprietary business secrets.

The witnesses in the Milken case include some of the most powerful figures in American business: John F. (Jack) Welch, Jr., the chairman of General Electric; John Malone, the chairman of Liberty Media and the former chairman of the cable operator TCI; Ronald O. Perelman, the chairman of Revlon; Gerald Levin, the chairman of Time Warner; Lawrence Ellison, of Oracle; and Rupert Murdoch, Ted Turner, and Bert Roberts, all of whom had extensive dealings with Milken during the period.

The picture that emerges of Milken's influence in the business world would be remarkable even if he weren't a convicted felon. That he was still on probation makes it more puzzling. Why would Milken even think of pursuing activities that might raise questions of legality and put him at risk of returning to jail? ("The Predators' Ball is now the Educators' Ball," a government lawyer told me.) Harvey Pitt, a former general counsel to the S.E.C., who represented MCI in the investigation, said, "It doesn't take a rocket scientist to realize he was certainly close to the line." Pitt also remarked, "It is extraordinary under the circumstances. Why did he do this?"

II—THE DEALS

On April 15, 1996, the S.E.C. called Milken as its first witness. Accompanied by his lawyers, he testified in Los Angeles. Milken seemed eager to cooperate, and proved surprisingly expansive—at least, as long as the questions focused on his strategic vision and his ideas about "content."

"Beginning in '93, I've had a philosophy that content, both entertainment content and computer-systems applications software content, would hold enduring value over time," Milken explained. He compared the plight of MCI and other telecommunications providers in the mid-1990s to that of cable operators in the early eighties, who found that they needed to gain some control over the films they delivered.

Milken made these points to Roberts and Murdoch, both of whom seem to have had the highest respect for his judgment. When Roberts took over MCI after the death of its founder, Bill McGowan, in 1992, he discovered a collection of clippings about Milken among McGowan's effects. Milken had played a vital role in financing McGowan's astonishing challenge of AT&T's monopoly over long-distance telephone service. Roberts, who had been McGowan's loyal number two for many years, was an engineering graduate whom *The Washington Post* once described as "positively nerdish," and he conspicuously lacked his predecessor's backslapping charm, fondness for bad jokes, and rapport with phone workers. Roberts called Milken after he was released from prison and offered him the clipping collection. Subsequently, in a conversation about content, Milken recalled, "I had stressed to him that I felt that there were certain things that just could not be reproduced in a generation"; that is, the libraries of the six major entertainment companies—Disney, News Corporation, Time Warner, Viacom, Matsushita (which owned MCA), and Sony (which owned Columbia Tri-Star). Roberts, in Milken's view, should make deals with one or more of them, and also with companies like Oracle and Microsoft, which create content in the form of computer software.

Milken had been pursuing similar themes in regular conversations with Murdoch, who had attended Milken's Predators' Ball. In 1986, Murdoch hired him to help finance his acquisition of Metromedia from another Milken client, John Kluge. Though Milken didn't share Murdoch's conservative political ideology, Murdoch, with his enormous holdings around the world in the communications industry, was exactly the kind of risk-taking client he liked to cultivate. Murdoch, for his part, testified that whenever they talked, Milken would have "six or ten very creative ideas [that] added value to our business. I always found that stimulating."

They resumed their conversations soon after Milken's release from prison, and Milken invited Murdoch to charitable events. "I just remember going with him to Harlem one night when they gave out Milken scholarships," Murdoch said. Milken, he went on, "thought there were great changes coming in communications and that we had opportunities and we should strengthen ourselves in every way to be ready for them. I remember him lecturing me quite often."

Milken began to excite Murdoch's interest in MCI. He told Murdoch that the content he owned and was creating, such as the 20th Century Fox film library and the Fox Network's programming, would soon be "traveling over what we know today as telephone lines, beamed from satellites, coaxial cable, fiber-optic cable," and that he should work on establishing alliances with communications companies that could distribute his intellectual property over phone lines.

While Milken explored these ideas with Murdoch, he was pressing Bert Roberts to "reinvent" MCI, as he put it in his testimony, for by this time MCI's destructive price competition with AT&T was eroding profit margins and growth was falling off. Milken told Roberts that he had to change MCI's business fundamentally and "get control of content." In an internal memo that resulted from that conversation and others like it, Roberts announced a major strategic shift for MCI, a "right-angle turn," which would make the company more aggressive. According to Milken, this reflected "my vision."

The new strategy created enormous opportunities for Milken. Indeed, he and Steven Fink proposed so many new ventures that even Roberts seems to have grown exasperated. In an internal memo that Roberts sent to Susan Mayer, who was the head of corporate development at MCI, he complained, "Milken and Fink think there is an unlimited supply of money and they keep jumping from deal to deal," and added, "I actually made them write down on a piece of paper a week or two ago all of the deals that they were talking about."

According to Milken, serious discussions between News Corporation and MCI began in early 1995, at a meeting at an airplane hangar that he maintained in Los Angeles. Milken used the hangar as a convenient conference room for executives with access to a jet. That day, Milken recalled, he was host not only to Murdoch and Roberts but also to Lawrence Ellison, of Oracle, and Merv Adelson, a cofounder of Lorimar and an investor, with Milken, in ICS Communications, a cable and phone company.

When Milken was questioned by the S.E.C., he described the meeting with Roberts and Murdoch as a "brainstorming" session. On being asked to describe his role in the negotiations, Milken said that he was a "facilitator," a "sounding board," and a strategist, but never an adviser or negotiator: "I had made it clear that we did not have the authority to speak for either party in this negotiation, nor would we structure this transaction, and the two companies had to get together and find some way to work together on whatever they decided to do."

At this point in Milken's testimony, the S.E.C. lawyers knew nothing about the 1995 awards luncheon, after which Fink helped close the deal between Murdoch and Roberts. Milken said nothing about it, except that it was his understanding that the agreement was ultimately negotiated by Murdoch and Roberts at a meeting in Murdoch's office in early May. He stressed that he wasn't present. "I am not sure of all the details," Milken said. "I just was not there. I know the two of them got together."

"Was anyone from MC Group present at the meeting or meetings?" an S.E.C. lawyer asked.

"I don't know," Milken replied.

"How did you learn about the meeting or meetings between Mr. Murdoch and Mr. Roberts when they structured the transaction?"

"I don't recall."

"Did you see any documents that related to the transaction prior to the public announcement?" the S.E.C. lawyer asked.

"I don't recall."

"For example, did you see any term sheets?"—written lists of terms being agreed to.

"I don't recall seeing any documents."

News Corporation and MCI announced the deal on May 10. Afterward, Milken testified, he received the $27 million consulting fee from Murdoch. He didn't say how the amount was determined, and added that he was not going to get a specific fee from MCI. Instead, he and MCI planned to "wait and see," but might "do something together in the education area."

One way Murdoch intended to strengthen the Fox Network was by getting the rights to broadcast National Football League games from CBS, a move that Milken endorsed. "It was my feeling that, as a branded name, Fox had a lot of momentum," Milken explained. "In my daughter's lingo, it was cool, it was hip, it was 'in.'" Finally, in December 1993, Fox outbid CBS for the NFL rights. But Milken was still concerned about the Fox Network's comparatively weak local affiliates, and Murdoch seriously considered abandoning Fox's television stations and buying CBS instead, mainly to get CBS's strong affiliate franchise.

Milken argued that Murdoch should target affiliates, not a network. "I felt with the Warner Brothers network coming on and the UPN network, that the power base, where independent television stations were beholden to the networks and the network was quote 'the king,' was going to switch," he explained.

At the same time, perhaps as a possible solution to Murdoch's needs, Milken was courting Ronald Perelman, the chairman of MacAndrews & Forbes, which owned (in addition to Revlon) New World, whose properties included a group of twelve television stations, among them eight CBS affiliates. Milken's financing of Perelman's successful 1985 bid for Revlon had put Perelman in the ranks of the nation's billionaires, and he also became a fixture in celebrity-gossip columns. On a visit to the Wharton School, Milken met with Perelman and his vice chairman, Howard Gittis. (Gittis also serves on the Cap Cure board.) At the meeting, Milken tried to interest Perelman in buying the Six Flags amusement parks, and he sounded him out about buying either Columbia Tri-Star or Universal Studios, then owned by Sony and Matsushita, respectively. Perelman seems to have been less impressed than Roberts and Murdoch. He wasn't interested in pursuing Milken's ideas and characterized the meeting as "a waste of time."

Undeterred, Milken invited Perelman and Gittis to a Cap Cure fund-raiser at the "21" club, in New York, in April 1994, and the next day met with them to discuss a donation to Cap Cure. "Every man suffers from this disease," he said, referring to prostate cancer. They agreed to give $1 million, and thought the meeting was over. Then, Gittis recalled, Milken said that he "would like to talk to us about the possibility of a transaction between Fox and New World."

Perelman apparently took Milken's suggestion more seriously this time, and turned the negotiations over to Bill Bevins, the chief executive at New World, who began talking with Murdoch through Milken. Bevins and Murdoch subsequently met at Murdoch's office in Los Angeles, with Milken present. In Milken's S.E.C. testimony, he took credit for the strategy behind the deal but said that he was mindful of his consent decree and the accompanying restrictions. He testified that to both Bevins and Murdoch he emphasized the fact that "I wasn't going to negotiate the transaction, wasn't going to structure the transaction. Both of them are fully aware of the problems that I had and that I've had restrictions." Milken said he arranged more meetings and talked to both sides for the next few weeks while the deal was being discussed.

On May 23, 1994, News Corporation announced that it would buy a 20 percent stake in New World, for $500 million. New World agreed to transfer its twelve station affiliates to Fox. In his testimony, Milken said that he vaguely recalled a discussion about financing the deal by issuing zero-coupon preferred stock but that he was not involved in structuring the transaction and never saw any term sheets or documents related to it.

Milken received $5 million from News Corporation and $10 million from New World in fees. When Milken was asked how he arrived at those numbers, he testified that he and Murdoch simply agreed that $5 million would be a "fair fee." (Milken explained that he charged New World twice as much as he charged News Corporation because he felt he deserved "a hundred percent of the credit" for the idea as far as New World was concerned, but a "less-percentage credit" for News Corporation.) Also, for a year Murdoch paid Milken a $100,000-per-month retainer.

Milken's fees went not to him directly but to companies he controlled: $5 million to EEN Communications Network and its principal subsidiary, Knowledge Exchange; and $10 million to MC Group. Few, if any, of Milken's business activities appear to have been conducted in his name. He made investments in ICS; Heron Realty, a London-based real-estate investment company; and Archon, a holding company whose major asset was Premier Radio. Milken's testimony suggests a network of cross-ownership by some of his clients and donors to his charitable causes. For example, Murdoch invested in several of these Milken ventures, including Heron, Archon, and ICS, into which he put $30 million; MCI also invested $30 million in ICS.

Word that Milken was working for Murdoch and Roberts quickly spread among former Milken clients, many of whom had remained loyal to him. In the second week of July 1995, Ted Turner, the mercurial chairman of CNN, flew to Los Angeles for a breakfast meeting with Milken. Turner said that he wanted Milken to advise him, too. Milken resisted. "I told him that I was not really interested in the consulting business, that we were trying to build an education business that he knew about, that I had limited time, particularly until March of '96, with my community-service requirements, that I was focused on prostate cancer," Milken testified. "His comment to me was that if I could do consulting for Rupert Murdoch it wasn't really fair that I wouldn't do consulting for him." Milken had financed Turner's acquisition of M-G-M/United Artists, in 1986, at a time when few on Wall Street took Turner and his Atlanta television station seriously. The Turner deal was an example of how Milken used Ivan Boesky to manipulate the market for his own ends, the government alleged. Boesky and other witnesses said Milken secretly directed Boesky to buy M-G-M stock and that, when the deal went through, they split the profits. Boesky and other witnesses had described the scheme to the government, explaining that Boesky's stock purchases gave Wall Street the illusion that an important arbitrageur believed the deal would succeed, which, in turn, helped persuade skeptical investors to buy the junk bonds necessary to finance it. This kind of fraud and insider trading, the government claimed, was typical of Milken's tactics during the 1980s. In addition to $3 million in profits that he allegedly split with Boesky, Milken earned $66.8 million in financing fees from Turner.

Now, however reluctant Milken may have been, Turner prevailed and began paying Milken's MC Group $100,000 a month in consulting fees. Under the terms of the agreement, Turner would pay Milken an "additional fee to be agreed upon between consultant and client with respect to any transaction between client or any other entity."

Milken testified that he began his consultations with a long discussion of what he believed the future held for Turner Broadcasting. As Turner put it, "He's got more ideas than a cat has lives." According to Milken, Turner asked him to explore a possible deal for the NBC network with Jack Welch, the chairman of General Electric, which owned NBC. Milken didn't know Welch, but, soon after that conversation with Turner, he attended a CEO conference in Annapolis, where Welch was on a panel, and introduced himself. "It was one of those milling-around scenes after a speech where people are all around, following up on Q&As from the audience," Welch testified. "He was probably one of the more publicized figures in the business world over the last decade, and I had never seen him before."

Welch recalled Milken saying, "Congratulations on the job you've done at GE," along with other "nice things" that "people say." At some point, Milken added that he was "a friend of Turner and Malone and had been involved in getting them to be public companies." Indeed, Milken said that he was the "financial creator" of Turner Broadcasting and TCI. As leaders in the cable industry, Turner and Malone were men almost guaranteed to interest Welch, given GE's ownership of NBC.

"Would you mind if I called you?" Milken asked. He began calling Welch in early August, and Welch, too, was quickly smitten. He offered, in his testimony, a remarkably candid account of how Milken gains a client's confidence: "Mr. Milken's calls were extraordinarily polite. . . . He was very seductive, very charming, goes out of his way to build a relationship, very ingratiating. So there was always a lot of small talk." Welch compared Milken to the kind of person "who's so seductive, by the time you're through you've told him about your innermost secrets, your sex life, your whole life. You've told him everything." He went on to say that Milken speaks "in these incredibly seductive, whispered tones of a personal relationship. You've just met your best friend."

Milken asked about Welch's family, of course, and his golf game, which he seemed to know about in some detail. "I can see how he took all these guys that he got as clients," Welch testified. "The guy's really a truly artful and very effective charmer. In a league few have attained, in my view."

Welch was aware that Ted Turner was restless and that he felt constrained by the large stakes in Turner Broadcasting owned by Time Warner and John Malone; in the late eighties, Malone had made a considerable investment in Turner Broadcasting to keep it afloat. Turner believed that Gerald Levin had been blocking the company's expansion and that Malone was resistant to any sale of Turner assets. "They were in a well-publicized stalemate with Mr. Turner," Welch said.

Milken had already told Welch about his close relationship with Turner and Malone. Now, Welch testified, "I was getting a lot of inside information as to what was happening. . . . Mr. Milken seemed to have . . . a very detailed knowledge of when Mr. Malone and Mr. Turner did this, that, or the next thing, and what they were thinking and how they were thinking." Milken, he said, "would sort of give me inside-baseball conversations. 'Ted is talking to John.' 'They're trying to figure out what to do.' 'John is talking to Gerry.' 'They met last week.'" In Welch's words, it was "almost like a reporter giving me information that was of interest to me because I was trying to find a way to play in this game." Welch went on, "I mean, if Ted meets with John, and they're trying to get Gerry to relinquish his blocking rights, I'm listening."

The point of all these calls was not lost on Welch. One possibility would have been for GE to buy Time Warner's stake in Turner, or John Malone's, or both, or to buy the whole company. Milken kept Welch in suspense with comments like "Ted is truly frustrated," "Something's got to break here," "I don't know which way it's going to go." But Milken didn't make a specific proposal, saying instead, "Ted really needs a network and likes you people, and I just know that some way, someday, you guys belong together." As Welch characterized it, "I was being kept as a dance partner at the back of the room."

The approach worked. By late August 1995, less than a

month after he began talking to Milken, Welch started preparing an offer to buy the Time Warner stake in Turner.

Similar conversations with Bill Gates, at Microsoft, and Andrew Grove, at Intel, were also under way. Turner accompanied Milken to a meeting at Intel headquarters, in Santa Clara, California, and Turner met with Gates in Redmond, Washington. Talks with Intel never really went anywhere, but Microsoft came close to a deal to invest $1 billion in Turner Broadcasting. As Turner put it, "There were all those different pieces. . . . You move this here and that there, and all we did was move them around on the board."

Before anything came of Milken's moves, however, Gerald Levin, the Time Warner chairman, approached Turner on his own, phoning him in August 1995 at his ranch near Bozeman, Montana, where Turner was vacationing. "I've got a surprise for you that I think you're going to like," Levin told Turner. He proposed flying to Montana to meet Turner for lunch. "That sounded good," Turner recalled. "I really didn't have any idea what he had in mind."

Just two days earlier, Levin had been talking to Milken about selling Time Warner's stake back to Turner, but Levin testified that the alternative he offered Turner was his idea alone. When Levin arrived at the ranch, the two men went into Turner's bedroom so that they wouldn't be overheard. As Turner recalled, Levin said, "We'd like to acquire Turner Broadcasting."

"I was very shocked," Turner testified. But his conversations with Milken, his frustrations over the ownership stakes in his company, and his failure to acquire a network had all prepared him for the possibility of a sale. He suggested a price per share. Levin "knocked a dollar off of it, which I agreed to, and we didn't get into real details," Turner said. "I asked him what he foresaw for me. . . . It was clear . . . that he was going to be the head honcho, but I agreed to it." Turner asked that the combined companies be called Time Warner Turner; Levin refused. He also asked for the title of vice chairman. Levin didn't agree to that, either. But he pointed out that, after the deal, Turner would be the largest share-holder in Time Warner and could have two seats on the board.

The two discussed the possible reaction of Malone, whose stake in Turner, and position on the board, gave him the power to block the deal. Strong willed, independent, and disliking public-ity, Malone had assembled the nation's largest cable system by outbargaining other cable operators, a notoriously freewheeling group, and had become a billionaire. He took equally tough posi-tions with cable-network operators, at one point throwing Via-com's VH1 network off his Denver cable systems. Malone didn't like surprises, and his sometimes volatile temperament was per-ceived as a risk to the deal. According to Levin, both he and Turner were concerned that Malone "might not be happy about" the deal, since Malone's stake in the merged Time Warner would be so diluted that he would have little influence.

The whole discussion, Turner estimated, lasted just thirty minutes to an hour. Still, it was "a very traumatic experience, sell-ing your company after thirty-five years," he said. "I was not myself for months afterwards."

Later that day, or the next, Turner called Milken with the news. "I told him everything of substance and consequence," Turner recalled. "I'm not the kind that holds anything back." Not surprisingly, Milken, given his previous efforts to convince Turner that he was too small to compete, was enthusiastic. "I felt this was a great idea," Milken said. The sale, of course, ended discussions with Intel, Microsoft, and GE.

Milken couldn't take credit for originating the transaction, but he could still "facilitate" it, as Turner put it. Turner asked Milken to "help me get it through" by persuading John Malone to support the deal. "Clearly, he knew John very well, and John really thinks highly of Milken," Turner said. "All of the good business-people do. It was only a logical extension of that that he would help us facilitate this very complex and difficult-to-put-together transaction."

Milken and Turner agreed that Turner should be the one to

tell Malone. (Turner explained, "You don't break up with your wife with your lawyer there. You tell her personally. You know, she might break down.") Turner did break the news to Malone, in an early-morning phone call. "He was speechless for a long period of time, which is very unusual for John, " Turner said. "He wanted to think about it for a few days." Two days after Levin flew to Bozeman, Milken joined Turner in a conference call with Malone, in the first of numerous conversations. Milken flew twice to Denver to meet with Malone, sitting in on the first critical, face-to-face meeting between Levin and Malone. They also met at least once in Atlanta. Milken's goals were to persuade Malone of the benefits of the merger and to develop a rapport between him and Levin. Milken testified that he was careful not to discuss securities issues that might violate his consent decree. At one meeting, he said, "I put up my hand and said, 'Hey, John, we are not here to discuss securities. That's not our function.'"

Though these meetings seemed to go well, Milken reported to Levin that Malone was experiencing a "psychological aversion" to going forward with the deal because he "was feeling betrayed by Ted Turner after having helped him for so many years." Milken arranged another meeting with Levin and Malone in New York, in September, at the same time as one of his Cap Cure fund-raising dinners. Before the meeting, Milken told Levin that it was Malone's wedding anniversary and that he should be sure to congratulate him. Malone was a "family man," Milken said, and Levin shouldn't neglect the "human side of John Malone."

The approach appears to have worked, and Malone finally signed off on the merger. Turner recalled that Milken talked to Malone repeatedly and "tried to get him to calm down and not be emotional and concentrate on the business aspects of the transaction . . . John and Gerry both knew that Mike was primarily working for me and for the management of the Turner Broadcasting System, but the respect that both of those parties held him in was so high that . . . they listened to him." Milken also succeeded in persuading Levin to give Turner the title of vice chairman.

It isn't clear when the subject of a fee for Milken entered the negotiations, but Levin's notes indicate that it was a subject for discussion with Malone sometime before a meeting in Denver. Invoking
the terms of the consulting agreement, Milken had proposed that
Turner pay him $100 million—an extraordinary 10 percent of the
value of the deal.

Turner testified that he couldn't remember when Milken had
broached the subject of the fee, but he said that the request left
him "speechless" and that he thought it was an "egregious"
amount. "I didn't say no, because I didn't feel I had the backdrop,"
he explained. "I wanted to talk with John and Gerry and the rest
of the board." Turner added that he couldn't remember much
about the circumstances of the request because "I went into traumatic shock afterwards."

"Do you remember where you were?" an S.E.C. lawyer asked.

"I don't remember . . ."

"When you went into this?"

". . . where I was, or I blacked out."

"Do you remember where you were when you blacked out?"

"No, I don't," Turner said. "I just blacked out mentally."

Turner said that Levin was similarly shocked. "I guess just
about anybody would be with a fee at that level," he said. The
Turner Broadcasting board balked at a payment of $100 million,
settling on $40 million instead. Turner offered to contribute
an additional $10 million out of his own pocket so that Mil-
ken would receive half his requested amount. The lead investment bankers for Turner—Credit Suisse First Boston and Merrill
Lynch—together received $6 million. On being asked to justify
the $50 million payment to Milken, Turner said, "They helped me
immeasurably and I really doubt that . . . anybody else could have
helped us and advised us on how to get John Malone and to get
this thing worked out."

Time Warner and Turner announced their proposed merger
on September 22. As reporters pored over its details, Milken's $50

million fee was noted by Steven Lipin, of *The Wall Street Journal,* and became public knowledge.

III—THE FORGOTTEN E-MAILS

Probably no one was more concerned about the *Journal* article than Thomas Newkirk, an associate director of enforcement at the S.E.C. Newkirk had come to the S.E.C. in 1986, just in time for the biggest scandals on Wall Street since the 1920s. As chief litigation counsel, he was involved in the Dennis Levine and Ivan Boesky insider-trading cases, and after Boesky implicated Milken he was involved in Milken's 1991 consent decree and the settlement of that case.

People forbidden to engage in the securities business can ask the S.E.C. if a contemplated activity is legal before carrying it out, and the agency either issues a "no action" letter—a free pass, essentially—or warns that the activity might indeed result in an enforcement proceeding. Milken had made no effort to obtain a "no action" letter. Newkirk discussed Milken's activities with William McLucas, the S.E.C.'s head of enforcement. After a six-month informal inquiry, the staff obtained a formal order of investigation from the full commission. The U.S. Attorney's office separately began an investigation into whether Milken had violated his probation. Thus, three years after being released from prison, Milken was again under investigation.

McLucas, Newkirk, and other lawyers involved in the case were taken aback by the breadth and significance of Milken's activities. It was hardly what they had anticipated when Milken entered into his consent decree, four years earlier. In his testimony, however, Milken consistently denied any involvement in dollar amounts, financing terms, exchange rates, or deal term sheets, and the recollections of his major clients supported him. That might well have been the end of the case. Then, in response to a document subpoena, MCI produced copies of a lengthy series of internal e-mails related to the deal with Murdoch's News Corporation. The e-mails arrived after Milken finished testifying; the delay was attributed to a computer retrieval problem. The S.E.C. lawyers read the e-mails with amazement. They suggested a sharply different role for Milken, one in which he not only advised the parties to the deal but actually negotiated terms and then drafted agreements—a clear violation, the S.E.C. lawyers believed, of his consent agreement. The exchanges between Bert Roberts and Susan Mayer, MCI's head of corporate strategy, were particularly explicit.

Susan Mayer to Bert Roberts, January 17, 1995, 2:12 P.M.:

> Was on the phone for an hour and a half with Milken and Fink and then just with Fink. . . . You'll remember that last week they told me they were working on a term sheet that would lay out a structure for working together. . . . Milken said they've been working on this for 50 hours via meetings with Murdoch and his team and they've identified four options but that they all need more shape.

Susan Mayer to Bert Roberts, February 10, 1995, 9:25 P.M.:

> I read [Fink] the riot act about the term sheet. . . . I asked him if he were willing to do a deal along the lines I had outlined tonight, and he said yes. . . . Having said that, however, we then got into a discussion of the amount of money we were willing to invest.

Bert Roberts to Susan Mayer, February 11, 1995, 10:49 A.M.:

> Keep the pressure on—and I'll reinforce your points on the stupid term sheet they sent.

Bert Roberts to Susan Mayer and others, March 15, 1995, 9:29 P.M.:

> Attached is Susan's rewrite of the Fink draft. . . . I told Susan to fax this to Fink/Milken tomorrow to keep the ball moving.

Bert Roberts to "All," April 14, 1995, 4:42 P.M.:

> I talked to Milken today and last night—he will be sending back our draft term sheet with markups and comments. . . . Mike went through a number of points under 5(i) and his thoughts on resolution seemed OK.

Finally, Mayer e-mailed Roberts:

> Got a copy of Milken and Fink's revised term sheet and spoke with Steve to make some corrections.

Milken had testified, under oath, that he didn't remember even seeing the term sheets, let alone marking them up. The e-mail traffic suggested otherwise. The S.E.C. lawyers moved swiftly to take testimony from Roberts, Mayer, and others at MCI. Roberts testified on May 30 and 31, 1996, in Washington, Mayer on May 15 and 17, in Washington and Los Angeles. Both Roberts and Mayer, along with other MCI witnesses, were represented by Harvey Pitt, the partner at Fried, Frank, Harris, Shriver & Jacobson who had defended Ivan Boesky in the insider-trading scandals of the eighties. But it quickly became apparent that Milken faced no danger from these witnesses, who displayed remarkable failures of memory even when confronted with their own e-mails.

Typical was this exchange between an S.E.C. lawyer and Roberts after Roberts reviewed copies of the February tenth e-mail from Mayer:

> S.E.C. lawyer: "Did you receive this e-mail message?"
> Roberts: "I don't recall."
> S.E.C.: "Is there anything here that leads you to doubt that you received this e-mail message?"

Roberts: "I don't recall receiving it."

S.E.C.: "Do you recall having had a communication with Ms. Mayer on or about February 10, 1995, about a communication she had with Mr. Fink regarding a term sheet?"

Roberts: "No, I don't recall."

S.E.C.: "Did you ever see a term sheet sent by Mr. Fink in connection with the News Corporation/MCI transaction?"

Roberts: "I don't recall any such term sheet."

The S.E.C. found Mayer's memory lapses equally striking. She testified that she couldn't recall sending or receiving any of the e-mails in her name or addressed to her. Reading from one of her many e-mails, an S.E.C. lawyer quoted her as writing, "Milken's last term sheet prevents us converting to ordinary voting shares," a reference suggesting that Milken was involved in structuring the deal.

"Do you see that?"

"Yes, I do."

"Did you ever refer to any term sheet as Milken's last term sheet?"

"I have no idea."

"Did you ever refer to any term sheet as Milken's term sheet?"

"I have no idea."

In one instance, Mayer said she couldn't say who "Michael" was in a reference to the News Corporation deal that read "Spoke with Michael."

"Is it Michael Milken?"

"As I said earlier, I don't remember sending this document."

At another point, Mayer testified that she couldn't say what a reference to "Fink" meant.

"Does that refer to Steven Fink?"
"Sitting here today, I can't tell that it does."
"Can you say that it doesn't?"
"I don't know what it refers to."

Nor did she acknowledge that a calendar entry—"Milken 11:30"—referred to contact with Michael Milken.

"Do you know another Milken?"
"Not that I can recall."
"Did you meet with Michael Milken on or about November 30, 1994?"
"I don't know. I don't remember."

Reviewing this testimony, McLucas, in the words of one lawyer on the case, "went nuclear." A litigator in the office also reviewed the transcripts and concluded that Mayer and Roberts had given "evasive, untrue, and misleading" testimony. (A lawyer for Mayer and Roberts declined to comment.)

In June, McLucas asked Pitt and MCI's litigation counsel to come to a meeting at his office in Washington. According to one S.E.C. lawyer who participated in the meeting, McLucas was furious at Pitt. He told the MCI lawyers that Mayer's testimony was not credible; they countered that Mayer was an inexperienced witness who had felt intimidated. After that encounter, Pitt withdrew from the case, and MCI reduced the amount of legal work it gave his firm. (Citing client confidentiality, Pitt has declined to give the reasons for his resignation.)

In October, the S.E.C. lawyers redeposed Douglas Maine, MCI's chief financial officer. In his earlier testimony, Maine had provided little of value to the S.E.C.; for example, he denied that he had received any term sheets from Fink or Milken. Now he proved a far more useful witness, remembering many of the e-mails and testifying that Milken was involved in deciding the terms of the News Corporation transaction. Milken and Fink "weighed in on the term sheets and the deal," Maine testified. And, to clarify earlier testimony, he said that he had in fact received a term sheet involving the News Corporation deal directly from Fink. "I certainly remember this document," he said, referring to a copy of it.

Maine also called into question Milken's assertion that he hadn't sought a fee for the News Corporation deal from MCI and that he and Roberts had agreed that they would "wait and see." Maine recalled that, not long after the deal was announced, he spoke with Fink on his car phone while driving outside Washington. "Well, what about an idea of a flat fee, or a one-time payment?" Fink asked. "We've, you know, done a lot of work."

Maine didn't remember whether Fink asked for a specific amount. Meanwhile, Roberts kept badgering Maine to come up with something for Milken, telling him to "hear them out" and at one point e-mailing him to call Milken about it.

E-mail traffic, however, indicates that those discussions came to an end around the time a journalist began calling to ask whether MCI had paid Milken a fee. On May 24, Mayer had received an e-mail and had forwarded it to Roberts, warning him, "It's possible we'll see a story in *The New York Times* tomorrow stating both MCI and News Corp. paid Mike Milken $20 million each for his assistance in the deal." She also e-mailed others, noting, "Maybe this sets the ceiling on what we have to pay Milken!" MCI denied that it had made any payment to Milken, and no *Times* story ran.

Other reporters called, including one from *Forbes,* which prompted a Milken public-relations adviser to issue a memo suggesting "talking points," to be used in dealing with inquiries from the press. Among the recipients were Roberts and Murdoch, and although the memo was dated June 21, after the executives testified, it seems to have embodied the same strategy used at the depositions. The memo read:

In regard to the News Corporation and MCI alliance, Michael's involvement was limited to sharing his vision with two old friends, introducing them, and helping them see the possibility of a future forged together. . . .

He didn't provide investment advice. . . . [The transaction] was finally negotiated between the two chairmen themselves.

He did not do anything that would even remotely violate his consent order. . . . All he did was consult, and make introductions. . . .

This approach gives everyone lots of wiggle room to talk about ideas and visions but not the specifics of the deal, which is either 1) not news or 2) not in any of our interests to make it news.

An article in the July seventeenth *Forbes* minimized Milken's role in the MCI deal. With so much publicity, MCI began to discuss ideas for paying Milken indirectly, perhaps by having MCI buy out his stake in ICS. But, Maine said, "none of them worked from an accounting standpoint." Still, Maine recalled, "every two or three weeks, Bert would pass by in the hallway, and [say,] 'Gee, Doug, have you thought of anything?'" But the effort "died on the vine," he said.

Other witnesses—even Milken's loyal aide Steven Fink—provided testimony that was harmful to Milken. Fink volunteered details of the behind-the-scenes meeting between Roberts and Murdoch at which he typed drafts of the agreements. Fink also testified that he told Milken about the meeting.

The S.E.C. lawyers now felt that they had sufficient evidence to pursue a complaint. They were also angry at Milken personally. One defense lawyer involved in the case told me, "What they reacted to the most was the sense they got from Milken that he doesn't respect them or the agency or the rules and laws they uphold. For better or worse, it colors their judgment. They see red." Milken was told that he was likely to face civil charges, and was invited to make a so-called Wells submission, arguing why the commission shouldn't proceed against him. In it he stressed that his lawyers had assured him that nothing he had done violated his consent decree. He also learned that he was the target of a criminal investigation into whether he had violated the consent decree and whether he and others "unlawfully misrepresented or failed to disclose" the full extent of his activities. The twin threats of renewed civil and criminal litigation, including the prospect of another prison term, quickly brought Milken's lawyers to the bargaining table. Though negotiations were often contentious, a settlement was finally reached, in part, his lawyers say, because of Milken's ongoing struggle with prostate cancer. They deny that he gave anything but truthful testimony. Milken agreed to pay the government the $42 million in fees he had received from the News Corporation/MCI and New World deals plus $5 million in interest. A lawyer for Milken noted that Milken was not required to pay any fines or penalties—the $47 million settlement was a "disgorgement" plus interest—and stressed that the S.E.C. never accused Milken of "knowingly" violating his consent decree.

The S.E.C. backed down on the Turner negotiations, conceding in effect that in that instance the agency might not be able to prove that he had violated his consent decree. The U.S. Attorney ended the criminal investigation, noting in a letter to Judge Wood that prosecution "is not warranted by the existing evidence and by the law."

Debate within the S.E.C. over whether to endorse the settlement was heated. But in the end the view prevailed that Milken's large financial settlement demonstrated the seriousness of the case against him and would serve as a sufficient deterrent. On February 27, 1998, the settlement was announced, and Milken, who was still on parole for his 1990 conviction, was released from probation.

Why Milken returned to making deals almost immediately after he was released from prison is a question possibly only he himself can answer. But, just as he has never admitted the scope of his illegal activities in the 1980s, he refuses to acknowledge that anything in his subsequent behavior might even give rise to questions about whether he violated the law. He testified that he made efforts to resist being drawn into consulting for Turner, but otherwise he appears to have embraced opportunities that seem to have taken him dangerously close to forbidden activities. Despite his avowed lack of interest in money, he pursued and accepted staggeringly high fees. Is it that he simply couldn't resist the thrilling process of making deals?

More troubling, perhaps, is another question: why did so many of the country's most highly regarded businessmen—men whose vision and acumen, presumably, had brought them so far— feel it necessary to pay millions of dollars for the services of a Michael Milken?

Last week, Stephen Kaufman, a lawyer for Milken, said that Milken has done no consulting and has accepted no consulting fees since the resolution of the S.E.C. investigation, in 1998. The S.E.C. hasn't monitored Milken, and no news reports or witnesses have raised questions about his activities.

In 1996, two years after Milken helped Murdoch's News Corporation buy 20 percent of New World from Ron Perelman and Howard Gittis, News Corporation tried to buy all of New World. Milken seemed eager to reprise his role in the earlier deal, in which he represented both parties; Gittis vetoed any involvement by Milken. In what he called "a hard conversation to have," Gittis told Milken that he could no longer work for MacAndrews & Forbes because the company had obtained a New Jersey gaming license, which prevented it from having any business dealings with a convicted felon. New World hired Goldman Sachs instead. According to Gittis's testimony, Milken continued to represent News Corporation in the negotiations, which were interrupted by the S.E.C. depositions. In 1997, News Corporation succeeded in acquiring New World.

However prescient Milken's vision of the future of entertainment and communications, the MCI/News Corporation deal didn't turn out well. Murdoch, even at the time of his deposition, described it as a "disaster." In 1999, News Corporation terminated its venture with MCI by buying back its shares, for $1.4 billion. Still, Milken and Murdoch remain close. Last September, Milken was Murdoch's guest at the Sydney Olympics.

Amid the failure of the News Corporation venture and other losses, MCI was acquired by the upstart WorldCom in 1998; Bert Roberts retains the title of chairman of MCI WorldCom, but the company has faced a serious erosion of its long-distance business and a sharply declining stock price. Susan Mayer also remains at the company.

Ted Turner is still vice chairman of Time Warner, which agreed to be acquired by AOL last January. Turner will remain vice chairman of AOL Time Warner and will retain two board seats. Although Turner supported the merger, he will have far less influence in the combined company. The value of his stake soared to $9 billion at the time of the merger, but it has since greatly declined.

Like Turner, John Malone ended up selling his company. AT&T acquired TCI in 1999. Malone retained the title of chairman of Liberty Media, which had been TCI's programming unit; joined the AT&T board; and became AT&T's largest single shareholder. After reaching a high of $60, AT&T shares recently plunged to below $20; and Malone has been agitating for AT&T to spin off Liberty as a separate company.

The news, last month, that President Clinton was considering a pardon for Milken sparked outrage at the S.E.C.—which hadn't been notified of Milken's request—and at the U.S. Attorney's office in Manhattan. Both sent blistering letters to the White House. "Few people have done more than Milken to undermine public confidence in our markets," the S.E.C.'s letter said. It pointed out that "almost immediately after release from prison . . . Milken secretly revived his activities as a broker," in violation of his consent decree. "There is compelling evidence," the letter continued, that, after the S.E.C. began investigating these activities, "Milken gave false and misleading testimony in that investigation" and "orchestrated false and misleading testimony of others, just as he obstructed justice before being apprehended and imprisoned."

Though the S.E.C. letter termed Milken's charitable endeavors "commendable," it concluded, "Philanthropy cannot provide a license to violate the law."

After decades of writing business columns, a veteran journalist might become jaded or a tad out of touch. Not Allan Sloan of *Newsweek*, who was honored for lifetime achievement in 2001 by both the Society of American Business Editors and Writers (SABEW) and UCLA's Gerald Loeb Awards for Distinguished Business and Financial Journalism. Sloan remains relevant, insightful, and delightfully pugnacious. Here he tackles the California energy crisis, the bungled DaimlerChrysler merger, and an important part of the economy that Allan Greenspan can't control. Sloan makes you laugh, but his underlying message is dead serious.

Allan Sloan

Profiting from the Darkness/ A Deal for the History Books/ Why Mortgage Rates Aren't Falling

PROFITING FROM THE DARKNESS

WHEN IT COMES TO FOOTBALL, "piling on" a player who's already been tackled is a major penalty that can set your team back a long way. But when it comes to markets, piling on by taking advantage of the weak is called "opportunism," and it can get you a big bonus.

Which brings us to California, where piling on enfeebled utilities and customers by power generators and power traders has become a way of life. Thanks to the idiotic way that California deregulated its electricity markets, the generators and traders of power in California have been making a fortune because electricity costs have gone through the roof. Meanwhile, consumers are getting pounded rather than protected, economic instability is spreading throughout the western United States, and some of the utilities that distribute power to customers are getting clobbered.

One big utility, Pacific Gas & Electric, has already gone broke and others may soon follow.

But while the market has produced a horde of losers—California's wholesale power bill is running at ten times the level of two years ago—there is a handful of big winners: companies that generate or trade power in the California market. Among the winners: Calpine, whose first-quarter profit quintupled, compared with last year's; Reliant Energy and Williams Cos., whose profits more than doubled; Mirant, up 84 percent, and Dynegy and Duke Energy, whose wholesale power profits doubled and quadrupled, respectively. Enron, the nation's biggest energy trader, had a 75 percent increase in wholesale-services profits but says little of that was from California. Some of these companies' profits would have risen far more—Mirant's would have quadrupled—had they not taken big earnings hits to cover the risk of not being paid for some of their California sales. If they finally get paid, their profits will be outtasight. You can see why some of these companies' stocks have heated up as California melted down.

To be fair, you can't attribute these entire increases to California—but you can be sure California accounts for a good portion of them. There are other, less obvious winners, too. Among them: the unregulated subsidiaries of some companies that own California utilities; aluminum producers that are making more money by closing their plants and selling their power allotments than they would have made by producing aluminum; farms that find it more profitable to resell electricity than to grow crops; and, in general, anyone in the western United States or Canada with an electron to spare and some way of getting it into California.

I'm not saying that these companies are immoral for making a fortune by taking advantage of California's problems. Breaking the law by creating an artificial shortage—which has been alleged, but not remotely proven—would be immoral. Taking advantage of a situation? That's what's known as amoral—having no moral values, either good or bad. It's not nice, but it's perfectly legal, and it's the way market players are expected to act.

So when California governor Gray Davis said last week that he was planning to have a "heart-to-heart" talk with California power generators, you just had to laugh. Because when it comes to business, those people have no hearts. They're not supposed to.

What created the problem in California is not only deregulation but a stupid deregulation plan carried out ineptly: the Kilowatt Keystone Cops, as it were. California put a cap on the rates that utilities could charge customers, but until recently, it forced utilities to buy all of their power in the short-term market. The utilities foolishly agreed to this deal. The problem: short-term markets are notoriously volatile. And notoriously ruthless. If there's a small surplus of power, you have desperate sellers trying to sell power, which can't be stored. But if there's a shortage, everyone piles on. Had California utilities been allowed to do the rational thing and buy most of their power in long-term markets, they would have paid more initially, but they and their customers would be in far better shape now. Compounding the problem is that while the state deregulated the wholesale rates the utilities paid for power, they capped the retail rates utilities could charge. Combine that with total reliance on the short-term market and—voilà!—you're totally at the market's mercy. And markets have no mercy.

In the old days, when utilities were regulated, there was often waste and inefficiency, but power was reliable and utilities cared desperately about keeping the lights on. Now we have markets that don't care about anything. Someday markets may give us total reliability at a cheaper price than regulation would. But in the meantime, get used to the piling-on concept. Just hope you end up on top of the pile.

A DEAL FOR THE HISTORY BOOKS

WHAT DO YOU GET when you combine a Mercedes S-Class sedan with a Chrysler PT Cruiser? No, you don't get a sleek, high-priced Euro-American hybrid vehicle. You get a car wreck, with Germans and Americans barking at each other about who's more to blame. In business terms you have the worst-executed big takeover since God invented corporations. To be sure, there are plenty of competitors for the worst-ever deal. But for a combination of a high profile, huge losses of shareholder value, total mismanagement, tone deafness, and the gutting of a proud old iconic company, DaimlerChrysler AG is unparalleled. Other worst-ever contenders, such as AT&T's 1991 purchase of mainframe-computer maker NCR or the disastrous mating of HFS and CUC to form Cendant in 1997, either were stupid on their face (NCR) or blew up because of unsuspected financial fraud (CUC). DaimlerChrysler, by contrast, should have worked. Financially, it was perfect. Daimler's stock was valued so much more highly than Chrysler's per dollar of earnings that Daimler could pay a 34 percent premium above the predeal price and still increase earnings per share, provided Chrysler's profits didn't fall sharply. And Chrysler, which had lopped off its international operations to help raise money during one of its periodic crises, needed a rich parent. That's because no matter how well Chrysler did, it was always one bad product cycle away from disaster. All Daimler had to do was not screw Chrysler up. But, of course, it did.

The problem at DaimlerChrysler is much more than lost market value—but lost value is the starting point. It's just stunning. Daimler-Benz stock was worth $48 billion on November 16, 1998, the day it issued an additional $36 billion of stock to buy Chrysler. As of Friday, DaimlerChrysler's market value was only $39 billion—less than Daimler alone was selling for, predeal. *Auf Wiedersehen* to $45 billion—more than Daimler paid for Chrysler. Ford and GM stock have also fallen since Daimler bought Chrysler, and the U.S. auto cycle turned. But they're down far less than Daimler. "It's common to lose the premium [over the predeal market price] that you pay," says Mark Sirower, head of Boston Consulting Group's mergers-and-acquisitions practice, "but it's rare to lose more than the entire market value of the purchase."

But market value is only part of the problem. Last quarter, Chrysler lost $950 million (including a $440 million charge on vehicles it had leased rather than sold), while other U.S. carmakers coined money. With the market's softening, further losses lie ahead. More than 25,000 layoffs loom. The Chrysler and Mercedes brands have been sullied. Chairman Jürgen Schrempp foolishly got himself caught between his 1998 statements to the S.E.C. that DaimlerChrysler would be a "merger of equals" and recent interviews in which he said he'd always intended to reduce Chrysler to a mere division. Did he lie to Chrysler? Or is he reinventing history now to cover up his blunders? Who knows? Next he'll say the company is only pretending to be messed up to make the competition overconfident.

And, of course, Las Vegas takeover tycoon Kirk Kerkorian is on the warpath. Schrempp, the multinationalist, seems to have confused German business culture with U.S. culture. In Germany pretty much the only stockholder to fear is Schrempp's biggest owner, Deutsche Bank, which is the nexus of Germany AG. (Germany, Inc., to English speakers.) But in the United States you worry about all big holders. Especially Kerkorian, DaimlerChrysler's third biggest holder, who's ferocious, well lawyered, and very proud. You dis him at your peril, as Chrysler's old management found out. And Schrempp dissed him big-time, by Kerkorian's lawyer's account. Kerkorian traveled to Berlin to see Schrempp this spring, but Schrempp had blown off the meeting and decamped to his ranch in South Africa. It's not clear what Kerkorian's game is. But for a relative pittance, he's whacked Schrempp, stirred the pot, and may be imperiling the chairman's hold on his job.

To close: two thoughts. First, I hope Chrysler turns around, given how many jobs are at stake. But with morale so low, the market softening, and German-American bickering going on, I wouldn't bet on it. Second, Jürgen Schrempp wanted a place in business history. He'll get it. But it won't be quite the place he had in mind.

WHY MORTGAGE RATES AREN'T FALLING

I F   Y O U   T H I N K that Alan Greenspan really controls interest rates, you haven't looked at the mortgage market lately. Uncle Alan has cut short-term interest rates by two percentage points so far this year and may cut them again at Tuesday's Federal Reserve Board meeting. But the rate on thirty-year mortgages—the most popular choice among home buyers—has barely budged. That rate averaged 7.22 percent last week, according to HSH Associates, only a freckle below the 7.31 percent it averaged for the first week of the year. (Fifteen-year rates, favored by refinancers, are down a bit more, to 6.73 from 6.94.) Greenspan started cutting rates on January 3.

Wait a minute. With the Fed cutting short-term rates like crazy, why haven't thirty-year mortgages gotten cheaper? The answer is that modifier you probably skipped over: "short-term." The Fed controls short-term interest rates, but it doesn't control long-term rates. Most people blithely assume that long rates and short rates move in tandem—but they don't. And long-term rates are the key to what lenders charge for long-term, fixed-rate mortgages. "The Fed influences short-term rates to a very high degree, but it controls long-term rates to a lesser degree and sometimes not at all," says David Berson, chief economist of Fannie Mae, the nation's biggest supplier of mortgage money.

The disconnect between short-term rates and long-term mortgage rates is logical, but most people don't know about it. "We're in a sound-bite world," says Keith Gumbinger, vice president of HSH Associates. "People hear that the Fed is cutting interest rates, and they think the Fed is cutting all interest rates. But it's not." That's why people bombard mortgage lenders with protests every time the Fed cuts rates but mortgages don't fall.

Here's the deal. The only economically significant rate the Fed controls directly is the federal funds rate—what banks charge each other for overnight loans. The Fed influences long-term rates by moral suasion, market clout, and influence but has no direct control of them. Because fixed-rate mortgages are long-term loans, they're heavily influenced by long-term rates, especially the rate on ten-year U.S. Treasury securities. If you look at an interest-rate chart, you'd see that as of Friday, ten-year Treasuries were yielding about 5.5 percent, up from 4.9 at the start of the year.

To see how little direct control the Fed has over long-term rates, consider last year. The ten-year Treasury rate and mortgage rates fell sharply, even though the Fed raised short-term interest rates.

Hello? What's going on here? It's simple. The stock market loves short-term-rate cuts, but the long-term-bond market hates them. "When you cut short-term rates, you're adding to the money supply, and that has the potential to be inflationary," says Joseph Rosenberg, the chief investment officer at Loews Corp. Long-term lenders fear inflation, which erodes the value of their money. Rosenberg, one of Wall Street's leading bondmeisters, says excessive Fed rate cuts in the fall of 1998 caused a thirteen-month bear market in bonds and may be setting off a similar bear market now.

The big beneficiaries of short-term-rate cuts are banks, which borrow huge amounts of short-term money, much of it to fund high-interest credit card loans. Corporate America loves short-term-rate cuts, too, because many of the folks who inhabit corporate America's upper echelons live for stock options. And Fed rate cuts are usually a short-term tonic for stock prices. (Stock prices may fall the day the Fed cuts rates, but they've usually risen in anticipation of the cut.)

The problem is that long-term rates are important, too. Rising long-term rates undermine the effect of falling short-term rates. For starters, anyone who's borrowing to finance a long-term project such as a manufacturing plant has to be an optimist—or sniffing something illegal—if she decides to finance it entirely in the short-term markets. Second, it's clear that for quite a while now, one of the factors stimulating consumer spending, especially on big-ticket items like cars, has been money that homeowners are taking out of their houses by refinancing mortgages. If the refi market is slowed significantly by rising mortgage rates (or even by their failure to fall), consumer spending could be hurt. Big-time.

So you can see that Alan Greenspan isn't the all-powerful free agent many people think him to be. He can't cut short-term interest rates blithely. He's got to worry about the long-term-bond market, as well as trying to stimulate the economy short-term. The bottom line: if the Fed cuts short-term rates this week, don't expect mortgage rates to tumble. In fact, don't be surprised if mortgages rise, because long-term rates spiked up last week. Don't blame Uncle Alan. It's not his fault; it's the way the world works.

The air is thin in the ultrarich world of Larry Ellison and Bill Gates, so it's not surprising that their lives make the rest of us feel a bit light-headed. Offering some amazing anecdotes about Oracle Corp.'s Ellison, Mark Leibovich of *The Washington Post* captures the CEO's splashy personal style and in-your-face business attitude, offering childhood reasons for such aggressive behavior. We learn what Ellison considers to be living well, and how very much it all means to him.

Mark Leibovich

The Outsider, His Business, and His Billions

LARRY ELLISON, the world's second-richest man, was entertaining friends aboard his 243-foot yacht off Capri when another yacht caught his attention. A mere 200-foot yacht. Belonging to Microsoft cofounder Paul Allen. The world's third-richest man.

As Allen's yacht set out on a twilight cruise to the village of Positano, Ellison instructed his captain to rev his boat's three engines to full speed. Within minutes, his craft overtook Allen's at 40 mph, leaving a huge and sudden wake that sent Allen and his passengers staggering across the deck. Ellison's yacht then returned to its anchorage with him and his friends belly-laughing.

A spokesman for Allen declines to comment on the episode, which occurred at the end of August. "It was an adolescent prank," says Ellison, who is fifty-six. "I highly recommend it."

This is the sort of thing that makes Silicon Valley's most successful entrepreneur such an easy caricature. He is the founder and

chief executive of Oracle Corp., the world's second-biggest software company and—as businesses shift their functions on-line—
one formidably positioned to profit from the Internet boom. His
net worth is $58 billion, according to the October issue of *Forbes*
magazine, and tied closely to the performance of Oracle stock. At
times this year, that sum has surpassed Bill Gates's fortune (it
dusts Allen's $36 billion). But when Ellison receives attention, it's
often for reasons irrelevant to his corporate bona fides.

Last June, he admitted that Oracle had hired a private investigator to snoop on a pro–Microsoft Corp. trade group in Washington. A few days later his longtime deputy, Ray Lane, left in a
public spat. Ellison continued a long-running battle with authorities at San Jose Airport for the right to violate its 11 P.M. curfew
with his Gulfstream V jet. A Florida man alleged in a lawsuit that
Ellison stiffed him out of a $700,000 commission when he bought
a $10 million yacht. A former housekeeper was accused of stealing
his Rolex. His McLaren F1 sports car was reportedly issued a fake
smog certificate. That was just last summer.

Yet Ellison wonders why his sweeping impact on the world
has been so obscured. Oracle's database software automates the
taken-for-granted functions of modern commerce: it provides
unseen tools that track data in automated teller machines, that
ease credit card transactions, that underpin on-line commerce.
Few people know how to use Oracle's software, but many encounter it indirectly every day.

Ellison, who founded Oracle twenty-three years ago, is both
the ultimate Silicon Valley entrepreneur and its consummate outsider. He typifies the extremes of the technology industry, its
wealth, brilliance, and speed as well as its ego, hype, and ruthlessness. But he did not emerge from the privileged suburban environment that nourished so many New Economy ambitions—the
Honolulu cul-de-sac that produced America Online's Steve Case,
the elite schools that trained Amazon.com's Jeff Bezos, the old-
money lineage of Bill Gates. "William Gates the Third," corrects
Ellison, deriding the only man richer than he.

Born to an unwed nineteen-year-old in Manhattan, Lawrence Joseph Ellison was adopted at nine months by distant relatives in Chicago. Louis Ellison was a Russian Jew who had changed his long surname to commemorate his passage through Ellis Island, a newcomer seeking acceptance and self-renewal. These themes he conveyed to his adopted son by assuring him he would always fail.

Beyond his outward refinement—his Armani suits, his Beverly Hills nose job—Larry Ellison's approach to business betrays a raw desperation. "I can't imagine anything worse than failing," he says. This, too, sets him apart. "For as competitive as it is in Silicon Valley, there's this idea that everyone should be playing like it's all a friendly chess match," says Marc Benioff, a former Oracle executive. "Larry doesn't think this for a second. He thinks of himself as a samurai warrior."

Last year Benioff left Oracle after thirteen years to start Salesforce.com, an on-line software service for sales operations. Ellison gave his blessing, plus a $2 million investment. He joined the board.

Three months ago, Benioff learned that Oracle had launched a competing business. He demanded that Ellison resign his board seat. Ellison refused.

"It would sound a lot cooler if you kicked me off," Ellison said, according to Benioff. "It would be a better story to tell my friends."

Ellison's version: "I said, 'Marc, I'm surprised you don't want to throw me off. It would get you more publicity, and that's what you've been using me for all along.'"

Both agree that Ellison, while resigning, quibbled over the Salesforce.com stock options he felt entitled to.

THE FOG OF DECEIT

Ellison places two fingers on his tongue and makes like he's gagging.

The topic: high-tech leaders who trumpet their enterprises as Crusades for Good—as if they had nothing to do with riches and victory. His rapid-fire speech slows to a cadence of disdainful sarcasm:

"Oh, well, the reason we're doing software here at Oracle is because someday children will use this software, and we wouldn't want to leave a single child behind. If I could just make the world a better place, what I really care about is making the world a better place, and that's why I'm doing this. And all my money's going to go to medical research so we can help people who are sick."

At which point he gags himself again.

"People say this and get away with it," he says, patting his temples with the tips of his long and manicured fingers. "I can't deal with the fog of deceit."

Deceit is a complicated notion with Ellison. He's been accused of practicing it in many forms—exaggerating the capabilities of Oracle products, embellishing the meanness of his boyhood neighborhood, and misleading people about which academic degrees he has earned.

At the same time, the rough transparency of Ellison's bravado flouts the PR obsession of his industry. He is asked when he knew the Internet would be big. A soft, fat question.

It was in the early 1990s, he says. He was visiting his daughter's kindergarten class, and he saw all the five-year-olds using it. The public relations woman monitoring the interview nods reassuringly.

By the way, his daughter's teacher was "an incredibly pretty single young lady," says Ellison, who has been thrice divorced. "Really, I never saw a kindergarten teacher look like that before." The image of toddlers in cyberspace is lost. The PR woman's smile is frozen.

Ellison is sitting in his eleventh-floor office at Oracle, a bright, large, and obsessively cleaned place decorated with Japanese paintings and ceramics. His face is both ugly and handsome, with cheeks worn red from sailing and busy brown eyes that turn soft when he smiles, squinty when he talks. His repaired nose sits in triangular symmetry with his long and bearded jaw.

No fan of tech-casual dress, Ellison wears a charcoal gray sports jacket over a black turtleneck. He rests his size-twelve feet on a glass table. He is six feet one, trim and somewhat body-obsessed. If he misses a workout, he is prone to vocal fits of self-loathing.

"To Larry, so much of his power comes from physical fitness," says Jenny Overstreet, his longtime assistant until she retired at age thirty-five in 1996. He talks about how his body feels and looks, Overstreet says—"like a woman saying, 'My thighs are fat today.'"

Ellison greets visitors with a soft but firm handshake and a courtly bow. He breaches no rule of decorum except that he is unfailingly late. Unapologetically late. And not a little bit late.

"Every time we'd go to lunch, he'd be thirty, sixty, ninety minutes late," says Stuart Feigin, Oracle's fifth employee, who calls his former boss "the late Larry Ellison." Ellison was ninety minutes late for this interview. He did not apologize; he only explained: he was in a meeting. He has a hard time getting out of meetings. He is "somewhat reassured" that two of the people he most admires, Winston Churchill and Bill Clinton, were and are habitually late.

Still, there are legions of Ellison lateness tales to suggest an edgier character. At an Oracle-sponsored demonstration for Defense Department clients in Herndon, a group of high-level Pentagon officials waited forty-five minutes until Ellison pulled up in a limousine. He kept Philippines president Fidel Ramos waiting more than an hour in his San Francisco mansion. When Ellison arrived, Ramos waited another fifteen minutes while Ellison changed clothes.

As a general rule, Ellison's scheduling commitments come with an eleventh-hour proviso: Larry Permitting. He has a five-year-old's attention span when he's bored and an ability to delve deep if he cares to. It makes him suited to running a company on

Internet time: his mind can pinball from topic to topic and focus when necessary. And he tends to say whatever is on his mind.

"Some people who like me would say there's a high degree of integrity," he says. "Other people would see it as incredibly self-destructive. Then the third group would say, 'I can't believe he's saying that; he's just an [epithet].'"

He says the first two groups would be right.

Rest assured, he wants to be loved, more and more as he gets older. "The reason you want to be loved," he says "is because you want to love yourself and feel self-esteem." Does he feel sufficiently loved?

"No, of course not." He's learned this over time and struggle (therapy? "None, nada; I tried marriage counseling once"), and he hates that he's perceived as mean, ruthless. "I don't think mean and ruthless people are loved." He has tried to improve, he says earnestly, almost plaintively; he is improving.

OUR PRIMEVAL ENVIRONMENT

"It's the ambiguity between inside and out," Ellison says. He's leading a tour of the compound he is building in the hills of Woodside, thirty miles south of San Francisco. At the moment, he's pointing to a rock that is both inside and outside a shower, but he returns repeatedly to the theme of planned ambiguity.

Guests will be kept guessing. Are the trees growing out of the main residence? Is the koi pond a discrete body or connected to the three-acre lake? Is that structure over the lake a bridge or a residence? Ellison points to a bathroom that opens out onto the woods. "It will be like taking a bath in a redwood forest," he says.

Inside or out? Where do you stand?

Six years in the making and much anticipated in architectural circles, Ellison's twenty-three-acre compound will be what Kublai Khan would have built if he'd had a Japan fetish and a budget that could reach $100 million. It will serve the tidy purpose of outdoing Gates's $50 million home on Lake Washington, the mention of which prompts Ellison to wince. He quotes his friend, Apple chief executive Steve Jobs: "I don't begrudge Microsoft their success. It's just that they have no taste."

The chief designer of Ellison's project is a Zen monk; it will replicate a sixteenth-century Japanese village. Expert craftsmen are building pieces of it in Japan, disassembling them, and shipping them to California for reassembly on-site. Ellison calls it "the most important Japanese project to be built in the last two hundred years."

He's wearing dark shades and a black tank top accentuating thick arms, and his black hair is tousled after a workout. His silver Mercedes-Benz S600 is parked in back, a hairbrush lying on the passenger seat.

Ellison has agreed to give a tour on one condition: no photographs on the grounds. He is a gracious and eloquent host, romping around the property as if leading an inspection of his idealized soul.

On a visit to Japan in the mid-1970s, Ellison says, he entered a garden and never felt more at home. This compound is intended to re-create that feeling.

At present, it is a large construction site: tractors zigzag across bare dirt; half-finished structures stand draped in plastic. But by late 2001, it will comprise an 8,000-square-foot main house, five guest residences and an underground network of basements and tunnels, a forest of cherry trees, streams, waterfalls, ponds, and a lake with boulders doubling as hot tubs; a teahouse, boathouse, natural amphitheater, indoor basketball court, and recreation center; a horse stable, three garages for Ellison's fourteen cars, and a sprawling garden to be maintained by a staff of twenty.

The lake will be filled with purified drinking water.

When the project is finished, Ellison will sell his $30 million Japanese-style home in nearby Atherton. He will keep the $25 million mansion in San Francisco for entertaining. He will live here with his fiancée, Melanie Craft, a thirty-year-old writer, an Icelandic pony, and two cats, Big Daddy and Maggie. His teenage son and daughter from his third marriage will have their pick of residences within the compound. He plans an influx of friends, artists, dignitaries. They will select meals with a mouse click, and food will be delivered by boat.

Overlooking the soon-to-be garden from a second-floor library, Ellison notes that the great Western structures—Notre Dame, Versailles—were designed to humble man before God and king. But the goal of Japanese architecture is to create a serene and familiar place. "By familiar, I mean natural," he says. "We just moved to cities a few thousand years ago. Before that, we were forest dwellers." The place is meant to integrate the most sublime creations of God and man.

"You can smell the oils of the cedar and the pine, and that's a very reassuring smell," he says. "That's our primeval environment," in contrast to the ambiance of his boyhood home, which he distills to "plaster and glass and gunshots."

The tour lasts two hours, inadequate for seeing the home's exquisite nuances—"like speed-reading poetry," Ellison says. Every time he enters a room, workers do a double take, as if expecting a command. Now he's pointing to a boathouse roof. "You can see how it comes together like the feathers of a bird." He smiles and giggles. "It's simply astonishing!" he says. "The sensuality is incredible."

Upon his death, Ellison will leave the compound to Stanford University, on the condition that "they don't touch anything." Ellison is terrified of dying. He doesn't get it; it mocks his rational bent and need for control. "I don't understand how someone can be here, then not be here," he says. "It's incomprehensible." He's more terrified of getting old. A portion of his charitable giving—which overall pales in comparison to Gates's—goes to fund research at the University of California on DHEA, a hormone that some people believe could retard aging. He has also given substantial sums to cancer research.

For now, he'll bid for immortality with this compound. "Sometimes it bothers me," he says. "I think it will outlive Oracle."

He walks into a bathroom next to a hand-carved wooden

bridge connecting two residences. "This wood is much too complex for me," he says, pointing to the basin of a sink. Fir and pine might work here, but not elm. Beautiful, but too grainy. "Get rid of it," he says to no one in particular.

"I have driven the poor people crazy," Ellison says, laughing. "They have suffered mightily."

BUT IS IT REALLY TRUE?

Obvious theories abound on what caused Larry Ellison.

"I think the distant and disapproving father created a maverick son," Jenny Overstreet says. Louis Ellison gave his son "so much fuel, so much anger, perseverance, and determination," says Overstreet, who now lives in a San Francisco mansion down the street from her former boss's. "It was great for all of us."

The trauma of abandonment? "So my biological mother abandoned me, and my mother who raised me abandoned me when she died of cancer," Ellison says. "I've thought of all this. It's one of those things that just sounds so good, the reasons are all there." He takes a deep and melodramatic breath.

"But is it really true?"

Starting from his birth, on August 17, 1944, Ellison's biography has been steeped in uncertainty. Errol Getner, his next-door neighbor in adolescence, says Ellison always told him that his father worked for the FBI. Over the years, Ellison has often spoken about the "projects" and "ghetto" he grew up in, and the gunfire. "He used to tell me that the two toughest kids from his neighborhood were Cassius Clay and Sonny Liston," says Gary Kennedy, a former top executive at Oracle. The future Muhammad Ali grew up in Louisville, Liston in Arkansas and St. Louis. Both spent time in Chicago later in their lives, miles from where Ellison lived.

People from Ellison's South Side neighborhood describe a cozy, lower-middle-class, and predominantly Jewish enclave. "If you took the TV shows *Happy Days* and *Brooklyn Bridge* and averaged them, we would be somewhere in the middle," says Chuck Weiss, a childhood friend who now works at Oracle. "We weren't quite as suburban as *Happy Days,* not quite as urban or ethnic as *Brooklyn Bridge.*"

Lillian and Louis Ellison lived in a two-bedroom apartment on Clyde Avenue. She was a bookkeeper, he was an auditor, and they survive in their son's memory as opposites: Larry describes her as a loving and committed mother, him as quiet and scornful. Louis, he says, had "an automatic and unthinking deference to authority figures and rules"; he was a "true believer." One thing he believed—or said a lot—was that his son would never amount to anything. "That was his form of greeting, as opposed to 'Hi' or 'Good morning,'" Larry says.

Louis had a daughter from a previous marriage, Doris, who was nineteen years older than Larry. She and her husband, Chicago judge David Linn, lived next door, and they were alternative mentors to Larry. He would bring friends over to view David's closet of fine suits.

Larry defied his parents' wishes that he have a bar mitzvah—signaling a lifelong indifference to Jewish customs. Hebrew school conflicted with his Little League practice.

His companions recall a child of outsized dreams. "Whatever he was doing, he was always projecting it bigger and better," says Jimmy Linn, Doris and David's son, five years younger than his uncle. Ellison was "extremely bright, but a little unbridled."

At South Shore High School, he was avidly curious, and he read voraciously. But he skipped classes, received frequent detention, and earned mixed grades. Once his biology teacher, Mrs. Coleman, threatened to flunk him for cutting class. "If I get the highest grade on the final, would you still flunk me?" Ellison said. Yes, she said, and forty years later, he re-creates their argument with a taunting edge. "If I know more about biology than anyone else in class, you're gonna flunk me?" he says, waving his hands, smirking. It is as if Mrs. Coleman, who died in 1975, were sitting next to him.

He has a harder time remembering when he learned that he was adopted. He was about twelve, and Louis told him in mid-conversation. Or maybe midargument. "My short-term memory was erased," Ellison says.

He didn't tell his friends. They were all male, athletic, and happy to indulge Ellison's gift for banter and pontification. One friend, Dennis Coleman, son of the biology teacher, recalls one of Ellison's oft-repeated manifestos: "There's no such thing as pleasure. There's only tension and the release of tension."

Ellison joined a Jewish fraternity, the Tommies, in high school, and played a lot of basketball and football. His formative teenage relationship was with Karen Rutzky, his girlfriend from age fifteen. Rutzky's parents did not like him, and "Larry was devastated by that," Doris Linn says.

But Ellison and Rutzky attended three proms and owned three matching shirts. Lillian gave her son money and he would take Rutzky out, buy her gifts. He gave her a Mary Poppins book. The inscription: "To Karen, a supercalifragilisticexpialidocious date and a truly tolerant person. Love always, Larry."

Their relationship continued after she left for the University of Michigan. He told her he planned to go to medical school, and asked her to quit school to support him. In their five years together, she refused two marriage proposals from him, she says. Ellison remembers just one.

And as with many relationships from his past, Ellison's memory differs starkly from the other person's. The details are long ago and unimportant. In sum: "I cared deeply about Larry," says Karen Rutzky Back, now of Los Angeles. But he lied to her serially, she says. "I got tired of being a detective about everything he said."

Ellison says the notion that he lied to her is "really breathtaking." He adds: "The fact that I stayed with Karen Rutzky for five years is one of the worst things anyone can say about me," he says. "Forget about always being late." Ellison rooted against University of Michigan sports teams for twenty-five years.

Over several hours of interviews, no subject animates Ellison more than Rutzky. For all his success, her rejection—and her parents' dislike—seems a lingering embodiment of all that made him feel unworthy. It also serves as a ready benchmark for his life's piece-by-piece reconstruction.

"You know, I was named one of *Playboy*'s top ten best-dressed people recently," he says. "I think my journey from those stupid matching shirts with Karen Rutzky to *Playboy*'s best-dressed list is a more heroic journey than going from the South Side of Chicago to running Oracle."

In 1962, Ellison graduated from South Shore High School and enrolled at the University of Illinois in Urbana–Champaign. At the end of his sophomore year, Lillian Ellison died of kidney cancer. Crushed, Larry left school.

In the summer of 1964, he and Chuck Weiss visited northern California. It seemed wild and freewheeling, perfect for escaping cohabitation with Louis. But he enrolled at the University of Chicago, where he spent one semester. He told friends that he had gotten into medical school. He even produced an acceptance letter. "The letter didn't look legit," says Dennis Coleman, noting that it was from the University of Southern California. "It was very short and had typos." Rutzky Back also recalls him showing an acceptance letter.

Ellison never applied to medical school, he says now. He didn't graduate from college, or come close. What about the acceptance letter? "It just couldn't be," he says.

Even his closest living relatives, Doris and Jimmy Linn, still believe he had been accepted to medical school. They recall David Linn's dismay when Ellison said he wouldn't be going: "You'll be the first man in five thousand years of the Jewish religion who was accepted to medical school but refused to go," he said.

Instead, Ellison bought himself a turquoise 1964 Thunderbird and drove west. He had no idea how he would support himself, but in an undergraduate physics class he had shown some aptitude in computer programming.

AMOUNTING TO SOMETHING

Toting a programming manual, Ellison moved from technical job to technical job—at banks, insurance companies, and small businesses. He made enough money to live on, and he loved the notion that he was "amounting to something" on his own.

In 1967, he met Adda Quinn at a San Jose employment agency, and they married after a few months, both at twenty-three. No one from Chicago attended the wedding, except for Weiss, who was living in San Francisco.

Ellison seemed determined to break clean from his past—although Quinn says he often mentioned Karen Rutzky. He got his nose fixed, smoothing out the lumps from long-ago basketball games. He enrolled in graduate classes at Berkeley, but would never finish. "He told me that he graduated from an obscure college in Sheffield, England," Quinn says. "He told me these big, whopping lies, and he stuck to them. He can follow these lies for years."

"I've never been to Sheffield, England," Ellison says. "So that's very peculiar." Yet in their seven years together, he never told his own wife that he lacked a bachelor's degree. They met at an employment agency, he explains, and he told people he had a degree in order to get jobs. And he could never come clean to his wife. "I lied," he says. "It's a bad thing. I'm embarrassed."

Quinn calls Ellison the most charming, brilliant, and non-boring man she has ever known. He also gave her an ulcer, she says, with his deceptions, his transient interests in jobs and classes, and his explosive temper. She says she feared for her safety as their marriage was ending: the couple kept guns in the house—they lived in a rough part of Oakland—and she thought Ellison was becoming increasingly erratic.

"I don't know how she could have feared for her safety," Ellison says, and calls himself a nonviolent person. "The fact that she ever thought I could shoot her is a little bizarre."

In 1971, Ellison invited his aging father to live with him. It was a kind and unexpected gesture, Quinn says, but their strain lingered. Louis was not disapproving, she observed; she never heard him criticize his son. But neither was he supportive, and Larry took that as disapproval.

"Louis would kind of look down, with this expression," Quinn says. "It would drive Larry absolutely crazy." Louis stayed until 1974, when he entered a nursing home, and died soon afterward.

The same year, Ellison's marriage to Quinn ended. He didn't want it to. They tried counseling. "I remember asking, how does this work?" Ellison says, "and I got this amazing gibberish answer. I'm like, okay, great, thanks. Uh, no." In one session, Quinn says, he vowed that he would make a million dollars. It was the first time she had heard him speak of becoming rich.

Years later, Ellison bought Quinn a car. He paid the mortgage on her parents' house. And when Quinn's second husband battled cancer, Ellison gave him a lucrative job. He is on good terms with all three of his former wives, he says.

Despite his scattershot job history, Ellison was becoming a good computer programmer. In the mid-1970s, he landed at a computing firm in Sunnyvale, Ampex, which, like many companies in the early days of Silicon Valley, did contract work for the federal government. Ellison contributed to a database project for the CIA. Code name: Oracle.

At the time, databases were usually "hierarchical": they organized data according to a "hierarchy" of information. If Pan American Airlines wanted to keep track of its flights—what are their flight numbers? where are they going?—the information would flow downward from a master heading marked "flights." Users would start at the top of a chart and work their way down to find the information they wanted.

But database technology was nearing a breakthrough. In 1970, International Business Machines Corp. researcher Ted Codd published a plan for a "relational" database, which could discern fluid connections between bits of data. With a relational database, a Pan American employee could tell, say, how many passengers on flight 209 had ordered vegetarian meals. Chrysler could see which models were selling best, and who was selling most.

Codd's paper prompted a race to create the best relational database. The key players were a group from IBM, called System R, and another from Berkeley, Ingres. In 1976, the IBM scientists completed their plan—and published it. That would be unthinkable today, but in the 1970s, software was a largely academic pursuit. "Our feeling was, the rising tide lifts all ships," says Michael Blasgen of the IBM team. "Since IBM was the biggest ship, we stood to benefit most."

No one benefited more than Larry Ellison.

ELVIS SIGHTINGS

"We can do this," Ellison thought as he read the IBM paper.

In 1977, at thirty-two, he had started a software development consultancy with two former colleagues, Bob Miner and Ed Oates. That same year, Bill Gates and Paul Allen started Microsoft. While Microsoft would transform computing for individuals, Ellison's team focused on businesses. Their goal was to build the first commercially viable relational database. With IBM's paper as a blueprint, Ellison felt that they could develop a better product and sell it first.

Ellison did nothing to hide his reliance on the IBM team. Blasgen recalls getting a letter from Ellison: "He basically said, give me a few details, I'll copy them, and that way our systems will be the same." The request was ignored.

Ellison, Miner, and Oates had limited resources; venture capital did not flow as it does today, and besides, Ellison had no interest in diluting his ownership. They began as a bootstrap operation: sign clients, do work, get money, develop their database product. They named the product Oracle, and put the first version on the market in 1979—three years ahead of IBM. Within five years, the company that would become known as Oracle Corp. was generating $12.7 million a year in sales.

On March 12, 1986, Oracle held an initial public offering. Shares debuted at $15 and closed that day at $20.75. Ellison's 34 percent stake was worth $93 million. Microsoft, which held its offering the next day, priced at $21 and closed at $28—putting Gates's stake at $300 million.

As Oracle grew, so did Ellison's craving for dominance, a notion fostered by frequent visits to the Far East. He once met a Japanese businessman who mocked his American counterparts for voicing "great respect" for their rivals. "In Japan, we believe our competitors are stealing rice out of the mouths of our children," the businessman said. "We must destroy our competition." Ellison returned to Oracle and invoked that conversation repeatedly.

While much of Oracle's success was a triumph of strategic and technical skill, it also stemmed from one of the most aggressive sales forces in computing history. The company's sales reps were pushed hard and paid well—Marc Benioff, at twenty-five, was making $300,000 a year in 1986; topflight sellers were making seven figures. "The management theory was simple," Benioff says. "Go out and don't come back before you have a signed contract."

The relational database market was in a land-grab period, analogous to what Internet commerce is undergoing now. Several sources recall Ellison exaggerating what his software could do and when it would be ready. "Were there things we promised in our early years that we couldn't do?" Ellison says. "I'm sure there were." When Ellison promised a customer something, he believed it at that moment, says Gary Kennedy, who oversaw Oracle's sales operation in the late 1980s. Benioff recalls, "Larry always said, 'I have a little problem with tenses.'"

Ellison during this period could be inspiring or abusive. "You would spend a lot of time anticipating what Larry would do next," says Unang Gupta, Oracle's seventeenth employee and a longtime executive. His hiring and firing patterns were unpredictable. Ellison viewed business relationships as transient, a phenomenon that extended to wives, two more of whom came and went before 1986.

In 1989, with more than 4,000 employees, Oracle moved to a verdant sprawl of ponds and glass towers twenty-five miles south of San Francisco. In a valley dominated by beige office parks, the lush campus became known as "the Emerald City" (also "Larry-land"), with Mercedes-Benzes, Jaguars, even Rolls-Royces lining the parking lots. Ellison, who drove a red Ferrari to work, began boasting about the hours of tennis he played on company time. He dated a procession of women, sometimes his employees. His rare appearances at headquarters were dubbed "Elvis sightings."

The good times came at a price. "Larry Ellison has created more millionaires than anyone in Silicon Valley," says Igor Sill, an executive search consultant who did work for Oracle from 1984 to 1990. "And most of them wind up hating him."

This is perhaps overstated, and it ignores the ambiguity of feeling that Ellison incites. Many who have fallen out with him speak generously in retrospect. "The people who dislike Larry, of which they are legion, tend to underestimate his brilliance," says Kennedy, who left, on bad terms, in 1990.

Ending life at Larry speed can be disorienting. "When you're doing anything so passionately, so emotionally, ending it is hard," Jenny Overstreet says. "I left in the most positive way possible, and it took me six months to come to grips with not being there."

Ellison feels profound loss when relationships end, no matter how. "Larry takes anyone leaving as a personal betrayal," says John Luongo, a longtime Oracle executive who left on good terms but at a point where the company was about to implode from its excesses.

Ellison speaks well of Luongo, and says he did not feel betrayed: "I felt, if anything, abandoned."

I LET EVERYONE DOWN

In 1990, Oracle started paying some sales commissions in gold. It would be the final indulgence of a company that seemed to be on a perpetual joyride.

Years of sales discounts, coupled with sloppy accounting methods, led Oracle to record revenues it had not received. The company reported nearly $971 million in sales in 1990—and yet had a large proportion of uncollected bills. It was forced to "restate" revenues in September of 1990, and after more than a decade of doubled sales each year, Oracle posted a loss of $12.4 million in 1991. Several executives and top managers fled. Ellison fired others. The company's stock value plummeted from $3.8 billion to $700 million. In November of 1990, shares of Oracle reached their all-time low, $4.88. Ellison's stake in the company was then worth $164 million, down from nearly a billion the previous spring.

When the company laid off 500 employees in 1991, he couldn't even leave his house. "I was too depressed," he says. "I let everyone down."

What had happened was easy, though unpleasant, to discern: Ellison had spent most of his mental energy on technology issues, neglecting such business fundamentals as finance and day-to-day operations.

After a period of soul-searching, Ellison resolved to run Oracle like an "adult" business. This meant his renewed engagement. It also meant bringing in seasoned executives, like Ray Lane, whom he hired in 1992 to shore up Oracle's operations. Lane, and new financial chief Jeff Henley, spearheaded Oracle's return to health in 1992. The company earned $61.5 million that year, on sales of $1.2 billion. Ellison survived what he calls "my near-corporate death," emerging more focused and, he says, humbled.

"I used to practice what I jokingly referred to as 'management by ridicule,'" he says. "People would be terrified to come into meetings." Ellison vowed to be more gracious, which coincided with another turning point in his life. After years of curiosity, he hired a private investigator to locate his biological mother, Florence Spellman of New Haven, Connecticut. He called her; they spoke briefly. She had no idea what her son had become. Ellison bought her a house in California. He paid her daughter's college tuition. They kept in contact until she died in 1999.

And yet, "It was very clear after meeting my real mother that she wasn't my real mother," he says. "My real mother was the woman who raised me; my real family were the people who raised me. . . . I felt completion in that I knew exactly who my family was."

Each year, Ellison invites Doris and Jimmy Linn for summer and winter yacht trips on the Mediterranean and Caribbean. Doris never flies commercial. In the years before he died, in 1996, David Linn rode to his judge's chambers in an Ellison-sponsored limousine.

"Everything that Larry has accomplished has had two psychic purposes," says one longtime friend. "To say thank-you to people who believed in him. And to say [expletive] you to the people who didn't."

IT'S THE WORLD, THE PLANET

Nothing holds more potential for Ellison's corporate immortality than the Internet. In 1995, he began insisting that Oracle gear everything to the emerging on-line world. Before there was an information age, Oracle dealt in information, and today, as companies produce oceans of data—whether it's Amazon tracking its customers or Ford processing bids from suppliers—Oracle has never been so central to the economy. The company owns 42.4 percent of the database software market, more than double the share of its closest competitor, IBM.

Ellison has never been more engrossed. He has overseen the

development of new software products that are transforming Oracle from a pure database company to a provider of "software services." The centerpiece is an "e-business suite," a single product that Oracle sells to businesses that lets them manage all data-related operations on-line.

When he speaks of the Internet, Ellison sounds almost messianic. He's making a sales pitch to some degree, but he also betrays a kind of soulful fear. Failing gets harder with age, he says. "There are only so many at bats you get."

The Internet offers a chance to subvert Louis Ellison's prediction for his son in the most extreme way. Only Bill Gates has amounted to more. Or has he?

Net worth is of course a fluid concept today, and in recent weeks, plunging stock values—including shares of Oracle and Microsoft—have complicated comparisons. But in early October, shortly after the *Forbes* survey was published, Ellison was skeptical that he was number two.

"*Forbes* spots Bill as many billions as he needs," Ellison says, sighing, resigned to the injustice.

There's just something surreal about being the richest, Ellison often says. "And it's not just the wealthiest guy in the United States. It's the world, the planet." He pauses to weigh the notion, as if it had never occurred to him before.

"I'm the wealthiest guy on the planet," he says. "That's very peculiar."

A battle is being waged in Africa, and children's lives are at stake. This dramatic *Wall Street Journal* article by Alix M. Freedman and Steve Stecklow introduces us to real people, not just statistics. It presents the irrational anger and unresolved conflicts that explain why needed baby formula is being withheld from mothers who have AIDS. Without nutritious baby formula, the virus is transmitted via breast-feeding to infants. While acknowledging the past misdeeds of corporations, it calls for immediate action to be taken.

Alix M. Freedman and Steve Stecklow

Bottled Up:
As Unicef Battles Baby-Formula Makers, African Infants Sicken

KAMPALA, UGANDA—When Busingye Scovia, who is infected with the AIDS virus, delivered a healthy baby girl last year, she was warned by hospital staff that breast-feeding could infect her newborn.

But no one at the hospital told her about an alternative: infant formula. As is true all over the developing world, hospitals here rarely supply formula to mothers—even those with AIDS. Instead, Ms. Scovia was sent home, where she continued to nurse her baby, Latshia. "I knew what I was doing was wrong," Ms. Scovia now says.

Eleven months later, Latshia tested positive for AIDS. Could this death sentence have been prevented?

Behind the scenes, this question has emerged as one of the most contentious among those trying to combat AIDS in sub-Saharan Africa. It's not because there's any doubt that breast-feeding can transmit the virus: to date, an estimated 1.1 million to 1.7 million infants have become infected this way, mostly in Africa.

Rather, the issue of whether and how infant formula should be made available to poor African mothers has become mired in an incendiary debate that appears to be driven more by politics and ideology than by science. On one side is the United Nations—and principally its member agency Unicef, which is charged with protecting the interests of children. On the other is the $3 billion infant-formula industry.

One major formula maker, Wyeth-Ayerst Laboratories, Inc., says it stands ready to donate tons of free formula to HIV-infected women. Number one ranked Nestlé SA says it too would donate, if asked. But Unicef refuses to green-light the gifts because it doesn't want to endorse an industry it has long accused of abusive practices in the developing world.

Relations between Unicef and the industry have grown, if anything, more bitter. Secret meetings to broker a free shipment of formula to 100,000 African babies broke down amid finger-pointing and unreturned phone calls. The imbroglio has also pitted two New York City Democratic political bedfellows against each other: former vice presidential candidate Geraldine Ferraro was retained by Nestlé to lobby former New York City Council president Carol Bellamy, now executive director of Unicef. Meanwhile, the industry hasn't donated a single tin of formula to HIV-infected mothers.

The bad blood between Unicef and the industry dates back to the 1970s, when Nestlé and other formula makers routinely blitzed developing world countries with ads featuring fat formula-fed babies and gave out free samples in maternity wards to attract women to their product. By the time the freebies ran out, women's own breast milk usually had dried up, too. Few could afford to purchase any formula, or they diluted it to make it last longer, sometimes starving their babies in the process. In protest, activists organized a worldwide boycott of Nestlé products, and Unicef refused to accept any cash donations from the big formula makers—as Unicef has done with other pariahs such as makers of land mines and cigarettes.

Eventually, the industry promised to mend its ways. Specifically, in the 1980s the major formula makers agreed to comply with a voluntary marketing code devised by Unicef and its sister UN agency, the World Health Organization. The fourteen-page document restricted advertising, specified labeling, and—most crucially—imposed a nearly blanket prohibition against distributing free and low-cost formula.

Since then, Unicef and the industry have battled over interpretations of the code, with the biggest formula companies arguing they comply as much as possible and Unicef vehemently disagreeing.

But this much is clear: the code was devised long before anyone ever contemplated the ravages of AIDS in Africa. Now, even some UN officials contend that Unicef's decades-old distrust of the formula industry should yield to a moral imperative to get formula to destitute, HIV-infected mothers. "They're having difficulty accepting that the world has changed," says Peter Piot, executive director of UNAIDS, an interagency UN program responsible for tackling the AIDS crisis. Mr. Piot, a researcher who was among the first to discover that AIDS can be transmitted among heterosexuals, says the UN must look beyond the "fierce battles" of the past in an effort to save lives.

Indeed, Nestlé says it has received "desperate" requests for free formula from some African hospitals. But the company says it's caught in a bind: if it donates the tins, it believes Unicef would view its action as a violation of the code—which could generate bad publicity and possibly fuel renewed boycott efforts. Theoretically, formula companies could just ignore the code and bypass Unicef, but that wouldn't work as a practical matter, the companies argue. The imprimatur of Unicef, which is best known in the United States for its annual trick-or-treating drive and peace-themed holiday cards, is vital in much of the developing world. There, the agency not only has a history of saving lives but also sometimes functions as a country's de facto children's health system.

In an interview, Ms. Bellamy, Unicef's chief, says she doesn't believe Nestlé and the other major formula makers have "a particular role" to play in the AIDS crisis. "What they should do is comply with the code," she says.

Studies suggest that only about 15 percent of pregnant women with HIV in Africa will transmit the virus to their children through breast-feeding. Also, Ms. Bellamy says, formula poses risks of its own if prepared without adequate sanitation: it can expose infants to diarrhea and other traditional killers of the developing world, while breast milk contains antibodies to help ward off such illnesses. So, even if formula protects a baby from AIDS, it could prove deadly later on. In addition, Unicef officials are worried about a phenomenon known as "spillover"—that providing formula to HIV-infected women would undercut support for breast-feeding among healthy women.

In Ms. Bellamy's view, Unicef has to focus on the vast majority of babies for whom breast milk is unquestionably the safest food. "We continue very much to advocate that breast is best," Ms. Bellamy says.

In 1998, in the wake of intense debate over the AIDS crisis, Unicef and other UN agencies agreed to modify their pro-breast-feeding stance in the developing world—but not to the point of endorsing donations of formula. The new policy, known as "informed choice," states that infected women throughout the world should "be empowered" to decide the best way to feed their babies and be advised on the benefits and risks of breast-feeding and alternatives such as formula. Though Unicef continues to lead the crusade for breast-feeding in the developing world, Ms. Bellamy says the agency is "supportive" of formula as an option for HIV-infected mothers. "We certainly don't rule it out," she says.

However, the policy says nothing about how the desperately poor, HIV-infected women who do choose formula are supposed to get it. In Uganda, formula is sold at supermarkets and in crowded food stalls at prices that are far beyond the reach of much of the population. Joyce Ganyana, an HIV-positive mother who lives in a Kampala slum, says she can't afford to buy a liter of cow's milk for 43 cents, let alone a one-pound tin of formula, which generally costs $6. "If I stop breast-feeding, the baby will fall sick and die because she'll starve," says Ms. Ganyana, forty, who ekes out a living selling vegetables. "Formula is for the rich ones who can afford it."

Many health workers in Africa and even some UN officials deride the informed-choice policy as little more than a cop-out. Health workers are rarely able to spend more than a few minutes with mothers whose education and resources often are extremely limited, and some mothers don't get any counseling at all. For instance, Latshia's twenty-five-year-old mother, Ms. Scovia, learned about formula only from neighbors after she had come home from the hospital. Before, she says, "I thought formula was a powder for old people."

Thousands of miles from Ms. Scovia's unfolding family tragedy, the political logjam shows no signs of loosening. Unicef and the industry are still fighting over various details of the 1981 marketing code, and attempts at reconciliation over the past five years have left the two sides barely on speaking terms.

For example, an argument has raged over whether the code applies just to developing countries or everywhere in the world. Unicef says the code applies globally, leading Nestlé to complain that its promotional giveaways in places such as Canada unfairly land it on the violators' list. Unicef says it's crucial that the code be applied worldwide because women everywhere should be able to choose how to feed their babies without undue pressure from formula marketers.

In the developed world, big formula companies are notably aggressive, showering new mothers in maternity wards with product samples and other gifts. Nestlé's U.S. Web site (www. verybestbaby.com) offers a free subscription to the company's magazine, which features coupons for formula. Such outreach can be extremely lucrative because once a mother starts feeding her baby with formula, she generally sticks to the same brand—and the company locks in a good customer for at least a year.

Unicef also says it has ample evidence of wrongful industry

marketing efforts in developing world countries such as Bangladesh and the Philippines, including cases of companies plying health clinics with free samples of formula and bestowing calendars, pen holders, and other promotional gifts on health care workers. Nestlé and the rest of the industry deny they are violating the code and claim Unicef relies for its information on a network of activist groups driven by a pro-breast-feeding ideology.

In addition, some inside Unicef fear the industry will try to exploit the AIDS crisis as a way to build its African market. The formula makers dismiss this, describing both current and potential sales in sub-Saharan Africa as minuscule.

When Ms. Bellamy, now fifty-eight years old, was appointed in 1995 by UN secretary-general Kofi Annan as Unicef's chief, both she and the industry hoped to mend the rift. Her predecessor, the late James Grant, had held meetings with the formula makers that had degenerated into mutual accusations, participants say. Ms. Bellamy told the industry's trade association she wanted to avoid this, and invited the companies to come to New York and detail how they marketed infant formula around the world.

Nestlé alone accepted, and in October 1997 its chief executive, Peter Brabeck, flew to New York from Switzerland. For the company, the stakes were high. Nestlé makes some of the world's best-known consumer products—from Perrier bottled water to Nestlé and Kit Kat chocolate bars. Though infant formula represents less than 5 percent of Nestlé's total annual sales of $43 billion, the company believed Unicef's long-standing criticism of its alleged code violations was stoking the fervor of anti-Nestlé activists, who continued to attack the company at its annual shareholder meetings and on the Internet. Nestlé claims that the boycott, which activists still invoke in nineteen countries, including the United States, hasn't affected sales. But it has been a public relations problem for the company, which markets formula under the brand names Nestlé Nan in Africa and Nestlé Carnation Good Start in the United States.

Mr. Brabeck, a career Nestlé employee who only months before had been promoted to CEO, was hoping for a friendly audience with Ms. Bellamy. But the session in a thirteenth-floor conference room at Unicef headquarters soon became anything but amiable. Mr. Brabeck says Ms. Bellamy disappeared after about an hour to take a telephone call and, inexplicably, never returned. Ms. Bellamy says she had a scheduling conflict and thought Nestlé knew this.

Left to run the meeting was Ms. Bellamy's deputy, Stephen Lewis, a vocal industry critic. The discussion soon dissolved into the familiar debate over whether the code applied only to developing countries. Mr. Lewis recalls telling the Nestlé CEO that "a lot of babies have died as a result of formula, and the violations have to stop." With that, Mr. Lewis says, Mr. Brabeck "jumped up and pounded the table, and yelled." Mr. Brabeck, now fifty-six, denies what Mr. Lewis calls a "tantrum," but concedes he conveyed frustration. "Perhaps my body language is stronger than my words," he says.

A testy exchange of letters followed. In November 1997, a month after the meeting, Ms. Bellamy wrote to Mr. Brabeck, citing a number of "not reconcilable" differences over the two sides' interpretations of the marketing code, concluding: "It does not seem to us to be useful to maintain such contact in the future." Mr. Brabeck says he recalls thinking: "The world's leading food and beverage company is just being thrown a door in its face and told, 'Go home.'"

In December, he wrote to Ms. Bellamy, whose term ends in 2005: "I am not prepared to let this unsatisfactory state of affairs persist." Five days later he fired off a letter to Secretary Annan, complaining that "Ms. Bellamy simply closed the door for any further conversation."

Mr. Annan responded that he shared Unicef's view that the code "applies to all countries" but said he hoped "for a continued dialogue in a constructive spirit" between Nestlé and the UN. Mr. Annan declines to comment.

The standoff persisted for nearly two years. Then, in January, Nestlé tried a new tack with Unicef: it retained Ms. Ferraro, who works as a business consultant. Mr. Brabeck says he wanted her to get to the bottom of the "strange and very difficult-to-comprehend attitude of Unicef" toward Nestlé. He charges that Unicef was treating the company "like a criminal." Counters Ms. Bellamy: "The only thing we consider Nestlé to be is a non-code-compliant infant-formula manufacturer."

Ms. Ferraro and Ms. Bellamy have been close friends since 1978, when Ms. Bellamy successfully ran for New York City Council president and Ms. Ferraro, then a local prosecutor, campaigned alongside her. Having heard "terrible things" about Nestlé, Ms. Ferraro says she was initially skeptical when the head of the advertising agency that represents Nestlé—and also owns her consulting firm—asked her to take the assignment. But she says she changed her mind after spending several months reviewing Nestlé's code-compliance procedures. "I want to get past this feud," says Ms. Ferraro, who declines to disclose her fee.

In March, the two women lunched in the UN delegates' dining room. Later, Ms. Ferraro lugged to Unicef's headquarters a shopping bag containing a lengthy Nestlé analysis on how its overseas sales force has been trained in code compliance. On June 8, Ms. Bellamy responded to her friend by letter, claiming there were "fundamental divergences" between the code and Nestlé's view of it. For example, Ms. Bellamy objected to Nestlé's assertion that the code doesn't apply to products like follow-up formula for older babies. Some Unicef officials accuse the companies of marketing these products heavily as an indirect means of promoting infant formula. "There is still much work to be done," Ms. Bellamy concluded.

Ms. Ferraro replied that she was "disappointed" by Ms. Bellamy's reaction but vowed not to give up. "If in Geneva at the human rights commission I could get Syria to join in a resolution condemning anti-Semitism, and in Beijing I could get the Holy See to agree to language accepting of nontraditional families . . . I'm optimistic we can resolve our differences," wrote Ms. Ferraro, who has continued to lobby Ms. Bellamy.

As the contretemps between Nestlé and Unicef dragged on,

another formula maker quietly began putting out feelers to the agency. In 1998, Wyeth, a unit of American Home Products Corp. that sells formula under the brand names SMA and Nursoy, caught wind that Unicef was planning to launch a pilot program at some African hospitals to try to reduce mother-to-child AIDS transmission. To conform with the new "informed choice" policy, formula likely would be offered as an option to participants. Wyeth sensed an opportunity, but the objective of saving babies' lives soon got overtaken by a dispute over public relations.

In November 1998, Daniel Spiegel, a Washington attorney for Wyeth, began conducting some very quiet conversations with top officials at UNAIDS, the UN interagency group. Mr. Spiegel, a former U.S. ambassador to the UN in Geneva, told UNAIDS that Wyeth wanted to donate formula to HIV-infected women in Africa.

The company believed it could make such a donation because of an exception in the marketing code that allows formula give-aways to babies "who have to be fed on breast-milk substitutes." The company assumed this could include AIDS babies and that a program administered by Unicef itself would use the formula safely, thereby averting the potential for bad publicity. UNAIDS began acting as a broker between Wyeth and Unicef to put the precedent-setting deal in motion.

"This was very new ground for everyone," recalls Jim Sherry, a UNAIDS official involved in the talks. "Because of AIDS, the public-health community was in a turnaround situation: formula had been like tobacco and suddenly it wasn't."

After lengthy negotiations, Wyeth and Unicef representatives finally met face-to-face on March 26, 1999, at the company's Philadelphia headquarters. Unicef, worried that Wyeth would try to exploit its donation for marketing purposes, insisted the free formula could carry no brand name. Wyeth agreed. The company also said it was prepared to provide free formula for six months to 100,000 infants, a figure based on Unicef's initial estimates of what its pilot program would require, and was willing to give more later.

At Unicef's request, Wyeth sent a draft proposal of its offer to the agency about a week later. But unknown to the company, the deal was fast unraveling. On April 28, Mr. Lewis, Ms. Bellamy's aide, received an e-mail from Unicef lawyer Peter Mason stating that Wyeth had suggested getting Unicef to commit to a thank-you letter. According to the e-mail, Wyeth's Mr. Spiegel expressed "outrage and shock" when told that Unicef might not agree to a letter, but said that the company might settle for a meeting with Unicef officials.

Liza Barrie, a Unicef spokesperson, says Wyeth also had requested a jointly issued press release and a photo opportunity with Ms. Bellamy and Wyeth executives. "It seemed that everything they were proposing could lead to a misunderstanding of our relationship with the company and our views of its practices," Ms. Barrie says.

Mr. Spiegel and Kevin Reilly, president of Wyeth's nutrition and vaccine division, counter that Wyeth made suggestions about recognition only after Unicef itself brought up the subject and that these weren't conditions of the donation. "All we wanted was an appropriate acknowledgment . . . that would conform with obviously a multimillion-dollar donation," Mr. Spiegel says. He adds that Wyeth made only one demand: "That we not make this donation and then be attacked by Unicef" for alleged past transgressions.

In the end, Wyeth needn't have worried: Unicef rejected its donation. Without giving any explanation, Mr. Mason simply stopped talking to the company. "He never got back to me," says Mr. Spiegel. Mr. Mason, the Unicef lawyer, says through an agency spokesman that Unicef and Wyeth had "informal and very regular conversations" and that "ultimately, it was pretty clear that Unicef wouldn't be going forward unless there was some new development."

Around this time, UNAIDS was also contacted by Nestlé, which had learned of Wyeth's overture and didn't want to be left out. At two meetings in Switzerland in March 1999, Nestlé said it favored an "all-industry approach," implemented by the industry's trade association, according to Niels Christiansen, Nestlé's vice president of public affairs, who attended both sessions. But after the Wyeth deal faded away, UNAIDS heard nothing further from Nestlé.

Having rejected Wyeth's offer, Unicef still needed to line up a supply of formula for its pilot program. The agency's options were limited, since it considered most of the major formula makers to be in violation of the marketing code. Unicef, whose $1.1 billion annual budget comes entirely from government and individual donations, concluded it could afford to pay for the relatively small amount of formula required by the program.

Before soliciting bids, Unicef checked with a group of pro-breast-feeding advocates that coordinates the continuing Nestlé boycott, and reviewed a 1997 report called "Cracking the Code" that was published by a coalition of charities, churches, and non-profit organizations, including the Church of England and the European offices of Unicef and World Health Organization (WHO). The report accuses Nestlé, Wyeth, and several other companies of "systematic" code violations in Poland, Bangladesh, Thailand, and South Africa, citing formula giveaways and other promotional activities aimed at mothers. (The industry's trade association dismissed the report as "unscientific, subjective, and prejudged.") Eventually, Unicef decided to buy its formula from a French dairy cooperative, Jammet Dietetique Nouvelle SA, whose brands include Jammet formula and whose parent company makes Yoplait yogurt.

Almost as soon as it was implemented in Uganda this February, the pilot program began to suffer what Dr. Iyorlumun Uhaa, a Unicef official in Kampala, calls "teething problems." Some of these snafus were of the sort that inevitably occur when a large bureaucracy such as Unicef tries to do business in the developing world. For instance, the warning labels on the formula boxes were only in English and French. The marketing code requires all labels to be "in an appropriate language," and almost all the Ugandan women who visit the clinics speak only local dialects, health workers say.

Other problems were more fundamental. Some health workers believe Unicef may have subverted its own program by insisting that the Jammet formula be packaged in generic boxes. In Africa, HIV-infected women face enormous stigma and often are abandoned by their partners when their condition becomes known. "Because this Unicef package isn't anywhere in the shops, the moment people see it, they start suspecting," says Kampala midwife Joyce Matovu. Some HIV-infected women who did accept the formula were so fearful it would reveal their condition that they purchased tins of Nestlé formula and refilled them with the generic powder, health workers say.

While acknowledging that their approach may have reinforced the stigma of formula, Unicef officials say they settled on a no-name product in a deliberately unattractive box to discourage healthy women from wanting to use it.

For the moment, Unicef's program does seem to be benefiting many women—though the 25,000 mothers in eleven countries who have participated represent just a drop in the bucket of the HIV-infected female population.

For example, after being counseled about the pros and cons of breast-feeding and formula at Nsambya Hospital in Kampala, twenty-three-year-old Betty Nanfuka chose formula and was taught how to prepare it. Now she recites how she boils water twice a day on charcoal left over from meals and mixes two scoops of water for every two "level" scoops of formula she puts into a clean flask. The HIV-infected mother says that to preserve her secret, she always feeds her baby inside the house.

Says Ms. Nanfuka: "If women are given a chance and told what to do, they can carry it out." So far, her baby, Maureen, has tested negative for the AIDS virus.

But if the Unicef official in charge of the pilot program prevails, not many more African women will have the same opportunity as Ms. Nanfuka. Urban Jonnson, Unicef's regional director for eastern and southern Africa, says that even if the pilot program proves successful and is expanded, infant formula "absolutely" won't be used. His rationale: "Infant formula is not the best alternative, even if it's free of charge." He says "home food" alternatives, like pasteurized breast milk, are cheaper. Nursing by another, noninfected woman is also an alternative. And, he adds, infant formula often leads to follow-up formula. "We don't want to create the dependence when the child grows older," he says.

Instead, Mr. Jonnson and a number of his Unicef colleagues are pinning hope on a recent and controversial South African study that suggests breast-feeding may be just as effective as formula in preventing HIV transmission, as long as the baby receives no other nourishment for six months. Anna Coutsoudis, the study's lead researcher at the University of Natal in Durban, hypothesizes that the antibodies contained in breast milk may shield infants against the AIDS virus. Under this scenario, anything other than breast milk—including formula—alters the digestive tract of babies, potentially making them more susceptible to disease.

Dr. Coutsoudis's finding has gained an enthusiastic following among Unicef officials because it would enable them to preserve their long campaign to promote breast-feeding, an effort credited with substantial declines in infant mortality. But even if Dr. Coutsoudis turns out to be right, exclusive breast-feeding can be problematic, too. For starters, a massive education effort would be required, since most African women who breast-feed also give their babies tea, water, and other food. Dr. Coutsoudis also concedes it will take at least two years to confirm her hunch, though she is urging African governments to call for exclusive breast-feeding now.

However, researchers who support the use of infant formula in AIDS cases remain skeptical of her research. They note a recent study also done in South Africa that suggests that breast-feeding can undermine the effect of new, low-cost AIDS drugs that block mother-to-child transmission.

For Unicef's Dr. Jonnson, who works in Nairobi, and other officials on the ground, suspicion of the formula industry runs deep. "I've seen all combinations of rotten behaviors from these companies," Mr. Jonnson says. "I don't think for a second that has changed dramatically."

Such suspicion was on vivid display this summer, when a potentially serious problem arose with Unicef's pilot program in Uganda. In early July, supplies of formula at Nsambya Hospital suddenly ran out. By that time, more than half of the 235 HIV-positive women enrolled in the program at the hospital had chosen to use formula, and some were simply told to fend for themselves. Unicef says the reason for the delay, which lasted several weeks, is that Ugandan staffers mistakenly wrote the wrong product code number on their order forms.

As the situation worsened, Jacqueline Thibault, a children's-aid worker from Switzerland, happened to visit the hospital. Told of the formula shortage, she decided to seek an alternative supply—from Nestlé. Ms. Thibault asked the company for enough infant formula to feed about 250 babies for six months. On July 24, Nestlé responded that it would be "pleased" to ship 4.4 tons of formula for free.

There were two caveats. Nestlé didn't want to pay import duty on the donation. And to ensure the donation would pass muster under the marketing code, the company said it wanted an "official authorization" from the Ugandan Ministry of Health "to prevent adverse actions against Nestlé."

Dr. Saul Onyango, who oversees the pilot project for the Ugandan Ministry of Health, turned to Unicef for advice. He says neither he nor his agency objected to the proposed donation but that when he told Unicef's Dr. Uhaa about it, Dr. Uhaa replied, "What? That is not acceptable." Dr. Uhaa says that a separate shipment of formula from Unicef finally did arrive in late July, and he was "suspicious" of the large quantity offered by Nestlé.

Two days after his discussion with Dr. Uhaa, Dr. Onyango informed a surprised group of Nsambya Hospital officials that the government wasn't going to authorize Nestlé's donation. "You have stepped into international politics," he told them. "That milk can't come in."

Lights, action, Schwab! Thirty years of pioneering and innovation by discount broker Charles Schwab has now expanded into the media business, with wealthy clients and AOL subscribers the target audience. Randall Lane of *Worth* examines this surprise competitor for *The Wall Street Journal* and CNBC, and raises the ethical question of whether salesmanship and journalism can mix.

Randall Lane

Why Charles Schwab Is the Newest Media Mogul

CHARLES SCHWAB waits just offstage. The makeup is on. The hair is parted carefully on the right, as it has been for decades. The cameras sit poised onstage. It's showtime! First comes the personable program host, Susanne Lyons, who moves quickly to introduce the star, "my hero for many years." Schwab emerges triumphantly. "Thank you for that warm welcome," he gushes in the easygoing drawl that's a holdover from his California upbringing. "And it's an incredible pleasure for me to be with you and, more importantly, all of our wonderful customers."

It comes off a bit corny—a kind of *MoneyLine* meets *Donny & Marie.* But once the topic turns to the markets, Schwab finds his rhythm. By the end of the hour, the show seems pretty slick, especially considering the producer. CNBC? Nope. Try Schwab's eponymous discount brokerage, which streams this program, a question-and-answer session with top CEOs, along with three other programs, over its Web site, Schwab.com.

The audience on this December day—some 200 specially invited high-net-worth Schwab customers who tuned in via the Internet—wouldn't exactly make Maria Bartiromo quake with fear. But she will pay significant attention the next time: less than a week after Chuck Schwab's show, his company began running content on America Online. Suddenly Schwab's broadband shows have a potential reach of 63 million users, dwarfing CNNfn and Bloomberg Television combined. Schwab's print articles have the potential to overwhelm *The Wall Street Journal, Forbes,* or this magazine in readership. In many ways, Schwab's talk on his Web site was just a baccalaureate. With the AOL deal, Charles Schwab, king of the discount brokers, has emerged as an important media player.

It's an evolution three years in the making. Even before AOL, Schwab's media reach was already extensive, spanning elements of print, television, and radio. Visit the Excite, MSN, or SeniorNet Web sites and you'll find Schwab content and tools. Check out *On Investing* magazine, a 1-million-circulation quarterly produced in association with Bloomberg, which is sent to Schwab's richer clients. Or listen via telephone to exclusive market updates. The company also has long been admired for its effective television advertising—another sign of media savvy.

But the three-year AOL deal moved Schwab into the stratosphere. It's a remarkable transaction even by AOL standards, less for the large dollar amount—though, at a cost insiders say is approximately $80 million, it's nothing to sneeze at—than for its scope. Technically, the Schwab arrangement is an advertising partnership, complete with banners, buttons, strips, and sponsorships. What Schwab insisted upon, and what two people familiar with the negotiations say AOL initially balked at, was that Schwab's content be featured prominently as part of the deal.

AOL has plenty of content partnerships with the likes of TheStreet.com, *BusinessWeek,* Reuters, and the Associated Press but never had a financial services advertiser demanded that an extensive amount of its content come along for the ride. After several months of sometimes intense negotiations—and a clear message from Schwab that excluding the media component was a deal breaker—AOL finally agreed to a package that included Schwab broadband, educational, mutual fund, and other investor-oriented content.

"We were never a big banner-and-button advertiser in the online space," says David Pottruck, a bricklike former college linebacker who serves alongside Chuck Schwab as the company's co-CEO. "It makes you a commodity, gives you name recognition without association. We wanted to be visible in a way that gave a value-added."

The media emphasis, however, doesn't mean that Schwab is becoming a media company. Far from it. At its core, the media business model, despite new technologies, has remained fundamentally unchanged for 200 years. Companies such as Hearst, CBS, and Clear Channel Communications create media products—newspapers or magazines, television programs or radio shows—that they think people will like. If the companies are successful, people spend time, and sometimes money, watching, reading, or listening, and the media companies can surround their products with paid advertising.

What Schwab is in fact doing is turning this model on its head. Instead of creating media to attract advertising, it's creating media to make its own marketing and advertising more effective. Instead of a revenue source, it's a marketing expense, and quite a costly one at that. The emcee of the Schwab broadcast, Susanne Lyons, was not some objective talking head but rather the firm's chief marketing officer. And note that Schwab didn't rush out to greet just any audience; he was addressing his customers.

Schwab is pioneering a dangerous path, one fraught with potential ethical dilemmas and singed hands. Another brokerage, E*Trade, dabbled in the media game within the traditional model, developing content and selling ads around it, only to pull back. In some ways, Schwab—which embraced the Internet more quickly and wholeheartedly than virtually any off-line company—feels that it doesn't have a choice. "We're dealing with a new frontier," Pottruck says. "It's like television advertising in the 1950s." With its media model, Schwab feels that it has found a killer app for the new arena.

Schwab's media infatuation was not born overnight. It has two parents: a corporate culture driven by change and a market necessity driven by competition. The company began in the early 1970s as a traditional stockbroker but switched course when the securities industry was deregulated in 1975. While most brokers used the move from fixed rates to raise commission prices, Schwab slashed them and began focusing on people who wanted to do their own research, make their own decisions, and pay as little as possible for trades. Thumbing his nose at his stiff rivals, Chuck Schwab promoted a customer-first philosophy that used salaried brokers and eschewed underwriting and stock promoting, removing the incentive to push stocks. "The traditional brokerage industry was all about keeping information out of the hands of individuals," Chuck Schwab says. "Information was the power that a broker had, and he kept it under lock and key."

As it rapidly expanded its services, opening branches and automating accounts, Schwab needed deep pockets, and in 1981 it was acquired by BankAmerica for $57 million in stock. The bank's cash helped, but its bureaucratic culture and Glass-Steagall restrictions did not. In early 1987, Chuck Schwab retook control of his company via a friendly $280 million leveraged buyout. By September of that year, Schwab had gone public, at a market capitalization well over $400 million.

As competitors crept into the burgeoning discount brokerage area, Schwab altered its mission, pushing beyond simple do-it-yourself stock trades to create instruments allowing customers to hold all their mutual funds in one account. Again, Schwab had read trends perfectly, riding the mutual fund boom. Again, competitors scrambled to copy what Schwab had successfully demonstrated.

Then along came the Internet. Schwab offers perhaps the seminal example of a true bricks-and-mortar business that has become an Internet player. Five years ago, every single one of its transactions was done the old-fashioned way, either over the telephone or at one of the company's 377 branches. Chuck Schwab himself sensed the potential and threw his firm early and furiously into on-line trading: testing began in 1994, and a prototype was ready by the fall of 1995. Today, 81 percent of transactions occur on-line, with no assistance from a Schwab agent. Thus, while the rest of the industry napped, Schwab was able to defend its market share against Internet start-ups such as E*Trade, Ameritrade, and Datek.

In defending that turf, however, Schwab has been, well, out-Schwabbed. In the fast world of day traders and Internet-stock speculators, Schwab is suddenly expensive. E*Trade, Ameritrade, and Datek charge between $8 and $10 a trade; Schwab charges around $30. Just as Schwab pilloried Merrill Lynch and Smith Barney three decades ago for offering a commodity service at a premium price, now the upstarts could do the same to Schwab.

At the other end of the spectrum, firms such as Merrill continue to cater to large, price-insensitive clients with their proprietary analysis, access to public offerings, and personal brokers and also have investment banking operations to fall back on. The new deep discounters don't give them much worry. Schwab is uniquely stuck in the middle, without the offerings of the high-end firms or the prices of the deep discounters.

Anticipating the problem, Schwab diversified boldly on a corporate level, buying white-shoe asset manager U.S. Trust for $2.9 billion in June 2000 and quickly covering the low-end market by scooping up day-trader favorite CyBerCorp for $488 million.

These acquisitions aren't doing a lot of good, however, for the core brand and its 7.4 million customers, who collectively hold almost $1 trillion in assets. In December, the company instituted a hiring freeze. Then, in January, several of the analysts following the company downgraded the stock, sending it into a spiral. The fortune of the company is inextricably linked with its flagship division, so standing pat isn't really an option. During the past year, the company took in more than $10 billion in net new-customer assets each month, according to Prudential Securities analyst Eva Radtke, an amount she terms "incredible." The company's stock price—which even at a recent $28.50 a share traded at a hefty price-to-earnings ratio of 45—is based on its taking in at least that much this year.

So Schwab must now respond to the Ameritrades as Merrill did to fend off Schwab two decades ago. It must differentiate. Proprietary media can accomplish two things: retain current customers by validating Schwab's costs with value-added material—the equivalent of analysts' reports for the masses—and creatively brand Schwab, giving it new avenues to attract the assets it needs. That's why the media initiative is so important to Schwab, why it paid so much for the AOL partnership, and why it will continue to tweak the perceptions of what media is supposed to do.

Schwab's physical plant certainly resembles the organizational structure of a typical media company. Although a signature building on Montgomery Street in San Francisco's financial district serves, on paper, as the company headquarters, the bulk of the work actually occurs on a hodgepodge of floors and half floors in a dozen buildings scattered throughout the city.

In a tall, thin building near Chinatown, directly across from the towering Bank of America building, home of Schwab's old corporate master, most of the company's media operations take shape. In a high corner office with a fine view toward Alcatraz, Joshua Rymer is a little anxious. He was brought in eighteen months ago to head Schwab's on-line customer-acquisition effort. Pamela Saunders, vice president of customer acquisition and business development and Schwab's veteran Internet marketer, sits with him. It's the morning of December 13, and at this very moment Schwab content is making its debut on AOL. "Today is when the clock starts ticking," Rymer says.

Schwab is ringing in what might best be termed the Schwab Relationship Era. After three years of dabbling in media, the company came up with the idea of emotional connection as its strategy for using media to convert and retain customers. As with most things at Schwab—the company is fanatical about testing and focus groups—the policy has its roots in numbers. Pottruck himself presides over monthly media-strategy sessions, and though he has been known to throw out new ideas, the bulk of his time is spent checking the status of focus groups and quantitative data such as page views and click-throughs to determine what's working and what isn't. "You learn by failure," he says.

There has been plenty of failure to go around. Schwab's first media deals, three years ago, were with Excite and iVillage (through Armchair Millionaire, once an investor feature on the portal). As Schwab moved to get a handle on media, it flooded these channels with targeted banner ads. Like most banner campaigns, the performance was lousy. Even targeted banners did little better than a 0.3 percent click-through back to the Schwab site.

Then Schwab began pairing its banner ads with Schwab-generated media. The difference was immense: by placing content within the banner space, the ads generated a response rate of more than 1 percent. By showing off its knowledge, Schwab could both hold the attention of the potential customer and help brand the company's mission. "Advertisers need a story to tell," Saunders says, "and you can't tell it with a banner ad."

Schwab went still farther. It began tailoring media to fit the banner ads and vice versa. Next, it began placing these combinations in contexts that matched the profile of the user: an article on managing retirement funds along with a banner touting IRA services running on SeniorNet, for example. Again, another pop, with some response rates coming in at around 2 percent, others higher, staggeringly so—the highest response rate ever recorded by Schwab was 24 percent for an article that ran on the American Association for Individual Investors site.

Numbers like that converted Schwab to the concept of using media—actual stories, chats, streaming video, and message boards—not as a salable product but as a visceral marketing tool.

Much of Schwab's ability to cast itself both as a neutral source for information and the best place for your account stems from the perceived personality of Chuck Schwab himself. Polite, personable, and genteel, he is the company's secret weapon. Even his very name has resonance: it was said that the respected industrialist Charles Schwab, who a century ago brought Andrew Carnegie and J. P. Morgan together to form U.S. Steel and later founded Bethlehem Steel, could talk the legs off a brass pot. The younger Charles Schwab, no relation, has a similarly effective pitch style. His role as a pioneer for the rights of individual investors, his low-key approach in television commercials, and his omnipresent name have combined to create someone who has, as Schwab's vice president of brokerage marketing, Alexandra Roddy, terms it, "a high E.Q." (emotional intelligence quotient) as well as street credibility among investors. "He gets very upset when he reads about firms that take advantage of the customers," says Carrie Schwab-Pomerantz, Schwab's daughter and now an executive at the firm. Every quality that Chuck Schwab embodies translates well into creating trustworthy media.

Accordingly, Schwab the person is front and center on the firm's Web site and in other media initiatives. Besides his streaming video appearances, Schwab, via a still picture, greets new visitors to the site. A soothing voice walks them step-by-step through the orientation process. It's a 56K version of the audio-animatronic Walt Disney welcoming people to Disneyland.

Walt Disney is an apt comparison. Like Schwab, he lent his company his name as well as his personal characteristics, which enabled it to shift business strategies when necessary. Like Disney's, Schwab's name will live on long after his death. It's also easy to see how Schwab's company could continue to use his image after he's gone, just as Disney sometimes comes in handy or a cartoon version of Colonel Sanders still flogs chicken on television. Some Schwab executives have even discussed, only half-kiddingly, the idea of creating a 2-D version of Schwab—the "autoChuck" or "askChuck"—that would pop up to help confused users in much the same way that Microsoft's annoying "paper clip guy" comes to the rescue.

In fully implementing its media strategy on its own site, Schwab has placed great emphasis on using content to cement and protect the relationships it has with its best customers. Ever since Schwab broke from the pack in 1975, it has possessed a reputation as a feeder brokerage that loses clients once they accumulate real money and seek proper services. Keying on that last word, Schwab created a program called Signature Services for the top 20 percent of Schwab users, those with more than $100,000 in assets, using media to impart privileges.

Like a frequent-flier gold membership, most of the media perks are invisible to the general Schwab audience. They aren't aware of the quarterly magazine with content from both Schwab and Bloomberg, nor do they hear about video broadcasts such as the CEO speakers series, which regularly features the likes of Intel's Andy Grove and Craig Barrett, Yahoo!'s Tim Koogle, and Oracle's Larry Ellison. A real relationship-driven value-added is apparent here, as these talks are given to small audiences, typically in the range of 500 to 1,000, who have access to the exclusive area of the Web site. It's the kind of access not even the big-name media-driven sites can deliver, and it's courtesy of Schwab himself, who issues the invitations personally (the gatekeeper to 7.4 million trading accounts rarely gets turned down). It's precisely such access, in fact, that proved a major selling point to AOL.

Lower on the pyramid, Schwab skews its content heavily toward analysis, how-tos, and expert advice but stays away from breaking news. On a practical side, this avoids the need to create the army of reporters that a Bloomberg or Reuters must maintain to stay ahead of the pack (Schwab has perhaps fifty staffers dedicated in some way to content). But in an emotional sense, the slant allows Schwab to cast itself in the role of advice giver and action suggester, the latter of which, of course, makes the reader more likely to become a customer. Most of the archives of 2,000-plus text articles that Schwab has developed—many credited to the Washington Research Group, an authoritatively titled organization that is really just Schwab's bank of D.C.-based analysts—tilt toward what traditional media companies would call service journalism. These helping-hand stories prove to be very popular on television and in magazines, but they're particularly effective on the Web, where a suggestion can lead to an immediate transaction.

Similarly, leaning on the idea that a better-informed account holder is more likely to actively invest, Schwab launched something called the Learning Center on its site last year. Users can access up to ten courses (twenty will be available by year's end), each of which generally takes about an hour, covering everything from selecting a mutual fund to determining a risk profile. The courses are tailored to adult learning patterns: they're self-directed and make the user apply the knowledge immediately via tests and mock trading. Of course, once the game is mastered, the user is gently invited to try the real thing.

There's cost-side benefit, too. "Here's the double whammy," Pottruck says. "Not only do we get a chance to do our education and content, it saves a lot of money, since we don't have to explain these things to customers face-to-face." This was especially true during the recent market downturn. "In the year 2000, we had more than 200,000 either attend a Webshop or register for an on-line class," Chuck Schwab says. "In the latter part of the year, when the markets got rocky, the pace of those registrations spiked over 40 percent."

This content-based outreach is also targeted toward specific niches. Learning from its iVillage partnership, which expired this past October, Schwab launched a special area for women, fronted by Carrie Schwab-Pomerantz, on its own site a month later. Tracking an interest in tax issues in the spring, Schwab, in partnership with Intuit, is launching a stand-alone site full of tax-related content, free TurboTax for Schwab customers, and, of course, a link back to the Schwab site.

Such relationship building goes beyond the Internet. Those who have a question or comment about a Schwab story or program can call the firm's 800 number and find someone at the other end who will actually help get them an answer. And much of the content tries to forge an in-person bond by pushing users through the doors of one of Schwab's branches to take a regular investing tutorial, 10,000 of which were offered last year. Are Schwab's motives here entirely altruistic? Of course not. Is it a good service? Probably. Great marketing? Unquestionably.

For someone schooled in the traditional media models and their emphasis on a church-state fire wall between content and advertising, as well as the sanctity of an objective press, walking around Schwab's byzantine media setup is inherently creepy. If Chuck Schwab is the business-suit version of Walt Disney, then his content areas have the feel of Disneyland: clean and sterile, with the overriding sense that free expression takes a backseat to the grand vision.

Part of that aura has to do with legal issues. While Chuck Schwab's influence as America's leading broker allows him to corral Andy Grove for an exclusive on-line chat, it is also subject to compliance laws. Stocks and funds cannot be touted in any way on Schwab's site. Accordingly, compliance officers monitor every word and picture that springs out of Schwab's media efforts, vetting every question, every posting, every article. "They suck out anything interesting," says one Schwab media veteran. "You say, 'It's great,' and they say, 'You can't say great.'"

The result is that much of Schwab's content winds up with as much edge as a butter knife while retaining just enough rah-rah to raise eyebrows. In doing so, it commits a cardinal sin in media: it can be boring. Disneyland is a great place for a weekend, not a month or a year. It's precisely the frenetic, sometimes inflammatory message board postings and the manic stock touting of many content-driven financial Web sites that bring people back.

Of course, at the end of the day, Schwab doesn't really care if its customers are coming back solely because they adore reading, watching, or listening to its media products. It wants them to come back to trade. And if you're to believe Schwab officials, such motivations, ironically, will keep its media operations objective. "We are only as good as our reputation among the people doing business with us," Pottruck says. "We can't overcome bad word of mouth." Push Schwab officials harder on this issue of trust and they'll invariably find refuge behind the shield of Chuck Schwab himself.

"Magazines are credible because they're independent, so the advertisers don't buy what they say. And newspapers are credible because you know the advertisers don't buy what they say," says Alexandra Roddy, who before joining Schwab did a stint on Knight-Ridder's business side. "Schwab is in an interesting space because we're not biased the way somebody who has an investment-banking side of the house might be. We're not pushing the catfish today just because it's getting a little rank."

The problem occurs when people can't tell the difference between media as objective news and media as marketing. Older media have faced similar issues, whether through television infomercials or magazine and newspaper advertorials—those splashy pages that have SPECIAL ADVERTISING SECTION splashed across the top but otherwise look and read like regular stories.

But these shades of gray are wider and darker on the Internet, which has proved to be a tough format for media's two main revenue sources: circulation and traditional advertising. Traditional media sites are increasingly willing to dabble with deals that garner money for pushing products or for directly referring customers to advertisers. It becomes harder to draw a clear differentiation between a media company that specializes in content and makes money on services and a services company that uses content to draw in new customers.

This will become harder still if consumers are willing to accept an unconventional brand as trustworthy—as is the case when the product is as professional-looking as Schwab's and is offered on an outlet as respected as AOL. AOL realized all this and yet managed to overcome its initial concerns. "Our consumers just want to know where it comes from," says Katherine Borsecnik,

AOL's senior vice president for strategic businesses. "As long as it's branded, they're interested in as much information as they can get"—caveat emptor as a replacement for an editor. "Our model has evolved a bit over time," Borsecnik adds. "There's no road map in this business."

Hoping to once again push the boundaries, Schwab antici-pates leveraging its new relationship across still more media as the AOL–Time Warner partnership moves forward. "We were making something of a bet that while it would be an okay deal with AOL alone," Pottruck says, "it would be a spectacular deal with the new AOL Time Warner." Think Schwab cable television shows or Schwab-driven magazine sections or a Schwab book imprint. Time Warner execs will no doubt have some thoughts on these matters.

On the Web, though, Schwab will be able to advance its efforts far more quickly, using new technology to better forge rela-tionships through content. Using cookies, Internet marketers can discover which Web sites you've visited and, correlating that information with surveys or previous purchases, take a guess at what you might be interested in. Schwab, however, won't be guessing: it knows. As the keeper of your portfolio, it knows how rich you are, your style of investing, your address, your tax liabil-ity, the stocks you own, the funds you've sold. The potential for customized content is almost endless. It's a marketer's dream, an ethicist's nightmare, and, quite probably, the next stage in an entirely new media model.

What decisions, right or wrong, go into the making of a best-selling product? Keith Bradsher of *The New York Times Business Day* has been on top of the Ford Explorer/Firestone Tire safety controversy from the start and here gives us an inside view of the auto-industry mind-set. Step by step, it shows how compromise and expediency, all-too-common aspects of corporate decision making, can have devastating results when safety hangs in the balance.

Keith Bradsher

Risky Decision: Study of Ford Explorer's Design Reveals a Series of Compromises

STEPHEN ROSS knew how dangerous it would be to wait.

His bosses at Ford would approve only one risky new project that year, 1986. If his new sport utility vehicle—the one he thought the Ford Motor Company needed right away to stay competitive—was to beat out a luxury sports car being promoted by more senior rival executives, he and his small team would have to come up with an inexpensive design.

So they improvised. Instead of a whole new design, which would be far too costly, they would simply bolt a roomy passenger cabin, stocked with leather seats and other family-friendly amenities, to the underbody of the existing Ranger pickup truck. The plan's crowning beauty was that the new vehicle could be built on the Ranger assembly line, using many of the same robots and auto parts.

"It's a lot riskier to do a complete new vehicle, particularly back then," Mr. Ross recalled. "In hindsight, we probably could have afforded it, but hindsight is always twenty-twenty."

Ford called it the Explorer, and it succeeded beyond anyone's wildest dreams. Months after it went on sale, in April 1990, it was America's number one sport utility vehicle; today, 3.2 million are on the road. And it was a gold mine: while Ford made less than $1,000 on the average sedan, the profit on an Explorer was nearly $8,000.

The Explorer was a marketing dream—the perfect vehicle for a baby-boom generation that wanted it all. You could use it as your family car, and it had the rugged, adventurous image of a truck. The problem was, it also had the Achilles' heel of a big, tall truck; it rolled over more easily than a car would.

The roots of that problem lie in Ford's original design decision to build the new sport utility on the bones of a pickup truck instead of all in one piece, like a car.

Most other sport utility vehicles are also built on pickup truck underbodies. Indeed, many have rollover death rates considerably higher than the Explorer's. But the Explorer has become the most visible example of the problem because of recent deaths in sport utility vehicles after treads peeled off their Firestone tires.

A review of recently obtained Ford documents, as well as interviews with executives, engineers, and marketers, shows how Ford designed itself into a box, then struggled to design itself back out. The biography of the Explorer reveals how executives at Ford, under great pressure to be in on the coming sport utility boom, decided to build their entry in a hurry and on a shoestring, but with only moderate attention to stability.

In succeeding years, amid rising concern about rollovers, Ford engineers strove to adapt that tippy, bouncy pickup design for a family vehicle that spent far more time racing down the highway than bumping along dirt roads. In the end, they had only limited success.

In most of the deaths linked to the Firestone tires, the vehicles were Explorers, and in almost every case they flipped over. Today, federal safety officials said the number of complaints of deaths linked to the tires had risen to 148. And while much attention has been focused on the tires, the accidents have also raised questions about the Explorer itself; in fact, tire problems have caused a tenth of the more than 1,200 Explorer rollover deaths since 1991.

An analysis of federal crash statistics by *The New York Times* shows the price that drivers of Explorers pay for a car with the lineage, and image, of a truck. The analysis shows that since 1991, occupants of Explorers have been 2.3 times as likely to die in rollovers—tire-related or not—as people in traditional cars. What is more, they are nearly twice as likely to die in rollovers as are occupants of Jeep Cherokees and Grand Cherokees, the only popular sport utilities long built like cars.

And the Explorer's fatal rollover rate has been rising considerably, according to the analysis. While the rates for cars and the Jeep sport utilities have stayed fairly steady (roughly 40 or 50 fatal rollovers per million vehicles), the rate for the Explorer rose from 53 per million in 1994 to 121 last year. Rates for other midsize pickup-based sport utilities have also risen, though not as much. Experts attribute the trend to a mix of factors, particularly growing numbers of younger drivers as middle-aged parents have switched to even bigger sport utilities. Tire problems did not push up the Explorer rate significantly until last year, when they accounted for 18 of the 121 deaths per million vehicles.

The Explorer may be the sport utility leader, but it is hardly alone, and its story illuminates the kind of trade-offs other automakers made as they tried to balance cost, safety, and market appeal. Most of the 21 million sport utilities on the road—including the Ford Expedition and Excursion; the Chevrolet Blazer, Tahoe, and Suburban; the Dodge Durango; and the Toyota 4Runner—were built on truck bases.

In the Firestone cases, Ford officials say a flaw in the tires, not the Explorer's design, was to blame. In designing the Explorer, they say, they consistently erred on the side of safety. Not only has the Explorer passed all the company's stability tests, they add, but it has the lowest rate of fatal rollovers of any similar-sized pickup-based sport utility.

"Our analyses continue to find that the Explorer is a very safe vehicle and has performed very well in the hands of its customers since its introduction ten years ago," said Ernest Grush, Ford's manager of safety-data analysis.

But many auto-safety experts have argued that there was a cocktail of blame behind the accidents—that after the tires failed, the Explorer's pickup-truck base and high center of gravity made it harder to control, while drivers often made the fatal mistake of swerving at high speed.

Mr. Ross said the company had considered stability issues in early designs. But another Ford manager on the original project said rollovers had not become a priority until a controversy erupted in the late 1980s over the rollover record of the Bronco II, which was also based on a Ranger underbody.

"At the time we locked up the design of the Explorer, we had no knowledge of the rollover problems of the Bronco," said the manager, who insisted on anonymity to avoid being identified by company executives or lawyers suing the company. "It all hit later."

And by then it was too late, for Ford and the other automakers as well.

"There was a flurry of 'Let's have a sport utility,' and look around for the nearest platform," said Brian O'Neill, president of the Insurance Institute for Highway Safety, which is financed by insurers seeking to reduce the cost of crash claims. "I don't think a lot of thought went into a lot of these designs. There was a bandwagon, a gravy train, that they couldn't afford not to jump on."

THE CREATION: FACING TROUBLE IN DETROIT

The mid-1980s were tough years for Detroit. Two oil shocks had nearly bankrupted Ford and Chrysler and humbled even General Motors. When the American economy began recovering in 1983, the soaring dollar allowed Americans to buy Japanese cars much more cheaply.

But as the gas prices fell, the American auto industry began to sense salvation in a group of obscure, and relatively fuel-inefficient, vehicles known as light trucks: sport utility vehicles, pickups, and minivans. Chrysler introduced the first modern minivan in November 1983, and the same autumn brought the Jeep Cherokee, the first four-door sport utility with the comforts of a car. Buyers snapped them up.

Observing popular culture, Ford recognized why Cherokees were selling so well. The rugged western look was in style for clothing, partly because of Ronald Reagan's popularity. The researchers paid particular attention to Hollywood, where the top box-office draws were films like *Top Gun, Rocky IV,* and *Rambo: First Blood, Part II.* Americans, the researchers concluded, wanted automobiles that communicated ruggedness, individuality, and an outdoor spirit.

The clear answer, Ford's light-truck team decided, was what, by the standards of the day, would be an unusually large sport utility vehicle.

"The Ford Explorer has the message, 'I'm big, I'm tall, I'm prepared to explore the world,'" said Dr. Clotaire Rapaille, chairman of Archetype Discoveries, a psychological research company that works for Ford and other automakers. Its name constantly brings that message home. "The letter 'x' means outside, exterior, exploration," Dr. Rapaille pointed out.

Ford's research found that potential Explorer buyers cared a lot about their image and that the image they hoped to be envied for often had little to do with the way they actually used their Explorers. While they were unlikely to drive off-road even on vacation, for instance, they wanted four-wheel drive because it suggested they took adventurous trips.

From a marketing standpoint, that week or so of vacation became "the most important week of the year," said Mr. Ross, now the vehicle development director for Ford's Land Rover subsidiary in Britain.

So as it rolled out the Explorer in 1990, Ford began a marketing campaign to build the Explorer's image as a versatile vehicle that could take its owners anywhere their fantasies led them. Television ads consistently showed the Explorer going on adventurous trips, traveling over rock fields and mountain tracks, instead of running errands, a much more common use. Soon Ford added references to luxury. One ad showed a couple splitting their time between a Manhattan penthouse and a country cottage. In 1995 and again this year the Explorer became the nation's best-selling family vehicle.

Of course, the adventure ads overlooked the Explorer's shortcomings in everyday driving. The rollover problem was the most significant. But there were others.

Off-road, for instance, four-wheel drive helps motorists free themselves from deep snow and mud, but it provides little, if any, advantage on roads that are merely wet or covered with light snow. And off-road vehicles tend to be harder to stop. The four-wheel-drive Explorer needs 164 feet to stop from 60 miles an hour, 20 to 30 feet more than a typical family car.

The driving habits of many Explorer owners did not help. An extensive Ford survey in 1993 found that sport utility buyers said they drove faster than other motorists drove, followed other vehicles more closely than other drivers did, and were especially likely to risk driving in bad weather.

Off-road driving also requires a high floor so that the vehicle does not scrape its gas tank and other important components on rocks and so that the wheels have plenty of room to bounce up and down. But a high floor limits cargo space and makes it harder for people to climb in and out, particularly the elderly.

The Explorer, in short, had a case of ambiguous identity. It said so right there in the "special notice" at the front of the owner's manual: "Your vehicle is not a passenger car."

THE PROBLEM:
UNPLEASANT SURPRISE IN ROLLOVERS

In early 1989, with the Explorer just a year from mass production, Ford executives found themselves with a puzzle.

Consumer Reports, enormously influential in the auto industry, had just criticized the Explorer's two-door ancestor, the Bronco II, for a tendency to roll over during certain high-speed turns. Having already designed most of the Explorer and ordered its parts, company documents show, Ford grasped anxiously for a solution.

Ford executives, by their own account, were surprised by the extent of the Bronco's problems. Even so, rollover problems had plagued sport utilities since primitive truck-based ones were built for the military during World War II. Indeed, costly rollover lawsuits involving truck-based Jeeps had pushed American Motors to design the Cherokee from scratch as a sport utility vehicle in the early 1980s.

But once a sport utility is built on a pickup-truck base, particularly a base designed for another vehicle, it is extremely difficult to make it as stable as a well-designed car-based model, most auto engineers say.

Car-based vehicles have two main advantages, they say. Their seats—and hence their centers of gravity—are considerably lower. And since they are built as a single unit, they are more rigid than vehicles whose passenger compartments and underbodies are manufactured separately.

No matter how firmly bolted together, tall vehicles based on pickup trucks are more prone to sway during sharp turns, said Roy Lunn, a legendary designer of Ford sports cars who later designed the Cherokee. This is especially true of the Explorer and other vehicles with "leaf spring" suspensions—a cheap, simple design dating back to buggy days.

To make a pickup-based sport utility as rigid as a car-based model, Mr. Lunn added, "you would have yourself such a heavy chassis that it wouldn't be practical, so you just live with it."

As the Ford engineers pondered their problem in 1989, they would have to live with that first design decision made three years before. To undo it would have set the Explorer back years more, and besides, this was the Explorer they wanted. So again, they improvised.

They came up with three options, company documents show. They could choose shorter suspension springs to lower the front end by half an inch and the back by an inch. They could recommend a fairly low tire pressure, which would give the Explorer a more stable ride (except when a tire failed)—as well as the softer ride favored by people accustomed to cars. And they could redesign the entire vehicle to mount the wheels two inches farther apart.

They chose the first two. And when prototypes passed Ford's stability test, they decided against the widening, which would have been extremely time-consuming and expensive. "Utilize as many of the chassis revisions as possible without delaying Job 1," said a Ford memorandum, using industry jargon for beginning mass production of a new model.

The decision making shows how they weighed costs and benefits—and, ultimately, were hemmed in by the original design as they tried to make that tippy truck into a safer family vehicle.

On the one hand, they did improve stability. On the other, the more radical option would have made it even safer. According to the government's new rollover ratings, which rank vehicles from one to five stars, the changes Ford made each added a quarter star. The widening would have added three-eighths more.

In the end, though, what they did not do was make the Explorer as stable as a traditional car or sport utility built on a car base, according to crash statistics and the rollover ratings, which compare the height of a vehicle's center of gravity with its width—the lower and wider the better. The Cherokee scores near the top of the two-star group in the five-star ratings, while the Explorer is at the low end. (A Ford Taurus sedan, by comparison, rates four or five stars, depending on the model year.)

Mr. Ross, the Explorer planner, said a pickup-based sport utility could be as stable as a car-based model. In the case of the Explorer, he said, Ford's primary stability goal had been to make it better than the other sport utilities on the market at the time.

Ford took a similar tack several years later, with the 1995 Explorer. The front suspension was redesigned to be somewhat less prone to rollovers, but the new suspension was also lighter, providing less weight down low in the vehicle. Ford rejected a costly move to lower the engine, so the Explorer's center of gravity actually rose slightly.

THE TRADE-OFFS:
ALONG WITH BENEFITS,
DESIGN LIABILITIES

Automobile design is a matter of trade-offs. And often, dealing with one problem only adds to another.

For instance, using the Ranger's underbody for the Explorer gave Ford the image it wanted, with the budget it needed. But while the Explorer looked roomy, its design actually limited the weight it could safely carry.

By extending the passenger compartment and installing a second row of seats, Ford made the Explorer more than 600 pounds heavier than the Ranger but did not upgrade the suspension and tires to carry the bigger load. That meant a typically equipped Explorer could carry 1,025 pounds, even less than the 1,100 pounds for a Taurus. Many Explorers are built to carry as little as 900 pounds—a 150-pound person in each of five seats and 150 pounds of cargo.

Sport utility vehicles are more prone to roll over when heavily loaded because the seats and cargo area are above the vehicles' center of gravity. By contrast, the stability of cars and minivans is less affected when they are full because the passengers and cargo are situated at roughly the cars' and minivans' center of gravity.

Whether overloading played a role in the Firestone tire failures is not clear. Some of the Explorers that crashed were stuffed with people and luggage; some were not. In general, though, overloading "can really affect your stability and handling," said Donald F. Tandy, an engineer who oversaw much of the early work on the Explorer.

Another trade-off involved the tires. Ford chose the same size tires it had long chosen for the Ranger. Those tires had the lowest possible rating for withstanding high temperatures. And when the company lowered the recommended tire pressure in 1989 to increase stability and soften the ride, it also further reduced the tires' ability to carry weight without overheating.

Tire pressure became an issue in the Firestone controversy, with Firestone arguing that the lower recommended pressure—twenty-six pounds per square inch, compared with thiry-five for the Ranger—had contributed to the tires' failure, especially where Explorers were being driven at high speeds in high temperatures.

For its part, Ford pointed out that Goodyear tires inflated to the same pressure almost never failed on Explorers and that Firestone had endorsed the recommendation for nearly ten years, until it recalled 6.5 million tires last summer. Even so, Ford recently raised the recommended pressure to thirty pounds.

Sometimes the trade-offs are not intended, and not understood until much later.

Ford believed the Explorer's size and design made it safe, Mr. Ross said, and Explorer occupants do have an unusually low death rate in multivehicle crashes. But he acknowledged that planners had scarcely considered whether the Explorer, while safer for its own occupants in a crash with a lower-riding car, was deadlier to other motorists.

Pickup-based designs are much deadlier to other motorists than are car-based models because these vehicles are heavier and taller and rely on two stiff, heavy steel beams that run the length of the underbody and curve up like the runners of a sleigh. Instead of crumpling and absorbing shock, these beams tend to slide up and over cars' bumpers and door sills, punching into the other vehicle's passenger compartment.

Quantifying that danger is difficult.

Ford says it has no specific statistics for the Explorer. Its senior traffic-safety researcher, Priya Prasad, said the designs of all light trucks were responsible for an extra 1,000 deaths a year in other vehicles.

One statistician, Hans Joksch of the University of Michigan, has studied the deadliness of the Explorer's design. Explorers cause 115 to 140 deaths a year in vehicles they strike, while big cars of the same weight cause 30 to 40. So the Explorer's design appears to cost about 100 extra lives a year—almost as many deaths each year as in tire-related crashes of Explorers over the entire decade.

THE NEW EXPLORER: MAKING SAFETY A HIGHER PRIORITY

Ford is trying to position itself as the industry's safety leader, so when it invited reporters last month to see the completely redesigned 2002 Explorer, engineers waxed particularly enthusiastic about new safety features.

The tires are larger, with a higher recommended pressure. The vehicle is two and a half inches wider—the option discarded in 1989 as too expensive and time-consuming. The stiff steel rails of a pickup-truck underbody remain, but Ford lowered them considerably when it exchanged the Explorer's primitive suspension for a sophisticated carlike one, a change that also improved the braking to car quality. And the new underbody can no longer be built on the same assembly line as a Ranger.

Taken together, these changes should mean that the Explorer would be less likely to roll over and less deadly to other motorists as well. But the decisions to incorporate them were actually made several years ago, before the tire cases threw a spotlight on the Explorer's stability.

Impressed by the success of the Durango, with its third row of seats, Ford decided to add a third row to the Explorer as well. The width, tire sizes, suspension strength, and maximum payload were increased mainly to accommodate the extra passengers and make the Explorer more competitive with other models, though stability was also considered, Ford executives said.

The rails were also redesigned to curve down just behind the grille. Mr. Prasad said this change seemed obvious only with hindsight.

More than half of all midsize and large SUVs have been redesigned in the last two years to be less deadly to other motorists.

Even so, Mr. Tandy cautioned that while engineers could do much to make certain models more stable, sport utilities would always be somewhat more rollover-prone than cars because of their greater height.

"Light trucks in general will have a higher rollover rate," he said, "because of all the things that make an SUV an SUV."

It's often better to be lucky than smart. Bill Gross is very smart, perhaps a visionary, but his ideas frequently melt into a pool of red ink. His incubator for Internet IPOs, now struggling through tough times, represents both the promise and the dark side of the new economy. We become acquainted with Gross's unflappable personality in this *Fortune* article by Joseph Nocera that lets us decide for ourselves if he's actually learned from his past mistakes. Nocera admires and castigates Gross, a reminder of our own love-hate relationship with technology.

Joseph Nocera

Why Is He Still Smiling? Bill Gross, the Founder and CEO of Idealab, Blew Through $800 Million in Eight Months (and He's Still Got Nothing to Show for It).

B I L L   G R O S S is one of the uniquely creative people I've ever met in my life. —Compaq cofounder Ben Rosen

Bill Gross is a modern-day P. T. Barnum. —Anonymous posting on f***edcompany.com

Bill Gross is both those things. He's also the most amazing entrepreneur I've met in twenty years of covering business, one of the smartest Internet thinkers I've encountered, a stupendously poor manager, and a tragic figure of the Internet bust. But that's getting ahead of the story.

So let's start with a few cut-and-dried facts. Gross, forty-two, is the founder and CEO of Idealab, a privately held "incubator" in Pasadena, with 100 employees there and in four satellite offices. Gross popularized the incubator concept when he founded Idealab back in 1996, spawning a movement that now includes several dozen imitators, with names like Divine interVentures and eCompanies. A few of the better-known start-ups to come out of Idealab are eToys, Citysearch, NetZero, CarsDirect, Cooking.com, FreePC, Tickets.com, and GoTo.com.

Now that the market has collapsed, it is common to scorn such dot-coms and their incubator parents as prime examples of dot-com mania. But it's worth remembering that not all that long ago people swooned over companies like eToys, anticipating the day when their brick-and-mortar competitors would plead for mercy. The Net cognoscenti, meanwhile, viewed incubators as one of those wonderful Internet-inspired innovations that would change business forever—"the Holy Grail" of company creation, as one former Gross disciple intoned. As the champion of the incubator, Gross was seen as a true visionary of the New Economy, right up there with Jim Clark and John Doerr.

That is the reputation Gross enjoyed last May, when I first started exploring this story. The market had turned—in retrospect, it's clear that the NASDAQ's long tumble started in March—but neither he nor I knew that then. Gross, who had raised $1 billion in private financing in late January, was absolutely certain that the market would come roaring back. In April, Idealab had filed a registration statement with the S.E.C., announcing its intention to go public. Typically, Gross thought that his IPO would be a lot more than just your run-of-the-mill public offering. The Idealab IPO, he said at the time, might well provide the spark to rekindle the entire market, just as eBay's IPO had revived the flagging bull back in the fall of 1998. And you know what? I believed him.

I believed him because I was dazzled by him. A small, wiry man, Gross had an infectious, boyish enthusiasm that was charming and irresistible. He spoke so rapidly—jumping from topic to topic as if he were hyperlinking—that it was hard to keep up with him, and had so much energy he seemed constantly on the verge of jumping out of his own skin. He bubbled over with irrepressible optimism.

And his brain! That's what really set him apart. You could practically see the ideas bursting out of it, one after another, each more offbeat, more original, more promising than the last. The sheer profusion of ideas—and the way he got excited as he described them—was a large part of his charisma, I later realized: it was his overpowering intellect, more than any personal charm, that drew people to him and caused them to buy into his vision.

And then there was the fact that he seemed to have serious business chops too; this mad scientist had the soul of an entrepreneur. He appeared to have an instinctual sense of how to operate in "Internet time." His model for starting companies seemed flexible, open, and Darwinianly efficient all at once. Old Economy execs flocked to his companies, hungry for the opportunity to operate in such a cutting-edge environment (especially when they were sure their options would soon be worth millions). And they were going to work for a man who loved what he did. "When we get an idea and start working on it, and then make a company out of it," he said excitedly—here he paused for a few seconds of dreamy contemplation—"that's just the most awesome thing." He made it sound like good sex. Back then, Gross seemed to embody everything that was cool and new and great about the Internet.

And then I kept reporting the story, and the stock market kept crashing, and Gross's companies started imploding, and he made a series of spectacularly stupid decisions, and he blew through $800 million with nothing to show in return. Which is why now, even though Idealab probably has enough money to survive this tough time—and even though some of its newer companies are quite promising—I understand that Bill Gross doesn't represent just the promise of the Internet. He represents its dark side as well. The essential condition of Bill Gross's business life is that he has always had more ideas than he knew what to do with. Some were brilliant, and some were loony, but the fact that they poured out of him practically unbidden is what drove him to start Idealab in the first place. A graduate of Caltech, Gross has always been half scientist and half entrepreneur; while still in college he sold stereo systems built around a speaker technology he had patented. As a star at Lotus Development in the 1980s and as the founder of

Knowledge Adventure, a successful multimedia company (it was sold to CUC for $100 million in 1997), Gross had to repress most of his ideas for the greater good. After all, most business success depends on a very different cast of mind from his: an ability to focus single-mindedly on one task and bring it to completion.

The arrival of the commercial Internet in the mid-1990s made Gross think that maybe, at long last, he had found a vehicle that might give his brain free rein. He could start a company that would bottle his ideas and turn them into successful Internet businesses. He'd "incubate" companies—yes, that's what he'd do! He'd turn the venture capital concept on its head—instead of raising money and waiting for ideas to walk in the door, he'd generate ideas and then go raise the money from the VCs. He and his crew would work over the business models, recruit the executives, help the companies get their Web sites up and running, and create separate equity pools for each company. Then, when the companies were ready, he's spin them out the door. That this was a radical way of creating companies did not give Gross a moment's pause. Why would it? Trying things other people hadn't thought of before was what he lived for.

Even before he founded Idealab, Gross started his first Internet company, Citysearch. It was September 1995—just a month after Netscape went public. Gross originally wanted to create a Web site that would post photographs of retail establishments in cities all over the country as a way to aid travelers. But Charles Conn, a McKinsey partner Gross had recruited to be CEO, wanted to go in another direction. "It wasn't really the picture that was central," Conn says now. "It was the idea of getting perishable information about cities. That, I thought, would work." No problem: Gross was perfectly happy to shift the model. This early experience would be repeated over and over again: Gross would start a company having no clue whether its business model would work; in fact, as often as not, he assumed it wouldn't work. But he was completely sanguine that he, and the executives he had recruited, could figure something out that would. He thrived on moving fast, testing what consumers responded to, changing midstream, and, of course, peppering everybody in every company with lots of ideas. As a result, Idealab has always had an undercurrent of chaos. Gross's first hire at Idealab, a young woman named Marcia Good-stein, learned how to become a businesswoman by trying to make order out of the chaos. Today, as Idealab's president and COO—my "alter ego," Gross calls her—she still plays that role.

As Idealab set up its first dozen or so companies, Gross tried to codify the incubation process. He had firm ideas about the need to be generous with equity, about the importance of passion among the top executives of an Idealab company, and about the amount of money Idealab should invest in a company. That amount was amazingly small—just $250,000—but the logic was actually quite sound. Gross believed that if an Idealab company couldn't land venture capital beyond that original sum, then the idea probably wasn't all that good to begin with. Another critical test was whether Idealab employees decided to join a new company; if no one internally was interested in pursuing an idea, then it probably was a lousy idea. Even with these rules, though, life at Idealab was unlike anything else in corporate America. It was more like business jazz, a free-flowing improvisation, with Gross as Charlie Parker, Louis Armstrong, and Duke Ellington rolled into one.

The world was astounded. Reporters marveled at how Idealab operated on "Internet time," going from idea to start-up in the blink of an eye. When Idealab start-ups like eToys and GoTo.com went public in 1999, the stocks skyrocketed. Other self-styled "serial entrepreneurs" made pilgrimages to Idealab's Pasadena head-quarters, where they would invariably be wowed by the setup. The whole process seemed so cool that some of these visitors set up their own incubators, using Idealab as the model. *Inc.* magazine went so far as to claim that Gross's incubator model had the potential to transform the very nature of company creation in America. In truth, that's what Gross believed himself.

Which is not to say that everything ran perfectly. There was a certain ruthlessness built into the Idealab model—not every company was bound to succeed, of course, which meant that people who had been lured from well-paying jobs could find themselves out of work six or nine months later. Since Gross knew far more about how to start a business than how to run one, there was a certain amateur-hour quality to Idealab. And there were tensions between Gross and some of his CEOs, who found his incessant suggestions and e-mails annoying and even counterproductive.

At the time, though, this was easy to overlook. In 1998, Gross was even asked to pen an article for the *Harvard Business Review.* His piece focused on what he had learned about creating companies. One key, he declared, was sticking to the $250,000 limit. Only once had he ignored that limit, he wrote, and that was with a company called Ideamarket. Gross had been so optimistic about the prospects for Ideamarket—which was intended to be a marketplace for intellectual property—that he continued to pump money into it, in dribs and drabs, until the total reached $810,000—when he finally pulled the plug. "I'm convinced," he wrote of that experience, "that too much help early on will ensure failure later. If companies don't know that they can run out of money, they won't be thinking of ways not to run out of money."

In Internet circles, the conventional wisdom holds that Gross's big mistake was in concentrating so heavily on e-commerce companies. There is some truth to this charge, but it's a pat truth and not particularly instructive. After all, many people were concentrating on e-commerce in the late 1990s; one of them, Amazon's Jeff Bezos, got himself named *Time* magazine's Person of the Year. Let's be honest here: we all once believed in e-commerce—journalists and investors and Net moguls alike—and we all turned out to be wrong. In retrospect, even with eToys now trading at sixteen cents a share, Gross's decision to focus on those companies seems pretty forgivable.

No, his real mistake was that he allowed his natural optimism to short-circuit his judgment. True, the Internet mania of 1999 and early 2000 warped a lot of people's judgment—but few were swayed to the extent that Gross was, and to such disastrous effect. His natural self-confidence morphed into a crippling arrogance, and because his personality was so magnetic, people who worked alongside him—people with lots of business experience, people who should have known better—were swayed right along with him. Caught up in the Bill Gross force field, they couldn't say no.

Like most Internet tragedies, this one began with the stock market and its crazy Internet valuations. Gross, alas, didn't believe that the valuations placed on Internet companies were crazy at all; on the contrary, he thought they were a well-earned validation of everything Idealab had been doing. When eToys went public in May 1999, for instance, it was worth $7.8 billion—and Idealab's original $200,000 stake was suddenly worth $1.5 billion. Idealab's search engine start-up, GoTo.com, went public a month later—and was worth $5 billion by November. Idealab owned about 20 percent of it.

According to Gross's original plan, after an Idealab company went public, the incubator would sell off some shares to replenish its coffers and to reward Idealab's employees and investors. But with the moment of truth at hand, Gross couldn't bring himself to sell the stock. He could cite lots of justifications. For instance, Idealab didn't like the tax consequences of distributing the stock. Besides, by holding on to the stock, Gross could claim that he was standing by his companies. Indeed, he began arguing that his refusal to sell exemplified an important difference between Idealab and a venture capital firm: his incubator didn't cut and run the minute a company went public.

But there was another calculation at work too: if eToys was worth $7.8 billion on its first day as a public company, just imagine how much more it could be worth in the future! In Gross's mind, Idealab companies could go in only one direction: up.

Gross's next bad decision, which came in the same general time frame, was to dramatically expand Idealab. Believing that

Idealab had largely perfected the art of company creation, Gross now thought he could juggle far more than the handful of companies he was starting each year.

Eventually Idealab became a pretty big company, with 250 employees and four brand-new offices in Boston, New York, Silicon Valley, and even London. As Idealab expanded, Gross wooed corporate heavyweights, such as Robert Kavner, an early investor who had been a bigwig at AT&T. Kavner joined Idealab as a member of its executive committee and the head of its Silicon Valley office. (Later even more august company signed on: both Compaq cofounder Ben Rosen and General Electric CEO Jack Welch joined Idealab's board.)

But as Idealab got bigger, Gross began to abandon all the rules he had once established to guide it. Remember the $250,000 limit? Suddenly Gross was no longer worried that "too much help early" would lead to failure later on. His new concern was that he didn't want to share the potential upside of Idealab companies with venture capitalists. So Idealab started investing large sums in its companies. And that passion he demanded in Idealab company executives? Within half an hour of meeting people he was telling them that they were destined to be rich if they joined an Idealab start-up. He also threw up a host of me-too companies, on the theory that anything others could do on the Internet, Idealab could do better. "The hubris," says one Gross watcher, "was incredible."

Of all the mistakes Gross made, three stand out as both particularly representative and particularly horrible. Not surprisingly, they all took place early last year, just as Internet mania was peaking. The first involves that $1 billion that Idealab raised in January 2000. Gross had no trouble finding sophisticated institutional investors, including T. Rowe Price, Dell Computer, and Banc-Boston Capital. In return for the investment they got 13 percent of Idealab, which valued the company at around $9 billion. But the money came with a catch: the investors insisted that Gross agree to a "ratchet." That is, if Idealab went public at a valuation of less than $9 billion—or even if it raised additional private financing—the investors would be given a bigger stake in Idealab to keep them whole. Indeed, if Idealab's valuation dropped low enough, they could conceivably wind up owing the majority of the company.

It boggles the mind to think that someone as smart as Bill Gross could agree to something so stupid. What could he have been thinking? But it's obvious what he was thinking: he was thinking that there was no way in the world that Idealab could ever go public at a valuation of less than $9 billion. But today, with Idealab's planned IPO a distant memory and its valuation presumably in the tank, Gross cannot tap the capital markets without turning over his incubator to the investors—a situation that will not change unless he can somehow renegotiate the ratchet away.

That wasn't the worst of it. No, the worst was that once he had the $1 billion, Gross began going through it like water. That was mistake number two. To be fair, the money had been raised partly to ensure that Idealab not run afoul of S.E.C. rules and find itself regulated as a mutual fund. To win this nod from the S.E.C., Idealab had to boost its stake in a number of its high-flying companies—which, given their valuations at the time, was bound to be expensive.

But still! Idealab plowed $200 million into CarsDirect, its unprofitable auto-buying site. It engaged in a stock swap to up its stake in GoTo.com, paying an average of $80 a share. There went another $220 million. It pumped $60 million into a me-too company called Homepage.com, a personal-home-page company. (Recently renamed Frontera, it is now in the Web-hosting business.) Another $10 million went to an Idealab entertainment company called Z.com. Idealab even began investing in companies it hadn't started, acting as pure VC. For instance, it put $16 million into Scout Electromedia, which was trying to make a little wireless device with regularly updated city information. By the time the spending spree was over, Idealab had gone through $800 million. In eight months!

And the third mistake? That had to do with one of Idealab's

more high-profile start-ups, Eve.com. Eve was another of those me-too companies Gross launched in 1999, a high-end beauty site that joined a raft of such sites being launched all over Silicon Valley. As e-commerce sites go, Eve was a hit—it quickly became number one in its category. The fact that it had no clear path to profitability—well, nobody worried about things like that in 1999, least of all Bill Gross. Which is why, when LVMH made an offer to buy Eve, for around $100 million, Gross once again took leave of his senses. Instead of letting Eve accept the offer—which would have been a huge win for Idealab—Gross instead made a counteroffer: Idealab would buy 80 percent of Eve for $110 million. Pleading with Eve's founding executives, Mariam Naficy and Varsha Rao, to sell the company to Idealab instead, he made his nuttiest deal yet: he guaranteed—yes, guaranteed!—that the stock options held by Eve employees would be worth a minimum of $50 million within eighteen months. As the largest option holders, Naficy and Rao were being told, in effect, that they would each get $17.5 million within a year and a half, no matter what happened to Eve. Not surprisingly, they accepted Gross's offer.

Can you guess what happened next? Of course you can. By the time the deal was sealed, it was May, and it was already clear that Eve wasn't worth anywhere near what Idealab had paid for it. (In April, Estée Lauder announced it would buy an Eve competitor for a reported $20 million.) Worse, when Gross focused in on Eve's business, he finally realized it didn't work. He brought in some retail turnaround specialists and promised to use some of the proceeds from Idealab's IPO to sustain the company. The next five months illustrated the downside of the Bill Gross approach. He was a whirlwind of ideas, none of which came close to saving Eve. For example, he wanted to turn Eve into a giant e-commerce portal, and he stuck two of his smaller e-commerce companies into Eve—a failing furniture site and a low-end jewelry site. The turnaround specialists, meanwhile, wanted to make Eve the on-line equivalent of the first floor of a big department store. But such a repositioning would be expensive, and as Gross gradually came to the realization that Idealab's IPO was not going to take place, he shut off the money spigot. He went to Naficy and Rao and asked them to put some of their guaranteed $17.5 million back into the company. The negotiations went nowhere.

By the end, there was recrimination on both sides, with each accusing the other of bad faith. In mid-October—with Idealab still on the hook for the options guarantee, and poised to lose $100 million in all—Gross shut Eve down. During the conference call to break the news, an Idealab executive told Eve employees that Idealab would help them find positions at other Idealab start-ups. The only response was the sound of derisive laughter.

By last fall Gross had developed a new refrain: We've learned our lesson. Looking backward for once in his life, Gross conceded that mistakes had been made. Yes, Idealab had run through the $800 million, and yes, Gross had seen his own reputation go from Internet hero to Internet goat. But almost immediately he decided that what had happened during the last year of Net mania had been good for Idealab—a giant learning experience that would make it a smarter, "more powerful" company. He would put his new "learnings," as he liked to call them, in place—and this time, he vowed, he wouldn't stray. Thus the new, sobered-up Idealab was going to return to its roots. It would no longer play venture capitalist but would go back to the discipline of the $250,000 limit. It would insist that executives joining Idealab companies be motivated by passion rather than the desire for instant wealth. There would be no more me-too companies. New companies had to have the potential for high margins and a proprietary edge of one sort or another. In other words, no more e-commerce.

During the course of several lengthy interviews, Gross openly discussed what Idealab had done wrong in one situation or another. "We were acting like VCs without the skill or the interest," he told me one day after Scout Electromedia had abruptly shut down—taking Idealab's $16 million with it. But only once did I hear him even glancingly concede his most obvious mistake: the hubris that had enveloped him during the boom. That one time came in a speech Gross made to his staff a few days after the IPO was withdrawn in October. Most of the speech was devoted to the learnings and how they were going to put Idealab back on top. But at one point he admitted that Idealab had gotten greedy and had believed its own press. "We thought we could do no wrong," he said sadly.

In the next minute, though, he was back to his old self. The company had just had a big brainstorming session and had come up with "several multibillion-dollar ideas," he proclaimed, making it sound, once again, as if he could conjure these at will. GoTo.com, whose stock had dropped from $80 to $10, "could be a $100 stock if they show profitability." Z.com, which was close to running out of money, had just cut its staff in half to lower its burn rate. "Now it has a chance to get to profitability," Gross said. Indeed, the more I saw of Gross, the more I was forced to wonder whether he had learned anything at all. Although he was pushing Idealab's companies to preserve cash, cut burn rates, and find profitable business models, he didn't seem to be applying the same rigor to Idealab itself. Its burn rate was $6.5 million a month—the same as during the height of the boom. It still had 250 employees. More startling to me was that during this same fall time frame, each of Idealab's four branch offices was moving into beautiful—and clearly expensive—new quarters.

Gross dismissed my concern about the new offices with a figurative flick of his wrist. "They only cost $1 million a month." He shrugged nonchalantly. "If each office comes up with just one $50 million company, they will justify their existence for the year. And I view a $50 million company as a complete failure."

His insouciance was startling, especially when combined with the fact that he still seemed so willing to launch companies without knowing whether their business models would work. When you looked at Idealab companies that had failed, wasn't their lack of a working business model a key factor? After all, look at Eve.com; if Gross had understood the beauty business in the first place, wouldn't he have had the sense to steer clear?

But Gross had his own set of counterexamples. Almost every Idealab company, starting with Citysearch, was operating with a business model that was different from the original conceit. Partly this was because the Internet was still so new that it was impossible to know what was going to work until you put something up and saw how people reacted. But it was also because of the way Gross's mind worked. For him, starting up companies was a voyage of discovery, in which half the point was to improvise some cool new way of making something work. (The other half, of course, was to create companies that would succeed in the marketplace.)

The most recent example was a company called Blastoff, which had been formed to send a rocket to the moon. (I'm not kidding.) It was obviously a loony idea, completely unfundable, as things turned out. But in the course of trying to figure out how to monetize a moon landing, some Blastoff engineers devised a way to use peer-to-peer technology to stream a little television picture to the corner of a computer screen. Gross swung into action; before long Idealab had a new company called DesktopTV, which was attempting to put a little television screen on computers—and stream in networks with greater speed and clarity than anyone had done before. Though it was early in the game, it looked as if DesktopTV had a real chance to succeed. And if Gross hadn't started Blastoff, you see, he would never have stumbled upon DesktopTV.

So in returning to its roots, Idealab was going to continue to rely on Bill Gross to come up with ideas that he could then turn into new companies. In good times or bad, that was never going to change—and it gave people at Idealab faith that the company had a future, despite everything that had happened. I realized this one day when I asked Marcia Goodstein whether it bothered her that Gross was starting so many new companies. She looked at me like I'd lost my mind. "I say thank God he is still coming up with companies," she replied. "That's what makes me understand that we are going to survive all of this."

And indeed, if you too turn your attention to the future—which is where Bill Gross wants you to look, after all—you'll see that she has a point. If Idealab were only the sum of its e-commerce companies, its situation would be truly dire. But it now has a handful of new start-ups with great potential; and in virtually every case they are the result of some fiendishly clever Bill Gross idea—and his willingness to try things other people have never imagined.

For instance, he devised a way to use clickstream data from ISPs to peek in on just about any Web site and see what consumers do when they get there. He has turned this idea into a company called Compete.com, which hopes to sell real-time data about Web sites to interested competitors. He's got the .tv Corp., which is the domain name business—it acquired the rights to the domain .tv from the tiny country of Tuvalu and is marketing .tv as a hip alternative to .com. He's got Airwave, which is trying to create a wireless network, using radio-wave technology, in places like coffee shops and gas stations, so that customers can be connected to the Web just by walking in the door and turning on their laptop or handheld device. He's got Faster.com, which uses peer-to-peer technology to allow people to cache their favorite Web sites directly onto their hard drives, giving them access much more quickly. To make this scheme work Gross even plans to "sell" bits of people's hard drives (with the users' permission) for caching purposes. Who else would think of something like that?

Most of these companies have attracted venture capital, even in this difficult climate. They've had success recruiting executives, even though the pay at Idealab companies remains heavily weighted toward stock options. They've all gained some "traction" in the marketplace. In other words, they've got real prospects.

Yet every time I found myself getting caught up in Gross's optimism about one or another of these companies, I'd suddenly be caught short. I'd be reminded of the awful mistakes he'd made in the very recent past. There was just no getting around it: he seemed perfectly capable of making the same mistakes all over again. His powerful personality contained both strains—the propensity to come up with truly brilliant ideas and the propensity to blow it. Ultimately, that is what made it so difficult to come to terms with Gross. "Sometimes with Bill, you smack your forehead and say, 'Wow!'" says one Idealab staffer. "And sometimes you smack your forehead and say, 'Yikes!'" With Gross, was it more important to look backward or to look forward? In all the time I worked on this story, I never came up with an adequate answer to that question.

Finally, last month, I had one last conversation with Gross and Goodstein. They told me that Idealab had, at long last, cut its monthly burn rate, from $6.5 million to $2.5 million. It had slashed its staff from 250 to about 100; though most had latched on with various Idealab companies, some had been laid off, and that had been hard. Perhaps most important, Idealab was going to stop funding the branch offices. They were in the process of lining up strategic partners and preparing to become self-sufficient. With these moves, Goodstein said, "We'll have enough money to last for many, many years."

I'm glad to hear it. There is much about Bill Gross that I admire. Idealab's new companies are grappling with some of the Internet's gnarliest problems, and I want to see how they play out. And I want to see what wild idea Gross will dream up next.

Actually, I can tell you that now. Within a few weeks, Gross says, Idealab is going to roll out a new company that he plans to call New.net. He's figured out a way to get around the government restriction on domains—in fact, Idealab is attempting to patent its method for doing just that. "We are launching with twelve domains," he says, among them .store, .firm, .kids, and .chat. Using New.net, people will be able to buy URLs with these domains, and as a result, the .com monopoly will be destroyed once and for all. "It going to be unbelievably huge," he exults. "It's going to revolutionize the Internet."

It sounds great, doesn't it? But then, with Bill Gross, it always sounds great.

Like the Wizard of Oz, what's behind the curtain at Yahoo! has little to do with its impressive public image. Kara Swisher, a thought-
ful observer of the technology scene for *The Wall Street Journal*,
delineates the pros and cons of this Internet company after a
major management change. She knows Yahoo! well enough to
cut to the chase by pointing out that a company can believe in
itself too much.

Kara Swisher

Boom Town: Yahoo! May Be Down, but Don't Count It Out

YAHOO! INC. has seen the enemy—and it is the company
itself.

The Santa Clara, California, company's announcement last
week that its chief executive, Tim Koogle, would step aside and
bring in a new CEO from outside is the first definitive sign that
Yahoo! recognizes its problems start at home. This also indicates
that it might actually have the guts to do what is necessary to realize its vast potential.

There is much trouble: Yahoo!'s once high-flying stock has
been cut to shreds, allowing it to buy less and less every day and
infusing investors with a poisonous mood; top management is in
turmoil and beset by defections; revenue prospects have been decimated by a slowing economy. And in the coming months, the
company must reshape itself drastically.

Many feel Yahoo! might have missed its big opportunity to
reach new heights back when its stock was doing just that last

year. Now it has precious little time to create new paid services to replace its popular free ones and must counter the perception that the game is up even for the industry leader.

But none of that means that Yahoo! should stop forging ahead. With tens of millions of daily users, a valuable brand name, easy-to-use and high-quality services, and a record of profitability, the company has a lot of strong attributes. So with a strong stomach, a willingness to transform its very soul, and a little bit of luck, this could turn out to be its finest hour.

First of all, it is time to lose the conceit that has long been a benefit for the company—its insistence that homemade Yahoo! is best. Over the years, this Yahoo!-way-or-the-highway approach has helped it define itself both internally and externally. While keeping its image consistent is important, the tendency of Yahoo! to think its vision was the only one doesn't give it enough flexibility to try new and better stuff. Ban the phrase that is often heard at Yahoo!: "That's not the way we do it here."

This leads into another issue that centers on the insularity of Yahoo!'s managers and staff, who are just too comfortable with each other and do not bicker nearly enough. This is a tone that seems to have been set directly at the top by the placid Mr. Koogle.

To be sure, his earnest demeanor and levelheadedness are a welcome change from a more brutal leadership style. However, it can also create a corporate mentality of nonconfrontation—a good idea in public, but not in private. Such a style has kept new ideas from percolating upward and held dissent to a minimum. Note to Yahoo!: Start arguing now. And that should begin right at the top with the company's inbred board.

Comprising a small coterie of insiders and friends of insiders, the board is too small, too chummy, and has too little outside experience to be truly effective. This is a problem for all Internet companies in general, but Yahoo! should have known better. It has taken far too long to strengthen its board with mouthy members who would give other board members the what-for and even scare the managers a little bit. Barry Diller, for example, a close confidant of Yahoo! executives, wouldn't hesitate to rip their heads off if need be. There are many others from the media, software, and more general corporate world who would be good for Yahoo!'s board.

These people would likely have pushed the company to get while the getting was good last year, when the power and influence of on-line companies were at a premium. Most agree that Yahoo! could have spent its stock more wisely and bought a more traditional media company to give a solid foundation to its impressive distribution network.

"I just don't get it; there's nothing there," AOL Time Warner Inc.'s president, Bob Pittman, would often mumble when a reporter brought the company up as a major competitor of the on-line giant. Mr. Pittman got himself a parcel of valuable content in AOL's deal to buy Time Warner, and something even more priceless: the idea that AOL actually owned something tangible.

As the mood of investors was shifting to decry the value of the more nebulous relationship Yahoo! has with its customers, Yahoo! should have been knocking furiously on the doors of then-scared media partners like Rupert Murdoch of News Corp. and Michael Eisner of Walt Disney Co. Now they dismiss Yahoo!'s value publicly—although they should still be very nervous—which makes Yahoo!'s negotiating position less than perfect.

Nonetheless, Yahoo! should probably acknowledge now that the best way out of this mess is a merger of some sort. It should avoid "strategic partnerships" since it never has done them well. That will mean Yahoo! will have to give up a great deal of power, but that is life after the dot-com downturn.

Right now, despite its turmoil, Yahoo! would be a great complement to many companies. Microsoft Corp. is a good example, especially if Yahoo! is combined with Earthlink or Excite@Home's cable TV networks and has an AT&T Broadband relationship. While Viacom Inc. and Disney are often bandied about as merger partners, what about a bolder deal with Thomas Middelhoff's Bertelsmann AG, which owns a lot of content? The German executive was an early and critical AOL investor and just struck a ground-breaking deal with the pioneering Napster.

Such a move would require Yahooligans to acquire a tougher skin and a more realistic outlook. This is especially hard for a lot of pioneers, but it is always better to admit that you may not be up for the job rather than fumble it. But sharing power is something Yahoo! has not wanted to do. Forget price; its inability to con-summate the deal to merge with on-line auction powerhouse eBay Inc. last year was all about power-sharing. Today, eBay executives will tell you flatly they need a merger a lot less than a year ago, and they are right.

Finally and most important, Yahoo! must focus all of its attention on creating solid, pay-me relationships with its users. It has taken far too long to do this and it is the only thing that mat-ters anymore, especially as the advertising market has soured. Yahoo! must convince its users that it delivers a series of goods and services that are worth paying for, regularly. This is basic business, of course, but is the only way Yahoo! can emerge from this trying time.

Unfortunately for Yahoo! and other Internet concerns, success (and high stock prices) covered a lot of mistakes. Yahoo! has to realize that while what they have done is incredible, it is also all about yesterday and sunnier times. It was then that top Yahoo! execs, Mr. Koogle, cofounder Jerry Yang, and President Jeff Mal-lett, used to refer to themselves as the "Three Amigos."

Today, they should perhaps remember that often the best thing you can do for friends is to be tough on them.

It may come as a surprise to you that you don't own your DNA, your own cells, or, for that matter, your own body. Did you even realize that you could take out a gene patent? Writing in *Esquire,* Wil S. Hylton gives us a wake-up call about the modern marriage of science and business. Better get used to the idea of life as an invention, he instructs us. The article walks us through the moneymaking potential of our human existence, which threatens to overshadow the potential good derived from genetic research.

Wil S. Hylton

Who Owns This Body?

THE SYMPTOMS CRASHED DOWN like an avalanche, and John Moore didn't know what to think. Bruises all over his body, bleeding gums, and the roll of flesh around his waist that he'd always figured for fat had gotten lumpy and red and sore.

He didn't know much about cancer, but when he finally dragged himself to a doctor in Anchorage in the summer of 1976, he learned more than he wanted to know. For one thing, he learned that he had it. For another, he found out his type was rare, something called hairy-cell leukemia. The doctor said it was attacking his spleen, so instead of absorbing aging blood cells the way a normal spleen does, his spleen was absorbing *all* his blood cells, cannibalizing him, swelling up in his gut and smashing his other organs against the walls of his body. The doctor said there wasn't much hope, but Moore wanted to give it a fight. He found a specialist at UCLA and flew down for a consultation.

Right off the bat, he liked Dr. Golde, who made such a point of cutting through bullshit that he let his patients call him Goldie. Moore trusted that, and when Goldie suggested that he should have his spleen taken out, he didn't hesitate. The surgery took three hours. A normal spleen weighs about fourteen ounces. Moore's spleen weighed fourteen pounds.

Within a few weeks, he was back on his feet, ready for a fresh start, and Seattle seemed as good a place as any. He was just thirty at the time, broad and strong, and it wasn't long before he found a nice girl there, married her, bought a ranch near the coast, and got himself a job as a salesman in the oyster industry. He tried to forget about the leukemia, the bruises, the bleeding gums, the cannibal spleen. For the most part, he did. The only reminders were his follow-up visits to see Goldie. They seemed never to end.

At first, Moore didn't think much of flying down to L.A. for his regular checkups. He knew cancer is something to keep an eye on. But after four years of it, he'd had enough. He didn't see why he had to travel a thousand miles every few months just to give blood and sperm samples. He offered to have the blood drawn in Seattle and shipped down to Goldie's lab, but Goldie said that wouldn't work. He mentioned that the price of the airfare was starting to hurt his pocketbook, but Goldie offered to pay for the flights. He brought up the fact that his folks were moving away from Pasadena and he wouldn't have anywhere to stay near L.A., but Goldie offered to get him a room at the Beverly Wilshire. Moore thought Goldie seemed mighty eager, but he agreed to keep coming down.

Then, after seven years of regular visits, Goldie's nurse brought him a contract to sign. Moore looked at it awhile, trying to figure out what the hell it was. Something about surrendering "any and all rights"; Moore didn't like the sound of that, so he circled the box that said "DO NOT" consent and gave it back. But when Moore got home to Seattle, he found another copy of the contract in his mailbox. This time it had a Post-it note attached, with an arrow pointing to the word "DO." He looked at the contract again. Again, it seemed strange. Again, he didn't sign it. A few weeks later, yet another contract arrived by mail. This time there was a nasty letter attached, Goldie telling Moore to stop being obtuse and sign the damned thing. He didn't like Goldie's attitude. Something was fishy, and he decided to find out what. He sent the contract to a lawyer.

Moore was at home when his lawyer called him back with some news. Turned out that Goldie had a few things going on behind Moore's back. Even before the surgery, Goldie had suspected that leukemia researchers would love to run experiments on Moore's spleen. So the doctor had instructed his surgical staff to remove some cells from Moore's spleen and make a culture. Then Goldie brought the culture back to his lab and kept Moore's cells alive, kept them reproducing, a tiny portion of Moore's body living inside a dish. Goldie took out a patent on Moore's cells in 1984, and then, without mentioning it to anyone, he shopped them around to a few pharmaceutical companies, eventually finding a taker. A company named Genetics Institute offered him 75,000 shares of stock, worth about $1.5 million, for Moore's cells.

Moore nearly fell over when his lawyer told him about that transaction. Later, after the shock wore off, he was just plain pissed. Not that he minded his cells being used in research. He minded being lied to and treated like a sucker. He minded being invaded and ripped off. Goldie hadn't ever told him about any cell line, or any patent, or any million and a half bucks, and Moore was starting to feel like a fool. He figured his best recourse was a lawsuit.

But when his case went before the California Supreme Court in July 1990, the judges weren't impressed. As far as they were concerned, Moore didn't have any right to sue Goldie for stealing his cells because the cells didn't belong to Moore in the first place. They might have come from his body, and they might have contained his DNA, but that didn't mean they were *his*. On the contrary. According to the judges, Moore's cells couldn't belong to him because if they did belong to him, then Goldie couldn't have a patent on them. "Moore's allegations that he owns the cell line and the products derived from it are inconsistent with the patent," the majority wrote, adding that he "neither has title to the property, nor possession thereof" and concluding that "the patented cell line and the products derived from it cannot be Moore's property."

John Moore didn't own his own body.

Neither do you. Not your body, not your blood, not even your genes. Not unless you've got a patent. And it's too late to get a patent on some parts of your body. They've already been sold.

Like, for example, the gene called BRCA1. There's a chance you have that gene. There's an even better chance your wife has it, or your sister or your mom, because that's the gene for breast cancer. If you could test yourself for BRCA1 right now, or if you could test your wife or your sister or your mom, you probably would, right? Just to be on the safe side. But you can't test yourself because you don't know how, and your doctor can't test you because he's not allowed—at least, not without permission from the person who owns the gene. And that person isn't you. It might be in your body, but it doesn't belong to you. It belongs to a company called Myriad Genetics in Salt Lake City. So if you want to know whether you have the gene for breast cancer, you're going to have to call somebody for permission. Then you're going to have to pay for the cost of the doctor's visit, plus a $2,500 fee to Myriad Genetics just to access its gene, the gene inside your body. Those are the rules of the patent game. That's what a patent means: exclusive access. And the last time somebody broke those rules, the last time somebody ran a test for BRCA1 without permission, Myriad Genetics went after them. And Myriad Genetics made them stop. And that was a university.

And that's just BRCA1. There are about a thousand other human genes that have been patented. Some of them are in your body, and many of them are important, like the one for Alzheimer's disease and the one for epilepsy and the one for brain cancer. If you happen to have one of those genes, it might interest you to know that researchers are paying to access them, too, sometimes millions of dollars just to continue the work of looking for a cure.

It's just not genes, either. There's a patent on the blood inside every human umbilical cord. So if, by chance, your newborn baby needs that blood, don't expect to get it for free. There's also a Swiss company called Novartis that has a patent on the stem cells in your American bone marrow. Don't expect to access those cells if you ever need a transplant, either, unless you're prepared to pay.

Some companies have patents on entire species of animals, like the species of mice and pigs that belong to DuPont. You can patent people, too, and not just John Moore. These days, you can get a patent on just about anybody; a patent issued in 1995 to the U.S. Department of Health covered the cell line of an unsuspecting member of the Hagahai tribe in Papua, New Guinea, whose resistance to certain diseases made him valuable to researchers. Other patents filed by the U.S. government at around the same time covered indigenous people from the Solomon Islands and from the Guaymi tribe in Panama.

As a matter of constitutional law, all of this is highly suspect. There's never been a vote by Congress to approve the patenting of human or animal life, there's never been an executive order by any president, and there's never been a decision by the U.S. Supreme Court on the patenting of any animal larger than a microorganism. In fact, just twenty-five years ago, you couldn't patent any of it: genes, cells, blood, marrow, even a clipped fingernail. Back then, the U.S. patent code looked a lot more like the code Thomas Jefferson wrote, the code that was designed to protect inventions—think cotton gins, whoopee cushions, Twinkies!—made on American soil. But that hasn't slowed down the patent code, which not only applies to U.S. soil but now lays claim to ninety foreign countries and even to "any object made, used, or sold in outer space."

If you're starting to get the impression that the U.S. patent laws have gotten out of hand, if you're starting to wonder how they got that way, how they stretched so wide so quickly without any public debate or government approval, the first question you ought to ask yourself is why you never thought about it before. The answer, most likely, is that you didn't know. You didn't know because nobody knew. Nobody knew because nobody cared. Life went on, oblivious.

And that's how it happened.

Jim Watson saw the whole mess coming. Not at first, of course. At first, he was in awe of the biological revolution, just as the rest of the world was. After all, it was his revolution, his discovery that sparked it, his insight, made in his lab, his glimpse into the mind of God. And so, for a short while, he put aside his natural cynicism and basked in the glow of his accomplishment.

It wasn't that nobody had ever seen DNA; it was that nobody knew what it was, or what it did, or even what it looked like. Microscopes had never been able to get closer than a blurry smudge, and as far as anyone knew for sure, that smudge might have been irrelevant cellular garbage. It took Jim Watson and his partner, Francis Crick, to figure out that DNA mattered.

Watson might have made the discovery even sooner, but it took him a few years to get through school. Not many years, just a few. He started college at fifteen, received his doctorate at twenty-two, began his career at twenty-three, and when he and Crick solved the riddle of DNA in 1953, he was just twenty-four, a pale, gawky kid from Chicago with a long neck and a narrow head of wispy black hair. He was an ambitious bastard, too, already thinking about the Nobel prize that his work would bring.

Watson and Crick had solved the first riddle of DNA. They had figured out that it was shaped like a string, or, rather, like two strings twisted together, a Twizzler-like structure they called the double helix. They had also discovered that those strings were made out of billions of tiny particles, called nucleotides, all linked together in a chain, one by one, in a very specific order. The trick that lay ahead was to understand the precise order of those nucleotides, why they were aligned in a specific way.

The discovery carried certain risks, however, the most obvious of which was that the order of nucleotides could be tinkered with, changing a person's genetic instructions and thereby rearranging his or her body or mind. Such modifications might do good in some cases, with the potential to cure hereditary diseases or deformations, but they could also take nature down a new and unseemly path. They could replace natural selection with a kind of deliberate genetic art.

At the very least, it was clear from the outset that genetic science had a special responsibility, and one of the earliest voices of caution was none other than Jim Watson. By 1975, he had established himself as officially dubious, and when he arrived at the Asilomar Conference on Genetic Ethics that year, he stood before an assembly of his colleagues and announced, "We can't even measure the fucking risks."

Watson was still just forty-five years old, but he was already disenchanted with his own success. Instead of pursuing fame and fortune on the cutting edge of his field, he had retreated in 1968 to an obscure laboratory in Cold Spring Harbor, New York, where he assumed the title of director and spent most of his time fundraising for the lab's endowment. In a few interviews and public appearances, he voiced contempt for the scientific community, issuing proclamations like the one he made in his memoirs: "A goodly number of scientists are not only narrow-minded and dull but also just stupid."

The truth was, Watson's retreat from the front lines *had* left a vacuum of creative ambition. In the three decades following his discovery of the DNA structure, not a single effort had been launched to produce a map of human DNA. Such a map would be essential for the budding field of genetics to blossom. It would provide a complete list of the nucleotides along the DNA strand, making it easier for scientists to locate and isolate specific genes. Because that's not easy to do. A gene does not have a distinct shape or contour, is not even a physically independent structure. In fact, the word *gene* is really just scientific jargon that describes a segment of DNA, a portion of the double-helix strand that happens to produce a protein. Each "gene" starts on a particular nucleotide and ends on another nucleotide further down the strand. Since there's no dramatic marker to announce the beginning or end of a gene, and since there are roughly 30,000 genes in human DNA, you can imagine how hard it is to locate them without a good map.

By the late 1980s, it was beginning to look as though nobody would ever draw that map. The project seemed dauntingly, if not impossibly, huge. Even with computers mapping one nucleotide per second, it would take 100 years to finish the job. But if anything was predictable about Jim Watson, it was that he would do the unexpected, and just when he had been counted out of the game, he emerged from his twenty-year slumber. Standing before Congress in 1987, he received a hero's welcome and a starting budget of $30 million to launch the Human Genome Project, a new division of the National Institutes of Health. He predicted a complete DNA map by the year 2005.

It wasn't long, however, before Watson's prickly nature caused a clash with his colleagues, most notably with a young scientist named Craig Venter. Like Watson, Venter was unusually blunt-spoken for a molecular biologist. A Vietnam vet who spent most of his teen years smoking pot and surfing the California coast, Venter had about as much respect for authority as he did for scientific convention. If anything, he and Watson were too much alike. Watson had solved the DNA riddle in less than eighteen months, and Venter was in just as big a hurry to map the human genome. He wasn't interested in plodding along, one nucleotide at a time: he was developing a way to isolate genes along the DNA strand. He had found markers on the double helix that gave clues about the locations of genes, and by focusing on those markers, he could identify the most important parts of the genome without wasting time on extraneous nucleotides.

The only problem with Venter's approach was that Jim Watson didn't like it. He didn't like the science, and he didn't like Venter, and he wanted to get rid of both. But Venter had friends in high places at the NIH. His approach to DNA mapping was faster than any other, and that had value in itself. By the early nineties, the patent code had already swollen, through a bizarre series of loopholes and judicial mistakes, to cover John Moore and maybe even raw human DNA. To the NIH, that spelled opportunity. The sooner Venter could locate genes, the sooner the NIH could patent them. And patents mean money. Big money. Money from pharmaceutical companies, from biotechnology companies, even from small laboratories hoping to do genetic research. Craig Venter meant more patents more quickly, and more patents meant more money, and that gave him a special cachet.

To Watson, the specter of genetic patents only made Craig Venter more distasteful. Watson complained to NIH administrators that they were privatizing nature, and when that didn't work, he took his beef to Capitol Hill, where, speaking to a roomful of senators in 1991, he blasted Venter's work as something that "could be run by monkeys." Venter and the NIH fought back, saying Watson was old news, old science, and that patents were the future of biotechnology. Heads butted and ideals clashed in a battle that history will remember as the inevitable conflict of two brilliant, unharnessable minds. But in the end, it was either Venter or Watson, patent or no patent, and in April 1992, Jim Watson was asked to resign from the Human Genome Project. He returned to the Cold Spring Harbor Laboratory to resume his duties as director, the man who had unlocked the secret of DNA, who had led the charge to decode it, pushed aside by the commercial forces that would eventually consume biology.

"What is this? It looks like an artificial anus." Craig Venter is grinning now. His tiny eyes gleam beneath the tangled mass of eyebrows that protrude like fingers from his brow. He is mostly bald, with a friar's ring of hair grown longer than most men would dare, and he's running a hand over the dome, looking at a record cover with a picture of a trumpet mouthpiece on it. *"Uuunngh,"* he grunts, tossing the record aside.

This is Craig Venter, fifty-four, the man who mapped the

human genome and who has been accused of attempting to own it, the man who left the NIH in order to compete with it, the man who has been called the "next Hitler" and who has, more than anyone else in the world, become the face of gene patents. This is Craig Venter at work, slung back in an executive chair, with his bare ankles crossed in front of him, surrounded by three black standard poodles, all barking and wrestling one another on the carpeted floor while three of his employees stand around the desk, all talking at once, to him and to one another, about three entirely different topics, with Venter listening to none of them and also to all three of them, responding occasionally to each of them, even while reading the mail and looking at the album cover and playing with the dogs and gazing out the window and generally giving the false impression that he is distracted, which he is not and rarely ever is.

Someone in the room is talking about Mount Everest. Someone else is talking about antibiotics. Venter picks up a pamphlet that he commissioned to announce the completed human-genome map, the second great secret of DNA, the one he unlocked, the reason he will probably win a Nobel prize. Venter unfolds the pamphlet, turns it over, then back. "Do I have any spare time tomorrow?" he asks an assistant who has, until now, been talking about a symposium in Europe.

She pauses, switching gears. "It's going to be a crazy day."

Venter shrugs. "They're all crazy." He tilts an ear toward a publicist on the other side of his desk, who has switched from the subject of Mount Everest and has begun prepping Venter for an upcoming press conference. He listens for a moment, then turns back to the assistant. "See if we can make time to call Umberto Eco," he says. "Just to make sure he's going to be at the symposium."

Refolding the pamphlet, he turns back to his publicist. "Who's going to be at this press conference?" he asks.

The phone is ringing. His cell phone.

"People like *The Guardian*," the publicist says, raising her eyebrow as she says the name of the left-wing British newspaper. The British press has been especially hostile toward Venter.

"Why would I want to talk to *them?*" asks Venter, reaching for the still-ringing cell phone.

"Well . . ." says the publicist.

A senior researcher steps into the room, a short man with neatly parted hair and a perfectly trimmed mustache.

Venter nods hello, yanks the phone from his hip, but doesn't hold it to his ear. "Okay," he says to the publicist as the researcher returns his nod. Venter wags the phone like a scolding finger. "I'll talk to the assholes, but you're coming with me."

The researcher smiles, acknowledged.

The publicist sighs, exasperated. "You're going to have to clone me," she says.

Venter on the phone: "Hello? Yeah. Just put in the estimation. The average accuracy—99.96. Yeah, percent."

Lowering the phone to his thigh, he hands the pamphlet to the researcher. "Hey, check this out."

Then to the assistant, "Who's this guy from Disney speaking at the symposium?"

Back on the phone: "Sure, and Jim said there's a listing in the table that there's no yeast seven-transmembrane receptors."

The researcher looking at the pamphlet: "Cool."

The assistant shuffling papers: "I printed out his bio."

On the phone: "That's a mistake. There are at least two in yeast." The dogs barking, Venter squinting his eyes, reaching under the desk to grab one of them by the snout while still on the phone, saying, "There's yeast-mating factor," the assistant digging for the bio, the researcher reading the pamphlet out loud, the publicist asking the assistant questions, the dogs breaking away into another snarling roughhouse, the desk phone beginning to ring . . .

Outside the room, stillness. Silence. The atmosphere you might fairly expect from a giant white building in a just-built Washington, D.C., suburb known as the Technology Corridor. There is the scent of detergent, of plastics and paint. Clean, whispering fluorescent lights. Prim young women and men walking briskly down the halls, giving artificial smiles and officious little nods to one another. It could be a law office or a dentist's waiting room except for the glass tunnel at the far end of the hall, spanning a landscaped garden, leading to one of the largest civilian supercomputers in the world.

He built that thing over there. He left the Human Genome Project in 1992 to build it. They wouldn't build it for him, so he built it for himself. His own human-genome project, his own genome processor, his own goddamn institute of health. Floor after floor of microprocessors, hard drives, alpha servers, you name it, all linked together, firing and rifling through more than 100 terrabytes of memory. This is Celera Genomics, Incorporated, the hardware of Craig Venter's imagination.

Because his imagination needed more room to breathe. Because the government computers were too small, and so were the government minds. Because they had liked him early on, until he needed more funding, more machines, more power. Because nobody—not even a fellow maverick like Jim Watson—believed him when he said there was a way to automate and accelerate the whole process. Because there were plenty of computer experts in the world, and plenty of mathematicians, and there were plenty of molecular biologists, some better in the field than he. But he was the one with the capacity to juggle all those fields in his mind, the algebra and biology and computational logic and probability and industrial sequencing, to keep all those mix-matched balls in the air long enough to see how they moved together. He was the one who drew inside and outside the lines of all those disciplines, who understood that a big enough computer and exactly the right algorithm and the forces of probability and logic and statistics could mesh together, allowing the computer to do the work for you, could let you sit back and drink a margarita while the human genome cracked open.

Maybe he didn't wire the supercomputer himself. And maybe he didn't write the software. Maybe he didn't devise the combinatorial algorithm for the data. But he was the one who woke up sweaty with the vision bashing through his skull, the train wreck of all those disciplines yielding an epiphany in the night: the human genome could be mapped in less than one year's time.

That's why he left the government project, and that's why the line formed behind him: a Nobel laureate named Hamilton O. Smith; some of the world's foremost computer-science geeks, including Gene Myers, the preeminent author of DNA-sequencing algorithms; even the director of the National Cancer Institute, Samuel L. Broder, all dropping out of their respective limelights, out of their various prestigious gobbledygook to form a technical-support group in Craig Venter's lab. It wasn't the money that brought them. Money never could. Besides, the moneymen were right there in line with the rest of the hangers-on, all clinging to Venter for the same reason: they bought his vision and wanted to see it happen.

Now Sam Broder stops in the glass passageway to explain why he did it, why he left one of the most coveted positions in the scientific world for this. A little man with downturned eyes and a faint, squeaky lisp, Broder is more the proper image of a biologist than his boss is.

"When I read in the newspapers that Craig was going to do the human genome," he says, his round eyes blinking proudly behind dense glasses, "I said, I've gotta do this. It was one of those areas where I knew that I would regret it the rest of my life if I didn't. Ten years from now, I would've looked back and said, I should've done it. The truth is, you can't go back. You don't get a second chance. I said to myself, I gotta do this. I gotta do this, because if I don't do it, I'll hate myself later."

Broder stops, smiles, gulps. His eyes are misty. "He's a genius. You can tell right away when you meet him. From the way he is. He's fearless. He's not like most scientists." Another employee enters at the far end of the passageway, and Broder's eyes dart to the floor. He waits for the man to pass, then looks up again. "You know, Craig gets a lot of criticism." A vaguely defiant smile, lips pressed together. "There have been people with very weird ideas about him, but I think in his heart . . ." The voice trails off again.

"If he had stayed at the NIH, his enemies would have slowed him down," Broder says finally. "So now we have to be a business to do the science we want to do."

The business of science is not exactly a thrill sport. Not to most people. Most people, for example, probably weren't paying very close attention when the Plant Patent Act was proposed in 1930. Most people were probably more concerned about, oh, say, the Great Depression than a law that would allow botanists to patent plants. But in Congress, the bill was a subject of fierce debate. This was about more than just plants, after all. At heart, it was about patenting life, and that required some consideration.

Until that point, living things had always been off-limits to the patent code, if for no other reason than that they were products of nature and products of nature cannot be claimed as inventions. For example, while it's okay to patent a method of purifying tungsten, it is not legal to patent the element itself. Tungsten is not an invention. The same had always been assumed about plants, but by 1930, the distinctions were beginning to blur. After all, nature may have invented the rose, but it certainly never produced the Betty Prior Hybrid Polyantha, a full-bodied rosebush that was bred for its resistance to disease and cold. Congress wanted to reward growers who were developing new strains, but it also knew that patenting plants was the beginning of a very slippery slope. You could start with the best intentions, but if you weren't careful, if you didn't pen the letter of the law just right, you could grease the way right down that slope into bizarre new territory— the patenting of hybrid insects, perhaps. Maybe even mammals. Maybe people.

To make sure that didn't happen, to plug any possible loophole in the law, Congress revisited the Plant Patent Act in 1970, adding a clause that specifically excluded bacteria. It had taken lawmakers forty years, but they had drawn a clear boundary on life patents: a plant could be seen as an invention, but other organisms could not.

Two years later, a scientist from General Electric showed up at the U.S. Patent and Trademark Office with an application for "a bacterium from the genus *Pseudomonas*." The application was quickly rejected. But GE wouldn't take no for an answer. As far as the company was concerned, the *Pseudomonas* bacterium was not just any bacterium; it was an invention, just as much as any hybrid rose. It had been genetically bred in a laboratory, did not exist in nature, and had a commercial function: it could eat oil out of salt water and could be used to clean up oil spills. GE decided to sue the patent office in hopes of changing the decision.

The courtroom was nearly empty when that case went before the U.S. Supreme Court on Saint Patrick's Day in 1980. The business of science is not exactly a thrill sport, and the national press was nowhere to be found. Arguments were brief and to the point. General Electric insisted that, no matter what the patent office said, its bacterium was an invention and should be protected by the patent code. The U.S. Patent and Trademark Office countered that, in spite of General Electric's marvelous bacterium, the laws of the United States were a clear and final authority that said bacteria were not patentable.

The decision that emerged from the judges' quarters nearly three months later would usher in a new era in American patent law. "The fact that microorganisms are alive is without legal significance," the majority wrote. "Respondent's microorganism plainly qualifies as patentable subject matter. His claim is not to a hitherto unknown natural phenomenon, but to a nonnaturally occurring manufacture or composition of matter—a product of human ingenuity having a distinctive name, character, and use."

Not only was the U.S. Supreme Court overruling Congress with its verdict, it was also overruling the U.S. Constitution, which states that only Congress has the power to change patent laws, a detail noted by Justice Brennan in his dissent: "It is the role of Congress, not this Court, to broaden or narrow the reach of the patent laws," he wrote. "Congress specifically excluded bacteria from the coverage of the 1970 Act."

Still, the majority had ruled, and the GE patent became official on a hot summer day in 1980. Here was the future, laid bare. Here was the Supreme Court making it legal to patent not only a bacterium but a whole new species of them. Here was the Supreme Court declaring a species of animal to be an invention. Here was the Supreme Court writing a new definition of life. Not that most people noticed or cared. Not that most people were even paying attention to the business of science. Not that a microorganism really counts as an animal, anyway. Not like it was a monkey or a fish or a mouse.

Jeff Green built a better mouse. Or, to be precise, he built a worse mouse, but he did it on purpose. He invented a mouse with cancer.

"What we did was overexpress oncogenes," he says, standing slightly stooped in a white turtleneck and faded black jeans, his longish brown hair and beard just unkempt enough to appear professorial. "We developed the first transgenic mouse model for prostate cancer doing this, and it turned out that we also developed an excellent model for breast cancer."

He's standing in a tiny government office on the campus of the National Cancer Institute in Bethesda, Maryland, an underfunded and overcrowded laboratory with research supplies stacked on the floors and counters. Behind him, there is a cartoon of a man holding a sign that says, WILL WORK FOR HEFTY SALARY AND PRE-IPO STOCK. At his feet is a small cardboard box. He reaches down to pick it up. "I think there might be one in here," he says, shaking the box lightly near his ear, setting it on a countertop and popping it open. A fat white mouse is inside, lying on its stomach, legs spread, with a peanut-sized hump on its shoulder. It doesn't move. Not a whisker. "Okay, so she's not very active," says Green. "But can you see that lump? That's a mammary gland. It's a female. This is what one of our mice looks like after the tumors progress." He studies it some more. "This animal is probably five or six months old. She's close."

Closing the box, Green takes a deep breath, sighs, and squares his shoulders. "We've essentially generated a new kind of animal," he says. "We've changed the genetics in a very defined way, so now we can breed these animals and predictably get the same kind of cancer in later generations. That's why it's a powerful tool; you don't have to go back and generate it again. It becomes incorporated into their genome."

That's the upside: that Jeff Green has plenty of mice with cancer, which is helpful when you study cancer, because mice get sick and die in a way that's similar to the way humans die, so if you watch the mice deteriorate, you can learn something about how cancer works. The downside, the thing that Jeff Green can't quite understand, is that somebody else already owns his mice, that somebody else has a patent on them, that even though he invented the mice and even though nobody has ever created mice quite like them, the mice are not his property and he cannot legally use them in his research because they belong to somebody else.

That somebody is Philip Leder, a genetic scientist at Harvard University. In the early 1980s, Leder invented his own cancerous mouse and named it OncoMouse. Much like Jeff Green's mouse, the OncoMouse had an overexpressed oncogene, and, also like Green's mouse, it got cancer. Those are the only significant similarities between Jeff Green's mouse and Leder's OncoMouse. They do not have the same genetic mutation or the same genetic code, they are not the same subspecies of mutated mouse, and they do not get the same type of cancer. But Leder was clever when he invented the OncoMouse. He knew that a few years earlier, GE's oil-eating bacterium had been patented and that the Supreme Court decision had left room for larger animals, so when Leder applied for a patent on the OncoMouse in 1984, he stretched that loophole to the limits. His attorney wrote the patent application so broadly that it covered not only the OncoMouse itself, a specific genetic creation, but also every other "non-human mammal" with an overexpressed oncogene.

In an earlier era, Leder's bloated patent application would

almost certainly have been denied. But at the time he filed his application, the U.S. Patent Office was still reeling from the GE bacteria verdict, revising its laws, struggling to figure out where to draw the line on animal patents, and, somehow, in the midst of the confusion, Leder's patent was granted. Now it was possible to patent not only a species of bacteria, not only a subspecies of mouse, but even a group of animals that wasn't in the same species, or even the same genus. Leder's patent was so broad that, in addition to covering mice, it also covered pigs, horses, monkeys, cattle—anything with an overexpressed oncogene. So broad that it covered Jeff Green's mice, the first mice with prostate cancer, before Jeff Green even invented them. Before they even existed.

Now, all things being equal, Leder might have been willing to let it slide, since he's generally a nice guy and since, after all, Jeff Green works for the government, not for profit. Problem was, by the time Green invented his mouse, Leder had already licensed the OncoMouse patent to DuPont, and DuPont wasn't eager to extend any professional courtesies to Jeff Green or the government or anybody else. DuPont wanted to charge $50 for every animal ever created or born with an overexpressed oncogene, and they had a legal right to do it.

"The mouse we made technically falls under that patent." Green shrugs. His work, for years, has skirted the law. If he had discovered a cure for cancer, the cure would have belonged to DuPont. Because the government didn't have permission to use those mice, didn't have permission from DuPont to continue with cancer research. Fortunately, says Green, just last year, after years of haggling, DuPont finally gave the government permission. Now the government can use mice for cancer research without being sued by DuPont. Now the government can, but a lot of research companies still can't.

"Other drug companies will stay away from using these mice," says Green. "If they use this technology or animals that were generated with this technology, then DuPont may have a legal right to their work." He shakes his head and laughs a laugh of disbelief, of polite disgust. "It would be nice if the system was revised."

The first time you ever heard John Moore's story, he was sitting at a bar in Seattle, telling a tale about a doctor stealing his cells, and you gaped at the sheer audacity. Now you know enough not to be surprised. Now you know about thousands of doctors and companies and government agencies doing the same thing, or worse, all clutching at Craig Venter's human-genome map as if it were a guide to pirates' treasure.

What amazes you now is not the patenting itself; it's that the whole thing passed you by, that life was being parceled out while your life went on, oblivious. But one man has been there through it all. Before Craig Venter mapped his first gene, before the oil-eating bacterium went to court, even before Jim Watson's big return, one man was keeping an eye on the business of science. He is a small and aging radical with a few tricks still up his sleeve, and you find him in his tidy office at the Foundation on Economic Trends in Washington, D.C., near Chinatown, a buttoned-down and squared-away old yippie with a neatly trimmed mustache and a cheap gray suit.

"Okay," he says, jumping up from behind a desk to shake your hand vigorously. The words come quick, in bursts. "Have you read *The Biotech Century*? What have you read? What do you think?"

The bookshelves, pressed against the wall of the adjoining room, are lined with his books. The first, *Who Should Play God?*, published in 1977, predicted things like surrogate wombs and test-tube babies and the commercialization of the gene pool, things that sounded absurd at the time, so absurd that Jeremy Rifkin quickly earned a reputation as an alarmist. Now he is taken more seriously. Now he speaks on the radio and wears suits to the office. Today, he has just returned from the World Economic Forum in Davos, Switzerland, where he was a featured speaker.

"There's a philosophical issue here that's the deepest of all

issues, but it's never talked about," he says. His voice is narrow
and thin and high. "In the last century, we fought over whether
you can have a human being as property. Slavery. We abolished it.
The Thirteenth Amendment." His eyes are dark and wide, his
hands small. He spreads them. "So you can't own a whole human
being, but now you *can* own all the parts. Genes, cells, chromo-
somes, organs, tissues, and whole organisms. What happens if we
patent all the building blocks of life? What role is there for faith
and theology, or even a concept of nature as being independent
and a priori? What happens if kids grow up in a world where the
government says life is an invention?"

But the truth is that these days, even Jeremy Rifkin is saying
that life is an invention. These days, even Rifkin is playing within
the system. After twenty years of agitating against the business
of science, he has learned that the way to slow its momentum is
not by protest but by patent. He has seen the power of DuPont's
OncoMouse patent, its potential to slow down research on prostate cancer, and he has seen the power of Myriad Genetics' patent
on BRCA1 and how it could slow down research on breast cancer,
and seeing that power has given Rifkin an insight: it's the same
power he wants to wield—the power to stop power.

And so in 1997 he applied for a patent on all human-animal
hybrids, a patent that would give him the exclusive right to determine who can mix human and animal DNA, the next frontier of
genetic research. Already, it's a frontier in fast development.
There's a company called Nextran mixing human DNA with that
of pigs, hoping to mutate pig livers into something a person could
use. There's another group of scientists at the University of Bath
in England experimenting with frog DNA, hoping to create
sustainable systems of human organs that can be harvested for
transplants. Rifkin's patent would cover both of those experiments, and he would wield his patent like a weapon, stopping
anybody from doing any research whatsoever with human-animal
hybrids.

So far, the prospects for his application don't look promising.

Actually, it was denied last year. But to an agitator like Rifkin, rejection is where the fun starts. "We have a challenge in the patent office now," he says eagerly. "Then it's going to the Patent Board, the U.S. Court of Appeals, and then probably the Supreme Court."

Outside, traffic is moving down the busy street, but you can't hear it, and you have to wonder if anybody out there can hear Jeremy Rifkin. Or if anybody would hear him even if they could. If they even should hear him now, talking about his rejected patent and his efforts to force it through. Life is being parceled out while, at the same time, life goes on, oblivious. Outside, traffic is moving down the busy street. Inside, even the radicals are filing patent applications.

It would be hard to find something more unpatentable than a gene. Genetic materials do not meet the criteria for a patent. They are not new; their function, for the most part, is unknown; and while it may be true that some living things, like the OncoMouse or the *Pseudomonas* bacterium, were invented by humans, the same cannot be said about the 1,000 human genes that have been found in nature and patented that way. They are, in the words of the Supreme Court bacteria decision, "a hitherto unknown natural phenomenon," which should make them unpatentable, like tungsten. They just don't fit the specs.

And yet, in the race to privatize life, the fact that genes should not be patentable makes them all the more important to patent. They have become the ultimate symbol: if a gene can be patented, anything can be. And so the bricks of life have come to mark the end, not the beginning, of the slippery slope.

The great irony of all this is that most of the early patents on genetic data were not filed by big business at all but by the government's Human Genome Project in 1992. And Jim Watson wasn't the only one to protest. The biggest opponent at the time was the Industrial Biotechnology Association, a consortium of private companies concerned about the effects gene patents would have on the flow of knowledge and research. It was only after the NIH defended gene patents that big business jumped into the game.

Even today, one of the most prolific patenters of human genes is the NIH. But big business is fast catching up. Companies like Incyte Genomics and Human Genome Sciences have filed for patents on hundreds of thousands of DNA sequences over the past five years, mostly on random patches of DNA that may or may not even contain genes. Incyte alone has applied for patents on more than 100,000 partial gene sequences, just hoping that somewhere along the stretch of DNA they have claimed there will be a few useful genes that they can hoard for themselves or sell. There will surely be money in licensing genes to researchers but nowhere near the windfall these companies will collect when one of "their" genes is used to cure a disease like cancer or cystic fibrosis or Alzheimer's or Parkinson's or Huntington's, all of which are associated with patented genes.

To get a sense of just what these patents may be worth, you don't have to look any further than the reports of investment banks. "We maintain our long-term buy on Incyte," says J. P. Morgan's equity research report. "Given its early position in gene finding and patenting and genomics databases, it has carved out a large, very valuable, and largely irreversible position."

Or Robertson Stephens on Human Genome Sciences: "HGS has one of the broadest portfolios of gene/protein targets in the industry . . . and an impressive patent estate to protect its discoveries. This translates into one of the largest intellectual property positions in the industry."

In fact, the one genetics company that doesn't brag about its patent collection is the company you'd probably expect to have the biggest collection of all: Celera. But the fact is, Craig Venter doesn't hold any gene patents. Not one. There was a time, a few years ago, when he did, when he applied for and was granted *provisional* patents on several thousands of gene fragments he had discovered. But they expire after one year, and Venter never upgraded them into full, twenty-year patents. He does plan to hold patents in the future, but the number of genes he'll patent will be in the low hundreds, not the hundreds of thousands like his competitors. He'll patent just the genes he wants to research himself so he won't have to pay a competitor for access. But, for the most part, patents aren't important to his business plan. Venter's goal is not to own the genes or even to provide access to them. His plan is to offer the best available analysis of the whole DNA strand, a running stream of information and insight, much like a trade magazine. Subscribers to his service won't get access to patented genes; they'll be exposed to a fresh collection of ideas and the most complete data available, including comparisons between the human genetic code and those of several other species.

Venter thinks of gene patents as a necessary evil, a way for researchers to recoup their financial investments without keeping their discoveries secret. "Patents are not secrecy," Venter says. "The patent law is basically there to encourage people *not* to hold trade secrets. When you patent, the information gets published." But the reason Venter has become a lightning rod in the growing debate is not because of his specific point of view or because he holds any gene patents. It's because he's one of the only people in the private sector who's willing to debate the issue at all. Actually, he's more than willing, even more willing than many academics. He's eager to engage the debate over gene patents, gene testing, gene discrimination, and anything else genetic. Because he's sick of hearing the eggheads do all the talking, and he's sick of the mentality that the business of science should be kept under wraps. He wants the public to know what's going on in the biotech revolution, and he wants to have an open debate about it, to confront not only its promises but also its threats. And so Craig Venter may be the only person in the whole field of genetics who's hungry for that discussion, who's so anxious to get a lively debate going that he's willing to fly around the world, often on his own tab, just to fan the flames.

Tonight, you can find him in the Gothic marble admitting room of a 500-year-old hospital in France, a room that has been filled with a dozen round tables, each one holding ten place settings. His flight arrived from D.C. this morning, and he's flying back tomorrow morning, and it's been thirty-six hours without sleep so far, maybe a few more, which means that Venter, who is famous among his staff for being indefatigable, is just now starting to get tired. You can see the day in the droop of his eyebrows, less wild and lively than usual, sinking and then jerking back up, snapping to as he twirls his spoon around in his three-fish soup and tries to make conversation with his tablemates.

He's been a celebrity all day at a conference on genetics in Lyons, surrounded by a sea of autograph seekers, and he's brought a CD-ROM to the event tonight. The cover has a picture of Da Vinci's man and says, "The Human Genome Map." The disc inside is blank. Venter's planning on leaving it behind at the end of the night, just to mess with the mind of some dummy.

He's finding ways to amuse himself, but he looks bored tonight, in an expensive blue suit that couldn't possibly fit worse over his slouchy, disinterested frame. The painkillers he took this afternoon have worn off, no longer blunting the edge of his ex-haustion, and although he asked around for some pot, he wasn't able to find any, so he has been forced to rely on wine—the third bottle's almost empty—which is muting the pain but, unfortu-nately, dulling his wit as well. He's fading. He's drifting. He's something that Craig Venter rarely is: shot.

Suddenly, a voice comes blaring through the speaker system, and Venter snaps to attention. "Now that we've fed the senses in this beautiful hall, and we've fed the stomach, we come to feeding the mind and the imagination," the voice announces. Venter wipes his eyes, trying to spruce himself up. "We've got a really wonder-ful lineup of contributors this evening. We have Denis Hoch-strasser, from the University of Geneva, a pioneer in proteomics. We have Jean-Marie Lehn, a Nobel laureate based at the Collège de France in Paris. We have Gert-Jan van Ommen, from the University of Leiden. And we have a bloke who I'm not sure if anybody has ever heard of, Craig Venter from Celera Genomics. So I think it's a great group of people to get together and kick some ideas around."

Hearing his cue, Venter rises, shuffles to the front of the room, and climbs onstage, where the other scientists are converging, greeting one another with niceties. Venter gives them all a quick nod, then flops down in a chair, shifting uncomfortably in his seat as each member of the panel introduces himself with a long-winded autobiography and a personal mission statement. Venter can barely suppress his yawns, and when it's his turn to make an opening statement, he leans into the microphone and mumbles, "Well, I've consumed a lot of wine, and I want to make sure I save some comments for later"; then he leans back, done.

A flurry of hands leap from the crowd with questions, and the moderator invites a young man to be first. "I'd like to address a topic to anyone on the panel," he says, "and that's the issue of ownership versus free access."

Venter rolls his neck, reaching for the microphone. This is what he was hoping for, a lively debate, right from the start, something to help wake him up. "I think it is a difficult challenge in terms of deciding where to draw the line," he says, "and I think the legal system has been slow to respond to the front lines of science."

"Would you say that certain segments of the genome are not available to everyone?" the guy asks.

Venter shakes his head. In a few days, he will publish the entire genome map on-line; anyone will be able to see the nucleotide sequence for free. Anyone will be able to see the collection of all human genes, including dozens of new, unpatented ones. Of course, the patented genes will still be restricted in commercial research, but there will be no secrets about where or what they are.

"No offense," Venter says, "but that's the number one fallacy I hear from people. When you submit a patent application, it gets published by the patent office. Patents are the opposite of secrecy."

At that, van Ommen leans forward, the spitting image of a

young Einstein, with his brow in a bunch. "But patenting does create problems for the scientist," he says in a thick Dutch accent. "When you find something, you want to publish it in *Nature* right away, but you can't. You first have to call a patent lawyer."

Venter gives him an annoyed look. Van Ommen raises his eyebrows. Venter takes a sip of water. The debate is under way. Another guy stands up in the audience, asking why Venter won't publish his DNA map, with some analysis, in a scientific journal. Venter assures him that he's got an article in the upcoming issue of *Science.* There's a young woman from Glasgow who's worried about the prospect of genetic discrimination, and Venter nods, saying, yeah, it's a concern of his, too, that he's lobbying Congress in the United States to set a global example with some kind of bill to stop genetic discrimination before it starts. There's a guy who wants to know how hospitals in the Third World will ever be able to afford the licensing fees to screen for patented genes, and Venter says it's a fair question, reminding the crowd that he doesn't hold any patents himself but admitting that he thinks companies should create a flexible pricing system, offering better deals to poorer nations. But just as the discussion is really starting to roll, a man stands up in the center of the room and brings it to a quick end.

"My two children suffer from a rare disease," he says. "I'm just a father. I got involved in this four years ago. I started a research foundation." His voice cracks. He catches himself, gives a slight smile. "I'm nervous," he says, swallowing. "Anyway, we found the gene, and we cloned an animal model." His voice breaks again. Again, he catches himself. "Whew," he says. "My hope and my expectation is that I will save my children's vision loss, and the 6,000 other patients' that I represent. And I think it's just . . . I think we all kind of get buried in the minutiae of patents and so forth, and I think it's important to recognize the power of this technology to solve and to protect human existence. We have to remember to think positive thoughts and focus on the difference this technology can make in people's lives."

Silence. A cough splits off the marble walls, and for the first time today, all eyes are off Venter. The moment lingers, the room hushed in support of this speaker, this father, this man announcing his hope, his calm confidence that genetics will better the world. The room is still, and Venter endures it as he has endured the stillness and silence for so long. As we have all endured the blind optimism that allowed business to consume science, that allowed life to be parceled out, even as life went on. Oblivious.

Attention, all lovers of California wines. Your enemy is the glassy-winged sharpshooter and it is truly to be feared. This *Harper's* magazine story by William Hamilton tells us why California wineries are in a defensive mode to fend off a threat to their profitability. Somewhere, a Frenchman is smiling. We're also taken on a trip to the Napa Valley to learn about the rich history and modern muscle of an important northern California industry.

William Hamilton

Day of the Locust: A New Pest Threatens to Wipe Out the California Wine Industry

WITH ITS EPONYMOUS WINGS folded under its carapace, the glassy-winged sharpshooter looks like a muddy SUV. Its ancient insect engineering and big, flathead power, however, suggest the nastiest of Harleys of the very baddest chapters of the old Hells Angels motorcycle clubs. This half-inch sapsucker from the American Southeast turns out to be the reason you have never tasted a glass of Florida wine.

When northern California's surging housing development needed more landscaping material than the state was producing, ornamental trees and shrubs were trucked in that direction by the big southern California nurseries. Straight up Highway 5— the great stem of north-south transport in this long state—right through the huge mainspring of California agriculture—the Central Valley—rolled trucks full of trees and turf and plants headed for the proliferating tracts of commuter homes that new job growth has brought on in places like the Silicon Valley. Hitching a ride on this foliage came the glassy-winged sharpshooter. Unfortunately, down in southern California's Riverside County, it had already developed a taste for grapevines.

The Napa Valley grew as many walnuts, prunes, and cattle as grapes when I was a boy there. It's all grapes now, only they're not often called that anymore, "grape" seeming too blue-collar a term for such a luxurious crop. Even the grape growers are now called just "growers," without the "grape." They call the little round balls they are growing "fruit."

Step onto an oak-bowered lawn outside St. Helena (my hometown) in the middle of the Napa Valley. Take a glass of wine, which is from those vineyards right out there. Hold the glass by the foot (the disc on the bottom of the stem that makes it possible to drink without a cupbearer) and swirl the wine around so you can watch it slide down the walls of the glass. Take a sniff. Have a sip. Walk over to your host, compliment the wine, and look out at his vineyards. Say, "How's your fruit?" This insider word usage will get you a different answer from "How are your grapes?" You'll hear about Brix and sugar and microclimates and noble rot—and perhaps about an obscure, ancient varietal from a Mediterranean region the grower is trying out over there in the foothill vineyard for his "meritage" blend.

Of course, not everyone in the wine industry has it all quite so attractively together as your host on this lovely lawn today. And since he was an investment banker before he bought the place and put in the winery, he had a few lessons to learn himself. Like the time he asked a big Central Valley grower how many tons an acre of cabernet he was getting. The vineyard veteran looked at the sophisticated newcomer a moment, taking in the Austrian corduroys, the Ivy League accent, and the little silver wire-framed eyeglasses, and answered the question with one of his own: "How many times a week do you fuck your wife?"

The Napa Valley won most of its fine wine reputation one afternoon in 1976 at what *Time* magazine called the "Judgment of

Paris." This expert blind tasting of France's greatest wines alongside some Napa Valley stuff arranged by the English wine merchant Stephen Spurrier had to be, at least in terms of marketing, one of France's lowest twentieth-century moments. Not even Spurrier had any idea of the global public-relations effect of French experts unwittingly choosing Napa's Stag's Leap Cabernet for first place over two premier cru classé giants—Châteaus Haut-Brion and Mouton Rothschild—and then picking another Napa Valley product, Château Montelena Chardonnay, for World's Greatest White wine honors, over Meursault-Charmes and Batard-Montrachet. Among the most flabbergasted were the Napa Valley proprietors of these suddenly greatest wineries in the world.

By assigning a Royal Commission in 1855 to classify the wines of Bordeaux according to quality, France invented the sales device (never more profitable than now) of a ranked list. Who is a dentist in Adelaide, Australia, or a Chicago professor, or even a Napa Valley vintner to argue with a title like "Le Grand Vin de la Château Latour, Premier Grand Cru Classé" issued nearly 200 years ago by a royal committee in a country that had been in the wine business for more than 2,000 years? A country credited with inventing kissing with the tongue? Spurrier had ingeniously appointed another committee of just such superior, native French experts as the 1855 one—a cordon-bleu panel who would probably spend a great deal of the rest of their lives in grim retrospect, not to mention beards, sunglasses, and new names. *Quel faux pas!* With the clunk of a head dropping into a guillotine basket, an old order fell.

The Napa Valley won its unexpected world title just as a marketplace for wine was opening in America with New World enormity. The United States Brewers Foundation's proud motto, "Beer Belongs . . . Enjoy It," run under happy pictures of family picnics washed down by brown bottles of brew painted by *Saturday Evening Post* cover artists, was beginning to lose its appeal. Sophistication had started to sell. James Bond, 007, didn't buy six-packs. Jackie Kennedy didn't look like she drank milk with her meals.

After the Judgment of Paris in 1976, not only the wine but also its home country, the Napa Valley, took on a new mien of success and chic. Walnut and prune orchards were going the way of Sonoma County's once flourishing breweries—under, and under new vineyards and wineries and country homes. Planting some grapes and starting a winery became the second career of oenophiles retiring from advertising and industry and finance and law. Architects and even landscape architects began to find work building photogenic homes and wineries in the beautiful Napa Valley, just over an hour from San Francisco.

Making wine turned out to be more work than most expected, but for some it worked out so spectacularly well that not even they remember much about their first careers. Wine was becoming a stylish success story. And then the boom began. The Silicon Valley banked in San Francisco.

At the Napa Valley Wine Auction last summer, a retired Cisco Systems executive paid $500,000 for a six-liter bottle of Screaming Eagle Cabernet. Screaming Eagle is only one of a number of Napa Valley wines so rare and prized that they sell completely out for vast sums before ever coming to a public market. Lucky subscribers to such limited productions often flip their purchases in eBay auctions for three or four times their purchase price.

In the comparatively less adrenaline-spritzed venue of a daily real-estate market, potential vineyard land in this region is selling for $100,000 an acre and more. A five-acre piece in St. Helena with an unremarkable house, some landscaping, and a pool just went for $4.1 million—a solid Beverly Hills figure. It costs around $50,000 to plant an acre, and vines don't produce fruit until they are between three and five years old. Under current regulations, the minimum size for a new hillside parcel in the Napa County agricultural watershed is 160 acres. Yet even with these financial and regulatory handicaps, such opportunities are hard to find. Sales are brisk and competitive. At what bars remain in the haute-culinary Napa Valley, real-estate stories have replaced the traditional fishing yarn. Everyone shakes his head over the last price paid, and anyone who hung on to a piece of property feels damn lucky. Like Andrea Palladio in the Roman boom times, and Richard Morris Hunt in nineteenth-century Newport, favored architects are building villas in the wine country by the tens of thousands of square feet. Because of the vast county parcel requirements, these palaces do not sit cheek-by-jowl the way they do in Newport's comical ghetto of châteaus. But they do seem to command every knoll, like a proliferating pack of steroidally enhanced architectural prairie dogs.

"He wants the wine cellar to have a glass wall looking through the waterfall at his valley view," architect Sandy Walker explained to me of a cathedral-sized floor plan on his drafting table. "And he shall have it!"

Without this mad wine-country lifestyle boom, this beautiful landscape (vineyards and wineries and mansions aren't the worst available eyesores) would probably have become another Bay Area suburb. The old crops of prunes and walnuts, the little cattle operations, the tacky old tourist attractions of hot springs, and even the one famous whorehouse that I remember from my boyhood would never have made the kind of money that holds off real-estate development. Without the kind of luck that got great Napa rather than great Sonoma or Australian or South American wine to Paris at the right time, what is now, like Disneyland, a huge tourist attraction in California (and home to Walt Disney's widow before she died) would have nothing to attract tourists. It would be pens of subdivisions with wooden chimneys and an occasional old, homeless-looking oak tree. But the wine boom saved it. Both as a luxurious country retreat and as a real business, the wine country prospers. Bottom lines here are real and huge and growing. The Bank of America as well as Silicon Valley banks have loaned eagerly to what has been a phenomenal success story. What could possible go wrong?

Down in southern California the orange groves pulled to build Disneyland in Anaheim themselves replaced a pioneer effort at

California winemaking. Started, like so many New World vineyards (including the first ones in Brazil, Australia, and the Napa Valley), by German immigrants, in 1857, the southern California wine industry was an immediate success. Grapes grew well, and wine and money from it were made in Anaheim until the 1880s, when the vines suddenly and mysteriously started drying up. The ripening fruit turned to raisins. Instead of flaming red and gold, one grim autumn the grape leaves crumpled up brown. By 1895, 35,000 acres of southern California vineyard were dead.

The blight was not phylloxera, the notorious root louse that wiped out the first vineyards of France and then those of California—a plague ultimately remedied by planting vineyards with a phylloxera-resistant native American rootstock onto which the noble varieties of wine grapes could be grafted (making, California vintners are proud to point out, all contemporary French wine American wine at root). The roots of the vines drying up in Anaheim were healthy. This was a different scourge. Luckily, whatever was killing off Anaheim's vineyards wasn't spreading. After wiping out every grapevine there, phylloxera's mysterious little sister pestilence seemed through. It became a wine-history footnote first known as Anaheim disease.

Since "Anaheim, Home of Anaheim Disease" was no town motto for a young and hopeful agricultural community, nominal honors for the disaster were eagerly passed on to a U.S. Department of Agriculture plant pathologist doing autopsies on the corpses of *Vitis vinifera,* the wine-producing grapevine. Newton B. Pierce proved that what would come to be called Pierce's disease was caused by a living organism that had invaded the vine's upper reaches, its trunk and branches. Correct as he was about this, Pierce couldn't figure out if the pathogen was a virus or a bacterium, or what was shooting it into the wood. It wasn't until nearly 100 years later that the killer was identified as a bacterium, *Xylella fastidiosa,* and its carrier as one of three native varieties of leaf-hopping insects popularly called "sharpshooters." The *Xylella fastidiosa* (a name that in happier circumstances might have been applied to the wine critic) is considered *fastidiosa* because it settles exclusively in the xylem, the water-bearing tissues plumbing a plant. In a *Vitis vinifera* xylem, it not only multiplies exponentially but litters, plugging up the entire circulatory system conduit by conduit, until the vine has strangled to death.

After Anaheim disease became Pierce's disease and orange groves replaced the vineyards of Anaheim, the southern California vineyard disaster faded into obscure anecdote. There was no major recurrence elsewhere in the state. Except for a 1940s outbreak in the San Joaquin Valley, and a persistent but contained presence throughout the state—including the premier *terroirs* of the Napa and Sonoma valleys, where the native blue-green sharpshooters' comparatively harmless picnics in the vineyards kept the incidence low—Pierce's disease became unobtrusive enough to be written off as just another of Mother Nature's annoying but bearable exactions of agricultural tribute. Through 1992 only the most technical histories of the California wine industry carry even index entries for Pierce's disease.

"Down on the valley floor they get frost, and up here in the hills we get these damn 'shooters; in agriculture there's always something out there about to make you miserable," was about how growers complained about the tiny insects they called sharpshooters all the way into the 1990s—not with a shudder but with a shrug.

Spectacularly and horribly, this situation has changed. Pierce's disease now has a comparatively humongous new agent, the Florida-born glassy-winged sharpshooter. Twice the size of the old locals with five times the range, and crazy about grapevines, the intruder has made Pierce's disease into a threat to California agriculture on the order of the San Andreas Fault.

In 1997, growers in the Riverside County city of Temecula noted the first cases of PD ever in their vineyards (Pierce's disease, PD, and its new vehicle, the glassy-winged sharpshooter, GWSS, are notorious enough to have become, like AIDS and NASDAQ, acronyms). Because the incidence was small, the few infected vines were replanted and attentions turned to other worries. The next year's growing season, however, revealed a marked increase. Scientists called in from the University of California at Riverside to test for Pierce's disease discovered a startling 27 to 97 percent infection in Temecula's vineyards. By 1999 hundreds of acres of vines were dead. Agricultural epidemiologists quickly determined that the *Xylella fastidiosa* bacterium was coming into the vineyards from adjacent citrus groves, and that the bugs delivering it were not from the three old, known California sharpshooter families.

Because, like a serial killer who behaves perfectly to his landlady, *Xylella* occupies other plants with less or no fatality, it can lie low. The Pierce's disease bacterium had long enjoyed an oblivious hospitality throughout the state. With nothing to carry it into vineyards, or almond groves or oleanders, where it kills its host, it isn't even apparent. The formerly domestic blackberry now spread especially along streamsides throughout the state thrives with *Xylella fastidiosa* aboard. But grapevines have no defense.

Inquiries to the office of one of the foremost Pierce's disease experts, Dr. Alexander Purcell, of the University of California at Berkeley, have reached such a volume that he has set up a long and increasingly tentacled Web site to deal with PD research and news. "*Xylella* does seem to stay in the cell it enters in some plants, spreading no further and after a couple of seasons completely dying out, but we don't know why," says Purcell. "All we know for sure right now is that the grapevine isn't one of them. Chronic Pierce's disease is 100 percent fatal to *Vitis vinifera*. There is no known cure."

Whereas the comparatively tiny native California sharpshooters can fly only a fifth as far as the glassy-winged sharpshooters and because they can get their PD-infected stylets into a grapevine only when it is relatively soft, as it is during the growing season—enabling growers to prune out most of the infected branches when dormant vines are cut back in the winter—the invader is a much more apocalyptic threat to vineyards. It can sink its stylet through a vine's permanent wood, releasing *Xylella* into xylems at any time of the growth cycle. Whereas aphids and leafhoppers and most stylet-sucking insects bypass the nutritionally thin sort of brew irrigating *Vitis vinifera,* this bug seems perversely engineered to feed specifically on it—specifically, and, to the wine industry, diabolically, evolved to destroy grapevines.

"I just don't want to even think about it. But I do, especially at around three in the morning, when I wake up filled with so much dread I can't get back to sleep," says Jay Heminway, the founder, proprietor, grower, and winemaker of Green & Red Vineyard, a producer of succulent zinfandel.

"We'll get rid of it," predicts Michael Mondavi, president and CEO of the great and global Robert Mondavi Corporation. "Unlike phylloxera, the glassy-winged sharpshooter operates aboveground, and it's almost as big as a fly. We'll get rid of it. We just have to keep it away from here until we figure out how. And it's not just the wine industry, you know, that's threatened by this. It's almonds and alfalfa, and, from what's happening in Brazil, we know citrus could be next. Just about all of California agriculture has a future riding on getting rid of this one. We did away with phylloxera—twice. We'll do away with PD and the glassy-winged sharpshooter the same way."

As I stood with the rangily attractive Cathy Roybal, deputy agricultural commissioner for Contra Costa County, in front of a model home at the brand-new Garin Ranch housing development in Brentwood, Contra Costa County—the first Bay Area county proximate to Napa Valley to have reported a glassy-winged sharpshooter infestation—the movie *Invasion of the Body Snatchers* came to mind. Cathy and her office had just completed a grueling three-week "GWSS delimitation" here. After detailing how the Discovery, Outreach, and Delimitation guidelines of the state's Glassy-Winged Sharpshooter Task Force work out here in reality—with an understaffed team, unfamiliar officials, and environmental protesters (who, she believes, were attracted by TV-news lights) trying to keep residents of the area from cooperating—Cathy agreed that the situation resembled that of the old movie.

"And it was probably because it started in these model homes that nobody noticed. Nobody lives in a model home." Then she got serious: "You know, this isn't the first time we've had Pierce's disease up here. This used to be great almond country. That's why we've got streets like Almond Way in Brentwood. But something brought PD into the almond groves. Killed off the whole industry. All the trees just suddenly dried up. They called it 'Golden-death.'"

California resembles a leg, slightly bent at the knee. South of Los Angeles, down near what increasingly resembles its Achilles' heel, lies Temecula, where the poison arrow first struck. Calls to the vineyardist at Callaway Vineyards, a winery with 740 acres of vines in Temecula, were eventually returned instead by a corporate spokesman hundreds of miles away (Callaway is owned by the British global conglomerate Allied Domecq), who told me that Callaway was "tired of being the poster boy for Pierce's disease." He said Callaway had plenty of other sources for grapes elsewhere from which to make wine until "this Pierce's thing is over." Apparently, the publicity Callaway got from its initial, cooperative attitude toward the press had turned on them: "poster boy" calls to mind a picture of a cripple, a useful image for charitable fund-raising but not for commercial sales.

Temecula lies halfway between Los Angeles and San Diego, at the juncture of two big highways. The first impression it gives is of new housing, housing starts, and land being bulldozed for housing. There are so many developments that a new sort of street sign hangs there, listing vertically the names of adjacent subdivisions: Chardonnay Hills, the Vineyard, Temeka Hills, Redhawk Vista, Vintage Reserve, and so on. WINE COUNTRY signs direct visitors through one development after another to a comparatively minute reach of vineyards and orange groves running toward the eastern hills. At Callaway Vineyards the fragrance of the crush was in the air. The vineyards looked patchy, but they had produced a record crop. "It hops around, you know?" a worker told me about the disease. "Some looks all right and then, right next to it, every-thing dead." For most of these vines, though, this abundant crop of 2000 would be their last.

Temecula provides an ominous model for the Napa Valley: an agricultural region is discovered to be hospitable to wine grapes. The charm of such a pretty place with such interesting agriculture and its proximity to jobs attracts real-estate development. Land-scaping for the new subdivisions carries in the glassy-winged sharp-shooters. The bugs poke stylets infected with Pierce's disease into the vines. Because there is no cure for PD—and because even if one were to be found in the next couple of years, the years more you would have to add on for a crop to grow and begin to pay interest on your outstanding loans would inexorably bankrupt these vineyards—Callaway is not replanting here. They have even changed the name of their otherwhere-sourced product to Call-away "Coastal" wines. As it was in Anaheim, so it is in Temecula. The place moves on to other uses. Temecula's final fate is already ravenously apparent: subdivisions. Like the Temecula Indians, who have been moved off their old territory, the very fine wine industry once growing on this ground that inspired such monikers as Chardonnay Hills and Vintage Reserve Estates may soon sur-vive only as names on local road signs.

In the Napa Valley this fall day, ladled by rain-gorged blue-green hills under cobalt blue skies, the yellow-leafed vineyards run like molten gold. The air is deliciously fragrant with the crush of grapes from a spectacular harvest. Not just prosperity is abound-ing but more real wealth than even financiers ever imagined. But driving up here from nearby San Francisco, after marveling at the views and maybe even lowering a tinted window to take in a breath of the delicious, grape-smoked air, people with land up this way are looking anxiously at their road maps. The spraying Cathy Roybal commanded was right next door in Contra Costa County. They say a glassy-winged sharpshooter was actually found in Sonoma. The map shows how inexorably the thing is moving up from way down there at the bottom of California, clear down the state at Temecula.

The state capitol in Sacramento has in its park one of the greatest stands of mature trees I've seen anywhere in the world. English elms there have achieved redwood specifications. There's a magnolia the size of a 200-year-old oak. The wonderful plantation set down in the 1880s gleams with health and majesty. It reminds you how California can apparently grow anything, with stupendous success. Across the street on October 26, in a state office building theater, the California Department of Food and Agriculture convened an open hearing to discuss the terrible danger to such fecundity from a new pest, the glassy-winged sharpshooter. The Title 3 Emergency Regulations pertaining to the Pierce's Disease Control Program (the action enabling the spraying of the infected subdivision in Contra Costa County) were to be discussed in an open forum. The format was five-minute speeches from interested parties. The venue brought together the preponderantly male representatives of the grape and nursery industries and a preponderantly female opposition to the "delimitation." The women spoke first.

Their props and catchphrases (one set up a tripod to videotape herself at the podium, another held with a practiced grip a poster of a child with what looked to me like a case of impetigo captioned IS YOUR WINE WORTH THIS? and another surrounded herself with SCENT FREE ZONE signs) announced that they represented groups with names like Central Coast Canaries, the Ad Hoc Committee for Clean Water, and Mothers Against Toxics. They seemed, at worst, to be veteran protesters on a well-worn environmental circuit. At best they had a point. The financial might of huge investment inevitably muscles out planning, zoning, and permit perspectives. A monoculture like the wine industry distorts the environment its way.

"How do we know this isn't just another scam being run by the big chemical and genetic-engineering industries, to get even more of our taxpayer dollars laundered through their buddies at the big universities, to cook up more toxic chemicals to poison us so they can get bigger, more synthetic yields and make more money?" they asked. "Why must taxpayers pay for corporate welfare?"

They have a point. To me, the problem seemed not so much their message as their image. At its most ludicrous, protest has become a kind of wolf-crying vaudeville circuit. Magick ("that's with a 'k,' she advised the recording secretary) said she spoke for the bacterium, which we had no right to call a pest. She allowed as how she had channeled the voices of the grapes down at Temecula. They had explained to her that they were shriveling up in an act of civil disobedience to protest the war declared against glassy-winged sharpshooters. Magick was well enough turned out to suggest that she was either a handsomely rewarded agent provocateuse fielded to make protest look silly or an authentic member of another powerful, unspoken element of the protest sector, Environmentalists with Trust Funds. Although Magick looked like she was ready to channel other voices in other rooms where demonstration news might be being made, the ominous questions of aftereffects from our synthetic alterations of agriculture are at issue here.

"Everybody blames us! Back when this started, the growers shook hands and said they'd help us with this problem. But they just got $40 million to help with their emergency and we are hurting and they aren't showing us a penny," complained Jim Poorbaugh, who was representing the huge Monrovia Nurseries. After describing the impossible tasks landed on nurseries by emergency-alerted politicians who had no idea what it was like to run a business, he finished on a hopeful note: "Long-term, crises never turn out as bad as they seem."

"If we can land a man on the moon, we can beat this pest," Phil Larocca, a grower who oversees 5,000 organic acres of wine grapes, said just as hopefully. One such hope is a Mexican wasp successfully released in five countries, where it seemed to enjoy sharpshooter eggs in its *desayuno de huevos rancheros*. The problem is time. Sharpshooter *huevos* appear on the entomological menu only twice a year. Not that many wasps exist yet. Can anything be found before the glassy-winged sharpshooter gets to Napa, where there is plenty of long-resident PD waiting to be spread around those world-class vineyards?

While the nurserymen are facing the problem of their deliveries being throttled by emergency regulations, the growers are facing extinction. In Sacramento the growers brought no props and weren't angry. They were deeply, sleeplessly, white-knuckle worried. Most of them only wanted everything anyone could think of to be done as quickly and massively as humanly possible to keep the glassy-winged sharpshooter at bay. As it had once upon a time with phylloxera, time might bring a solution, a cure, a resistant vine, a sharpshooter predator—the kind of miracle science has pulled off so often, at least in the movies. Otherwise, inevitably, the glassy-winged sharpshooter will spread Pierce's disease in Napa and Sonoma the way it has in Temecula. America's world-class wine will go down like cotton to the boll weevil. The Napa and Sonoma valleys will become just more bedroom hives for Bay Area employment opportunity.

County commissioners and other agricultural officials spoke of their efforts to halt the spread of the GWSS infestations. One of the more ironic problems they encountered was the result of prosperity: the effect of high employment on the availability of temporary staff. Initially, there simply weren't enough clerks available to process the paperwork necessary to orchestrate the $40 million of declared emergency funds.

As Peter Newton, of the Napa Valley's highly sophisticated Newton Vineyards, pointed out to me, not only are the growers and vintners of Napa rich; they mainly got that way as savvy and determined business veterans who have won a global reputation. Of course, they are ready to defend their deep and famous interests here, by whatever means they must.

The spraying chemicals carbaryl and chlorpyrifos are both on the Pesticide Action Network's list of "California Bad Actor Pesticides." The rest of the agents that might be used to gas the alien insects from the American Southeast are almost equally notorious. If it comes to spraying, a confrontation between corporate strategists and furious domestic protesters will ignite TV screens across the country.

What the vintners fear almost as much as GWSS is not protesters but lawyers questioning the Title 3 Emergency Regulations adopted for the Pierce's Disease Control Program. Growers dread the possibility that, if legal hearings started to measure the private against the public good, the rights of homeowners to refuse access, and the aftereffects of the sort of pesticide spraying managed in Contra Costa County, the glassy-winged sharpshooter would not obligingly suspend its biology to await the outcome.

During the next hearing, a regional one at the Napa Valley's Charles Krug winery that was important enough to bring Bill Lyons, the state of California's secretary of agriculture, just such a possibility turned up. The local prince of trust-funded environmentalists, Peter Mennen (of the underarm Mennens, fresh from a victorious lawsuit that has effectively stopped the planting of hillside vineyards, despite the consensus that in the Napa Valley hillside vines make the very best wines), drew glares. Sitting with him was his notorious cat's-paw, Napa Sierra Club political officer Chris Malan. Perhaps because she had just drawn a letter of disavowal from her own club for calling grape growers "alcohol farmers" at the Sacramento hearing, Malan left the speaking to her patron. In the faded blue cotton and long gray hair of a retired folksinger, Mennen first challenged the glaring growers by asking if this were really a public meeting. They scowled and vibrated. Then he assured them that the glassy-winged sharpshooter was not going away. They gurgled with rage. Then he asked why taxpayers were paying to kill nature. In a coat and tie, the beefy secretary of agriculture made a carnivorous contrast to the reedy heir. Beaming, he walked protectively near Mennen and reminded the room how respectful they must remain of one another. When others spoke, Mennen and Malan, apparently present to impart but not to gather information, left.

Is the mighty monoculture of the wine industry worth spraying to preserve? Are the environmentalists unintentionally inviting in their own worst enemy, housing, by opposing spraying here? Will the battle over spraying end up in court? The townships of Sonoma, Sebastopol, and Windsor already have issued bans on any chemical spraying. Will such local legislation hold up against a statewide agriculture emergency?

In winter, the glassy-winged sharpshooter sleeps. The extent of its northern migration is about to become clear. The hopeful say it's just too cold up in northern California for the GWSS. The pessimists point out that the bug has been discovered in Oregon, where it's been living for over a year. How long the glassy-winged sharpshooter can be kept at bay, how long it will take to control, and what protest can do to limit the weaponry used in the forthcoming war against it will soon become apparent.

When phylloxera devastated California's first wine industry, fifteen years passed before a solution was found. If a true agricultural Armageddon kills or maims our current California wine industry badly enough, would we have that kind of time to wait? Will the rest of the world be able to keep Pierce's disease out? Australia has just announced a scientifically useless, if public-relations friendly, ban on the importation of California table grapes (glassy-winged sharpshooters don't occupy grapes; they prevent grapes from forming). I asked Dr. Purcell, the UC Berkeley expert, if Pierce's disease had ever turned up in Europe. "Yes," he said. "It has been reported and confirmed in Europe. PD is in Kosovo. You can find all the details on my Web site."

If too many cooks spoil the broth, many of the products from the world's best-known companies should leave a sour taste in our mouths. "Parent" companies farm out so much of their work to suppliers these days that it's increasingly difficult to determine who made what. Kerry A. Dolan and Robyn Meredith of *Forbes* peel away the labels and let us take a peek behind them. Their research draws into question the time-honored tradition of paying more for brand names.

Kerry A. Dolan and Robyn Meredith

Ghost Cars, Ghost Brands

SOME FAMOUS ENTREPRENEURS failed spectacularly trying to start car companies from scratch. Preston Tucker brought out the Tucker in 1946 and went bankrupt three years later. John DeLorean had his gull-wing sports car and failed in 1982. Henry J. Kaiser could produce his beloved Henry J. only from 1952 until 1954.

Now Robert A. Lutz, the former vice chairman of Chrysler and a thirty-five-year veteran of the auto industry, has started Cunningham Motor Co. He aims to deliver a sexy sports coupe with a 600 hp engine and a $250,000 price tag sometime in 2004. The car will be called the Cunningham C-7, after America's postwar racing legend, Briggs Cunningham, Jr., whose son is Lutz's partner. Lutz is showing off a prototype now and is rounding up venture capital.

Does Lutz have a prayer of succeeding? He does because, unlike those other three would-be carmakers, he will put not a penny into a factory. Cunningham Motor will farm out production to some outsider, most likely a car-parts maker. The design, engineering, and even most of the retailing will be contracted out. Lutz, an ex-Marine who flies fighter jets for fun, plans just twenty employees for a company with targeted annual revenue of $100 million.

"Cunningham will be the world's most virtually integrated car company," says Lutz. His role is more movie producer than manufacturing mogul: "You have the idea for the movie. You give them the money, and you've signed off on the script."

Times have changed since Henry Ford made the River Rouge complex in Dearborn, Michigan, into the ultimate in vertical integration, with iron ore going in at one end and shiny Model As coming out the other. Now vertical dis-integration is the order of the day—in autos, in handheld computers, in pharmaceuticals, in ink-jet printers, in health foods, in cameras. The company with the brand name or a clever marketing idea isn't necessarily the one with the factory. Why put capital into a factory when you can put it into something much more valuable—like a brand?

The whole personal-computer era can be seen as one giant triumph of dis-integration, as IBM's circuit-boards-to-boxes-to-software mainframe business gave way to the layered computer industry we see today: Intel making the electronics, Dell the boxes, and Microsoft the software. Taking this dis-integration a step further, many firms selling electronic appliances are outsourcing large chunks of their manufacturing. Lucent Technology is handing off $8 billion worth of its manufacturing to outside parties, about 45 percent of its output. Rival Cisco Systems, though it does have four of its own factories, was committed from its infancy to going outside. Now all of its subassembly manufacturing and 42 percent of final assembly of its switches and routers are done by a variety of the largest contract manufacturers. Nearly 80 percent of Kodak's reloadable cameras and all of its digital cameras are sourced in Asia.

Compaq Computer makes only about 10 percent of the computers it sells to consumers. It relies on an outside provider to field a chunk of its customer service calls and had a Taiwanese firm, HTC, help design its iPaq pocket computer. Nearly all of Hewlett-Packard's printers are made by someone else. So are the majority of HP's calculators, PC's, and low-end servers. The company even outsources some of its sales and marketing efforts. Engineering is what defines this company, not workers in hair nets picking tiny screws out of parts bins. Says Corey Billington, vice president for HP's sourcing: "We don't think we gain competitive advantage by driving forklifts faster."

Outsourcing has been around for a while—witness the Coca-Cola Co., which has for decades enjoyed a particularly handsome return on capital because it has outsourced the machinery-intensive bottling work to other entities. Yet there is no mistaking the trend. Whereas the twentieth century was one in which vertically integrated companies were powerful, the twenty-first is the century of virtual companies. But why? Why is it that so many manufacturers have recently taken a dislike to factory work? There are three reasons.

One is that, to a degree that was not true in Henry Ford's day, the money is in the brands, not in the machinery. Hewlett-Packard's tangible book value—its factories, inventories, and receivables, minus liabilities—is $14.5 billion. Its market value is $58 billion, four times as much. Wall Street is saying that engineering, brand recognition, and other intangibles are together worth three times as much as assets you can see and touch. The phenomenon is not peculiar to this company. The ratio of price to tangible book value for the S&P 500 is 7.1; that is six times what the ratio was in 1979, according to Standard & Poors.

Next reason for the growth of outsourcing: globalization. No surprise that contract manufacturers for electronic gear have sprung up in Malaysia and China, where skill levels are high but labor costs only one-fourth what it does in the United States. In Detroit the outsourcing may begin with a transfer of work from a unionized big-three plant (total labor cost, more than $53 an hour) to a unionized but economically weaker parts company (where the UAW can extract only $26 an hour). The next stage is the shift of work to Mexico ($2.50 an hour). GM's former parts-making subsidiary, Delphi, which opened its first plant in Mexico in 1978, now has 55 plants there.

Third reason not to own a factory: only the biggest companies can keep it busy enough. That doesn't explain what Ford Motor is up to, but it definitely explains Cunningham. Lutz hopes to sell 400 of his luxury cars a year; a car a day does not make an efficient assembly line. Hain Celestial, the natural foods outfit, has other manufacturers produce 45 percent of its sales. Revenues total only $400 million spread across 2,500 products, so it needs to go outside to get economies of scale.

Henry Ford made his own tires, steel, and glass. Ford Motor, now running in the other direction, spun off its parts-making operation, Visteon, last summer, then hired that company to supply 25 percent of the 2002 Ford Explorer, including a fully assembled dashboard, the rear axle, the fuel tank, and the carpets. Says Ford chief executive Jacques Nasser: "I don't think a customer minds, as long as the particular component or system is true to the brand values." The Visteon deal shaved off over $1.5 billion of assets. Nasser is putting Ford's capital elsewhere, spending $9 billion to buy just two intangibles, the names Jaguar and Volvo.

General Motors will soon be making just the outside and underbodies of its cars and trucks; it is putting various auto supply companies in charge of the interior of each of its vehicles. Some of GM's 1,100 engineers now working on car interiors will move to desks at suppliers' offices. GM didn't even bother to design and engineer the Chevrolet SSR pickup it will start selling late next year. Instead, it farmed that work out to ASC Inc., a Detroit-area auto supplier that will help train workers at the GM factory where the 15,000 Chevys will be built each year. Workers assembling the Mercedes M-class in Vance, Alabama, build just 20 percent of the sport utility vehicle. The rest comes in big pieces ready-made by suppliers and trucked to the assembly line, where Mercedes workers bolt them on.

In his day job Bob Lutz is chief executive of battery maker Exide, where he is on the other end of the outsourcing movement. Lear, a $14.1 billion auto supplier, has hired Exide to help package its batteries within the interior modules that Lear is selling to automakers. This trend led Exide, with $3 billion in revenue, to design the Exide Select Orbital battery, a battery shaped like a six-pack of beer that can be configured to fit in tight spaces under the hood or inside the vehicle. Another auto supplier, $1.1 billion MSX International, is growing fast by acting more like a consulting firm for the auto industry. It supplies engineers, not camshafts, to the world's automakers and increasingly takes on outsourced projects in the telecommunications and health care industries.

Outsourcing, which once meant mainly the simple offloading of auxiliary activities like groundskeeping, the corporate canteen, or the data processing center, is very different today. It now entails what are—or once were—a business's core activities. "It's a case of the vertical business model dies and another one begins," says Eugene Polistuk, chief executive of Toronto-based Celestica, one of the new breed of contract manufacturers that dominates electronics products.

There has long been a place for private-label or house-brand makers of everything from washing machines to mayonnaise—sometimes the brand companies themselves would peddle excess output that way. But now it's the premium-label products themselves being ghosted. And in technology that's pretty advanced stuff. Swedish telecom giant Ericsson made news in January by opting to farm out an estimated $3 billion worth of mobile phone sets. At the service end Verizon, AT&T, and Sprint now use contract help in some cases to deploy and manage their cellular phone networks.

The surge in outsourcing has made fortunes for shareholders in companies like Solectron in Milpitas, California, and Flextronics International in Singapore. Despite the recent deflation in the technology sector, Solectron's stock—to the delight of finance chief Susan Wang—is up seventyfold since 1990. "We're still in the early stages of growth in manufacturing outsourcing," says Lehman Brothers analyst Louis Miscioscia, who sees the value of outsourced electronics goods more than doubling to $280 billion three years from now. The chief executive of Sweden's Electrolux, Michael Treschow, has told analysts he'd like to get out of building refrigerators, if only there were an independent supplier.

No surprise, many brand-name companies are shy about the fact that they touch their own products so lightly. You don't see Sun Microsystems, Apple Computer, and Gateway as well as food producer and apparel-maker Sara Lee and drug star GlaxoSmithKline—all of which outsource a healthy portion of their production or activities—talking about this aspect of their business. Even companies that are proud of handing off work, like Dell Computer, withhold most details.

In the pharmaceuticals industry outsourcing has become a $30 billion business, according to consulting firm Arthur D. Little. About half that sum goes to manufacturing firms like Greenville, North Carolina–based DSM Catalytica, which offer both chemical ingredients and finished products, including cartons, bottles, and packaging. A good chunk of the rest flows to contract research organizations like Quintiles Transnational in Durham, North Carolina, and Covance in Princeton, New Jersey, which test and market drugs. Quintiles, which had revenues last year of $1.66 billion, manages 9 percent of all the clinical trials done worldwide.

Though generic firms and new companies tend to outsource more than Big Pharma, the practice is growing there, too. Among DSM Catalytica's clients are Pfizer, Merck, and GlaxoSmithKline. Quintiles and Covance both do work for the world's fifty largest drug companies.

One driver is Big Pharma's desire to reduce expenditure on fixed assets. "Imagine you're a big pharmaceutical company with three drugs in late-stage trials and the next year you have none," explains J. P. Morgan H&Q analyst Ken Miller. Expanding or launching capacity in-house involves recruiting, training, and sta-

tioning employees. Quintiles and Covance are there to absorb the
ebb and flow. They cut time to market, too. Whereas it might take
a large pharmaceutical firm eighteen months to recruit 500 patients
for a study, "we do it in six months," says Quintiles chairman Dennis Gillings. That adds one more year that the brand owner can be
selling on a twenty-year patent.

It's no secret that the footwear and apparel sectors contract
widely—working conditions at subcontractors often attract unfavorable notice. For all the sweatshop noise, the rag trade knew this
setup made sense long ago—it never occurred to the Gap to hire
an apparel worker. Nor is it a surprise that companies like Mattel
and Hasbro get most of their toys from outside factories, many in
Asia. But did you know that about half of Samuel Adams beer
comes from contract brewers (and that parent Boston Brewing
produces on contract for two other brands)? And, in the financial
realm, that the company behind PNC and First Union credit cards
is giant MBNA? Cincinnati-based Redox, a virtual detergent-
maker that acquired lesser Procter & Gamble brands like Oxydol
and Biz, relies on contract manufacturers such as Korex in Michigan, which in turn also produces for other big laundry brands.

So-called fabless semiconductor companies—like Altera and
Xilinx—arose in the 1980s to design specialized chips while leaving the wafer line work to all-purpose foundries in Taiwan and
elsewhere. Cisco Systems was a pioneer in fabless electronic gear,
taking advantage of the Internet to connect customer orders directly to the shipping docks of its contract manufacturers. Handspring, the company behind the Visor personal digital assistant,
followed the Cisco model from the start: It has no factories of its
own. None of its employees has any physical contact with products. When orders for Visors come in over the Web site (which is
hosted by yet another firm), the information is fed first to its fulfillment partner, which keeps the inventory, and then directly to
Handspring's contract manufacturers, Flextronics and Solectron,
which also package and ship the product. To make it all work
smoothly, Handspring brought in the contract manufacturers

while designing the Visor. Result: the breakthrough product hit the market only fifteen months after the company was founded.

Leveraging resources? "We're projecting revenues this year of $400 million, and we only have 400 employees," says a Handspring spokesman. "When our chief executive Donna Dubinsky was at Apple Computer, they had 1,500 employees and half the revenue."

But the main reason to outsource is the imperative to do what you do best—what economists call comparative advantage. Fifteen years ago Ericsson was still designing and manufacturing the screws that went into its wireless phones. "Nobody would imagine doing anything like that today," asserts Björn Boström, Ericsson's senior vice president of supply and data processing. Of course not. Spend too much time on screws and some competitor will score a hit with a cooler handset.

Henry Ford happened to be a manufacturing genius, but he was not particularly adept at judging customers' needs. What's Bob Lutz good at? He has a wizard's touch for marketing, he has impeccable taste in cars, and he is so well connected in the auto industry he can tap into whatever talent he needs. Factory layouts are for someone else to worry about.

Stock fraud is inherently complex and therefore difficult to investigate and prosecute. This story by Susan Harrigan of *Newsday* traces one of history's largest scams all the way back to the chance meeting of its two masterminds. With a story line worthy of *The Sting*, it describes the hatching of the scheme, the fleecing of the naive victims, the extravagant lifestyles made possible by ill-gotten gains, and the government's strategy to put an end to it all. It sounds a familiar warning to investors: some investments are too good to be true.

Susan Harrigan

Castles Made of Sand

CASTLES MADE OF SAND

THE FOUNDERS OF THE BIGGEST, most infamous stock "boiler room" in recent history met when they rushed to help a child who had fallen off a playground slide at the Bay Club condominiums in Bayside.

Jordan Belfort and Daniel Porush, who both lived at the Bay Club, fell into conversation on that Sunday in December 1988, and Belfort soon mentioned that he was making $50,000 a month selling small stocks at Investors Center, a brokerage in Hauppauge.

"That was over ten times more than I was making," Porush said later. Within two days, he visited Investors Center, thought, "I can do this," closed his own ambulette service business, and went to work with Belfort.

The pair would go on to create Stratton Oakmont, a Lake Success–based brokerage that cheated thousands of individuals out of about $250 million, spawned "rogue" brokers who spread its methods to other firms, exposed holes in the nation's safety net for investors, and made a mockery of securities regulators who tried to stop it.

When Stratton opened in early 1989, Belfort and Porush decided almost immediately that "nothing worked but fraud," Belfort said. So the pair concocted a sophisticated scheme to inflate the prices of stocks and sweep the profits into their own pockets, financing what they called a "broker Disneyland" that included mansions, a yacht, golf at world-class courses, and dazzling parties featuring charcoal pits full of lobster tails.

But their sunlit existence hid a darker reality. Both brokers used drugs heavily, and Belfort injured his wife and risked hurting his daughter during one drug-fueled incident.

Richard Walker, director of enforcement for the U.S. Securities and Exchange Commission, said he was "humbled" by the seven years it took to close Stratton, which hired top legal talent to fight the civil penalties that are the mainstay of the nation's system of stock regulation.

"The big lesson is that vigorous criminal enforcement is critical to stopping these things," Walker said. "The civil regulatory process takes too long."

But developing a criminal case against Belfort and Porush took a long time, too. Protected by a tight-knit group of friends and associates, they weren't arrested until September 1998, almost two years after Stratton closed. They have pleaded guilty to stock fraud and international money laundering.

Now the two men, who have remained mysterious figures despite Stratton's notoriety, are telling their stories in court as star witnesses for the prosecution in the trials of several alleged Stratton accomplices.

From testimony, as well as interviews and documents, *Newsday* has pieced together the first detailed account of how two middle-class men from Queens and Long Island took advantage of naive investors flooding into the great bull market of the 1990s to build Gatsby-esque lives of lavish parties, travel, and expensive toys—only to see it all undermined by their own overwhelming avarice and dishonesty.

Becoming an honest businessman "was something that was always in my mind, every day," Belfort said. "I was too greedy to stop."

In coming months, the credibility of Belfort and Porush will be vital to deciding whether a number of people, including one of America's most prominent footwear designers, go to jail. In an unprecedented effort to prosecute alleged insiders in small-stock schemes, the government has accused four people, including Steven Madden, founder of Long Island City–based Steven Madden Ltd., of helping the two ex-brokers commit fraud.

The trial of another alleged Stratton accomplice, New Jersey accountant Dennis Gaito, ended in a hung jury in November. Gaito is to be retried in April, and Madden's trial is scheduled for May. The other individuals accused of helping Belfort and Porush are Harry Shuster, former head of the company that operates Grand Havana cigar clubs, who will be tried in July, and Elliot Lavigne, a former fashion executive, for whom no trial date has been set. All have pleaded innocent.

Although prosecutors say it's common to use admitted felons as witnesses, some defense attorneys say Belfort and Porush aren't believable by juries. The two are hoping to mitigate prison sentences that could total more than twenty years, and by their own admission they are chronic liars. "We lied to stockbrokers. We lied to customers. I lied to the government when being investigated. We lied to each other," Belfort said at the Gaito trial.

The two men have lost their families, their friendship, and their golden business touch. While awaiting sentencing, Belfort has been running a troubled nutritional-products business. Porush sells sports memorabilia.

Beyond their testimony in the Gaito trial, neither would comment for this story. Gregory O'Connell, an attorney who represents Belfort, said his client "deeply regrets his wrongdoing," which caused "a catastrophe in his life." Charles Stillman, a lawyer for Porush, said the ex-broker feels "great remorse" for what he did during "a bad stage in his life."

PRINCES OF "PUMP AND DUMP"

People who are familiar with the reputations of Belfort and Porush and meet them for the first time have sometimes commented with surprise that the two look like choirboys. It's a reference to their relatively slight statures and youthful looks, but also to the fact that they resemble what they are—two products of the American mainstream.

Belfort, thirty-eight, is dark-haired, baritone-voiced, and possessed of considerable charm in contrast to the light-haired, sandy-voiced, and more brusque Porush. The son of two accountants, Belfort was born and raised in Bayside, attended Bayside High School, and graduated with a major in biology from American University in Washington, D.C.

After dropping out of the Baltimore College of Dentistry after three months, Belfort worked as a meat salesman and then owned and ran Manchester Farms Meat and Seafood Co., a now-defunct Woodside-based business that delivered its products door-to-door. But he expanded too quickly, declared personal bankruptcy, and in 1987 began working at a series of brokerages that sold small stocks.

Porush, whose father is a doctor, was born in Brooklyn. He grew up in Lawrence and graduated from Woodmere Academy in 1975. The inscription under his senior class yearbook picture paraphrases Mae West—"Whenever I have to choose between the better of two evils, I choose the one I haven't tried yet." After attending Dickinson College and Boston University for a total of four years and a summer, Porush left without a degree, worked as a courier, and had just started an ambulette service when he met Belfort.

After Investors Center closed, Belfort and Porush used space in a friend's car dealership to open a branch of the firm that eventually became Stratton Oakmont, using customer leads stolen from their previous employer. By late 1989, they and a partner who had worked in Belfort's meat business had purchased the parent brokerage and relocated to an office building on Marcus Avenue in Lake Success.

Belfort said he and Porush quickly realized they couldn't succeed honestly. "My expertise was in sales. I didn't know how to trade stocks, or find and structure deals," he said. "It was a very seedy world in the over-the-counter [stock] market. . . . People popped out of the woodwork" suggesting dishonest deals.

Working with small firms that they found or that were referred to them by acquaintances and promoters, the two men perfected a fraudulent technique of bringing companies public. Stratton became what John Coffee, a Columbia University securities law professor, called "the best-known example in history of a pump-and-dump scheme."

Such a scheme requires getting control of the supply of a stock being offered to investors so that no one will sell too early and thereby lower the price. Then the firm artificially increases demand and runs the price up (the pump) by having hundreds of salespeople call investors all over the country and make false promises about the stock's performance.

Once the price rises, insiders sell out (the dump) and leave the public holding nearly worthless shares.

FLIPPERS, RATHOLES, BIG SHOTS

Stratton achieved control of a stock's supply partly by selling a huge chunk of each company's initial public offering, or IPO, to three types of insiders it called "flippers," "ratholes," and "big shots." Most had secret arrangements about when they would sell, which are illegal under U.S. securities laws.

Flippers were individuals who bought stock in an offering with a secret agreement that they would sell it back to Stratton immediately after trading opened, for a profit of about 25 percent.

Ratholes, also called nominees, were people who bought stock at the low offering price as fronts for Belfort and Porush, who were, as Stratton principals, forbidden by securities laws to invest in their own IPOs. Later, after the price had been manipulated as high as possible, the nominees would sell out for a high price on the public market and split the profits with Belfort and Porush. Stratton offerings frequently doubled in price, or better, before such selling took place.

Big shots included golf pros, restaurant owners, friends, family members, and others for whom the brokers wanted to do favors. Also called "preferred clients," they sold on the public market at a higher price than flippers but at a lower price than ratholes.

Stratton's creators also controlled the supply of stock in public offerings by allowing some friends and acquaintances to make loans to companies they were bringing public. The loans were convertible into stock, which ostensibly was subject to "lockup" agreements that it couldn't be sold for a substantial period of time without Stratton's consent. In fact, the lenders already had secret agreements to sell the stock back to Stratton within days or hours after an offering, prosecutors said.

Federal prosecutors have accused Steven Madden and Elliot Lavigne of acting as flippers, nominees, and lenders who violated securities laws in domestic stock manipulations by Stratton. Porush also said at the Gaito trial that the "big shots" in Stratton offerings included a number of executives at Steven Madden Ltd. Participating in Stratton offerings "was part of the package at Steven Madden," Porush said. "It was a nice enticement to join his firm."

Steven Madden Ltd. declined to comment on Porush's statement, and no one else at the company has been charged.

Once a huge chunk of a stock offering had been disbursed to

insiders, hundreds of salespeople in a large room at Stratton called "the boardroom" sold the rest to outside investors, using high-pressure sales tactics and scripts containing fraudulent statements to drive up the price.

A number of former Stratton brokers and cold-callers (people who call strangers), some of them quite young at the time, said they didn't know they were violating securities laws. Belfort and Porush testified that only a few brokers knew Stratton controlled the stocks' supply.

The scene in the boardroom was pure bedlam, according to people who witnessed it. With no space between desks, "guys were on top of one another," said one investor who arrived at Stratton unannounced. "It was like a sweatshop."

Brokers and cold-callers stood on their desks and screamed into telephone headsets. The noise was "so bad you thought you were in the middle of the Chicago Stockyards," one former Stratton broker said.

Before every offering, Belfort and Porush appeared in the boardroom to whip up enthusiasm and urge salespeople not to take no for an answer.

"They were powerful speakers and had golden tongues," said one former Stratton broker, who didn't want to be named. "They wore thousand-dollar suits. They'd stand in front of the boardroom with microphones and feed us a line you wouldn't believe. They'd say, 'This is broker Disneyland. People are only coming after us because they're jealous.'"

"The common saying at Stratton was 'deal and burn,'" said a former Stratton cold-caller. "The guys on the phone were taught to lie. . . . I personally pushed a Kentucky guy into a deal simply by yelling at him during my second week." To build up their aggression, he said, brokers and cold-callers would break baseball bats in half and wrestle, sometimes throwing each other across the room. Supervisors would tell cold-callers that the people on the other end of the line were "all big [rich] and all in the market."

Stratton also motivated brokers by paying them big bonuses

on sales of stocks it wanted to pump. "There were nineteen-year-old guys in the room with no education, with $100,000 to $200,000 in their pocket . . . who owned five or six exotic cars," the former cold-caller said.

Stratton's frenzied sales tactics succeeded partly because of a middle-American fascination with stocks, and especially IPOs, that developed as the bull market gathered steam in the early 1990s, said Joseph Borg, Alabama securities commissioner and head of a multistate task force that investigated the brokerage. "They were really ahead of their time seeing the trend of Americans getting into the markets," Borg said of Stratton's creators.

Belfort said it was so easy to sell IPOs that he got a speeding ticket dropped in 1990 by telling a policeman he owned a brokerage firm. "He agreed to forget the tickets if I would make him money in the stock market," Belfort said. "He then told a couple of his friends about it, and about four police officers ended up opening accounts at Stratton Oakmont and receiving new issues, making money."

PITS FULL OF LOBSTER TAILS

All those investor dollars supported lifestyles for Stratton's two top honchos that at times seemed to resemble scenes from the 1987 movie *Wall Street.*

Belfort, who made at least $50 million from Stratton during its seven-year-life, held parties for employees at his home in the Hamptons that one former Stratton worker said were "kind of like a teaser—all this could be yours if you work hard." People who attended said Belfort served gourmet food, including caviar and pits full of lobster tails, dispensed unlimited top-shelf liquor, and offered swimming in his pool and at a nearby beach.

Belfort owned a Westhampton home that he bought for about $1 million and later sold, and a Southampton property for which he paid $5.5 million. His main residence was a gated mansion on several acres in Old Brookville. When he turned over the Old Brookville and Southampton properties to the government in 1998, Belfort said they were worth a combined $11 million.

His fleet of cars included a Mercedes-Benz, a Porsche, and a Ferrari. He was driven to work in a limousine, complete with a bar and television set. He wore a Bulgari watch, and his wife, Nadine, a former model, had accumulated so much jewelry that she was able to turn over more than $800,000 worth of it to help make his 1998 bail.

Then there was something even the *Wall Street* character Gordon Gekko didn't have—a 166-foot-long motor yacht originally built for the French designer Coco Chanel and remodeled by a Texas millionaire before Belfort bought it in 1993. It had a helicopter, seaplane, kayaks, personal watercraft, and a trapshooting gun used for shooting at clay pigeons. After it sank in the Mediterranean in 1996, Lloyd's of London, the yacht's insurer, paid Belfort between $6 million and $7 million.

Porush, who said he made about $30 million from Stratton frauds, led a slightly less ostentatious, but still affluent, life. He owned a home in Oyster Bay Cove, a house on Dune Road in Westhampton Beach, and a condominium in Palm Beach, Florida. Like Belfort, he had a taste for expensive cars, driving at least two Mercedes-Benzes, two BMWs, a Porsche, and a Bentley.

For all the possessions, loose money was plentiful. Belfort, who kept money in sock drawers as well as a safe, regularly ordered $100 bottles of wine and once bought Gaito, the accountant, a $5,000 bottle. One ex-employee said that as a prank, Belfort offered colleagues $10,000 if they would shave their heads. And Porush told federal investigators that while the yacht was sinking, Belfort, who was on board with his wife, called and told him there was between $5 million and $10 million buried in the yard of his Old Brookville home that Porush could use to take care of Belfort's children. Belfort denied burying any money.

The two men took lavish trips. One, on a chartered jet paid for by Stratton, included a stopover in Scotland and golf at two world-famous courses, Turnberry and Troon, on summer days when it was light until midnight. Belfort once rented all of Castle Ashby, a twenty-six-bedroom manor in Northamptonshire, England, to house friends and family members during a vacation. He also took brokers on gambling trips to Las Vegas and Atlantic City.

And remembering the less fortunate, in January 1992, Stratton gave $100,000 to a child-abuse prevention center in Woodmere. "Anybody that has a business on Long Island and is successful has an obligation to give something back," Belfort told *Newsday* at the time.

THE S.E.C. AND THE GOLDEN CROWBAR

But cracks were developing in Stratton's facade. In March 1992 the Securities and Exchange Commission filed suit in federal court in Manhattan accusing Stratton and some of its principals, including Porush and Belfort, of abusive sales practices, market manipulation, and unauthorized trades.

Instead of settling the charges and paying a fine, as most brokerages do in such a situation, Stratton embarked on an odyssey of delay and litigation. It hired top legal talent and fought the charges until February 1994 when, on the brink of a court trial, it finally settled with the agency without admitting wrongdoing.

Although it had originally demanded $11 million, the S.E.C. settled for $2.6 million from Stratton and fined Belfort, Porush, and another principal $100,000 each. It also permanently barred Belfort from the securities business, forbade Porush from acting as a supervisor for a year, and ordered the firm to hire an S.E.C.-approved independent consultant to review its operations and recommend changes.

The result: Stratton had its "best year ever" in 1994, according to Porush, turning out seven more manipulated initial public offerings between February and the end of the year. "We came out just great," Porush said. "In our minds, we won." Despite his bar from the securities industry, Belfort spoke to Porush every day and approved all deals.

The S.E.C. consultant, Carl Loewenson, Jr., didn't have the power to subpoena records or compel testimony, and Stratton personnel deliberately misled him. One former Stratton employee said he and other salespeople would simply sweep everything incriminating off their desks and watch their language whenever Loewenson and other S.E.C. personnel walked in. The minute they left, it was business as usual.

"The leader would go to the front [of the room] and say, 'We've got more money than they make in a year,'" the former Stratton employee said. "There was disrespect for the S.E.C."

At the request of Stratton Oakmont, a federal judge ordered most of Loewenson's report to be kept sealed until last fall, when it was made public at the request of attorneys for Harry Shuster, one of the alleged Stratton accomplices. According to the report, Loewenson noticed violations including "flipping" agreements, sales scripts containing illegal price predictions, and a cold-caller verbally abusing a customer by saying, "You have two ears to listen and one mouth to talk. Why don't you shut up and listen?"

The report also noted that the supervisor who was supposed to make sure brokers complied with securities laws had been named in at least twenty-two customer complaints, more than twice as many as the broker with the next-highest number.

It was "troubling," the report said, that hanging on the wall behind that supervisor's desk was a "Golden Crowbar" award. Among stock fraud perpetrators, to "crowbar" someone means to deliberately spoil their trade.

Before settling with the S.E.C., Porush and Belfort had agreed to a noncompete agreement under which Stratton would pay Belfort $180 million, in equal monthly payments of $1 million, for fifteen years. Because the two had known at the time that Belfort would be barred from the securities industry and thus unable to compete, the agreement was a sham and "simply a way to funnel illegal profits to me," Belfort said.

The duo also had developed a new business plan. While Porush ran the firm's day-to-day operations, Belfort would find new ways for the two of them to make money.

Belfort was interested in running Dollar Time, a Hollywood, Florida, company he controlled that owned dozens of variety stores selling items for $1.

"For me, being in the fraud business, it was enticing to actually try to have a legitimate business," Belfort said. In 1994, he came back to Stratton as a Dollar Time executive for a "road show" designed to whip up broker enthusiasm for selling the company's stock. "He was a legend to the brokers, so they got all excited," Porush said.

But Belfort said he soon realized that "someone defrauded me" at Dollar Time. He said someone connected with the company "looted" it but he covered up the theft because "the S.E.C. might think I took it." Eventually, he said, he lost $1.5 million he had invested in Dollar Time along with as much as $2 million invested by his friends.

Ultimately, Dollar Time was to cause more grief for Belfort and Porush. A money-laundering scheme involving that company was the Achilles' heel that allowed another two-man team—an FBI agent with a penchant for making charts and a Brooklyn prosecutor with European connections—to arrest the two Stratton principals on charges so serious that they turned state's witnesses.

For now, however, Belfort became interested in making B movies. In early 1995 he moved to Los Angeles to be a producer, working with Shuster and one of Shuster's sons in a film company they ran. Their output, which went quickly to video, included *Santa with Muscles* (with Dan Porush listed as executive producer) and *Secret Agent Club,* both starring Hulk Hogan. In addition to producing, Belfort tried his hand at writing and editing scripts.

SETTING UP SATELLITES

On April 19, 1995, Belfort was back in New York for a meeting at Millie's Place restaurant in Great Neck to discuss a growing crisis at Stratton.

In the summer of 1994, Loewenson, the S.E.C. consultant, had issued his recommendations, which included tape-recording all of Stratton's conversations with customers and eliminating the bonuses it paid brokers for selling certain stocks. But Stratton astonished regulators by refusing to comply. Its lawyer, Ira L. Sorkin, said the recommendations were "impractical and irresponsible" and may have violated the S.E.C.'s original order.

Stratton's defiance forced the S.E.C. into the lengthy process of obtaining a court order to make Stratton adopt the new procedures. In January 1995 a federal judge issued a preliminary injunction requiring the brokerage to comply with the S.E.C.'s order. In March, the judge issued a permanent injunction against Stratton, triggering automatic delicensing proceedings in a number of states.

Partly because of publicity surrounding the battle with regulators, Stratton's liabilities were soaring as a result of numerous investor complaints. By the end of 1995, the amount of money being demanded in arbitration against the firm had risen to $30 million, nearly triple the amount two years earlier.

By the time Belfort, Porush, and a few advisers sat down at Millie's Place, "the handwriting was on the wall," Belfort said. "The days of Stratton were definitely numbered. So Porush and I agreed to close Stratton's doors and . . . cockroach."

Cockroaching meant setting up satellite firms, moving as many Stratton brokers there as possible, and continuing to cheat investors. "If someone turns on the light in a dark room, they scatter," Porush said. "You live on vicariously."

Shortly after the meeting, however, Porush changed his mind and embarked on an eighteen-month battle to keep Stratton open.

"I had a lot of friends that worked there and a lot of money tied up in the place," he said. "I was fighting to the bitter end to survive."

Porush said he spent much of his time trying to make arrangements and deals with various state regulators. But he still managed to manipulate eight more stock offerings. And the National Association of Securities Dealers, a broker trade group and self-policing organization, said in a later complaint against Stratton that even though its sales calls were being recorded, supervisors allowed or even encouraged brokers to engage in fraud. Some brokers were recorded touting questionable stocks without discussing the risks, refusing to honor customer sell orders, and making illegal price predictions.

"I'm telling you right now the stock will be around $18 to $25 per share," one broker said on a tape reviewed by the NASD. "I think it's the best growth company right now, period, end of story, on the NASDAQ."

While Porush was struggling to keep Stratton open, Belfort was betraying him by "shorting" Stratton offerings because he thought—wrongly, he said—that Porush had gone behind his back in some business dealings. Belfort said he made hundreds of thousands of dollars through the shorting, which involves selling borrowed stock in hopes of a price drop.

In December 1996 the NASD finally expelled Stratton from the industry, effectively closing its doors. The specific cause cited was overcharging customers in a 1993 offering. That complaint had been filed in late 1995 and early 1996, one of twelve the NASD brought against Stratton during its existence.

Asked why it took so long to close Stratton, Barry Goldsmith, executive vice president of the NASD's enforcement arm, said it was time-consuming to develop the kind of serious and complex case that would result in a Stratton ban. Also, he said, Stratton was expert at delaying regulators with litigation and offers of settlement.

"Today, all the regulators are far less tolerant of the kind of action Stratton was engaged in," Goldsmith said. "We all learned a little bit from them."

By the time Stratton was closed, seven states, including New Jersey, had revoked its brokerage license, and numerous others were close to settlements severely restricting its operations. But New York State, which could have put Stratton out of business by delicensing it, didn't do so. Unlike many other jurisdictions, New York law requires regulators to file a civil suit to lift a license, rather than providing an administrative procedure.

"I ALMOST KILLED MY DAUGHTER"

After Stratton closed, Porush opened a small office in Great Neck and looked for a "business opportunity" for most of 1997. "I didn't know what to do with myself," he said.

He hung out some with Belfort but they weren't close, partly because Belfort, as a recovering addict, wasn't supposed to spend time with people with whom he used to do drugs. By the end of the year, Porush had separated from his wife and moved to Florida, where he got a job selling sports collectibles.

Drugs had always been around at Stratton, during and after working hours, and Porush said that by the end of 1995 he was using quaaludes three or four times a day. "I'm sure it didn't enhance my ability to run a business," he said. "Maybe it enhanced my ability to cope with the guilt and other nonsense." He said he also used cocaine and ecstasy.

Belfort said he used quaaludes and cocaine and sometimes gave them to friends who worked for him, although he denied using them as a broker incentive. He testified that in 1996, he injured a woman in a traffic accident while driving under the influence of quaaludes.

But in early 1997, Belfort reached bottom. On the morning of April 17, when he had been taking quaaludes, cocaine, and the tranquilizer Xanax for three days straight, he decided to take his four-year-old daughter to Florida. He pushed his wife, who tried to stop him, down a small flight of steps, bruising her ribs. Then he put his daughter in the passenger seat, stepped on the accelerator, and drove into the garage door, which had begun descending.

"That, for some reason, woke me up," Belfort said. "I was almost like in a blackout, a trance. And I stopped and I got out of the car, and I just stood there and waited. . . . Eventually, the police came."

The incident ended with Belfort agreeing to seek help. His drug addiction, he testified, "was destroying my life, destroying my family's life. I almost killed my daughter, putting her in a car without a seat belt, high on drugs. I was going to either die or go to a drug rehab."

A short time later, Belfort spent a month at a drug rehabilitation center. He said he hasn't used drugs or alcohol since. The Belforts later divorced.

In December 1997, Belfort started a Jericho-based company that distributed vitamins and other nutritional supplements. The firm had problems selling its products and "got kind of taken to the cleaners on inventory," he said in taped conversations that were introduced as evidence at the Gaito trial.

But at least customers were happy. Belfort's new business "stood by its money-back product guarantees and made prompt refunds," his lawyer said.

CHEATED OF CASH, ROBBED OF TRUST

THE LAVISH LIFESTYLES of Jordan Belfort, Daniel Porush, and other top brokers at Stratton Oakmont were paid for by the broken dreams of tens of thousands of individual investors.

Smooth-talking brokers persuaded people all over the country to pay too much for risky small stocks that Stratton wanted to manipulate then refused to sell until insiders had taken profits and the price had plummeted.

To find out how the experience affected victims' lives, *Newsday* revisited a number of people it interviewed in the past about their experiences with Stratton. Although many of the investors are still hurting in a material sense, they also have a less tangible wound—a general loss of trust. They feel betrayed not only by their brokers but by those charged with protecting investors, including stock market regulators and the Securities Investor Protection Corp. (SIPC), a tax-exempt agency mandated by Congress to recover customer assets when brokerages fail or when investor assets are stolen.

Dorothy and Louis Dequine, eighty-eight-year-old Pensacola, Florida, residents, lost $252,000 in 1994 when a Stratton employee swapped their stocks for worthless securities without authorization. They have yet to receive a penny from SIPC.

So far SIPC, which is financed by the brokerage industry, has reimbursed only 41 of 3,337 people who filed claims in Stratton's liquidation proceedings, and it says it plans to repay only 9 more. The agency takes the position that its mandate doesn't cover most types of fraud, such as losses due to failure to execute a trade or broker misrepresentation of a stock. Losses due to unauthorized trading are covered only if customers can prove they complained promptly—and reimbursement is likely to come in the form of the original stock, which may lack any value, rather than cash.

The Dequines complained about their treatment by Stratton in writing. But SIPC said it would reimburse them only with their original stocks, which now have no value because Stratton had artificially supported their prices. Moreover, it demanded that the Dequines first pay the agency $10,000 to unwind the unauthorized trades.

After the Dequines' lawyer, Tim Dennin of Manhattan, appealed the SIPC ruling, a federal bankruptcy judge overturned it in January, saying such a result "would raise the concept of Pyrrhic victory to a new level." The judge said the Dequines should receive cash, but earlier this month SIPC appealed that decision.

"We believe all of the people who ought to be paid in this case have been paid," said Stephen Harbeck, SIPC's general counsel. "Certainly anyone who disagrees with that will get to be heard by the judge."

The Dequines, who had looked forward to traveling in Europe in retirement, have been able to take one trip in recent years, to visit their son in Colorado. "I haven't given up," said Louis Dequine, a former Golden Gloves boxing champion, "but it's made me lose faith in brokers in general."

Steven Orton, an Alpharetta, Georgia, insurance agent, lost more than $68,000—an investment earmarked for his children's education—in 1994 when a Stratton broker ignored his orders to sell stocks that were dropping in value by $5,000 to $6,000 a day. "It's a horrible corner to be in," Orton said. "You feel kind of like a deer frozen in the headlights of an oncoming car." At one point, the broker suggested that Orton "reevaluate" his marriage if his wife complained about the investments.

Orton won a $68,500 award from Stratton in a 1996 arbitration but couldn't collect because the firm went bankrupt. Nearly two years ago, SIPC notified him that his losses were not protected by the agency because they stemmed from broker fraud.

Orton managed to send his children to college but said the episode has shaken his belief in salespeople of all types and changed the way he looks at government. The U.S. system of securities regulation and investor protection is "nonexistent," he said. "It's a joke. Sound and fury signifying nothing."

Claude Stemp, a former air force officer who flew bombers in Vietnam, lost $62,000 of his own and his parents' funds in 1996, a year after Stratton bowed to a court injunction and taped all sales calls as the Securities and Exchange Commission had ordered. One broker, Stemp said, called him as early as 5:30 A.M. to push stocks he said were sure to rise, then refused to sell the shares when the price began falling. Part of the broker's pitch still rings in Stemp's ears: "Everything's taped. You don't have to worry."

SIPC told Stemp two years ago that failure to sell wasn't a covered claim. Now, instead of using his flight privileges as an air force retiree to travel to Europe, Stemp, sixty, works full-time as a teacher of troubled high school students in southern California and plans to do so until he is at least seventy. He recently took out a second mortgage on his house to pay for care for his ailing mother.

"My ability to trust people has gone down the tubes," Stemp said. When he saw last year's movie *Boiler Room,* about a high-pressure brokerage, "I just about cried," he said.

Stephen McClaran, a resident of Hawaii, keeps almost all of his savings in the bank after losing more than $60,000 in 1994 when a Stratton broker ignored orders to sell a stock Stratton was manipulating upward. "You don't get over it very easily," McClaran said of his experience with Stratton, which included an admonition that he couldn't sell his stock because it would "cause the market to collapse." McClaran won $16,000 from Stratton in an arbitration but hasn't been paid and hasn't been reimbursed by SIPC.

William Moison, a real-estate broker in Los Altos, California, got a call in May 1990—when Stratton was less than one year old—from a Stratton salesman who told him he represented an "old, established banking firm" that catered to a few select high-net-worth individuals. Moison ended up losing every penny of the $117,000 he invested because the salesman made unauthorized purchases of stocks Stratton was pumping and ignored sell orders.

Moison hasn't applied for repayment from SIPC because he settled with Stratton for a smaller amount than he lost and was paid. He still invests in the stock market but only with West Coast brokers, "someone I can meet and touch." Moison calls his Stratton experience "scary."

"To have people like these doing business so shoddily, so openly, and so flagrantly" for so long "is beyond belief in this country," he said.

HOW TO CHECK OUT A BROKER

The National Association of Securities Dealers' regulation Web site, www.nasdr.com, or its hotline, 800-289-9999, will tell you if and where a broker is registered and send you a disciplinary history if one exists. There is no charge, and the disciplinary history may arrive in a day or less if you are using e-mail.

More information about a broker's record is available from the New York State Attorney General's office, Investor Protection and Securities Bureau, 212-416-8200. The information costs twenty-five cents a page and may take seven to ten business days to arrive.

BOOM TO BUST

IN THE SPRING OF 1997 federal prosecutor Joel M. Cohen and FBI agent Gregory A. Coleman met in Cohen's Brooklyn office. Both were frustrated by the government's inability to bring criminal securities fraud charges against Jordan Belfort and Daniel Porush, creators of Lake Success–based Stratton Oakmont, the most infamous stock "boiler room" operation in recent history.

Four years earlier, Alvin Abrams, a New Jersey stockbroker whom Belfort called one of his mentors, had pleaded guilty to stock fraud and told the government about Stratton stock manipulations in which he had been involved. Ever since then, federal investigators had been trying to gather enough evidence to prosecute Stratton's kingpins, including issuing subpoenas to their employees and associates. Almost no one would talk. Stratton was a "very tight-knit, closed circle" of people, a person familiar with the case said.

But as they met in Brooklyn, Coleman told Cohen there were signs that Belfort and Porush had slipped up and left a trail of incriminating evidence in another, relatively tiny part of their operations—a scheme to smuggle cash overseas.

Making a high-risk decision, Cohen and Coleman abandoned the traditional bottom-up strategy of gathering evidence from low-level personnel and went for the top.

A year and a half later, Belfort and Porush pleaded guilty not only to money laundering and international securities fraud but also to domestic stock manipulation involving thirty-four companies for which Stratton acted as an underwriter. In hopes of cutting their prison sentences, they gave prosecutors information that has led to the arrests of four other people so far, including Steve Madden, one of the nation's top footwear designers. Experts say it's the first time the government has ever prosecuted alleged insiders in small-stock schemes.

"In many ways, if you want to use the organized-crime analogy, [Belfort and Porush] were like the head of the biggest family in organized crime," said Cohen, a former prosecutor in the Eastern District of New York who now defends people accused of white-collar crimes as an attorney in the Manhattan office of Greenberg Traurig. "All kinds of people were kissing their rings."

Now the two ex-brokers who once led opulent lives are warming government-issue chairs as they serve as star witnesses for the prosecution in the trials of their alleged accomplices. But because the first such trial—that of an accountant—recently ended in a hung jury, some defense attorneys are calling the government's strategy misguided.

Putting Belfort, an admitted criminal and former drug addict, on the stand is "sort of like a serial killer testifying against the guy who drove the getaway car," said Stephen B. Wexler, an attorney in Mitchel Field who defends stockbrokers. "How do you accept the testimony of the head bad guy?"

Eric Corngold, head of the business and securities fraud unit for the U.S. Attorney's office in Brooklyn, said that office has been "repeatedly successful" in presenting complex securities-fraud cases to juries and that it's common practice in criminal trials to use testimony by people who have pleaded guilty. The government will retry the case next month on all counts.

"The argument [prosecutors] often make is that if we could bring priests or rabbis as witnesses, we would," Corngold said. "But those aren't the people who have the evidence."

Stratton, closed for securities fraud in December 1996, stole at least $250 million from investors by operating a classic "pump-and-dump" scheme. The firm would gain control over the supply of a thinly traded small stock, then pump up demand and prices by having a large roomful of brokers make high-pressure telephone sales pitches to small investors. After the price had risen sharply they would sell their holdings, stop promoting the stocks, and leave the investors holding nearly worthless shares.

To achieve control of an issue, Belfort and Porush used a network of people who acquired stocks cheaply before they went public and had secret arrangements to sell them at specific times. They included people called "flippers," who agreed to sell stock back to Stratton for a profit immediately after trading opened, as well as "nominees," who held on to it until prices had peaked, then sold on the open market and split the profit with Belfort and Porush.

Madden, the founder of Long Island City–based Steven Madden Ltd., was indicted in June on charges including being either a flipper or a nominee for Belfort or Porush in more than twenty stock offerings underwritten by Stratton and an affiliated brokerage, Purchase-based Monroe Parker.

A native of Cedarhurst, Madden is a former golfing buddy of Belfort's and a childhood friend of Porush's, who described Madden in court as "deep into the fraud with us."

Madden, who had pleaded not guilty to the charges, is scheduled to go on trial May 21. He could not be reached for comment. His attorney, Joel Winograd, called the charges "ridiculous."

"Mr. Madden was a friend of and knew nothing of what they were doing with respect to criminal activity," Winograd said. "People involved in criminal doings don't tell their friends about it."

An executive of Monroe Parker, a now-closed Stratton clone that participated in many of its frauds, said during the trial of four Monroe Parker brokers last year that Madden once handed him

$80,000 in a brown paper bag in the locker room of the Engineers Country Club in Roslyn. The money was a payoff for being allowed to participate in fraudulent deals, said the executive, Bryan Herman.

Winograd called the alleged incident "a figment of Mr. Herman's imagination" and said Madden "categorically denies" it occurred.

According to a federal grand jury indictment, Madden committed fraud in connection with Stratton's December 1993 initial public offering of his own company. It says the shoe designer had an undisclosed, prearranged deal to sell a large block of stock he owned in Steven Madden Ltd. back to Stratton less than a month after the IPO, despite a "lockup agreement" that said he couldn't do so without getting Stratton's formal consent. Madden received $674,120.40 for the stock, the indictment said.

Madden also is accused of helping Belfort and Porush hide the fact that they owned a majority of shares in Steven Madden Ltd. when it went public. According to the indictment, he falsely told NASDAQ market officials—who refused to permit the IPO unless the brokers' positions were sharply reduced—that Belfort, Porush, and a third principal had sold most of their shares to BOCAP, a company Madden controlled. In reality, Madden had "a secret and unlawful agreement" that the Stratton brokers still effectively owned the shares, prosecutors said.

In court testimony, Belfort said he and some associates "got a laugh" out of the fact that NASDAQ believed he had really divested his Madden stock. "It was discussed . . . in terms like, 'Can you believe those idiots?'" Belfort said. NASDAQ officials declined to comment.

In 1996, Belfort sued Madden to force him to turn over the BOCAP-held shares. Madden, whose lawyers denounced Belfort as a "former meat salesman," said in an affidavit that Belfort had tricked him into signing documents that he didn't read. "I have never been comfortable with complicated or technical legal or business documents," Madden said.

In January 1998, Madden settled the lawsuit by agreeing to

pay Belfort $4.3 million and Porush $1.6 million to drop claims to the BOCAP stock.

The other people accused of helping Belfort and Porush also have pleaded not guilty. They are:

Elliot Lavigne, a former chairman of the Perry Ellis clothing company unit of Salant Corp., accused of being a Belfort nominee in Stratton offerings as well as a flipper. Lavigne's lawyer, Benjamin Brafman, said Lavigne will "vigorously defend" himself against the charges and called his client "a very, very serious victim" of the Stratton principals. No trial date has been set.

Harry Shuster, a former chief executive of two California companies, including one that operates Grand Havana cigar clubs in Manhattan and Los Angeles. He is scheduled to be tried in July on allegations that he helped Belfort and Porush illegally buy and resell stocks meant for overseas investors. His lawyer, Alan Cohen, said Shuster was "used and deceived" by Belfort.

Dennis Gaito, a New Jersey accountant whose first trial resulted in a hung jury last fall. His retrial is due to begin April 2 on charges that include helping the Stratton principals launder money and falsifying some of Stratton's audit reports to the U.S. Securities and Exchange Commission. Belfort testified that Gaito's nickname was "the chef" because he had "a true love . . . of cooking up numbers."

Gaito's attorney, Ronald Fischetti, called Gaito's mistrial "a very severe blow" to the government's strategy because it showed that Belfort and Porush have no credibility with jurors. "If they didn't believe them the first time, they certainly won't believe them the second," he said.

But a number of legal experts said it's a standard, and usually winning, practice to use admitted wrongdoers as witnesses in criminal trials. "Who else but one of their own can you get?" said Constantine Katsoris, a professor of corporate and securities law at Fordham University Law School. "There's no other witnesses. You're really stuck with people you wouldn't use as character references."

Katsoris and other law professors said that to successfully try such cases, prosecutors need to tell jurors everything about the witnesses' pasts, rather than allowing defense attorneys to reveal unexpected details and make it look like the government is hiding something.

Although Stratton generated headlines during its seven-year struggle with regulators, Belfort and Porush remained relatively mysterious figures until recently, when the two ex-brokers testified at the Gaito trial. That testimony, as well as interviews and documents, shows that for all their apparent finesse as stock manipulators, the two were finally tripped up by a combination of greed, bad luck, and mistakes worthy of the Keystone Kops.

"I totally screwed up," Belfort said in one taped conversation with Gaito about money laundering.

The scheme to smuggle money overseas was created by Belfort as a way to make some extra profit for himself and Porush, even though Stratton was still going strong. It was supposed to let the two take advantage of Regulation S, an S.E.C. rule intended to make it easier for companies to sell securities abroad. Under the rule, stocks sold to overseas investors don't have to be registered, saving the issuing companies fees and legal costs. As a result, overseas investors who bought the stocks were charged less.

The situation created a golden opportunity for someone to pose as an overseas buyer and then profit by reselling stocks for a higher price back in the United States—especially if Stratton Oakmont's brokers could be used to manipulate the price upward.

"As usual . . . we took the laws and figured out how we could use them and abuse them to make ourselves money," Porush said. (Regulation S has since been amended to make such abuse more difficult.)

In 1994 and 1995, Belfort and Porush sold four phony "Reg S" offerings in two companies they controlled to offshore entities that were fronts for the two Stratton principals, financed with money they had smuggled out of the United States. Then they resold the stock in the United States, using Stratton brokers to push the price as high as possible.

For advice on setting up the scheme, Belfort made the fateful decision to consult Gary Kaminsky, chief financial officer for Dollar Time Inc., a Hollywood, Florida, company. Belfort had gained a controlling stake in Dollar Time in 1993, and it was one of the companies used to make phony Reg S issues. Unknown to Belfort, however, the U.S. Customs Service was running a sting aimed at other money-laundering activities in which Kaminsky was involved. It used, according to the *Miami Herald*, a bogus drug-money-laundering client known as "Steve Smoke."

In November 1994, Kaminsky was arrested for operating a global money-laundering network, along with others, including Jean-Jacques Handali, a Swiss banker who also had helped Belfort and Porush. Kaminsky and Handali pleaded guilty and cooperated with authorities, although it took a long time for their statements about helping two Long Island brokers to filter back to New York. It was one of the pieces of evidence that Coleman, the FBI agent, presented to Cohen, the prosecutor, in 1997.

Kaminsky's attorney, Charlton Stoner, declined to comment. Handali's lawyer, Paul Lazarus, said his client was doing "what Swiss bankers do" and was "to a large extent . . . the victim of manipulation of the American government and their agents."

Porush handed the FBI another major break in August 1994 when he drove a Bentley to the Bay Terrace Shopping Center in Bayside and, in broad daylight, handed a bag of cash to a person who arrived in a limousine. That person, who was on the Stratton payroll, was supposed to give the money to couriers who would smuggle it overseas.

But a security camera photographed the transaction, and a guard, deciding that a drug deal was going down because of the expensive cars, called police. The person in the limousine was caught with $200,000 in cash, and Porush, who had left, was identified by a photo of his license plate. Although it was unsolved at the time, a Nassau County investigator filed a report on the incident that Coleman later read.

Other cracks in the money-laundering scheme were created by the sudden death in 1994 of one of Belfort's fronts, an aunt of his wife's who was a retired schoolteacher living in England. Belfort's frantic attempts to unwind transactions in that account and get his money back also left a trail of evidence, according to law enforcement sources, who said the aunt didn't know she was being used as part of a fraud.

The aunt wasn't the only family member who became enmeshed in the Reg S scheme. Belfort said during the Gaito trial that his wife's mother, who died last month, was one of several couriers who took large amounts of cash to Switzerland without reporting amounts over $10,000 to U.S. Customs authorities, as is required. He said he didn't think she knew about the Reg S fraud.

"I didn't really think it through at the time," Belfort said of the possibility that his mother-in-law could be punished for her actions. "I thought that it was going to fall on my shoulders."

Belfort's ex-wife, Nadine Belfort, declined to comment.

Porush said, also at the Gaito trial, that he used a brother-in-law who was a citizen of the Ivory Coast as the false owner of another Swiss bank account. Porush said the brother-in-law didn't know he was doing anything illegal.

None of the Belfort or Porush relatives has been charged with any crime.

Shortly after their meeting in 1997, Cohen and Coleman went to Florida to talk with Kaminsky and the Swiss banker, Handali. Then they flew to Europe, where Cohen's previous experience and connections as the U.S. Justice Department's Paris-based liaison with French authorities turned out to be helpful. To gain Swiss cooperation, he eventually argued the case to the Swiss Supreme Court, which ruled in his favor and "opened the floodgates" to receiving banking records and other information, Cohen said.

To keep track of and explain what proved to be an extremely complicated series of transactions, Coleman pieced together a humongous chart showing where the money went and carried it around with him. Made of eight-by-eleven-inch sheets of paper held together by Scotch tape, it eventually became twenty feet long and nearly five feet wide.

On September 2, 1998, Belfort was pulling out of the driveway of his home with his daughter to go to a video store when two men got out of a car and said that they were from the FBI and that he probably should turn around and drop his daughter off at the house. After he did so, they arrested him for money laundering and international securities fraud.

"I wasn't surprised," Belfort said. "I knew for a long time that it was only a matter of time until someone came knocking on my door."

Porush was arrested at the same time in Florida and was later flown to New York in shackles.

When Cohen got back to his office after the arrests, the risky strategy he and Coleman had formulated eighteen months earlier began to pay off. Lawyers for Belfort and Porush had both left phone messages asking if they could come in and talk, and within days the two former Stratton kingpins were cooperating with the government.

While they wait to be sentenced, something that won't happen until they finish testifying, the formerly high-living ex-brokers are leading new, decidedly unglamorous lives.

Porush is divorced, remarried, and working at a Florida company that sells sports memorabilia.

Belfort is living on Long Island and winding up the affairs of his nutritional products company. In 1999, he violated conditions of his bail by calling a casino helicopter to take him to Atlantic City to gamble. But the helicopter took him by mistake to a casino where he wasn't known, and the casino, finding it suspicious that he lacked identification, called law enforcement authorities. Because of the incident, Belfort's bail was revoked and he spent nearly five months in jail.

Nadine Belfort, who began divorce proceedings after her husband's arrest, has moved with their children to California, where she helps run a maternity fashion company that she and a partner founded in 1993.

Asked by a defense attorney last fall to describe his current possessions, Belfort, the former owner of luxurious homes and numerous exotic cars, said he had "no house and one car."

During a break in the Dennis Gaito trial, for which he had spent roughly 100 hours going over tapes and transcripts, Belfort rose from his seat on an uncomfortable bench outside the court-room and paced the hallway.

With an exasperated expression, he offered a two-word sum-mary of his current existence: "Professional witness!"

MADDEN KEEPS ON HIS FEET DESPITE STOCK FRAUD CHARGES

STEVE MADDEN, founder of a burgeoning shoe business that sold more than $200 million worth of its chunky-heeled products to trendy young women last year, launched his company with a mere $1,100 in capital and one employee in early 1990.

The hyperenergetic, baseball-cap-wearing Madden, who turned forty-four last week, is a native of Cedarhurst. After dropping out of the University of Miami in the late 1970s, he fell in love with shoe designing while working as a stock boy in Lawrence and later as a salesman at Jildor, a chain of stores on Long Island.

When he needed money to expand the fledgling Steven Mad-den Ltd., it was natural he turn to Stratton Oakmont because Daniel Porush, one of its principals, was his childhood friend, according to an affidavit Madden filed during a court battle with Jordan Belfort, Porush's partner, several years ago.

"When I first met Steve, he was selling shoes out of the trunk of his car," Belfort testified in a more recent court case. "I asked him how much money he needed to get started and get a real busi-ness going. He came up with about $1 million."

A partnership owned by Belfort, Porush, and a third Stratton principal invested more than $100,000 in Steven Madden Ltd. and then arranged private placements of the company's stock that raised its total capital to $1 million, Belfort said. And in December 1993, Stratton took Steven Madden Ltd. public at $4 a share, raising about $5.6 million for the company after commissions and expenses.

The IPO is one of more than twenty Stratton stock offerings in which Madden has been accused of committing securities fraud by secretly agreeing with Stratton's principals to sell stock at pre-arranged times. If convicted, Madden, who has pleaded not guilty, could face up to twenty-five years in prison.

His indictment for stock fraud doesn't appear to have hurt the operations of Steven Madden Ltd., which recently reported that net income rose 40 percent in its fiscal year that ended December 31. The company has expanded aggressively, adding fifteen locations in 2000, and last week it announced plans to open is sixty-seventh store nationwide, in San Francisco.

Steven Madden Ltd. recently launched a line of men's shoes, and last year it introduced the "Stevies" brand for girls between five and twelve. Fiscal 2000 sales of $205 million were up 26 percent over 1999, and the company is forecasting that this year's sales will increase as much as 20 percent.

The stock, which fell 40 percent after Madden was arrested last June, has recovered and currently trades for about $14 a share, still well below its two-year high of more than $22 in April 2000.

The day after his indictment, Madden resigned as chairman of the board. But he remains chief executive, and judging by his numerous comments in news releases, he remains actively involved with the company.

Madden didn't respond to requests for an interview, and company officials declined to comment. The company's president, Rhonda Brown, said in an e-mail to *Newsday* last August that Steven Madden Ltd. remained "focused on executing its business and strategic plans" and was "quite comfortable as we move forward."

Jessica Schmidt, an associate analyst with Ferris Baker Watts, the only investment bank that follows Steven Madden Ltd., said the company "has been posting strong results even though he may have been distracted." The company has a deep management team, she said, and even if Madden is convicted, "they should be able to handle things."

In its most recent quarterly report filed with the Securities and Exchange Commission, Steven Madden Ltd. said that as of September 30, it was the subject of seven lawsuits related to the charges against its CEO. The company said it believes it has "substantial defenses to the claims."

But while its public statements have been as tough as shoe leather, Steven Madden Ltd. hired the investment bank Bear Stearns last fall to "assist in exploring strategic alternatives to maximize shareholder value." Analysts speculated that one likely alternative is for the company to be sold to another shoemaker or a fashion house.

"When there are questions about the integrity of the man running the company, it sends people to the exits," Erik Gordon, an expert on corporate mergers who teaches at the University of Florida's Warrington College of Business, said at the time. He also called the fashion business for young women "one of the most fickle markets in the world."

Running a successful restaurant is a dream shared by many. Unfortunately, something was poisoning the profits at Louise's Trattoria, and the new CEO didn't have long to find out what it was. Samuel Fromartz of *Inc.* lets us join him as amateur sleuths on the trail of lost profits. We experience the sinking feeling of a good business gone bad while uncovering a deception good enough to fool even an expert. Call it cookin' the books.

Samuel Fromartz

The Mystery of the Blood-Red Ledger

IN AUGUST 1997, after a twenty-two-year career in the restaurant industry, Fred LeFranc finally got the call. An investor was buying Louise's Trattoria, a $22 million Italian-dining chain with fifteen restaurants in the Los Angeles area. The investor wanted LeFranc as his CEO.

Louise's, which dished up homemade pastas, pizzas, and entrées, had won a following in ritzy Santa Monica, Beverly Hills, Brentwood, and Pasadena. But popularity had not translated into profitability. That's why the prospective owner wanted LeFranc. LeFranc's job: to pump up the struggling restaurants and expand.

The career move seemed tailor-made for LeFranc, who had helped grow a few companies in the past. The first was El Torito Restaurants in southern California, where he had worked for ten years. Later he had served as chief operating officer at Una Mas, based in Palo Alto. In the latter position, he had helped expand the Mexican-food chain from eight restaurants to twenty-five and had merged it with the Pollo Rey chain, doubling the size of the business.

Restaurants were in LeFranc's blood. He had dropped out of his premed studies at Chicago's Northwestern University at the age of nineteen, breaking the heart of his mother, who had emigrated from Mexico and dreamed that her son would become a doctor. He began waiting tables at the Chicago Hilton, eventually working at the legendary Pump Room, where Frank Sinatra would show up at 1 A.M. with his entourage in tow and keep the joint hopping until dawn. LeFranc never looked back.

At age forty-one, LeFranc decided to take the top suite at Louise's, eager to grow a new company and try out in a small arena a raft of management theories he'd been testing for years. He got a 5 percent stake in the company, so he could eventually cash out in a sale or a merger. Plus, he'd be back in southern California, close to where his two teenage children were living.

On September 1, 1997, he moved into the main offices of Louise's, which were located far from the restaurants themselves, in a patch of cheap office space near an oil refinery in Torrance. Even before he could tour all the restaurants and shake the hands of his managers, the California State Board of Equalization froze the company's bank accounts, seeking $225,000—about three months' worth of overdue sales tax. Unable to write checks to suppliers on the frozen accounts, Louise's filled for Chapter 11 bankruptcy protection. It was LeFranc's ninth day on the job.

He was shocked. "What did I get myself into? This was not part of the deal," LeFranc recalls thinking. Quickly, he called a meeting with his employees and reassured them that Louise's was still afloat. But over the next harrowing months, he delivered another message: in a company blindsided by surprises, Louise's would now follow a policy of truth telling. "And the truth is, we're fucking bankrupt," he told the workers. (When LeFranc is driving home a point, he gesticulates and you can hear the remnant of a Chicago accent.) Honesty would be a two-way street, he said. He would require the managers to be up front about their operations, just as he would be about the company's finances. The approach was especially crucial at that point, because it was the only way to identify problems, correct them, and surmount the crisis, he said.

Then he hit the road to get credit terms restored with his suppliers.

LeFranc never says he felt betrayed or misled about the state of affairs he walked into. But he admits that like the rest of the employees, he didn't realize the depth of the chain's problems. He didn't know that former managers had been using tax receipts to cover expenses. And there was a lot more he wouldn't learn—until much later.

In the $376 billion restaurant industry, pretax income averages only 6 percent, according to the National Restaurant Association, the industry's main trade group. With unforgiving margins like those, making a go of any restaurant is a herculean effort. And the odds of turning around a bankrupt restaurant are slim. Against that backdrop, LeFranc was in for a fight against both time and hungry competitors. He had to cut losses and generate cash, let deadweight employees go and boost the morale of the people he would keep, and, finally, figure out how to lure customers back to the establishment. He would call upon two skills he'd learned over the years but had never tested in such a harsh environment: using technology to manage a business in maniacal detail and empowering workers to make decisions on their own. Although LeFranc had formidable experience, he had never had to tackle so many crises simultaneously—and against such odds.

Louise's was founded in 1978 and grown by restaurateur Bill Chait, who acquired it seven years later. Chait, according to several people, had an almost instinctive grasp of the business, anticipating and riding the wave of the Italian-food craze that began in the late 1980s. Chait's brother, Jon, financed the chain's second restaurant; over the years, Bill Chait sought and received $14 million in venture capital and loans from Bank of America and

Bankers Trust and used the money to expand the chain. But like many other restaurant organizations, Louise's found that undisciplined growth would be its undoing. "They started building restaurants and spending money faster than it was coming in," recalls Jon Chait.

Before LeFranc came aboard, Louise's had already closed four restaurants on the East Coast. LeFranc would eventually reduce the total number of restaurants to thirteen. But despite the chain's obvious problems, it already had its fans. "They had real strong attributes, like high-quality takeout years before it was the norm," says Jim Parish, a Dallas restaurant-investment consultant who advised one of Louise's investors in 1997, when the troubles surfaced. But Parish found the management team lacking. "You need to be aware of costs and build it into your daily discipline. None of that existed," he says.

Louise's had also followed a top-down management model in which employees were expected to do as they were told. LeFranc encountered that culture as soon as he visited the restaurants. "I used to ask the managers, 'What do you think should be done?'" he says. "And they looked at me with an expression like, 'What's the right answer?' And I would say, 'No, really, what do you think?' They just weren't used to being asked that question."

In 1997, Jon Chait, who was then managing director of Manpower, thought Louise's was promising enough to buy it from his brother and the venture-capital investors, who held a 20 percent stake. He knew, though, that he would need a professional to take over for his brother, whom he describes as a passionate entrepreneur who was bored by managerial details. (Bill Chait declined to comment for this story.) Using a headhunter, he found LeFranc.

But things would hardly go as Jon Chait had planned. After Louise's filed for Chapter 11, the bankruptcy judge threw out Jon's deal to buy the company for $4.5 million. Instead, because there were other people interested in buying the chain, he ordered an auction. Jon ended up paying $7 million for Louise's, which added yet one more financial burden. Under the terms of the sale, which was completed in January 1998, when Louise's exited bankruptcy, Jon put up $3.5 million in cash and gave the creditors a note for another $3.5 million to satisfy their debts. The note paid the creditors principal and interest of about $68,000 a month, which would come out of Louise's already stretched coffers.

THE HUNT

In his previous jobs, LeFranc—an analytical man in any case—had learned to rely on the grittiest of details. To run a successful restaurant, he believed, he needed to manage what to others might seem like minutiae: the frequency of supply deliveries, the way food is stored in the walk-in refrigerators, the unit costs of pre-made tomato sauce, seasonal-staffing schedules, targeted marketing promotions, guest counts, average check sizes, and the margins on a plate of food. But the former owners had measured few if any of those details. In the chaotic months after the bankruptcy filing, LeFranc had hardly any of the information he needed. He was flying blind.

To add to his troubles, accounts payable was in shambles, and his first chief financial officer quit shortly after the filing. In March 1998, LeFranc lured James McGehee, a controller he had worked with at Una Mas, to come aboard. On McGehee's first day as Louise's controller, a second CFO, on the job for just two weeks, walked into McGehee's office and wished him luck. He, too, was leaving.

McGehee, who suddenly became CFO, put a temp to work sorting out stacks of invoices left in the wake of the bankruptcy filing. "In the second week I was there, I caught a duplicate payment of $110,000," he says. He hired everyone he could find, including LeFranc's two kids, to help input the invoices. It took him three months to put together an earnings statement. Louise's was losing $157,000 every twenty-eight days. But where were those losses coming from?

Although LeFranc couldn't immediately pinpoint the source of the bleeding, the more he dug, the more he learned. One early focus was the company's commissary, which imported olive oil, cheese, and other ingredients from Italy and then made sauces, salad dressings, and pastas by hand. The commissary was Louise's central-supply operation, selling its goods to the restaurants.

At first glance, the setup looked surprisingly healthy. The restaurants paid the commissary a price for supplies that left their food costs at 28 percent to 29 percent of revenues. "Then December comes rolling around, and the food costs jump to 50 percent," LeFranc says. "It's like my stomach goes into a knot."

And for good reason. He discovered that the commissary was selling supplies to the restaurants below cost and accumulating losses each month. Then, in December, to erase the $150,000 in losses it had built up all year, it would dramatically raise its prices.

Once he figured out what was going on, LeFranc priced the commissary's products at their true cost. The higher prices pushed up the restaurants' food costs to 35 percent, and all of a sudden operations didn't look so buoyant.

In May, LeFranc traveled to Italy to meet the suppliers that were at the root of those costs. "They treated us like kings. And I was very polite. I learned a lot, and as soon as I came back I said, 'OK, we're not going to do business with them anymore,'" he says.

He decided to outsource basic foodstuff—sauces, dressings, and pastas—to less expensive American companies, and he shut the commissary down. LeFranc also reduced distributors' deliveries to the restaurants from six to three days a week. With fewer deliveries, transport costs declined, and LeFranc was able to wring out better terms for supplies. The new delivery schedule also helped the accounts-payable department, since it meant fewer invoices, down to about 3,000 a year from 20,000. Finally, LeFranc moved the company's headquarters to West L.A. to be closer to the restaurants and, not incidentally, to cut his rent almost in half.

With the reengineering of supplies, deliveries, and eventually the menu, food costs fell more than nine percentage points, to around 25.5 percent of revenues. By November 1998, eleven months after it had emerged from bankruptcy, Louise's was cash-flow positive.

Stopping the bloodletting was one thing. What was less clear was whether LeFranc could create a self-monitoring organization that could survive and grow.

THE MAP

The key to running such an organization was getting accurate information, which at the broadest level meant an income statement. But to get a really detailed plan that might guide the team forward, LeFranc and his managers would have to parse the profit-and-loss statement into hundreds of components and measure each individually. The cost of pizza dough, the wages of a new chef, the price of napkins—all of it would need to be tallied for each restaurant, creating the detailed contours of an earnings map.

The problem with gathering that wealth of information, however, was that it could be expensive. And LeFranc's top-level staff was lean. He had cut headquarters by about 40 percent, down to just himself and seven administrators. He didn't like the top-down model anyway, since he felt it stifled initiative and had contributed to the company's troubles. Instead, he wanted managers to become de facto CEOs of their restaurants, using the information they collected to plan and measure their performance. LeFranc would reward the managers based on cash-flow results. For some, the bonuses would push a $55,000 annual salary up to $80,000.

To get his program running, LeFranc taught his team to not just read but also analyze an income statement, not something restaurant managers commonly do. He also put his managers through a time-management course designed by Stephen Covey, author of *The Seven Habits of Highly Effective People,* and had them set goals for both the company and their own careers. He trained the chefs as well, since they were responsible for food and labor costs in the kitchen. Many of them had worked their way up from entry-level dishwashing jobs. "We had to teach some of them how to use a calculator," says CFO McGehee.

Change didn't come easy. LeFranc brought in management consultant Nancy Bross to teach the managers planning and goal setting. "All I got were blank stares," Bross recalls. In LeFranc's first year, turnover among managers hit 85 percent.

A few of his employees, however, welcomed the new regime. One of the bookkeepers at the former commissary was a young man named Roger Ortiz, a self-taught whiz at Excel spreadsheets. Impressed by Ortiz's work, LeFranc promoted him from his $10-an-hour job tracking food supplies and trained him as a financial analyst. With McGehee's help, Ortiz began crunching all the numbers that increasingly were letting LeFranc sleep well at night.

LeFranc provided all his managers with personal computers and DSL lines in the restaurants so they could feed data quickly to Ortiz. The managers began tallying revenues, expenses, and guest counts daily, entering the figures into spreadsheets. Each Monday morning they e-mailed the spreadsheets to Ortiz, who then imported the data into his master Excel files and created a report that ran to forty pages. He broke out year-to-date figures for the entire company as well as for each restaurant, did comparisons between year-ago results and the company's plan, and charted the effect of marketing promotions. On Monday afternoon Ortiz would ship the report to all the managers. (LeFranc plans to have Ortiz post the reports to a shared server soon so that managers can access the reports without e-mailing them back and forth.)

The system of data sharing had some unintended but beneficial consequences. The managers at two of the biggest restaurants began competing hard against each other to post the highest results. And LeFranc started holding monthly meetings for all managers at which they explained their results to one another. All were accountable, most notably to their peers.

THE WELCOME MAT

The burning question for the newly self-directed team, however, was whether it could ramp up sales in a company that had been tainted by bankruptcy. The task was particularly hard because of what LeFranc admits was a bad decision he had made early on—keeping the company name. "I didn't go there because it was such a radical change," he says ruefully. So the team went forward with larger signs and a sporty logo featuring the tarnished moniker.

After the bankruptcy filing, the company's sales had dropped 8 percent to 10 percent. Then, in the fall of 1998, when LeFranc reduced the menu from sixty to thirty items to lower food costs, sales dropped another 7 percent within four months. (Since he had turned cash-flow positive during that time, he was sacrificing sales for profits.)

To get his customers back, LeFranc had to find out who they were. So he turned to Gazelle Systems, a Newton, Massachusetts, company he had come across at an industry convention in 1997. It had just four employees at the time, but LeFranc was blown away by its technology. Gazelle could develop a demographic profile of the restaurants' customers—where they lived, where they shopped, and how much they earned and spent. The software company could determine whether the customers were married or single, male or female, parents, or sports fans. It also could find out how frequently they visited Louise's and how much they spent. Although large retailers and catalog companies relied on such information, no one, to LeFranc's knowledge, had ever applied such data-mining technology to a restaurant.

Gazelle downloaded customer-purchase information from the restaurants' point-of-sale (POS) system and then matched it with in-depth demographic records in data banks that marketing companies offered for sale.

Gazelle's data helped LeFranc overhaul his marketing approach. With maps pinpointing where his customers lived, for example, he could target specific streets with promotional material. "Instead of doing a direct mail of 495,000 pieces, we door-dropped 20,000 pieces," LeFranc says. "For a third of the cost of the mailing I got double the response." The number of "trials," as new customers are called in the industry, rose.

The CEO had learned that 54 percent of his customers were women, which prompted him to put lighter fare on the menu—salads, pastas with light sauces, and vegetarian dishes. He began to offer seafood dishes designed by a well-known Maui chef—sea bass with white-bean tomato salad, and salmon on a bed of garlic mashed potatoes with pineapple-cilantro salsa. LeFranc calls such food "California Italian."

It also turned out that 60 percent of the restaurants' customers had children aged eight to sixteen, and 30 percent of those parents were single—and time strapped, LeFranc assumed. That meant a huge potential for the company's takeout business. To grow the chain's already substantial takeout trade, LeFranc had one of his managers set up a toll-free phone number that would detect where a customer was calling from. The system would route the call to the nearest Louise's location.

During the bankruptcy, "we never had time to focus on just sales building, as we can now," says the CEO. "We were always juggling priorities." With the team's full attention, sales grew 4.8 percent in the fourth quarter of 2000 and peaked with an 11.5 percent gain in December. In early 2001 sales rose another 6.7 percent.

When a guest sits down for a lunch of grilled swordfish over fettuccine with a piquant tomato sauce at a Louise's in West Los Angeles, all the elements that LeFranc has put together are in evidence. The food arrives quickly; the steaming fish is juicy. And the sauce—whose tomato base is outsourced to a supplier—tastes homemade. The CEO has reason to complain only when a waiter clears an appetizer plate and leaves a guest without a fork for the main course. It's a small point, but LeFranc notices it—just as he notices everything else.

Ultimately, the triumphs of LeFranc's business are measured in tiny increments—shave a percentage point on food costs, lift customer counts by 1 percent or 2 percent, get another $1.25 per average check, strive for three seatings a night instead of two. At some point, perhaps this year, LeFranc and his staff will have made all those changes. Revenues will be about as high as they can go, given the size of the restaurants, and margins will be healthy. Then Louise's can begin expanding once again—but this time without disastrous results.

The difference now is that LeFranc, the detail man, will be in charge. He figures he can open up another five locations without adding corporate overhead, so cash flow from those new restaurants would pour straight to the bottom line. Owner Jon Chait is in favor of the plan. "It's hard to have a restaurant business that's standing still," he says.

In any industry, turnarounds are grueling. In the restaurant business, they're brutal. Without persistence, luck, and a bloodhound's attention to detail, they're fated to fail. LeFranc had all those things. So now he's finally back where he started—ready for growth.

If you have insomnia, Ron Popeil is probably an old friend. Son of the inventor of the Veg-O-Matic, the man from Ronco is the mesmerizing guru of late-night infomercials that tout culinary inventions such as the Showtime Rotisserie & BBQ. This National Magazine Award winner fleshes out the Popeil family history, Ron's lonely childhood, and his irrepressible personality while explaining just how he runs his one-of-a-kind empire. With the precision of a Feather Touch Knife, Malcolm Gladwell of *The New Yorker* slices into Popeil's past, present, and future.

Malcolm Gladwell

The Pitchman: Ron Popeil and the Conquest of the American Kitchen

THE EXTRAORDINARY STORY of the Ronco Showtime Rotisserie & BBQ begins with Nathan Morris, the son of the shoemaker and cantor Kidders Morris, who came over from the Old Country in the 1880s, and settled in Asbury Park, New Jersey. Nathan Morris was a pitchman. He worked the boardwalk and the five-and-dimes and county fairs up and down the Atlantic coast, selling kitchen gadgets made by Acme Metal, out of Newark. In the early forties, Nathan set up N. K. Morris Manufacturing—turning out the KwiKi-Pi and the Morris Metric Slicer—and perhaps because it was the Depression and job prospects were dim, or perhaps because Nathan Morris made such a compelling case for his new profession, one by one the members of his family followed him into the business. His sons Lester Morris and Arnold (the Knife) Morris became his pitchmen. He set up his brother-in-law Irving Rosenbloom, who was to make a fortune on Long Island in plastic goods, including a hand grater of such excellence that Nathan paid homage to it with his own Dutch Kitchen Shredder Grater. He partnered with his brother Al, whose own sons worked the boardwalk, alongside a gangly Irishman by the name of Ed McMahon. Then, one summer just before the war, Nathan took on as an apprentice his nephew Samuel Jacob Popeil. S. J., as he was known, was so inspired by his uncle Nathan that he went on to found Popeil Brothers, based in Chicago, and brought the world the Dial-O-Matic, the Chop-O-Matic, and the Veg-O-Matic. S. J. Popeil had two sons. The elder was Jerry, who died young. The younger is familiar to anyone who has ever watched an infomercial on late-night television. His name is Ron Popeil.

In the postwar years, many people made the kitchen their life's work. There were the Klinghoffers of New York, one of whom, Leon, died tragically in 1985, during the *Achille Lauro* incident, when he was pushed overboard in his wheelchair by Palestinian terrorists. They made the Roto-Broil 400, back in the fifties, an early rotisserie for the home, which was pitched by Lester Morris. There was Lewis Salton, who escaped the Nazis with an English stamp from his father's collection and parlayed it into an appliance factory in the Bronx. He brought the world the Salton Hotray—a sort of precursor to the microwave—and today Salton, Inc., sells the George Foreman Grill.

But no rival quite matched the Morris-Popeil clan. They were the first family of the American kitchen. They married beautiful women and made fortunes and stole ideas from one another and lay awake at night thinking of a way to chop an onion so that the only tears you shed were tears of joy. They believed that it was a mistake to separate product development from marketing, as most of their contemporaries did, because to them the two were indistinguishable: the object that sold best was the one that sold itself. They were spirited, brilliant men. And Ron Popeil was the most brilliant and spirited of them all. He was the family's Joseph, exiled to the wilderness by his father only to come back and make more money than the rest of the family combined. He was a pioneer in taking the secrets of the boardwalk pitchmen to the television screen. And, of all the kitchen gadgets in the Morris-Popeil pantheon, nothing has ever been quite so ingenious in its design, or so broad in its appeal, or so perfectly representative of the Morris-Popeil belief in the interrelation of the pitch and the object being pitched, as the Ronco Showtime Rotisserie & BBQ, the countertop oven that can be bought for four payments of $39.95 and may be, dollar for dollar, the finest kitchen appliance ever made.

A ROTISSERIE IS BORN

Ron Popeil is a handsome man, thick through the chest and shoulders, with a leonine head and striking, oversized features. He is in his mid-sixties, and lives in Beverly Hills, halfway up Coldwater Canyon, in a sprawling bungalow with a stand of avocado trees and a vegetable garden out back. In his habits he is, by Beverly Hills standards, old school. He carries his own bags. He has been known to eat at Denny's. He wears T-shirts and sweatpants. As often as twice a day, he can be found buying poultry or fish or meat at one of the local grocery stores—in particular, Costco, which he favors because the chickens there are ninety-nine cents a pound, as opposed to $1.49 at standard supermarkets. Whatever he buys, he brings back to his kitchen, a vast room overlooking the canyon, with an array of industrial appliances, a collection of 1,500 bottles of olive oil, and, in the corner, an oil painting of him, his fourth wife, Robin (a former Frederick's of Hollywood model), and their baby daughter, Contessa. On paper, Popeil owns a company called Ronco Inventions, which has 200 employees and a couple of warehouses in Chatsworth, California, but the heart of Ronco is really Ron working out of his house, and many of the key players are really just friends of Ron's who work out of their houses, too, and who gather in Ron's kitchen when, every now and again, Ron cooks a soup and wants to talk things over.

In the last thirty years, Ron has invented a succession of

kitchen gadgets, among them the Ronco Electric Food Dehydrator and the Popeil Automatic Pasta and Sausage Maker, which
featured a thrust bearing made of the same material used in bullet-
proof glass. He works steadily, guided by flashes of inspiration.
This past August, for instance, he suddenly realized what product
should follow the Showtime Rotisserie. He and his right-hand
man, Alan Backus, had been working on a bread-and-batter
machine, which would take up to ten pounds of chicken wings or
scallops or shrimp or fish fillets and do all the work—combining
the eggs, the flour, the bread crumbs—in a few minutes, without
dirtying either the cook's hands or the machine. "Alan goes to
Korea, where we have some big orders coming through," Ron
explained recently over lunch—a hamburger, medium-well, with
fries—in the VIP booth by the door in the Polo Lounge, at the
Beverly Hills Hotel. "I call Alan on the phone. I wake him up. It
was two in the morning there. And these are my exact words:
'Stop. Do not pursue the bread-and-batter machine. I will pick
it up later. This other project needs to come first.'" The other
project, his inspiration, was a device capable of smoking meats
indoors without creating odors that can suffuse the air and perme-
ate furniture. Ron had a version of the indoor smoker on his
porch—"a Rube Goldberg kind of thing" that he'd worked on a
year earlier—and, on a whim, he cooked a chicken in it. "That
chicken was so good that I said to myself"—and with his left hand
Ron began to pound on the table—"This is the best chicken sandwich I have ever had in my life." He turned to me: "How many
times have you had a smoked-turkey sandwich? Maybe you have
a smoked-turkey or a smoked-chicken sandwich once every six
months. Once! How many times have you had smoked salmon?
Aah. More. I'm going to say you come across smoked salmon as an
hors d'oeuvre or an entrée once every three months. Baby-back
ribs? Depends on which restaurant you order ribs at. Smoked
sausage, same thing. You touch on smoked food"—he leaned in
and poked my arm for emphasis—"but I know one thing, Malcolm. *You don't have a smoker.*"

The idea for the Showtime came about in the same way. Ron was at Costco about four years ago when he suddenly realized that there was a long line of customers waiting to buy chickens from the in-store rotisserie ovens. They touched on rotisserie chicken, but Ron knew one thing: they did not have a rotisserie oven. Ron went home and called Backus. Together, they bought a glass aquarium, a motor, a heating element, a spit rod, and a handful of other spare parts, and began tinkering. Ron wanted something big enough for a fifteen-pound turkey but small enough to fit into the space between the base of an average kitchen cupboard and the countertop. He didn't want a thermostat, because thermostats break, and the constant clicking on and off of the heat prevents the even, crispy browning that he felt was essential. And the spit rod had to rotate on the horizontal axis, not the vertical axis, because if you cooked a chicken or a side of beef on the vertical axis the top would dry out and the juices would drain to the bottom. Roderick Dorman, Ron's patent attorney, says that when he went over to Coldwater Canyon he often saw five or six prototypes on the kitchen counter, lined up in a row. Ron would have a chicken in each of them, so that he could compare the consistency of the flesh and the browning of the skin, and wonder if, say, there was a way to rotate a shish kebab as it approached the heating element so that the inner side of the kebab would get as brown as the outer part. By the time Ron finished, the Showtime prompted no fewer than two dozen patent applications. It was equipped with the most powerful motor in its class. It had a drip tray coated with a nonstick ceramic, which was easily cleaned, and the oven would still work even after it had been dropped on a concrete or stone surface ten times in succession, from a distance of three feet. To Ron, there was no question that it made the best chicken he had ever had in his life.

It was then that Ron filmed a television infomercial for the Showtime, twenty-eight minutes and thirty seconds in length. It was shot live before a studio audience, and aired for the first time on August 8, 1998. It has run ever since, often in the wee hours of the morning or on obscure cable stations, alongside the get-rich schemes and the *Three's Company* reruns. The response to it has been such that within the next three years total sales of the Showtime should exceed $1 billion. Ron Popeil didn't use a single focus group. He had no market researchers, R&D teams, public-relations advisers, Madison Avenue advertising companies, or business consultants. He did what the Morrises and the Popeils had been doing for most of the century, and what all the experts said couldn't be done in the modern economy. He dreamed up something new in his kitchen and went out and pitched it himself.

PITCHMEN

Nathan Morris, Ron Popeil's great-uncle, looked a lot like Cary Grant. He wore a straw boater. He played the ukulele, drove a convertible, and composed melodies for the piano. He ran his business out of a low-slung, whitewashed building on Ridge Avenue, near Asbury Park, with a little annex in the back where he did pioneering work with Teflon. He had certain eccentricities, such as a phobia he developed about traveling beyond Asbury Park without the presence of a doctor. He feuded with his brother Al, who subsequently left in a huff for Atlantic City, and then with his nephew S. J. Popeil, whom Nathan considered insufficiently grateful for the start he had given him in the kitchen-gadget business. That second feud led to a climactic legal showdown over S. J. Popeil's Chop-O-Matic, a food preparer with a pleated, "w"-shaped blade rotated by a special clutch mechanism. The Chop-O-Matic was ideal for making coleslaw and chopped liver, and when Morris introduced a strikingly similar product, called the Roto-Chop, S. J. Popeil sued his uncle for patent infringement (As it happened, the Chop-O-Matic itself seemed to have been inspired by the Blitzhacker, from Switzerland, and S. J. later lost a patent judgment to the Swiss.)

The two squared off in Trenton, in May 1958, in a courtroom

jammed with Morrises and Popeils. When the trial opened Nathan Morris was on the stand, being cross-examined by his nephew's attorneys, who were out to show him that he was no more than a huckster and a copycat. At a key point in the questioning, the judge suddenly burst in. "He took the index finger of his right hand and he pointed it at Morris," Jack Dominik, Popeil's longtime patent lawyer, recalls, "and as long as I live I will never forget what he said. 'I know you! You're a pitchman! I've seen you on the boardwalk!' And Morris pointed his index finger back at the judge and shouted, 'No! I'm a manufacturer. I'm a dignified manufacturer, and I work with the most eminent of counsel!'" (Nathan Morris, according to Dominik, was the kind of man who referred to everyone he worked with as eminent.) "At that moment," Dominik goes on, "Uncle Nat's face was getting red and the judge's was getting redder, so a recess was called." What happened later that day is best described in Dominik's unpublished manuscript, "The Inventions of Samuel Joseph Popeil by Jack E. Dominik—His Patent Lawyer." Nathan Morris had a sudden heart attack, and S. J. was guilt-stricken. "Sobbing ensued," Dominik writes. "Remorse set in. The next day, the case was settled. Thereafter, Uncle Nat's recovery from his previous day's heart attack was nothing short of a miracle."

Nathan Morris was a performer, like so many of his relatives, and pitching was, first and foremost, a performance. It's said that Nathan's nephew Archie (the Pitchman's Pitchman) Morris once sold, over a long afternoon, gadget after gadget to a well-dressed man. At the end of the day, Archie watched the man walk away, stop and peer into his bag, and then dump the whole lot into a nearby garbage can. The Morrises were that good. "My cousins could sell you an empty box," Ron says.

The last of the Morrises to be active in the pitching business is Arnold (the Knife) Morris, so named because of his extraordinary skill with the Sharpcut, the forerunner of the Ginsu. He is in his early seventies, a cheerful, impish man with a round face and a few wisps of white hair and a trademark move whereby, after cutting a tomato into neat, regular slices, he deftly lines the pieces up in an even row against the flat edge of the blade. Today, he lives in Ocean Township, a few miles from Asbury Park, with Phyllis, his wife of twenty-nine years, whom he refers to (with the same irresistible conviction that he might use to describe, say, the Feather Touch Knife) as "the prettiest girl in Asbury Park." One morning recently, he sat in his study and launched into a pitch for the Dial-O-Matic, a slicer produced by S. J. Popeil some forty years ago.

"Come on over, folks. I'm going to show you the most amazing slicing machine you have ever seen in your life," he began. Phyllis, sitting nearby, beamed with pride. He picked up a package of barbecue spices, which Ron Popeil sells alongside his Showtime Rotisserie, and used it as a prop. "Take a look at this!" He held it in the air as if he were holding up a Tiffany vase. He talked about the machine's prowess at cutting potatoes, then onions, then tomatoes. His voice, a marvelous instrument inflected with the rhythms of the Jersey Shore, took on a singsong quality: "How many cut tomatoes like this? You stab it. You jab it. The juices run down your elbow. With the Dial-O-Matic, you do it a little differently. You put it in the machine and you wiggle"—he mimed fixing the tomato to the bed of the machine. "The tomato! Lady! The tomato! The more you wiggle, the more you get. The tomato! Lady! Every slice comes out perfectly, not a seed out of place. But the thing I love my Dial-O-Matic for is coleslaw. My mother-in-law used to take her cabbage and do this." He made a series of wild stabs at an imaginary cabbage. "I thought she was going to commit suicide. Oh, boy, did I pray—that she wouldn't slip! Don't get me wrong. I love my mother-in-law. It's her daughter I can't figure out. You take the cabbage. Cut it in half. Coleslaw, hot slaw. Pot slaw. Liberty slaw. It comes out like shredded wheat. . . ."

It was a vaudeville monologue, except that Arnold wasn't merely entertaining; he was selling. "You can take a pitchman and make a great actor out of him, but you cannot take an actor and always make a great pitchman out of him," he says. The pitchman must make you applaud *and* take out your money. He must be able to execute what in pitchman's parlance is called "the turn"—the perilous, crucial moment where he goes from entertainer to businessman. If, out of a crowd of fifty, twenty-five people come forward to buy, the true pitchman sells to only twenty of them. To the remaining five, he says, "Wait! There's something else I want to show you!" Then he starts his pitch again, with slight variations, and the remaining four or five become the inner core of the next crowd, hemmed in by the people around them, and so eager to pay their money and be on their way that they start the selling frenzy all over again. The turn requires the management of expectations. That's why Arnold always kept a pineapple tantalizingly perched on his stand. "For forty years, I've been promising to show people how to cut the pineapple, and I've never cut it once," he says. "It got to the point where a pitchman friend of mine went out and bought himself a plastic pineapple. Why would you cut the pineapple? It cost a couple bucks. And if you cut it they'd leave." Arnold says that he once hired some guys to pitch a vegetable slicer for him at a fair in Danbury, Connecticut, and became so annoyed at their lackadaisical attitude that he took over the demonstration himself. They were, he says, waiting for him to fail: he had never worked that particular slicer before, and, sure enough, he was massacring the vegetables. Still, in a single pitch he took in $200. "Their eyes popped out of their heads," Arnold recalls. "They said, 'We don't understand it. You don't even know how to work the damn machine.' I said, 'But I know how to do one thing better than you.' They said, 'What's that?' I said, '*I know how to ask for the money.*' And that's the secret to the whole damn business."

Ron Popeil started pitching his father's kitchen gadgets at the Maxwell Street flea market in Chicago, in the mid-fifties. He was thirteen. Every morning, he would arrive at the market at five and prepare 50 pounds each of onions, cabbages, and carrots and 100 pounds of potatoes. He sold from six in the morning until four in the afternoon, bringing in as much as $500 a day. In his late teens, he started doing the state- and county-fair circuit, and then he scored a prime spot in the Woolworth's at State and Washington, in the Loop, which at the time was the top-grossing Woolworth's store in the country. He was making more than the manager of the store, selling the Chop-O-Matic and the Dial-O-Matic. He dined at the Pump Room and wore a Rolex and rented $150-a-night hotel suites. In pictures from the period, he is beautiful, with thick dark hair and blue-green eyes and sensuous lips, and, several years later, when he moved his office to 919 Michigan Avenue, he was called the Paul Newman of the Playboy Building. Mel Korey, a friend of Ron's from college and his first business partner, remembers the time he went to see Ron pitch the Chop-O-Matic at the State Street Woolworth's. "He was mesmerizing," Korey says. "There were secretaries who would take their lunch break at Woolworth's to watch him because he was so good-looking. He would go into the turn, and people would just come running." Several years ago, Ron's friend Steve Wynn, the founder of the Mirage resorts, went to visit Michael Milken in prison. They were near a television and happened to catch one of Ron's infomercials just as he was doing the countdown, a routine taken straight from the boardwalk, where he says, "You're not going to spend $200, not $180, not $170, not $160. . . ." It's a standard pitchman's gimmick: it sounds dramatic only because the starting price is set way up high. But something about the way Ron did it was irresistible. As he got lower and lower, Wynn and Milken—who probably know as much about profit margins as anyone in America—cried out in unison, "Stop, Ron! Stop!"

Was Ron the best? The only attempt to settle the question definitively was made some forty years ago, when Ron and Arnold were working a knife set at the Eastern States Exposition, in West Springfield, Massachusetts. A third man, Frosty Wishon, who was a legend in his own right, was there, too. "Frosty was a well-dressed, articulate individual and a good salesman," Ron says. "But he thought he was the best. So I said, 'Well, guys, we've got a ten-day show, eleven, maybe twelve hours a day. We'll each do a rotation, and we'll compare how much we sell." In Morris-Popeil lore, this is known as "the shoot-out," and no one has ever forgotten the outcome. Ron beat Arnold, but only by a whisker—no more than a few hundred dollars. Frosty Wishon, meanwhile, sold only half as much as either of his rivals. "You have no idea the pressure Frosty was under," Ron continues. "He came up to me at the end of the show and said, 'Ron, I will never work with you again as long as I live.'"

No doubt Frosty Wishon was a charming and persuasive person, but he assumed that this was enough—that the rules of pitching were the same as the rules of celebrity endorsement. When Michael Jordan pitches McDonald's hamburgers, Michael Jordan is the star. But when Ron Popeil or Arnold Morris pitched, say, the Chop-O-Matic, his gift was to make the Chop-O-Matic the star. It was, after all, an innovation. It represented a different way of dicing onions and chopping liver: it required consumers to rethink the way they went about their business in the kitchen. Like most great innovations, it was disruptive. And how do you persuade people to disrupt their lives? Not merely by ingratiation or sincerity, and not by being famous or beautiful. You have to explain the invention to customers—not once or twice but three or four times, with a different twist each time. You have to show them exactly how it works and why it works, and make them follow your hands as you chop liver with it, and then tell them precisely how it fits into their routine, and, finally, sell them on the paradoxical fact that, revolutionary as the gadget is, it's not at all hard to use.

Thirty years ago, the videocassette recorder came on the market, and it was a disruptive product, too: it was supposed to make it possible to tape a television show so that no one would ever again be chained to the prime-time schedule. Yet, as ubiquitous as the VCR became, it was seldom put to that purpose. That's because the VCR was never pitched: no one ever explained the gadget to American consumers—not once or twice but three or four times—and no one showed them exactly how it worked or how it would fit into their routine, and no pair of hands guided them through every step of the process. All the VCR makers did was hand over the box with a smile and a pat on the back, tossing in an instruction manual for good measure. Any pitchman could have told you that wasn't going to do it.

Once, when I was over at Ron's house in Coldwater Canyon, sitting on one of the high stools in his kitchen, he showed me what real pitching is all about. He was talking about how he had just had dinner with the actor Ron Silver, who is playing Ron's friend Robert Shapiro in a new movie about the O. J. Simpson trial. "They shave the back of Ron Silver's head so that he's got a bald spot, because, you know, Bob Shapiro's got a bald spot back there, too," Ron said. "So I say to him, 'You've gotta get GLH.'" GLH, one of Ron's earlier products, is an aerosol spray designed to thicken the hair and cover up bald spots. "I told him, 'It will make you look good. When you've got to do the scene, you shampoo it out.'"

At this point, the average salesman would have stopped. The story was an aside, no more. We had been discussing the Showtime Rotisserie, and on the counter behind us was a Showtime cooking a chicken and next to it a Showtime cooking baby-back ribs, and on the table in front of him Ron's pasta maker was working, and he was frying some garlic so that we could have a little lunch. But now that he had told me about GLH it was unthinkable that he would not also show me its wonders. He walked quickly over to a table at the other side of the room, talking as he went. "People always ask me, 'Ron, where did you get that name GLH?' I made it up. Great-Looking Hair." He picked up a can. "We make it in nine different colors. This is silver-black." He picked up a hand mirror and angled it above his head so that he could see his bald spot. "Now, the first thing I'll do is spray it where I don't need it." He shook the can and began spraying the crown of his head, talking all the while. "Then I'll go to the area itself." He pointed to his bald spot. "Right here. OK. Now I'll let that dry. Brushing is 50 percent of the way it's going to look." He began brushing vigorously, and suddenly Ron Popeil had what looked like a complete head of hair. "Wow," I said. Ron glowed. "And you tell me 'Wow.' That's what everyone says. 'Wow.' If you go outside"—he grabbed me by the arm and pulled me out onto the deck—"if you are in bright sunlight or daylight, you cannot tell that I have a big bald spot in the back of my head. It's quite a product. It's incredible. Any shampoo will take it out. You know who would be a great candidate for this? Al Gore. You want to see how it feels?" Ron inclined the back of his head toward me. I had said, "Wow," and had looked at his hair inside and outside, but the pitchman in Ron Popeil wasn't satisfied. I had to feel the back of his head. I did. It felt just like real hair.

THE TINKERER

Ron Popeil inherited more than the pitching tradition of Nathan Morris. He was very much the son of S. J. Popeil, and that fact, too, goes a long way toward explaining the success of the Show-time Rotisserie. S. J. had a ten-room apartment high in the Drake Towers, near the top of Chicago's Magnificent Mile. He had a chauffeured Cadillac limousine with a car phone, a rarity in those days, which he delighted in showing off (as in "I'm calling you from the car"). He wore three-piece suits and loved to play the piano. He smoked cigars and scowled a lot and made funny little grunting noises as he talked. He kept his money in T-bills. His philosophy was expressed in a series of epigrams: to his attorney, "If they push you far enough, sue"; to his son, "It's not how much you spend, it's how much you make." And, to a designer who expressed doubts about the utility of one of his greatest hits, the Pocket Fisherman, "It's not for using; it's for giving." In 1974, S. J.'s second wife, Eloise, decided to have him killed, so she hired two hit men—one of whom, aptly, went by the name of Mr. Peeler. At the time, she was living at the Popeil estate in Newport Beach with her two daughters and her boyfriend, a thirty-seven-year-old machinist. When, at Eloise's trial, S. J. was questioned about the machinist, he replied, "I was kind of happy to have him take her off my hands." That was vintage S. J. But eleven months later, after Eloise got out of prison, S. J. married her again. That was vintage S. J., too. As a former colleague of his puts it, "He was a strange bird."

S. J. Popeil was a tinkerer. In the middle of the night, he would wake up and make frantic sketches on a pad he kept on his bedside table. He would disappear into his kitchen for hours and make a huge mess and come out with a faraway look on his face. He loved standing behind his machinists, peering over their shoulders while they were assembling one of his prototypes. In the late forties and early fifties, he worked almost exclusively in plastic, reinterpreting kitchen basics with a subtle, modernist flair. "Popeil Brothers made these beautiful plastic flour sifters," Tim Samuelson, a curator at the Chicago Historical Society and a leading authority on the Popeil legacy, says. "They would use contrasting colors, or a combination of opaque plastic with a translucent swirl plastic." Samuelson became fascinated with all things Popeil after he acquired an original Popeil Brothers doughnut maker, in red-and-white plastic, which he felt "had beautiful lines"; to this day, in the kitchen of his Hyde Park high-rise, he uses the Chop-O-Matic in the preparation of salad ingredients. "There was always a little twist to what he did," Samuelson goes on. "Take the Popeil automatic egg turner. It looks like a regular spatula, but if you squeeze the handle the blade turns just enough to flip a fried egg."

Walter Herbst, a designer whose firm worked with Popeil Brothers for many years, says that S. J.'s modus operandi was to "come up with a holistic theme. He'd arrive in the morning with it. It would be something like"—Herbst assumes S. J.'s gruff voice—"'We need a better way to shred cabbage.' It was a passion, an absolute goddamn passion. One morning, he must have been eating grapefruit, because he comes to work and calls me and says, 'We need a better way to cut grapefruit!'" The idea they came up with was a double-bladed paring knife, with the blades separated by a fraction of an inch so that both sides of the grapefruit membrane could be cut simultaneously. "There was a little grocery store a few blocks away," Herbst says. "So S. J. sends the chauffeur out for grapefruit. How many? Six. Well, over the period of a couple of weeks, six turns to twelve and twelve turns to twenty, until we were cutting thirty to forty grapefruits a day. I don't know if that little grocery store ever knew what happened."

S. J. Popeil's finest invention was undoubtedly the Veg-O-Matic, which came on the market in 1960 and was essentially a food processor, a Cuisinart without the motor. The heart of the gadget was a series of slender, sharp blades strung like guitar strings across two Teflon-coated metal rings, which were made in Woodstock, Illinois, from 364 Alcoa, a special grade of aluminum. When the rings were aligned on top of each other so that the blades ran parallel, a potato or an onion pushed through would come out in perfect slices. If the top ring was rotated, the blades formed a crosshatch, and a potato or an onion pushed through would come out diced. The rings were housed in a handsome plastic assembly, with a plunger to push the vegetables through the blades. Technically, the Veg-O-Matic was a triumph: the method of creating blades strong enough to withstand the assault of vegetables received a U.S. patent. But from a marketing perspective it posed a problem. S. J.'s products had hitherto been sold by pitchmen armed with a mound of vegetables meant to carry them through a day's worth of demonstrations. But the Veg-O-Matic was *too* good. In a single minute, according to the calculations of Popeil Brothers, it could produce 120 egg wedges, 300 cucumber slices, 1,150 potato shoestrings, or 3,000 onion dices. It could go through what used to be a day's worth of vegetables in a matter of minutes. The pitchman could no longer afford to pitch to just 100 people at a time, he had to pitch to 100,000. The Veg-O-Matic needed to be sold on television, and one of the very first pitchmen to grasp this fact was Ron Popeil.

In the summer of 1964, just after the Veg-O-Matic was introduced, Mel Korey joined forces with Ron Popeil in a company called Ronco. They shot a commercial for the Veg-O-Matic for $500, a straightforward pitch shrunk to two minutes, and set out from Chicago for the surrounding towns of the Midwest. They cold-called local department stores and persuaded them to carry the Veg-O-Matic on guaranteed sale, which meant that whatever the stores didn't sell could be returned. Then they visited the local television station and bought a two- or three-week run of the cheapest airtime they could find, praying that it would be enough to drive traffic to the store. "We got Veg-O-Matics wholesale for $3.42," Korey says. "They retailed for $9.95, and we sold them to the stores for $7.46, which meant that we had $4 to play with. If I spent $100 on television, I had to sell twenty-five Veg-O-Matics to break even." It was clear, in those days, that you could use television to sell kitchen products if you were Procter & Gamble. It wasn't so clear that this would work if you were Mel Korey and Ron Popeil, two pitchmen barely out of their teens selling a combination slicer-dicer that no one had ever heard of. They were taking a wild gamble, and, to their amazement, it paid off. "They had a store in Butte, Montana—Hennessey's," Korey goes on, thinking back to those first improbable years. "Back then, people there were still wearing pea coats. The city was mostly bars. It had just a few three-story buildings. There were 27,000 people, and one TV station. I had the Veg-O-Matic, and I go to the store, and they said, 'We'll take a case. We don't have a lot of traffic here.' I go to the TV station and the place is a dump. The only salesperson was going blind and deaf. So I do a schedule. For five weeks, I spend $350. I figure if I sell 174 machines—six cases—I'm happy. I go back to Chicago, and I walk into the office one morning and the phone is ringing. They said, 'We sold out. You've got to fly us another six cases of Veg-O-Matics.' The next week, on Monday, the phone rings. It's Butte again: 'We've got 150 oversold.' I fly him another six cases. Every few days after that, whenever the phone rang we'd look at each other and say, 'Butte, Montana.'" Even today, thirty years later, Korey can scarcely believe it. "How many homes in total in that town? Maybe several thousand? We ended up selling 2,500 Veg-O-Matics in five weeks!"

Why did the Veg-O-Matic sell so well? Doubtless, Americans were eager for a better way of slicing vegetables. But it was more than that: the Veg-O-Matic represented a perfect marriage between the medium (television) and the message (the gadget). The Veg-O-Matic was, in the relevant sense, utterly transparent. You took the potato and you pushed it through the Teflon-coated rings and—voilà!—you had French fries. There were no buttons being pressed, no hidden and intimidating gears: you could show-and-tell the Veg-O-Matic in a two-minute spot and allay everyone's fears about a daunting new technology. More specifically, you could train the camera on the machine and compel viewers to pay total attention to the product you were selling. TV allowed you to do even more effectively what the best pitchmen strove to do in live demonstrations—make the product the star.

This was a lesson Ron Popeil never forgot. In his infomercial for the Showtime Rotisserie, he opens not with himself but with a series of shots of meat and poultry, glistening almost obscenely as they rotate in the Showtime. A voice-over describes each shot: a "delicious six-pound chicken," a "succulent whole duckling," a "mouthwatering pork-loin roast . . ." Only then do we meet Ron, in a sports coat and jeans. He explains the problems of conventional barbecues, how messy and unpleasant they are. He bangs a hammer against the door of the Showtime, to demonstrate its strength. He deftly trusses a chicken, impales it on the patented two-pronged Showtime spit rod, and puts it into the oven. Then he repeats the process with a pair of chickens, salmon steaks garnished with lemon and dill, and a rib roast. All the time, the camera is on his hands, which are in constant motion, manipulating the Showtime apparatus gracefully, with his calming voice leading viewers through every step: "All I'm going to do here is slide it through like this. It goes in very easily. I'll match it up over here. What I'd like to do is take some herbs and spices here. All I'll do is slide it back. Raise up my glass door here. I'll turn it to a little over an hour. . . . Just set it and forget it."

Why does this work so well? Because the Showtime—like the Veg-O-Matic before it—was designed to be the star. From the very beginning, Ron insisted that the entire door be a clear pane of glass and that it slant back to let it in the maximum amount of light so that the chicken or the turkey or the baby-back ribs turning inside would be visible at all times. Alan Backus says that after the first version of the Showtime came out Ron began obsessing over the quality and evenness of the browning and became convinced that the rotation speed of the spit wasn't quite right. The original machine moved at four revolutions per minute. Ron set up a comparison test in his kitchen, cooking chicken after chicken at varying speeds until he determined that the optimal speed of rotation was actually six rpm. One can imagine a bright-eyed MBA clutching a sheaf of focus-group reports and arguing that Ronco was really selling convenience and healthful living and that it was foolish to spend hundreds of thousands of dollars retooling production in search of a more even golden brown. But Ron understood that the perfect brown is important for the same reason that the slanted glass door is important because in every respect the design of the product must support the transparency and effectiveness of its performance during a demonstration—the better it looks onstage, the easier it is for the pitchman to go into the turn and ask for the money.

If Ron had been the one to introduce the VCR, in other words, he would not simply have sold it in an informercial. He would also have changed the VCR itself so that it made sense in an infomercial. The clock, for example, wouldn't be digital. (The haplessly blinking unset clock has, of course, become a symbol of frustration.) The tape wouldn't be inserted behind a hidden door—it would be out in plain view, just like the chicken in the rotisserie, so that if it was recording you could see the spools turn. The controls wouldn't be discreet buttons; they would be large, and they would make a reassuring click as they were pushed up and down, and each step of the taping process would be identified with a big, obvious numeral so that you could set it and forget it. And would it be a slender black, low-profile box? Of course not. Ours is a culture in which the term "black box" is synonymous with incomprehensibility. Ron's VCR would be in red-and-white plastic, both opaque and translucent swirl, or maybe 364 Alcoa aluminum, painted in some bold primary color, and it would sit on top of the television, not below it, so that when your neighbor or your friend came over he would spot it immediately and say, "Wow, you have one of those Ronco Tape-O-Matics!"

A REAL PIECE OF WORK

Ron Popeil did not have a happy childhood. "I remember baking a potato. It must have been when I was four or five years old," he told me. We were in his kitchen, and had just sampled some baby-back ribs from the Showtime. It had taken some time to draw the memories out of him, because he is not one to dwell on the past. "I couldn't get that baked potato into my stomach fast enough, because I was so hungry." Ron is normally in constant motion, moving his hands, chopping food, bustling back and forth. But now he was still. His parents split up when he was very young. S. J. went off to Chicago. His mother disappeared. He and his older brother, Jerry, were shipped off to a boarding school in upstate New York. "I remember seeing my mother on one occasion. I don't remember seeing my father, ever, until I moved to Chicago, at thirteen. When I was in the boarding school, the thing I remember was a Sunday when the parents visited the children, and my parents never came. Even knowing that they weren't going to show up, I walked out to the perimeter and looked out over the farmland, and there was this road." He made an undulating motion with his hand to suggest a road stretching off into the distance. "I remember standing on the road crying, looking for the movement of a car miles away, hoping that it was my mother and father. And they never came. That's all I remember about boarding school." Ron remained perfectly still. "I don't remember ever having a birthday party in my life. I remember that my grandparents took us out and we moved to Florida. My grandfather used to tie me down in bed—my hands, my wrists, and my feet. Why? Because I had a habit of turning over on my stomach and bumping my head either up and down or side to side. Why? How? I don't know the answers. But I was spread-eagle, on my back, and if I was able to twist over and do it my grandfather would wake up at night and come in and beat the hell out of me." Ron stopped, and then added, "I never liked him. I never knew my mother or her parents or any of that family. That's it. Not an awful lot to remember. Obviously, other things took place. But they have been erased."

When Ron came to Chicago, at thirteen, with his grandparents, he was put to work in the Popeil Brothers factory—but only on the weekends, when his father wasn't there. "Canned salmon and white bread for lunch, that was the diet," he recalls. "Did I live with my father? Never. I lived with my grandparents." When he became a pitchman, his father gave him just one advantage: he extended his son credit. Mel Korey says that he once drove Ron home from college and dropped him off at his father's apartment. "He had a key to the apartment, and when he walked in his dad was in bed already. His dad said, 'Is that you, Ron?' And Ron said, 'Yeah.' And his dad never came out. And by the next morning Ron still hadn't seen him." Later, when Ron went into business for himself, he was persona non grata around Popeil Brothers. "Ronnie was never allowed in the place after that," one of S. J.'s former associates recalls. "He was never let in the front door. He was never allowed to be part of anything." "My father," Ron says simply, "was all business. I didn't know him personally."

Here is a man who constructed his life in the image of his father—who went into the same business, who applied the same relentless attention to the workings of the kitchen, who got his start by selling his father's own products—and where was his father? "You know, they could have done wonders together," Korey says, shaking his head. "I remember one time we talked with K-tel about joining forces, and they said that we would be a *war machine*—that was their word. Well, Ron and his dad, they could have been a war machine." For all that, it is hard to find in Ron even a trace of bitterness. Once, I asked him, "Who are your inspirations?" The first name came easily: his good friend Steve Wynn. He was silent for a moment, and then he added, "My father." Despite everything, Ron clearly found in his father's example a tradition of irresistible value. And what did Ron do with that tradition? He transcended it. He created the Showtime, which is indisputably a better gadget, dollar for dollar, than the Morris Metric Slicer, the Dutch Kitchen Shredder Grater, the Chop-O-Matic, and the Veg-O-Matic combined.

When I was in Ocean Township, visiting Arnold Morris, he took me to the local Jewish cemetery, Chesed Shel Ames, on a small hilltop just outside town. We drove slowly through the town's poorer sections in Arnold's white Mercedes. It was a rainy day. At the cemetery, a man stood out front in an undershirt, drinking a beer. We entered through a little rusty gate. "This is where it all starts," Arnold said, by which he meant that everyone—the whole spirited, squabbling clan—was buried here. We walked up and down the rows until we found, off in a corner, the Morris headstones. There was Nathan Morris, of the straw boater and the opportune heart attack, and next to him his wife, Betty. A few rows over was the family patriarch, Kidders Morris, and his wife, and a few rows from there Irving Rosenbloom, who made a fortune in plastic goods out on Long Island. Then all the Popeils, in tidy rows: Ron's grandfather Isadore, who was as mean as a snake, and his wife, Mary; S. J., who turned a cold shoulder to his own son; Ron's brother, Jerry, who died young. Ron was from them, but he was not of them. Arnold walked slowly among the tombstones, the rain dancing off his baseball cap, and then he said something that seemed perfectly right. "You know, I'll bet you'll never find Ronnie here."

ON THE AIR

One Saturday night a few weeks ago, Ron Popeil arrived at the headquarters of the television shopping network QVC, a vast gleaming complex nestled in the woods of suburban Philadelphia. Ron is a regular on QVC. He supplements his infomercials with occasional appearances on the network, and, for twenty-four hours beginning that midnight, QVC had granted him eight live slots, starting with a special "Ronco" hour between midnight and 1 A.M. Ron was traveling with his daughter Shannon, who had gotten her start in the business selling the Ronco Electric Food Dehydrator on the fair circuit, and the plan was that the two of them would alternate throughout the day. They were pitching a Digital Jog Dial version of the Showtime, in black, available for one day only, at a "special value" of $129.72.

In the studio, Ron had set up eighteen Digital Jog Dial Showtimes on five wood-paneled gurneys. From Los Angeles, he had sent, via Federal Express, dozens of Styrofoam containers with enough meat for each of the day's airings: eight fifteen-pound turkeys, seventy-two hamburgers, eight legs of lamb, eight ducks, thirty-odd chickens, two dozen or so Rock Cornish game hens, and on and on, supplementing them with garnishes, trout, and some sausage bought that morning at three Philadelphia-area supermarkets. QVC's target was 37,000 machines, meaning that it hoped to gross about $4.5 million during the twenty-four hours—a huge day, even by the network's standards. Ron seemed tense. He barked at the team of QVC producers and cameramen bustling around the room. He fussed over the hero plates—the ready-made dinners that he would use to showcase meat taken straight from the oven. "Guys, this is impossible," he said, peering at a tray of mashed potatoes and gravy. "The level of gravy must be higher." He was limping a little. "You know, there's a lot of pressure on you," he said wearily. "'How did Ron do? Is he still the best?'"

With just a few minutes to go, Ron ducked into the green-room next to the studio to put GLH in his hair: a few aerosol bursts, followed by vigorous brushing. "Where is God right now?" his cohost, Rick Domeier, yelled out, looking around theatrically for his guest star. "Is God backstage?" Ron then appeared, resplendent in a chef's coat, and the cameras began to roll. He sliced open a leg of lamb. He played with the dial of the new digital Showtime. He admired the crispy, succulent skin of the duck. He discussed the virtues of the new food-warming feature—where the machine would rotate at low heat for up to four hours after the meat was cooked in order to keep the juices moving—and, all the while, bantered so convincingly with viewers calling in on the testimonial line that it was as if he were back mesmerizing the secretaries in the Woolworth's at State and Washington.

In the greenroom, there were two computer monitors. The first displayed a line graph charting the number of calls that came in at any given second. The second was an electronic ledger showing the total sales up to that point. As Ron took flight, one by one, people left the studio to gather around the computers. Shannon Popeil came first. It was 12:40 A.M. In the studio, Ron was slicing onions with one of his father's Dial-O-Matics. She looked at the second monitor and gave a little gasp. Forty minutes in, and Ron had already passed $700,000. A QVC manager walked in. It was 12:48 A.M., and Ron was roaring on: $837,650. "It can't be!" he cried out. "That's unbelievable!" Two QVC producers came over. One of them pointed at the first monitor, which was graphing the call volume. "Jump," he called out. "Jump!" There were only a few minutes left. Ron was extolling the virtues of the oven one final time, and, sure enough, the line began to take a sharp turn upward, as all over America viewers took out their wallets. The numbers on the second screen began to change in a blur of recalculation—rising in increments of $129.72 plus shipping and taxes. "You know, we're going to hit $1 million, just on the first hour," one of the QVC guys said, and there was awe in his voice.

It was one thing to talk about how Ron was the best there ever was, after all, but quite another to see proof of it, before your very eyes. At that moment, on the other side of the room, the door opened, and a man appeared, stooped and drawn but with a smile on his face. It was Ron Popeil, who invented a better rotisserie in his kitchen and went out and pitched it himself. There was a hush, and then the whole room stood up and cheered.

In a world of instant information and relentless marketing, it's understandable that personal privacy is a preoccupation. But it's evolving into a business worth billions of dollars. Toby Lester of *The Atlantic Monthly* takes an in-depth look at the emergence of privacy services as a major profit center for mainstream corporate America. He also considers whether privacy is good for business, and business good for privacy.

Toby Lester

The Reinvention of Privacy

A RELATIVELY UNSUNG VIRTUE of the U.S. Patent and Trademark Office is that its databases can be viewed collectively as a sort of cultural seismograph, registering interesting spikes of entrepreneurial enthusiasm. A patent application filed on January 10, 1995, is part of one such spike. Issued as U.S. Patent 5,629,678 ("Personal tracking and recovery system"), the patent is summed up in an abstract that begins,

> Apparatus for tracking and recovering humans utilizes an implantable transceiver incorporating a power supply and actuation system allowing the unit to remain implanted and functional for years without maintenance. The implanted transmitter may be remotely actuated, or actuated by the implantee. Power for the remote-activated receiver is generated electromechanically through the movement of body muscle. The device is small enough to be implanted in a child.

Until recently such an idea might have seemed better suited to science fiction or political allegory than to real life. But in December 1999 the patent was acquired by a Florida-based company named Applied Digital Solutions, and it is now the basis of an identity-verification and remote-monitoring system that ADS calls Digital Angel. "We believe the potential global market for this device," ADS announces on its Web site, "could exceed $100 billion."

New surveillance and information-gathering technologies are everywhere these days, and they're setting off all sorts of alarm bells for those who worry about the erosion of privacy. The result has been a clangor of dire predictions. Books have recently appeared with such titles as *Database Nation: The Death of Privacy in the 21st Century* (by Simson Garfinkel), *The Unwanted Gaze: The Destruction of Privacy in America* (by Jeffrey Rosen), and *The End of Privacy: How Total Surveillance Is Becoming a Reality* (by Reg Whitaker). Polls suggest that the public is gravely concerned: a 1999 *Wall Street Journal*–NBC survey, for instance, indicated that privacy is the issue that concerns Americans most about the twenty-first century, ahead of overpopulation, racial tensions, and global warming. Politicians can't talk enough about privacy, and are rushing to pass laws to protect it. Increasingly, business and technology are seen as the culprits. "Over the next fifty years," the journalist Simson Garfinkel writes in *Database Nation,* "we will see new kinds of threats to privacy that don't find their roots in totalitarianism, but in capitalism, the free market, advanced technology, and the unbridled exchange of electronic information."

There's a general sense, too, that businesses in the modern free market are indifferent to the threats their new technologies pose to privacy. That sense seemed powerfully confirmed in early 1999, when Scott McNealy, the chief executive officer of Sun Microsystems, was asked whether privacy safeguards had been built into a new computer-networking system that Sun had just released. McNealy responded that consumer-privacy issues were nothing but a "red herring," and went on to make a remark that still resonates. "You have zero privacy anyway," he snapped. "Get over it."

But something very interesting is happening: the market for goods and services that protect privacy is surging. Entrepreneurs are realizing that privacy and technology are not fundamentally at odds—and that, in fact, expectations of privacy have in large measure always been created or broadened by the arrival of new technologies. People are coming to accept the notion that the protection of privacy is a pervasive and lasting concern in the computer age—and that, indeed, it may turn out to be *the* true enabler of the information economy.

Companies old and new are getting into the business. The number of newly registered privacy-related trademarks and patents has risen dramatically in the past few years; they include everything from banking services and computer technologies to window treatments and even an independent software agent ("for protecting consumers' privacy") called Privacy Just Got Cool. Anonymous Web-browsing and e-mailing services are available from companies called Anonymizer, Hushmail, IDcide, PrivacyX, and ZipLip. An outfit called Disappearing has developed an e-mail system that allows users to send messages that permanently unwrite themselves after a previously specified amount of time. Sales of personal paper shredders are up. Personal bodyguards are increasingly in demand. American Express has just unveiled a system called Private Payments, which generates a random, unique card number for each on-line purchase. A California law firm now offers to prepare something it calls the Privacy Trust, which, it claims, "successfully conceals ownership of bank and brokerage accounts, the family home, rental properties, and interests in other entities." Money may soon begin to be "minted" solely in electronic form, creating "digital cash" that could make credit cards (and the data gathering they make possible) obsolete. There is serious talk of building privacy protection into the infrastructure of the Internet and of using such protection, paradoxically, to make the flow of information freer than ever before.

Billions of dollars are at stake. A new sector of the economy seems to be coming into being. Among entrepreneurs and venture capitalists it already has a name. It's known as the privacy space.

THE DECADE OF TRACKING
AND MONITORING

The privacy debate is, essentially, a debate about the control of personal information. What's unsettling about Digital Angel, for example, is not that the remote electromechanical monitoring of a human being is possible. In fact, it's easy to see the potential benefits of such a technology: doctors and hospitals could use it to keep an unobtrusive twenty-four-hour watch on patients at home; military commanders could use it to monitor the exact locations of soldiers in battle. What is unsettling to a lot of people is the idea that personal data—in this case, one's very life signs—might be converted into information that could be exchanged, bought, or sold for secondary use without one's knowledge or consent. Conceivably, for instance, insurers or drug companies might pay a lot of money for access to the very specific information in hospitals' Digital Angel databases.

These examples are hypothetical, but the issue most certainly is not: there are plenty of ways in which personal data is already gathered and exchanged for secondary use. People give away vast amounts of valuable information about themselves, wittingly or unwittingly, by using credit cards, signing up for supermarket discount programs, joining frequent-flyer clubs, sending e-mail, browsing on the Internet, using electronic tollbooth passes, mailing in rebate forms, entering sweepstakes, and calling toll-free numbers. Such behaviors are essentially voluntary (although a somewhat abstract case can be made that they are the product of what has been called "the tyranny of convenience"), but many other ways of participating in everyday life basically *require* the divulging of information about oneself. A person can't function in

American society without regularly using a Social Security number, which has become a de facto national ID number—and which, as such, is the key to all sorts of private information. If one needs a mortgage, as almost everybody buying a home does, one has to turn over pages of detailed background data, some of which banks can then sell to whomever they like. People who buy prescription drugs now leave a trail of highly sensitive (and therefore valuable) personal information that is often gathered up and sold. The proliferation of surveillance cameras in public places means that one's comings and goings are increasingly a matter of public record.

The now very familiar reaction to all of this was recently reprised for me by the privacy activist Richard M. Smith, who has made a name for himself by exposing false or misleading claims made by companies about their privacy practices. "This coming decade is going to be known as the decade of tracking and monitoring," I was told by Smith, who recently became the chief technology officer of a watchdog organization called the Privacy Foundation. "Technologies are going to come on-line to monitor us in ways we would never have imagined ten years ago. It's going to be with us throughout our lives. The past five years on the Internet have been the prototype of what's going to happen in the off-line world. Cell phones. Smart cards. Digital TV. Biometrics. It's happening. There are going to be millions of things tracking us that we've never even dreamed of."

It's a complicated equation, of course. "The same technologies that have raised concerns about a 'surveillance society' have historically made possible many benefits that most citizens would prefer not to surrender," Phil Agre, an associate professor of information studies at the University of California at Los Angeles, has written, in *Technology and Privacy: The New Landscape* (1997), a thought-provoking collection of essays edited by Agre and the privacy advocate Marc Rotenberg. Even Alan Greenspan, the chairman of the Federal Reserve Board, has weighed in on the topic. In a 1998 letter to Congressman Edward J. Markey, Greenspan wrote,

The appropriate balancing of the increasing need for information in guiding our economy to ever higher standards of living, and essential need of protection of individual privacy in such an environment, will confront public policy with one of its most sensitive trade-offs in the years immediately ahead.

The gloomy assessment of that trade-off today is that privacy concerns are losing out and that something needs to be done about the problem right now, before patterns are established and built into the infrastructure of the economy. (In some respects this argument is made for the benefit of future generations, because voluminous information about people alive today has already seeped out into the public domain.) The national mood has led to a flurry of privacy-related activity in Congress. Pending Senate bills include the Consumer Privacy Protection Act, the Privacy and Identity Protection Act of 2000, the Notice of Electronic Monitoring Act, the Consumer Internet Privacy Enhancement Act, the Secure On-line Communication Enforcement Act of 2000, and the Freedom from Behavioral Profiling Act of 2000.

Not everybody, however, has faith in the government's ability to legislate control of—or even to understand—an issue as complicated and as rapidly changing as privacy in the information age. American industry has therefore come out in favor of self-regulation—assuming that businesses, in response to a form of peer pressure, will individually and collectively develop reasonable methods of protecting privacy. (To date the most visible results of this approach are the fairly easy-to-find privacy policies posted on company Web sites.)

The relative merits of legislation and self-regulation are fiercely debated and will no doubt continue to be so for some time. But this story is not about that debate. Rather, it is about the fact that many businesses view the coming several years—the period during which the debate will probably play itself out—as an opportunity to seize lucrative leadership in the privacy space.

"AN EMERGING BUSINESS IMPERATIVE"

"What so many businesses don't get," Ann Cavoukian, the information and privacy commissioner of Ontario, Canada, told me not long ago, "is that you shouldn't be having an adversarial relationship with privacy. Privacy is good for business. I've argued this from day one. If you're in the information business today, you've *got* to lead with privacy."

We were sitting in Cavoukian's office, on the seventeenth floor of a high-rise in midtown Toronto, chatting and nibbling chocolate-covered biscuits. The room was huge, immaculate, and tastefully appointed in the somewhat generic way that the offices of important government officials often are. We sat next to a coffee table, on tightly upholstered furniture; CNN flickered silently on a television in the background. A wall of windows provided a commanding view of the city.

I had sought out Cavoukian because I had just read the book she wrote with Don Tapscott, *Who Knows: Safeguarding Your Privacy in a Networked World* (1997), and had been impressed by its pragmatic approach. One sentence in particular had struck me: "Protection of privacy is not just a moral or social issue; it is also an emerging business imperative." This ran counter to most of what I had read, and I wanted to hear more.

Cavoukian—an energetic woman of Armenian descent who happens to be the sister of the children's songwriter Raffi—radiates enthusiasm, especially when the topic is privacy. This is as it should be: her job, as commissioner, is to educate the public about privacy matters and to ensure that all government agencies in Ontario abide by the province's freedom-of-information and protection-of-privacy laws. Her office's mandate doesn't yet include oversight of the private sector, but pending legislation may soon change that. In any case, she's clearly committed to engaging local companies in a meaningful dialogue about privacy.

Cavoukian's reach extends far beyond Ontario. She and her

staff have developed enough of a reputation for leadership and innovative thinking that companies from the United States—where her job has no equivalent—regularly seek her advice. The day before my visit a delegation from American Express had come to discuss the company's brand-new suite of privacy initiatives.

"What I caution people against," Cavoukian said, "is throwing in the towel. It's still early days, and we can't give up just because people say, 'You have no privacy, get over it.' So much has been written about the erosion of privacy that it makes you want to say, 'Enough!' Let's take all that as a given, and focus on the exciting new things that are happening. In this decade we're going to see the emergence of a new breed of privacy-protective company. It's leading-edge."

Cavoukian shifted forward in her seat excitedly. "There's a book that predicted much of this back in 1997, when there was a lot of privacy erosion happening without much protection. It was one of those turn-of-the-millennium books (what's going to happen, lots of predictions, that sort of stuff), by two business types, Jim Taylor and Watts Wacker, called *The 500-Year Delta: What Happens After What Comes Next*. I loved their take on things. They said, and I can quote this because I use it so much, 'Here's a prediction you can take to the bank: Within a decade, privacy management will be one of America's great growth service industries.' Their argument was that privacy is becoming increasingly scarce, and as it becomes more scarce, it's going to become more valuable—and *that* means you'll soon find new businesses that are developing to try to protect it. I thought that was great. And you know what? It's starting to happen. For example, have you heard of Zero-Knowledge Systems, in Montreal?"

Cavoukian went on to describe the company as "in a class by itself" and "the Mercedes-Benz of anonymizer-technology companies." It sounded intriguing.

HITTING A FLY
WITH A SLEDGEHAMMER?

"It's a neat space to be in," Dov Smith told me as we walked through the offices of Zero-Knowledge Systems. "The privacy space." Young and soft-spoken, Smith is the company's director of public relations, and he was giving me a tour of its brand-new headquarters, which occupy three floors of an upscale office building in Montreal's Latin Quarter. The design was spare, in a Bauhaus sort of way that implied a recent and significant influx of venture capital. Doors were made of glass, and clicked open only when employees flashed special cards at nearby sensors. Imposing stacks of sleek black computer equipment stood behind big hallway windows, quietly flashing little red and green lights. Tiny black halogen lamps hung over clusters of colorful retro chairs and tables in the central hallways, which formed a square around a large glassed-in atrium.

"We like to think of ourselves as a Silicon Valley company in Montreal," Smith said proudly. He showed me vending machines stocked with free juice and soda; a cappuccino bar with a pool table, a Ping-Pong table, and a dartboard; an in-house cafeteria run by a local restaurateur; and bunk beds for anybody who might need to crash. Massage was of course also available—for a high-tech start-up these days, Smith said, it is "almost de rigueur."

Zero-Knowledge is a privately held company that was cofounded in 1997 by two brothers, Austin and Hamnett Hill, and their father, Hammie. It claims, quite simply, to be "leading the privacy revolution." Currently the only product the company offers is something it calls Freedom 2.0, which combines a free computer program with an international network of participating Internet service providers. Some basic privacy and security services are free, such as a personal fire wall and an ad manager, but for $49.95 one gets access to a premium service that essentially amounts to an impenetrable on-line cloaking device. By wrapping information in multiple layers of the strongest encryption available and passing it through the Freedom network, Zero-Knowledge allows customers to establish as many as five untraceable pseudonymous digital identities, or "nyms," with which to browse Web sites and send e-mail.

Plenty of other companies have in the past couple of years jumped into the on-line anonymizing business. Many provide their services free, in fact. But none offers the pseudonymous segmentation of identity that Zero-Knowledge makes possible, and none makes the claim, as Zero-Knowledge does, that information about its users simply cannot be retrieved. Many anonymizer companies concede that if presented with a subpoena, they can, and indeed must, supply information about a given user's browsing habits and identity. This prompts skeptics to point out that if a company can access data about its users, then others (unprincipled government agents, hackers, snooping employers, litigious ex-spouses, criminals, and so on) can too, with or without a subpoena—and that means privacy isn't protected.

To avoid that bind Zero-Knowledge has invested a lot of time and money in developing cryptographic privacy solutions that, it claims, guarantee that it has no data on and—as its name implies—knows absolutely nothing about its users. "Some people might think we're hitting a fly with a sledgehammer," Dov Smith told me. "I mean all of this crypto for e-mail and Web browsing. But we wanted to establish ourselves. We think we can become the dominant player in a multinational business that cuts horizontally through every market."

That stopped me short. It seemed quite a claim for a company operating in what had to be the rather limited niche of anonymous Web browsing and e-mailing. It called to mind a conversation I had had not long before with Ruvan Cohen, the president and chief operating officer of iPrivacy, a new and ambitious New York–based company that aims to enable private on-line buying and shipping—a tricky feat that almost nobody else is now attempting. "A lot of these companies float privacy up the flagpole," Cohen said about the anonymizers, "and then nobody comes. So to have 5,000 customers, or even 20,000 customers, the best of whom are Chinese dissidents and Kosovar rebels who don't want to be tracked when they're surfing, and the worst of whom are pedophiles and drug dealers—that's not a business that I would particularly want to be in. The truth is, how do you make money in an e-mail business? How do you make money in surfing? The only way you can do it is advertising. And the only way you can get advertising is if you're going to have customer information—and if you're going to use it. To me, the logic of that business model tends to fall apart." I agreed, and planned to press Austin and Hamnett Hill about such questions.

As we wrapped up our tour, Smith deposited me in a conference room and handed me a collection of articles that I "really should read" about the importance of cryptography, specifically for Zero-Knowledge but also for the privacy world in general. Then he went to find the Hill brothers.

THE CYPHERPUNKS

In 1787, while serving as the U.S. ambassador in Paris, Thomas Jefferson sent a report to James Madison on the volatile situation in pre-Revolutionary France. "These views are said to gain upon the nation," he wrote. "The 1647 678.914 for 411.454 is 979.996.607.935 of all 789. The 404 is 474.872. And an 223 435.918 of some sort is not impossible."

The message was diplomatically sensitive, and to keep its contents private Jefferson had resorted to using a secret cipher that he knew only Madison could unlock. (Decrypted, the message read, "These views are said to gain upon the nation. The king's passion for drink is divesting him of all respect. The queen is detested. And an explosion of some sort is not impossible.")

According to Bruce Schneier, the author of *Applied Cryptography* (1995), the development and use of such codes was until recently "the province of learned people everywhere." After World

War II, however, cryptography essentially became the secret and exclusive province of government. In fact, the cryptographic systems produced by computers in this country were considered so powerful and so important to the national interest that they were classified as munitions, and their export was eventually banned by the Department of State. But the advent of personal computers changed everything. Suddenly the idea emerged that cryptography could and should protect not only national secrets but also private personal data stored on and transmitted between computers. In 1991 a software engineer named Philip Zimmerman created and made freely available a powerful encryption program called Pretty Good Privacy. PGP soon made its way overseas, and the U.S. government—which strongly resisted the idea of putting top-grade cryptography into public hands, for fear of its abuse by unsavory elements—opened a criminal investigation into Zimmerman for, among other things, having exported a munition. Defenders of PGP and other forms of encryption rallied behind Zimmerman and made his case a cause célèbre, arguing that the expression of ideas in cryptography, like any other form of expression, is protected by the First Amendment. (*Applied Cryptography,* a sort of how-to manual, was written and published very much in that spirit.) The government investigated Zimmerman for three years before yielding to the inevitability of publicly available cryptography and dropping the case.

Zimmerman became the model for a new breed of privacy activist—namely, one who uses computer technology to protect privacy. In 1992, inspired by his example, a band of mathematicians, computer scientists, and software engineers based primarily in the San Francisco area began to discuss ways to defend personal privacy in the computer age. They were brought together by an intense ideological commitment to privacy and free speech, and by an anarchistic mistrust of government and big business. They dedicated themselves to creating and widely disseminating the best cryptography possible, for all to use. They called themselves the Cypherpunks.

"Privacy is necessary for an open society in the electronic age,"

Eric Hughes, one of the original Cypherpunks, wrote in the opening of "A Cypherpunk's Manifesto," which he put on-line in 1993. The document continued,

> People have been defending their own privacy for centuries with whispers, darkness, envelopes, closed doors, secret handshakes, and couriers. The technologies of the past did not allow for strong privacy, but electronic technologies do.
>
> We the Cypherpunks are dedicated to building anonymous systems. We are defending our privacy with cryptography, with anonymous mail forwarding systems, with digital signatures, and with electronic money. . . .
>
> Cryptography will ineluctably spread over the whole globe, and with it the anonymous transactions systems that it makes possible.

The Cypherpunks' philosophy is extreme—they believe that cryptography and anonymous transactions should and will inevitably make the idea of the nation-state wither away—and their numbers are relatively few, but their influence has nevertheless been impressive. Their successful efforts to spread cryptography around the globe were a major factor in the U.S. government's decision in 1999 to relax its restrictions on the export of cryptography. And they have worked on and enabled a host of technologies that businesses—Zero-Knowledge Systems among them—are beginning to use to protect privacy on-line.

THE CADILLAC OF ANONYMIZERS

Eventually Austin and Hamnett Hill shambled in to meet me. In their late twenties, the brothers are already millionaires, from having created and then sold Canada's third largest Internet service provider. They both had goatees and wore black shirts and seriously baggy jeans. They had the habit of finishing each other's sentences. My first impression was that I was meeting two members of a white-guy rap group, but it faded fast. They had some very interesting things to say.

I started by asking how they had decided to create a privacy-protection business:

"The genesis of the idea," Austin said, "came from things like the PGP debates, which had a real civil-rights feel. We looked at that when we were selling our last business. People were so passionate about it, and we realized we had a chance to change what the Internet will look like ten years from now. We loved the idea that we could do something that would actually make a difference in the world—and that we might make a lot of money doing it. So we said, 'Okay, this is only going to get worse. The more computers are intertwined with our regular lives, the bigger these issues are going to be—'"

Hamnett jumped in. "Going in and redoing back-end systems and architecture and all that didn't seem to be realistic, so we started to try to think about what the best way was to chip away at this big block."

"Right," Austin resumed. "We said, 'What if we could take something like encryption but make it so simple that it would be to the privacy world what Netscape was to the Web—in other words, a platform that kicks off widespread change? What if we could build the ultimate consumer privacy tool?' That's how we came up with the idea for Freedom."

He paused and looked me in the eye. "It's the Dolby analogy," he said. "Who's Dolby's competitor?"

I couldn't think of one.

"Nobody can answer that question! You just kind of expect that audio equipment will have Dolby. People will soon have the same expectations with regard to their digital devices. They'll ask, 'Are they privacy-enabled?' You may not understand it, and it may just be a menu item, but you want to know that it's there, and that it's built in by default.

"Anyway, we thought that if we could come out with this tool, so that people could express their concerns or their passions about privacy by actively *using* something, we could get huge brand loyalty, and we'd be at the heart of the debate. We wanted to make ourselves *the* experts, *the* leaders in the privacy space. Then it wouldn't matter where things went, because people would come to us to solve the privacy problem, and we'd figure out a way to make a really good business."

Austin's cell phone rang, and he left the room to take the call. Hamnett picked up where his brother had left off.

"We were just like, 'Hey, get the best brains in privacy—the best technologists, the best policy people—and focus on them.' The first group we *had* to get on board was the Cypherpunks, because they really do the best thinking about crypto systems, particularly about how those systems apply to social issues like privacy, and because they can just rip you apart if you don't do things right."

By all accounts, Zero-Knowledge has so far been extraordinarily successful in building its staff. It has managed to lure several of the world's top cryptographers and software developers, and its absolutist commitment to privacy protection does seem to have won over the Cypherpunks—so much so that a leading Cypherpunk and cryptographer, Ian Goldberg, is now the company's chief scientist. Zero-Knowledge has also recently hired one of Canada's best-known policy experts—Stephanie Perrin, a longtime government official who was one of the prime movers in the development of Canada's privacy policies and legislation. Perrin is responsible for public affairs, keeps tabs on the legislative environment, maintains ties with governmental and nongovernmental organizations, and oversees the development and monitoring of Zero-Knowledge's overall privacy policy.

These efforts have paid off. Zero-Knowledge is awash in investment (as of this writing it has received more than $30 million), and its reputation as the Fort Knox or the Cadillac of anonymizers seems firmly established. I still wondered, though, as I listened to Hamnett, whether all of this made good business sense. When Austin returned, I asked.

"Not a lot of people understand the privacy space," Austin

said. "Freedom's going to be only a small part of what we end up doing. It's just our first entry into the space. You know, a lot of people think privacy's like the weather: everybody talks about it, there's not a lot you can do about it, so the best you can do is build a niche market selling umbrellas. That's what some people think we're doing. It's a view that's rather limiting—but we're actually working hard not to change it for a while."

The brothers chuckled conspiratorially.

"We think privacy is going to be one of the biggest industries out there," Austin continued, "because it's a foundation-level industry that touches every single aspect of personal information. Think about how much business is predicated on the flow of personal information! If you need to add privacy as a foundation under all of that, what is that industry worth? It's huge. Billions and billions and billions. We're very glad to see other privacy players stepping into the mix, by the way, because it means that privacy really is becoming an industry. And an industry that has a marketplace of solutions has more chance for success."

A DISTRESSINGLY LEAKY SYSTEM

In the weeks after my visit to Zero-Knowledge, I began to think about the historical relationship between technology and privacy. What interested me most was that people have always seemed to associate the arrival of new technologies with the invasion of privacy. It's a phenomenon that the privacy activist Robert Ellis Smith describes at some length in his new book, *Ben Franklin's Web Site: Privacy and Curiosity from Plymouth Rock to the Internet* (2000), a fascinating study of attitudes toward privacy in American history. "Each time when there was renewed interest in protecting privacy," Smith writes about the modern era,

> it was in reaction to new technology. First, in the years before 1890, came cameras, telephones, and high-speed

publishing; second, around 1970, came the development of personal computers; and third, in the late 1990s, the coming of personal computers and the World Wide Web brought renewed interest in this subject.

To find out more about the relationship between technology and privacy, and particularly between computers and privacy, I sought out Phil Agre, the UCLA professor. I asked him if part of the reason computers seem to be such a threat is that they were inadvertently designed without privacy concerns in mind—somewhat in the way they were inadvertently designed without the year 2000 in mind.

"Privacy wasn't left out unintentionally," Agre responded. "The main tradition of computer systems design originated in military and industrial contexts, where surveillance and control were taken for granted as good things. It was also informed by the ideology of technological rationalization, according to which there is a 'one best way' to organize the world, which it is the engineer's job to discover and impose. The command-and-control assumptions of that worldview are deeply ingrained in the practices of systems analysis and design that are taught in school to thousands of engineering students every year, and that are reified in thousands of legacy computers that new computers need to be compatible with.

"That said, one area where the 'unintentional omission' story makes sense is the Web. Personal computers were shaped by a false idea about the person—roughly, the idea that each person is an island. They were also shaped by the need for great simplicity, given how small and weak the first personal-computer hardware was. So those early PCs didn't have real operating systems. The operating systems of mainframe computers had, and have, serious ideas about security—for example, means of preventing users from reading one another's files or trashing the system. But all those techniques went out the window on the personal computer. Not only was there no room for them but they were thought unnecessary, because there was only one user. But then personal computers were attached to computer networks. The computer network was treated as a peripheral device, like a printer, and the whole idea that one was opening the computer out into a potentially untrustworthy domain was hard to comprehend, much less deal with technically."

In other words, we have inherited computer systems and communications technologies that—partly by design and partly by chance—are not inherently privacy-friendly. Lots of transparency has been engineered in, lots of security has been left out, and we're stuck with a system that from a privacy standpoint is distressingly leaky.

It is interesting to note here that no right to privacy is specified in the Constitution. This comes as a surprise to many people, who tend to assume that privacy is one of the bedrock rights upon which American society is built. But as Smith points out in *Ben Franklin's Web Site,* until the late nineteenth century, Americans for the most part thought of privacy as a physical concept: if one needed to protect it, or just wanted more of it, one simply moved west, where there were fewer people likely to know or care what one was doing. By the closing years of the nineteenth century, however, things had changed: the frontier's limits had been reached, the population was growing rapidly, and a blitz of novel technologies had arrived.

Two of these were cameras and high-speed printing presses. For the first time, spontaneous, unposed pictures could be taken, quickly printed in newspapers and books, and distributed widely, all without the subjects' consent. This possibility was highly unsettling to many people (as it still is in remote cultures less familiar with photography), and it led to an article by Samuel D. Warren and the future Supreme Court justice Louis D. Brandeis—"The Right to Privacy," published in the *Harvard Law Review* on December 15, 1890—that began to define privacy for the modern age.

"Recent inventions and business methods," Warren and Brandeis wrote, call attention to the next step which must be taken for the protection of the person, and for securing to the individual what Judge Cooley calls [in a famous treatise on torts that was published in 1879] the right "to be let alone." Instantaneous photographs and newspaper enterprise have invaded the sacred precincts of private and domestic life; and numerous mechanical devices threaten to make good the prediction that "what is whispered in the closet shall be proclaimed from the house-tops."

. . . The intensity and complexity of life, attendant upon advancing civilization, have rendered necessary some retreat from the world, and man, under the refining influence of culture, has become more sensitive to publicity, so that solitude and privacy have become more essential to the individual; but modern enterprise and invention have, through invasions upon his privacy, subjected him to mental pain and distress, far greater than could be inflicted by mere bodily injury.

Warren and Brandeis's masterstroke was to document in the common law the presence of a "principle which protects personal writings and any other productions of the intellect or of the emotions" and to argue that "the law has no new principle to formulate when it extends this protection to the personal appearance, sayings, acts, and to personal relation, domestic or otherwise." In other words, the two men broadened the legal conception of privacy to include not only the tangible but also the intangible realm.

THE PRIVACY PRAGMATISTS

The argument set forth in "The Right to Privacy" has been enormously influential. One cannot help hearing echoes of it in, to take just one important example, the landmark privacy decision set forth by the Supreme Court in the 1965 case *Griswold v. Connecticut*. Striking down state laws that made the use of contraceptives by married couples illegal, Justice William O. Douglas wrote, in the majority opinion, "Specific guarantees in the Bill of Rights have penumbras, formed by emanations from those guarantees that help give them life and substance. . . . Various guarantees create zones of privacy."

Not long after that ruling the legal scholar Alan Westin published the groundbreaking study *Privacy and Freedom* (1967)—a book that, years ahead of its time, jolted the nation and the government into an awareness of privacy concerns in the information age. Arguing in the tradition of Warren, Brandeis, and Douglas, Westin made a compelling case that the Bill of Rights guaranteed a zone of privacy not only for one's person, one's sayings and acts, and one's relations but also for information about oneself. "Privacy is the claim of individuals, groups, or institutions," he wrote, "to determine when, how, and to what extent information about them is communicated to others."

Ever since the publication of *Privacy and Freedom,* Westin has been sought out as an expert on information privacy and business. Over the years he has served as a privacy consultant for more than 100 companies—including American Express, Bank of America, Equifax, and IBM—and as a member of state and federal privacy commissions. Since 1993 he has been the editor and publisher of the influential bimonthly newsletter *Privacy and American Business.* During the past two decades he has worked on forty-five national public-opinion and leadership surveys on privacy. One of the results of his work on those surveys is that he has developed a widely cited taxonomy of American consumers, based on their attitudes toward privacy.

Westin divides the population into three categories. On one end of the spectrum are what he calls "privacy fundamentalists" (approximately 25 percent). They are deeply concerned about privacy rights and potential invasions of privacy, and they therefore reject any consumer benefits that require oversight of their activity or the release of data about themselves. The appeal of Zero-Knowledge, it would be fair to say, is to date largely limited to privacy fundamentalists.

At the other end of the spectrum are "the privacy unconcerned" (12 percent)—people who don't care to think about privacy, don't see any problem with giving their information away, and don't worry at all about how that information might be used. ("If McDonald's offered a free Big Mac for a DNA sample," Bruce Schneier told me, describing this attitude, "there would be lines around the block.")

Most people (63 percent) fall into an intermediate category that Westin calls "privacy pragmatists." Such people are always balancing the potential benefits and threats involved in sharing information and are particularly concerned about what Ann Cavoukian described to me as "function creep"—that is, the secondary use (deliberate or inadvertent) of information that was originally divulged for one purpose only. Depending on what privacy pragmatists get in return for their information, they are willing to forsake different degrees of privacy protection.

From a business standpoint, this category is absolutely crucial. "The struggle over privacy today," Westin told me, after gruffly dismissing the idea that anonymizers will ever have broad appeal, "is the struggle over the minds and hearts of the privacy pragmatists. And infomediary work is where that struggle is going."

The word "infomediary" first attracted widespread attention when it appeared in the January–February 1997 issue of the *Harvard Business Review,* in an article titled "The Coming Battle for Customer Information," by John Hagel III and Jeffrey F. Rayport. The authors wrote,

> We believe that consumers are going to take ownership of information about themselves and demand value in exchange for it. . . . Consumers probably will not bargain with vendors on their own, however. We anticipate that

companies we call *infomediaries* will seize the opportunity to act as custodians, agents and brokers of customer information, marketing it to businesses on consumers' behalf while protecting their privacy at the same time.

That article and a book that grew out of it—*Net Worth: Shaping Markets When Customers Make the Rules* (1999), by Hagel and Marc Singer—introduced a new business model for the information age. Already, lavishly funded companies with such names as Persona, Privada, and Lumeria have begun to put it to the test.

"WE'RE YOUR AGENT"

I called up Fred Davis, the founder and CEO of Lumeria, which has its headquarters in Berkeley, California, to find out more about the infomediary business. Davis is a longtime computer visionary and entrepreneur who has been involved in, among other ventures, the start-ups of the Ask Jeeves search engine, the technology company c/net, and *Wired* magazine. He has also been the editor of *MacUser* and *PC Week* magazines and is the author of thirteen computer books, including *The Windows 98 Bible.* He's a manic character who seems to operate in a permanent fast-forward mode, speaking in unstoppable gushes of enthusiasm and self-promotion. All I had to do was mention that I was interested in privacy and he was off and running.

"Sure! I'm always happy to talk about my favorite subject!" he told me. "Privacy is perhaps the biggest social issue of the Internet age, and today's practices don't just suck, they're downright unconstitutional! The Internet was never designed to be private, and in the early days there were attempts to take advantage of the fact that the technological infrastructure was designed to have everything open, and that there was no social infrastructure. People want to close their eyes to this, but you know what? Gays and people of color are targeted for hate crimes, and abortion doctors are targeted, all based on information that gets out over the Internet. Hello? What? It's a serious problem.

"Basically, when we started up, three years ago, I said, 'I don't want my privacy invaded anymore, and I don't want anybody stealing or selling my information without (a) my permission and (b) their cutting me in on the sale.' What we figured out pretty quickly was that we needed to help people protect their identity. The knee-jerk reaction to privacy problems has been to take your identity away completely. That's what these anonymizers do. But that's a horrible thing too. Think about it: if we make everybody anonymous, they're going to lose the value of their identity, and they're not going to be able to benefit from who they are. That's what this whole *Net Worth* book was about: there's $5 *billion* sitting on the table for the company that figures out how to give people control back over their information! It's huge! If we pull this off, we're a Fortune 500 company!"

I asked how Lumeria had been designed.

"Our model was that the individual should be able to control what information is shared with what entities—people, Web sites, commerce partners, whatever. What we needed was a system that could present information about you without revealing who you are, not even to us at Lumeria. So what I did was, I went out and hired a bunch of hackers and security nuts and said, 'Let's reengineer. Let's create a system that is comprehensive enough so that even when *all* of your information—browsing habits, medical data, bank accounts, school transcripts—becomes digitized and moves into the Internet age, you can have a unified way to control and reveal and protect it.' Basically, we created a new piece of Internet infrastructure for the secure communication and authentication of transmissions across the Internet. It took us a few years and millions of dollars to develop it, but now it's here, and it's pretty cool. The consumer has complete control for the first time. And the legislative future plays into our hands. Soon we'll be a compliance mechanism for new privacy regulations. It's a great sell. It's a no-brainer. Businesses won't have to understand all of the great things we do for our customers. It's just, the feds are going to bust you if you don't use it!"

Davis went on, and on, sometimes in great technical detail and always at lightning speed, but as I understood it, the gist of his plan for Lumeria was this: A customer will store personal data in what is called a SuperProfile. The more specific the information stored (about such things as age, sex, family status, sexual orientation, income level, assets, consumer preferences, and current shopping interests), the more valuable that profile will become to advertisers, who will pay handsomely to participate in Lumeria's network. They will do this because Lumeria will give them the chance to do highly targeted, permission-based marketing—to offer special deals on, say, new cars or housepainting services or plane tickets—exclusively to people of a predetermined demographic profile, and often only to people who have already expressed an interest in the very things being advertised. Most of the money from advertisers will go directly to Lumeria's users; Lumeria will take a small cut.

According to Davis, this is a win-win proposition. Advertisers will save billions of dollars formerly spent on wasteful direct-mail, radio, TV, and print advertising campaigns and will be better able to cultivate long-term relationships with preferred customers, by giving them exactly what they want. Consumers will be able quickly to get information about and find the best deals on whatever products they're interested in—and will get paid for doing it, simply by being a part of Lumeria's network.

I asked Davis whether gathering all of that data from consumers wouldn't create what is often referred to in the security business as a "honeypot"—an alluring mass of valuable information about consumers that is a natural target for privacy invasion.

"The thing is, remember, we don't have a database," he said. "We're not like some of these other guys, who put their information in a database and then just say they won't reveal it. What if you *buy* their company? Then what? Then you have their data! Our system is different: it distributes data across the Web. Nothing resides in a central database, and we have no way of gaining or granting access to your data. Only you do. We're just a platform for infomediation, and this means that every one of our value propositions is consumer-facing. We work for you, the consumer, as an agent to extract the maximum value for your identity. We help you copyright your profile. Not only that, we take your click trail and consider that a unique work of authorship. We'll even allow members to police the system, create mini–class actions, and—finally!—make prosecuting privacy violations cost-effective. That's aggressive. We're fighting fire with a neutron bomb. We're your agent."

THE SPREAD OF PRIVACY CONSULTANTS

Anonymizers and infomediaries aren't the only players in the privacy space. One of the hottest new jobs in certain sectors of the economy is that of chief privacy officer, or CPO. This is by no means just a Silicon Valley fad; rather, it represents a certain maturing of businesses' approach to privacy. "It's really healthy," Austin Hill told me. (Hill helped to start the trend, in fact, by hiring Stephanie Perrin, his policy expert, and by designating her Zero-Knowledge's CPO.) "What we're discovering," he added, "is that lots of places are hiring CPOs, often as a result of public-relations concerns, but then these guys are turning around and telling them, 'Hey, you've got some real problems. We've got to pay attention to this stuff.'"

All companies whose business in one form or another involves the management of personal information will probably end up having chief privacy officers in the near future. American Express, AT&T, and Microsoft already have them. So do companies as varied as Delta Airlines, Mutual of Omaha, the Royal Bank of Canada, and Equifax. Ahead of the game as always, Alan Westin has very recently created the Association of Corporate Privacy Officers, currently the only organization of its kind, and has begun to run a highly acclaimed training course for new CPOs. I asked him about the emergence of this new line of work.

"In the United States," he said, "the private sector has announced that it isn't in favor of federal privacy regulation covering the whole privacy sector. So what we've had is some sector-specific legislation, in financial services and health, but self-regulation elsewhere, especially on the Internet. Internet companies are now supposed to develop their own privacy policies. But as soon as you say you're going to self-regulate, you've got a problem. Who's going to develop the policy? Who's responsible for tracking legislation? For tracking competitors? Who's going to train employees? Who can do risk assessments? Who can do damage control in the press if there's a privacy firestorm? People pretty soon saw that they needed CPOs."

Even if not every company will need to hire a CPO, the signs are that the services of privacy consultants are going to be in regular demand from now on—to help companies develop overall privacy policies, to examine new and existing information-management systems for "seepage," to assess compliance with new legislation, to provide outside verification of a company's privacy-protection claims. New companies are emerging to provide a whole range of such services—an impressive example is Fiderus, based in North Carolina, which was founded by a former worldwide director of security and privacy for IBM, and which claims to be "the first company in the world to focus entirely on services and solutions for security *and* privacy." Zero-Knowledge has recently announced a new service, to be called Managed Privacy Services, that will combine consulting and technical solutions in order to "enable businesses to comply with privacy legislation, maximize customer relationships, and build consumer trust." But existing companies, too, are launching themselves wholeheartedly into the business. Big Five accounting firms have begun doing privacy audits in an attempt to cash in on their long-standing reputation as trusted, impartial third parties. More than 200 companies have already submitted to audits by PricewaterhouseCoopers, including Microsoft's travel Web site, Expedia.com. Even though the main value of such audits at this point is that they build public confidence, business seems brisk all around. "We've seen a dramatic increase in demand for our privacy services in the past couple of months," I was told by Gary Lord, a partner and the chief technologist of the information-risk-management practice at KPMG, one of the Big Five firms. Rather than looking at the costs associated with addressing privacy issues, "companies are asking, 'What is the cost of us *not* doing this?'"

I called a prominent privacy consultant, the legal scholar Fred Cate, to ask about this surge of mainstream corporate interest in providing privacy services. Cate teaches information law at Indiana University and is the author of *Privacy in the Information Age* (1997) and *The Internet and the First Amendment* (1998). "These days you're nobody if you're not a privacy consultant," he told me. "There's no law firm, no accounting firm, nobody *at all,* who's willing to admit to you that they don't know anything about privacy. It's big, big business. That's something to remember about all of us, you know: there are selfish reasons to beat the privacy drum in addition to whatever 'legitimate' reasons there are. I make money as a privacy consultant. These companies all make money because people are worried about privacy. The advocates raise funds because privacy's a key issue. And politicians get enormous positive ratings simply by talking about privacy."

A staggering number of bills to help rein in the corporate use of personal information are under consideration around the country. "People I've talked to on the Hill believe that privacy will be one of the hottest issues, if not *the* hottest issue, for the next three to five years," I was told by Stephen Lucas, a leading privacy-policy adviser who is also the CPO for Persona. "It's hard to find a person on the Hill who isn't involved in this issue in some way, shape, or form. During the 105th session of Congress more than 100 privacy-related bills were debated at the federal level—and more than *1,000* bills at the state level."

The flurry of interest certainly is remarkable. But Fred Cate, for one, worries about the wisdom of proceeding with such haste to address an issue that, because it is evolving so quickly, is vexingly hard to get a handle on. "People are being fed expectations—by the media, by politicians, by privacy advocates, by companies trying to sell privacy services—that they've never had before," Cate told me. "And as soon as somebody tells you to worry about something, it's hard not to. But it's not a bad idea to understand a subject before you regulate it. We're not talking about biological or chemical warfare here. Waiting another year would not be the end of the world. We've already got a gazillion laws that protect privacy, and to a certain extent they work or don't work based on your faith in the political system."

EXTREME SOLUTIONS

In *Seeing Like a State: How Certain Schemes to Improve the Human Condition Have Failed* (1998), the Yale political scientist James C. Scott has written, "The modern state, through its officials, attempts with varying success to create a terrain and a population with precisely those standardized characteristics that will be easiest to monitor, count, assess, and manage." This aspect of government is a natural one—personal information is as necessary and as valuable to efficient government as it is to efficient business. But there are plenty of people who take a decidedly dark view of it, and who therefore have very little faith in the ability of the political system to protect privacy. Recent revelations, in the midst of the rush to pass privacy-protection legislation, that the FBI has been developing and putting to use a sophisticated and questionably legal global computer-eavesdropping system—regrettably called Carnivore—haven't helped matters any. In the resulting clamor references to Big Brother abound.

One person who has very little faith in the government's commitment to privacy, particularly when it comes to financial matters, is Robert Hettinga, an entrepreneur in Boston. I was referred to Hettinga by Phil Agre, who intriguingly described him as "the head cheerleader for a loose circle of financial cryptographers who

want to build a parallel global financial system that the government cannot tax or audit." According to Agre, "This is not an
implausible goal."

I met Hettinga one day last summer, at a luncheon meeting of
the Digital Commerce Society of Boston, which he founded in
1995, and we struck up a conversation about privacy. Soon after, I
called him on the phone to hear more of what he had to say. After
making it clear to me that financial privacy wasn't really his goal
but simply an inevitable result of his business plan, Hettinga
explained the essence of his company, the Internet Bearer Underwriting Corporation (IBUC), which he established in 1999.

"The idea that financial privacy can be cheaper than transparency started out as a straw man," he told me, "but every time it
got knocked down, it got back up a little bigger. Now it's the size
of, you know, that marshmallow man in *Ghostbusters.* But anyway,
here's my rant. I like to claim that the reason that we have to put
up with taxes, and with regulations that invade our privacy, and
with people calling us to sell stuff, and with spam and all that, is
that we have to keep records of who we do business with, in case
they lie to us. It's embedded in how we do business these days. It
used to be that you would hand over a token in exchange for goods
of some sort. That was called a bearer transaction. You didn't need
to know anything about the person you were doing business with,
because you knew what money looked like, and the transaction
executed, cleared, and settled all at once. That's how cash works,
by the way. It's anonymous and very efficient. Until World War II
it was the primary means of payment for all but the largest transactions. But when telephone and mainframe computers allowed
transactions to execute and settle at a distance, we ended up making trades by recording them in a ledger or a database and then
locking away whatever physical securities there were in a vault
somewhere. That's called book-entry settlement. It's hugely invasive of privacy, but it's about three orders of magnitude cheaper
than 'my Brinks truck to your cage,' so it's what we do."

Hettinga bubbled along exuberantly. "The rise of book-entry

settlement has helped create a more invasive government, because the state, as lie enforcer, if you will, becomes an integral part of the entire economy. You have to know who it is you're doing business with so that you can send them to jail if they lie to you. But within the past fifteen years or so Internet financial cryptographers have created fairly good anonymous digital-cash protocols. This means, once again, that there's no need to know or care who you're doing business with, because transactions can execute, settle, and trade all at once. So now we're back to bearer transactions—*Internet* bearer transactions—and the costs of doing business can drop dramatically. You reduce transaction costs, and that reduces firm size—down to the device level, eventually. With Internet bearer settlement you don't need lawyers, or accountants, or even billing. All that goes away. The need for regulation goes down. In the end you get privacy because it's just cheaper, not because it's private."

Hettinga's sights are for the time being set on enabling what he described to me as a fraud-resistant form of "micropayments"— or, as he put it exactly, "functionally anonymous bearer-cash systems that do very small streaming transactions." ("We can do down to a thousandth of a dollar fairly easily," he told me. "Probably a millionth of a dollar, sooner or later.") "Minting" money in these denominations was simply not cost-effective until recently, but there are already lots of potential applications. To take just one appealing example, Hettinga suggests that IBUC micropayments could resolve the current debate among consumers, musicians, and the music industry about the exchange of music over the Internet. Consumers would pay only a tiny amount each time they downloaded a piece of music, but collectively musicians and the music industry would still make plenty of money, perhaps even more than before.

Hettinga's ideas may seem radical, but they're nothing compared with what is perhaps the most extreme scheme now being put to the test for keeping private data out of the hands of government. A new Cypherpunk-motivated company, called HavenCo, has plans, already being implemented, to set up an offshore data haven on a rusting and abandoned World War II anti-aircraft platform some six miles east of the coast of England. In 1967, when the platform was considered to be outside British territorial waters, it was "occupied" by a former British army major named Roy Bates, who named it the Principality of Sealand and declared it an independent state. Bates soon designated himself, his wife, and their son as Sealand's "royal family" and began issuing passports, coins, and stamps. Things were generally lackluster for the new nation, however, until 1999, when representatives of HavenCo negotiated with Bates and his son for the right to place a data haven on Sealand—and got "specific hands-off guarantees," HavenCo's chief executive officer, Sean Hastings, told me in an e-mail, "from the local government authorities" (the royal family, that is). The result, Hastings claims, is that HavenCo is "making real privacy available."

A MATTER OF TRUST

Making *real* privacy available? That's something that everybody now entering the privacy space claims to be doing, in one way or another. But most of what's happening at this point is still theoretical at best, and all sorts of difficult questions remain unanswered. How much legitimate cause for concern is there about privacy? Is it really something we should worry about—more than, say, racial tensions or global warming? Do we have less privacy than ever before—or do we have more? Are new technologies the problem—or the answer? Can privacy be good for business, and business good for privacy? Is it a commodity that can be bought and sold, or is it an inalienable human right?

The debate over these questions illustrates one irreducible truth: privacy is not so much a legal or technical concept as a social one. "The dominant feature of the current privacy debate," Fred Cate told me when I asked him to try to sum things up, "is its irrationality. The drivers are emotional." I think he's right. The crucial question about privacy today is the same as it has always been—namely, whom should you trust?

A lot of people instinctively don't trust technology, especially in the hands of businesses, to protect privacy. But, as Robert Ellis Smith and others have pointed out, contemporary notions of privacy have in many cases evolved not despite new technology but because of it. "Privacy," the influential journalist and editor E. L. Godkin famously wrote, in *Scribner's* magazine in 1890, "is a distinctly modern product, one of the luxuries of civilization." Phil Agre made a related point to me, a bit more bluntly. "The idea that technology and privacy are intrinsically opposed," he said, "is false."

There seems to be plenty of evidence to justify that claim. One of the earliest technologies, writing, enabled a new and enduring form of private communication. The printing press popularized reading, an intensely private affair. The wristwatch privatized time. Cheap and widely available mirrors allowed, literally, a new level of private self-reflection. The gummed envelope boosted expectations of privacy in the mail. The technological advances of the Industrial Revolution led to the creation of a prosperous middle class that could afford to build houses with separate rooms for family members. The single-party telephone line allowed for direct, immediate, and private communication at a distance. Modern roads and mass-produced automobiles made private travel possible. Television and radio brought news and entertainment into private homes.

Then, of course, came personal computers, the Internet, wireless devices, biological engineering, and more—the full effects of which on the evolution of our notions of privacy are yet to be determined. This evolution will be one of the more interesting developments to watch in the twenty-first century. Nothing is clear yet, of course; but if history is any guide, a good place to get a sense of what's to come will be the databases of the U.S. Patent and Trademark Office.

Even one of the most famous names in investment banking can lose its cachet when times change, competitors grow, and the chairman is out of touch. The odds of rebuilding that reputation and recapturing the riches that go with it are handicapped in this story by Stephanie Baker-Said and Jacqueline Simmons of *Bloomberg Markets*. It examines a company that's attempting to build a future based on individual attention for its clients but which is losing its own partners as well.

Stephanie Baker-Said and
Jacqueline Simmons

The Last Emperor

WHEN LAZARD LLC PARTNERS MET at the Victorian mansion of Michel David-Weill on Long Island, New York, in October 1999, it was the first time in the firm's 152-year history that all of its top investment bankers had gathered in one place.

The partners had good cause for finally getting together. David-Weill, who was then both chairman and CEO, had announced his plan to merge Lazard's historically separate London, Paris, and New York houses, and the partners were pushing their chief executive, now sixty-eight, to name his successor. The ultimate question on the table was how their relatively small firm—focused on mergers advice and money management—could survive in an era of monster financial services companies.

Before sipping champagne at David-Weill's waterfront house—which is so sumptuous that a Matisse hangs above a coatrack in the hall—200 partners and directors had met at a nearby conference center to listen to the business plans of the top four contenders to succeed David-Weill: New York partner William Loomis, London partner David Verey, Paris partner Bruno Roger, and European partner Gerardo Braggiotti.

In the end, the partners left the meeting disappointed. The merger of the Lazard units did take place five months later—in March 2000. But David-Weill failed to relinquish the CEO title for another eight months, and Lazard's merger advisory business continued to stagnate.

More than a dozen bankers quit the firm in 2000, including Deputy Chairman Steven Rattner, who left in February. Many longtime clients, particularly in New York, have moved to rivals like Goldman Sachs Group Inc. and Morgan Stanley Dean Witter & Co. Lazard has slumped to number ten in global mergers advice from number three in 1997, according to Bloomberg data. Pesky minority investors like corporate raider Vincent Bolloré and UBS Warburg, the investment banking subsidiary of UBS AG, have agitated for simplification of Lazard's structure of interlocking holding companies.

"There isn't room for medium-size investment banks such as Lazard, because they don't have the capital," says Philip Middleton, a partner at accounting firm KPMG in London. "Lazard needs to craft a very clearly differentiated strategy because they aren't going to win on size or clout."

In November 2000, David-Weill yielded to calls to name a chief executive by appointing Loomis, fifty-two. That surprised some partners, who knew very little about Loomis. In any case, few of them wondered who would still be running the show. "I remain chairman," David-Weill said at a news conference in Paris after Loomis was named. "The chairman, which I am, has relatively extended powers."

In many ways, Lazard, founded by David-Weill's family in 1848 as a New Orleans dry goods company, is an anachronism. The firm earns the bulk of its revenue and profit from advising such companies as drugmaker Pfizer Inc. and utility-turned-media-company Vivendi SA on mergers. About 20 percent of pretax profit comes from managing $90 billion for institutional investors. Lazard doesn't have legions of traders selling stocks and bonds. Nor does it offer its merger clients bridge loans, as rivals do.

Some clients remain satisfied with Lazard's limited focus. "We use them regularly, and we have been very happy each time," says Guillaume Hannezo, chief financial officer of Vivendi, which Lazard advised on the $39 billion purchase of Seagram Co., owner of Universal Studios, and pay-television operator Canal Plus SA. Vivendi's chairman, Jean-Marie Messier, is a former Lazard banker.

Lazard may be too small to compete with the likes of Goldman Sachs and yet too big to sustain itself as an M&A boutique like Greenhill & Co. With a mere $600 million in capital compared with Goldman Sachs's $41.2 billion, Lazard doesn't have the resources to underwrite the large stock and bond issues that are often needed to finance large transactions.

Other investment banks much larger than Lazard are getting snapped up. In November, Credit Suisse Group bought Donaldson, Lufkin & Jenrette Inc. from Axa SA for $13.4 billion, and UBS bought Paine Webber Group Inc. for $15.8 billion. Laurent Marie, an analyst at Crédit Lyonnais SA in Paris, values Lazard at $5.1 billion based on a comparison of the firm's earnings with those of rivals such as Goldman Sachs, Morgan Stanley, and Merrill Lynch.

Still, David-Weill says he will keep Lazard independent as he tries to stem the exodus of partners and clients such as Glaxo Wellcome Plc. In late 2000 he rebuffed overtures from Deutsche Bank AG, which wanted to buy the firm and put Lazard in charge of the German bank's flagging mergers business, a person close to the talks says. David-Weill denies he held talks with Deutsche Bank. "We have no desire to sell," he says. "We don't need to." A former partner says it's all but impossible for David-Weill to give up control. "Lazard is David-Weill," the person says. "It's his identity and social standing. I think he'd let the firm dwindle down to a secretary rather than sell."

David-Weill doesn't have to sell if he doesn't want to. He directly controls 22.4 percent of the firm in league with three former partners—Antoine Bernheim, André Meyer, and Jean Guyot—and their families. This group also controls another 17 percent of Lazard through a cascade of closely held and publicly held holding companies.

David-Weill, who has run Lazard since 1977, has struggled to keep the firm competitive since 1997, when star dealmaker Felix Rohatyn left to become U.S. ambassador to France. Rohatyn, a forty-nine-year veteran of Lazard, built his reputation advising Harold Geneen on the acquisitions that built the ITT Corp. conglomerate in the 1960s. Rohatyn went on to advise Pfizer, RCA Corp., and Paramount Communications Inc. David-Weill inherited Rohatyn's seat on the board of ITT, which later sold off parts of the company—often with Lazard's advice again—and changed its name to ITT Industries Inc.

Lazard has lost several other partners besides Rohatyn. David-Weill's son-in-law Edouard Stern, who was being groomed as a future CEO, quit in 1997 after David-Weill proved reluctant to give him control. Subsequently, Ira Harris, Lazard's Chicago rainmaker, and Michael Price, the firm's senior telecommunications banker, quit. Kendrick Wilson, who worked with bank clients and was once a CEO candidate, left in 1998 to join Goldman Sachs.

The most notable departure in 2000 was that of Rattner, who was also Lazard's media banker. Rattner quit along with three colleagues to start a private investing firm called Quadrangle Group. Rattner believed the three-way Lazard merger would fail unless a CEO was appointed to run the new company, people close to the firm say; instead, David-Weill set up a seven-member executive committee composed of three Europeans, three Americans, and himself. Another big loss in 2000: Richard Emerson, head of technology and telecommunications, who quit to join Microsoft Corp.

The defections haven't significantly eroded Lazard's capital. The firm withholds 10 percent of each partner's earnings every year to be put into its capital pool; partners who leave take their share of the pool with them, so the sums aren't great.

As bankers leave, so do clients. Since the beginning of 1998, when bank merger specialist Wilson departed, there has been $399 billion in announced and completed mergers involving a U.S. bank; Lazard has advised on only eight small transactions with a combined value of about $2.1 billion, according to Bloomberg data. In one of its last big bank transactions, Lazard advised BankAmerica Corp. on its $540 million acquisition of Robertson Stephens & Co. in 1997.

John Nelson, who quit Lazard in 1998 to become chairman of Credit Suisse First Boston in Europe, took his old client Kingfisher Plc with him. He advised the U.K. retailer on its $9.6 billion bid for Asda Group Plc last year, which fell through after Wal-Mart Stores Inc. made a rival offer.

Lazard missed out on the second-biggest takeover of 2000, when one of its old clients, Glaxo Wellcome, paid $68 billion for drug rival SmithKline Beecham Plc. Nicholas Jones of Lazard had advised Glaxo two years earlier, when previous talks with Smith-Kline broke down. This time, Glaxo turned to Goldman Sachs. "A lot changed over the past two years, and Goldman Sachs had developed an expertise in international pharmaceuticals," says Martin Sutton, a Glaxo spokesman. Since then, Lazard has advised Smith-Kline Beecham on some of the asset sales regulators required before approving the merger.

Some longtime French clients—including Thomson-CSF and Cie. de Saint-Gobain SA—have looked elsewhere for advice—even though Bruno Roger, Lazard's top Paris-based banker, sits on their boards. Thomson-CSF used Credit Suisse First Boston when it bought Racal Electronics Plc for $1.3 billion in July 2000. Saint-Gobain turned to Rothschild & Cie. when it bought Meyer International Plc for $2.05 billion in June 2000.

David-Weill's response to questions about lost clients? "People don't do 100 percent of their business with one principal banker these days," he says.

The man trying to keep happy his remaining partners—and, through them, his clients—embodies an earlier era of investment banking. David-Weill—whose five-foot-seven-inch frame is topped with a shock of gray hair and who often has a large cigar hanging from his mouth—is an old-fashioned power broker. He uses corporate connections and influential contacts in government to win business for Lazard. He also sits on the boards of such companies as Groupe Danone, a food producer, and Publicis Groupe SA, the world's fifth-largest advertising company. Yet he rarely, if ever, gets involved in doing deals.

That hasn't stopped him from making all of the key decisions at his firm. Until recently, David-Weill would strike secret compensation arrangements with more than a dozen partners, Lazard bankers say. Some partners who didn't like their take at the end of the year would go to David-Weill to demand more. He would usually fend off such requests by saying, "Perhaps you're right, but who should I take it from?" Former partners say whoever got David-Weill's ear first won.

Before the merger of the Lazard houses, David-Weill also had the final say when it came to solving conflicts of interest when two clients wound up on different sides of the same transaction. When, for example, Grand Metropolitan Plc was in talks to merge with Guinness Plc in a $40 billion deal in 1997, Lazard could advise either Guinness or LVMH Moët Hennessy Louis Vuitton SA, the biggest shareholder in both British companies at the time, which opposed the merger.

London-based partner Marcus Agius had Guinness as a client. Paris-based partner Georges Ralli had the relationship with LVMH. Back then, the London and Paris offices had their own profit-and-loss accounts, so any loss of fees at the expense of another Lazard office caused friction. David-Weill heard from both sides and decided the firm should go with Guinness, people familiar with the matter say. The reasoning was that Guinness approached Lazard London first. The company that resulted from that combination is now called Diageo Plc. Lazard hasn't done work for LVMH since, though it has advised LVMH chairman Bernard Arnault on his Internet investment group, Europatweb SA.

———

David-Weill, who was born in Paris, is the last descendant of Lazard's founders. He was educated at the Lycée Français de New York and the Institut d'Études Politiques de Paris, an elite political school that French president Jacques Chirac also attended. Some former partners say David-Weill remains a distant and out-of-touch character. Bankers in London used to jokingly call him "Mr. Ow Are You?" because of his thick French accent, they say. People weren't being malicious; they just found it humorous that a billionaire Frenchman would make rounds at the office, trying to be one of the guys.

David-Weill earned about $65 million in 1999, or about 13 percent of Lazard's pretax profit of about $500 million. In 2000 the firm's pretax earnings probably rose less than 20 percent, to less than $600 million, a person familiar with the firm says. With his cut of the pie, David-Weill lives a lavish lifestyle. He's known to take two puffs of a $30 Cuban cigar and squash it out. His cigar habit began at age seventeen, those close to him say. In addition to his Long Island home, called Viking Cove, he also owns a Fifth Avenue apartment in New York; a villa in Cap d'Antibes, France; and a house in Paris. He recently sold a home in Jamaica.

David-Weill also has an office in New York's Rockefeller Center with an expansive view of midtown Manhattan. In contrast, Lazard's offices in Paris are shabby and dimly lit compared with those of competitors. The furniture is out of style and the walls are covered in worn brown wallpaper. Across town at Goldman Sachs, the rooms are spacious and bright, with large French windows that open onto a park.

"We don't put a lot of money into the offices because we want the money for ourselves," says a Paris partner. Lazard's working partners have the rights to 60 percent of the firm's profit—that is, what doesn't accrue to David-Weill's group or minority stockholders. Even David-Weill's Paris office is modest, partners say. The one thing that sticks out is a painting of his grandfather—David David-Weill, who ran Lazard from 1900 to 1940—by French painter Jean Édouard Vuillard.

David-Weill has four daughters, aged twenty-three to forty-three, none of whom work at the firm. David-Weill hasn't said whether they will inherit his stake, though many Lazard employees say they expect that will be the case. "It would be a mistake to leave it to his estate," says Roy Smith, a New York University professor and former Goldman Sachs partner. "Even Michel has to understand that it doesn't make sense to have family trusts own a big stake in the firm when there are no family members in the business."

David-Weill acknowledges that the firm's compensation scheme fails to tie bankers in for the long term and makes Lazard an easy hunting ground for the competition. He is considering giving partners the opportunity to profit from a series of revamped private equity funds managed by Lazard and offering them options on profits from about one-third of the Lazard stake he owns with former partners and their families, or 7.5 percent. "You need to have enough carrots to go around," Smith says. "Just think what they could do to entice people if David-Weill gave up some of his stake in the firm."

In addition, David-Weill needs to convince bankers—and clients too—that there's room for Lazard in a world in which investment banks are increasingly offering one-stop shopping for everything from cheap loans to mergers advice. "The more our clients turn to the big houses with large bureaucracies where the principal business is trading and raising capital, the more they're going to want an independent financial adviser," he says.

Lazard has always insisted on independence. Until the New York, Paris, and London partnerships merged, the three houses had coexisted for more than a century as autonomous entities that worked together only when they had to. David-Weill tried combining the partnerships in the late 1980s, but he dropped the plan after resistance from New York and infighting over how the firm would be structured.

In 1995, in another attempt to bring the three offices together, David-Weill started a capital markets business that operated globally. The following year, the houses began putting one-third of their profits into a pool shared by all. In 1997 the firm merged its asset management businesses.

Lazard wasn't just split along geographic lines. Each business unit—such as real estate and private equity funds—operated as a separate fiefdom run by one partner who reported directly to David-Weill. Rattner set about to change this arrangement after he was appointed deputy CEO in New York in 1997.

Rattner forced Art Solomon, who oversaw as much as $9 billion in assets as Lazard's real-estate chief, to report to him rather than to David-Weill. Solomon had always run his business as he wished. In early 1999 he clashed with Rattner by trying to spin off Lazard's entire real estate investment business, which had several large funds. According to people familiar with the situation, Rattner started an audit of one of the funds—the $1.5 billion LF Strategic Realty Investors II Fund—and discovered it had invested in assisted-living centers that had plummeted in value. As a result, Rattner fired two of Solomon's colleagues—Murry Gunty and Robert Freeman—and asked Solomon to step back and become nonexecutive chairman of the real-estate group.

In retaliation, Solomon invited five investors into Lazard's New York offices to rally support for his case. He called an unsuspecting Rattner into a conference room, where they were all waiting. "We wanted to know what the hell was happening to our investment," says one of the investors who was at the meeting. "We never would have invested in the funds had we known there were such troubles at Lazard." Rattner told the investors to come back in a few days, and as they were leaving, he brought Solomon into his office and fired him. Rattner later told colleagues he'd been "ambushed." Solomon sued for wrongful dismissal. Rattner and Solomon declined to comment for this article. Lazard settled the suit out of court in June 1999 for about $11 million to avoid publicity, those familiar with the situation say. One of the real-estate partners, Tony Meyer, stayed on to clean up the mess.

Just as the suit was being settled, David-Weill promulgated his merger plan. Although most partners said the changes were long overdue, there was no formal voting; it was presented as a fait accompli.

Under David-Weill's new system, partners share fees worldwide rather than keep the bulk of what they bring in for their individual offices. Conflicts are sorted out by a committee overseen by Ralli and Kenneth Jacobs, the two global coheads of mergers. New York is expected to generate about half of the profit for 2000, according to partners. Partners said in December that there was no clear sense of how much they would take home, and they were eyeing the performance of other offices. Fees from Vivendi's $30 billion purchase of Seagram will be shared with the rest of the firm, for instance, upsetting some Paris partners. "It's not an easy process going from three separate organizations into one," says Verey, the senior partner in London and a member of the executive committee, "but it's gone amazingly smoothly."

Pulling together three autonomous offices and naming a CEO isn't all that David-Weill has had to contend with. He's also had to placate grousing minority shareholders such as French financier Vincent Bolloré and UBS Warburg. Bolloré, forty-eight, first started acquiring shares in a Lazard holding company, Rue Impériale de Lyon SA, in June 1999, betting the value of the shares would rise as Lazard started to reorganize.

Bolloré's decision to buy a stake in one of the Lazard holding companies galvanized other minority shareholders, including UBS Warburg, into calling for change. UBS Warburg first began buying stakes in three Lazard holding companies about five years ago, betting that France's structure of corporate cross shareholdings would unravel as the country's equity markets developed, thereby unlocking the value of their assets. UBS Warburg acquired 7 percent of Azeo SA, 10 percent of Société Eurafrance SA, and 5 percent of Société Immobilière Marseillaise SA.

UBS Warburg was publicly silent until Bolloré arrived. In May 2000, after Bolloré had built his stake in Rue Impériale to 31 percent, UBS Warburg managing director Jon Wood, an Englishman based in the Bahamas, started demanding that David-

Weill boost the share price of the other Lazard holding companies by merging them or buying back shares. Bolloré also began acquiring Eurafrance shares about that time.

Bolloré's decision to buy into the Lazard cascade was taken without the advice of his longtime adviser, retired Lazard partner Antoine Bernheim. Bolloré, a French corporate raider with a history of buying into companies and forcing management to take steps to boost their share prices, had used Bernheim to build his empire in tobacco, specialty papers, and transportation.

As he was fending off Bolloré, David-Weill was trying to placate UBS Warburg, which had complained that shares of the three holding companies were trading at less than their asset value. In November, David-Weill met Bolloré over breakfast in Paris to discuss a plan for merging Eurafrance and Azeo. Later that month, Eurafrance offered to buy out Azeo at 90 euros ($79) a share, almost double the Azeo share price in January 2000. UBS Warburg said the bid undervalued Azeo's assets. It also criticized Eurafrance's plan to fund the acquisition by giving Milan-based Mediobanca SpA the first right of refusal to buy its $1.76 billion stake in Italian insurer Assicurazioni Generali SpA at a discount.

It was after the breakfast meeting with Bolloré that David-Weill began quiet negotiations with Crédit Agricole—a bank set up in 1894 to provide financing for French farmers—to buy out Bolloré's 31 percent stake in Rue Impériale shares. Crédit Agricole paid Bolloré $500 million, helping him almost double his investment in less than eighteen months. "Bolloré made a load of money," says Sophie L'Hélias, a Washington-based shareholder activist who says she represents owners of Eurafrance stock that she declines to identify.

David-Weill then orchestrated a truce with UBS Warburg, agreeing to a stock buyback for Eurafrance in an effort to boost the price of the shares. "We welcome the intention of Eurafrance to actively pursue its policy to reduce the holding company discount," USB Warburg said in a statement. Still, the company said it would keep pressing Lazard to unlock the value of the holding companies' assets. "He still has problems with restructuring the business, but at least now, he'll do things at his own pace," says L'Hélias.

There's more work to be done at Lazard. Present and former partners say it's unclear how much new CEO Loomis will help Lazard renew itself. David-Weill still wields the power, and Loomis was chosen largely because of his ability to appease everyone, not because he had a great record as a banker, they say. In a memo sent to partners, David-Weill said Loomis will help run the firm "under my guidance."

David-Weill says that he picked Loomis because he's well liked and can provide cohesion. Other top partners agree. "It wasn't a difficult decision," says Verey. "Loomis was the obvious choice."

David-Weill couldn't have chosen someone more different from himself. Before getting into banking, Loomis traveled around South Asia on a creative writing fellowship. He joined Lazard in 1978 as a junior banker as part of a raid on his former employer, Lehman Brothers, orchestrated by David-Weill. A native of California, Loomis was sent to San Francisco to build Lazard's West Coast banking business, but he ended up returning to New York before the office opened. Loomis declined to be interviewed for this article.

Loomis, who has never worked in Lazard's Paris or London offices, is not well known outside the New York office. He inherited ITT as a client from Rohatyn and has had Limited Inc., a U.S. clothing chain, as a client; he's close to Limited chief executive Leslie Wexner.

So far, David-Weill's efforts to shore up Lazard's ranks have not been effective. In 1997, the year Rohatyn left, David-Weill approached Bruce Wasserstein about buying Wasserstein Perella & Co., a merger advisory firm even smaller than Lazard, according to a person close to the talks. David-Weill dropped the idea after some Lazard partners objected that Wasserstein would have too prominent a role in the firm. In October 2000, Wasserstein agreed to be bought by Dresdner Bank AG for $1.56 billion.

Lazard has brought in some high-profile figures from outside investment banking, including U.S. ambassador to Germany John Kornblum and Vernon Jordan, a lawyer with personal ties to U.S. president Bill Clinton. Neither is an established banker who can bring a roster of clients with him.

Lazard is far from dead. The firm advised Pfizer on its $120 billion merger with Warner-Lambert Co. in June 2000 and is representing Thames Water Plc on its proposed takeover by Germany's RWE AG for $9.8 billion. One of the firm's biggest clients is Vivendi. Since January 1999, Lazard has advised Vivendi on almost a dozen transactions, including the $39 billion purchase of Seagram and Canal Plus. Danone—whose board includes David-Weill—is also a major client. Lazard advised the firm when it was looking to buy Quaker Oats Co. and Nabisco Holdings Corp. in 2000. Neither deal worked out.

David-Weill bets Lazard can keep and attract bankers who don't want to work in the anonymous bureaucracies of big firms. Still, he rests his hopes on a partnership structure that increasingly seems obsolete. In May 1999, Goldman Sachs went public after 131 years as a partnership, enriching its partners—Goldman shares rose 72 percent in the first nineteen months of trading—and gaining a permanent capital base. One smaller rival—177-year-old London stockbroker Cazenove & Co.—in November 2000 announced plans to go public and abandon its partnership structure after concluding it was limiting the firm's ability to lure senior talent and raise capital for expansion.

David-Weill and the bank he runs are now increasingly surrounded by giant rivals who seem intent on mimicking each other's business plans. The Lazard chairman says he's convinced his firm can survive in its current form. "The demise of Lazard has been predicted before, but it hasn't happened," says Roy Smith of NYU. "They may slide off the cliff one day, but I'm tired of being wrong about them." David-Weill, who took a nineteenth-century approach to banking and made it work in the twentieth century, must show that he is equally adaptable in the years ahead.

Most of our offhanded daily observations are quickly forgotten. Investigative business journalism digs deep to determine the validity of perceived problems and whether larger trends are at work. Thousands of discount-store customers have been hurt and some killed by falling lumber, detergent boxes, and other items. While stores have been sued for millions, the toll continues to mount. Davan Maharaj of the *Los Angeles Times,* through interviews and examination of court records, was the first to break this major story. Every reader can relate to it.

Davan Maharaj

"Sky Shelves" Can Be Lethal for Shoppers

FEW OF THE MILLIONS OF SHOPPERS who each day crowd into the retail canyons of big discounters such as Home Depot and Wal-Mart expect to be crushed in an avalanche of merchandise.

But that's exactly what happened to Mary Penturff.

The seventy-nine-year-old Santa Monica woman was looking for lattice to stake her morning glories in November at a Los Angeles Home Depot when a nineteen-year-old forklift operator accidentally tipped a load of lumber stacked several feet above her. She was crushed to death in front of her horrified daughter.

"You expect to die or get injured if you go to war or if you speed on the freeway," said the daughter, Rebecca Hamilton. "The last thing you expect when you enter your neighborhood store is that you won't come out alive."

Penturff's accident was just one of thousands of injuries and deaths involving shoppers that resulted from falling merchandise in warehouse-style stores, according to a *Times* examination of court records from around the country. The incidents have been piling up for at least fifteen years, since boxes of Final Touch fabric softener toppled from a shelf at a Sam's Club store near Tulsa, Oklahoma, in 1995, killing a woman who was shopping for cleaning supplies.

Despite numerous lawsuits and millions of dollars in jury awards and settlements against various discount retailers and warehouse superstores, the toll continues to mount. Only last month, a forty-one-year-old Connecticut man was killed at his neighborhood Home Depot when a 2,000-pound pallet of landscaping timbers fell and pinned him to the ground.

The mushrooming of retail superstores—where forklifts prowl aisles, stacking pallets of merchandise from floor to ceiling—has brought lower prices and convenience to cities and small towns across America. But thousands of consumers who have ventured into these retail centers to run routine errands have encountered tragedy instead.

Wal-Mart has acknowledged in court records that during a six-year period ending in 1995, its claims department reported that falling merchandise was responsible for about 26,000 customer claims and 7,000 employee injuries.

Home Depot refused to provide specific numbers, but a company official testified in 1998 that the retail haven for do-it-yourselfers was receiving 185 injury claims a week, many involving falling merchandise. During an eighteen-month period in 1995–96, sixty-eight customers sued Home Depot for injuries sustained from items falling off shelves.

"People don't understand the danger they're in when they enter these stores," said Stephen Rasak, a Torrance attorney who last week won a $900,000 settlement from Home Depot for Penturff's two surviving daughters. "They're assuming these places are just like supermarkets, but little do they know they're walking into a minefield."

Officials with Wal-Mart, Home Depot, and several other

warehouse-style retailers say their stores are reasonably safe, that accidents are rare, and that they're constantly striving to prevent mishaps.

"Accidents are just that, they're just accidents," said Jerry Shields, a Home Depot spokesman, noting that the number of customers injured from falling goods are a fraction of the 30,000 transactions recorded each week at a single Home Depot outlet.

Wal-Mart makes the same argument.

"When you consider we have 100 million customers a week, the number of falling-merchandise cases is very small," said Les Copeland, a spokesman at Wal-Mart's headquarters in Bentonville, Arkansas. "We wish these particular accidents never happen. Unfortunately they do. But our overall track record is very good."

But safety experts and lawyers representing injured shoppers say these superstores often flout their own safety rules, sacrificing consumers' safety by stacking heavy and dangerous objects up to twenty feet above the floor without restraining devices.

These retailers, experts say, operate in an industry in which stores are seldom inspected for safety violations and penalties are paltry. And even when a fatal or serious accident occurs, fines, if any, are minimal

While there are many rules and regulations designed to protect employees from workplace accidents—indeed, an entire federal government agency is devoted to worker safety—consumers get little consideration. Remedies are often left to the civil courts, which have recently been flooded with hundreds of damage suits. Wal-Mart, Home Depot, and other retailers have successfully defended many of these suits, but often they pay confidential sums to settle or are ordered by juries to pay multimillion-dollar verdicts.

The retailers decline to say how much they pay in lawsuits from people hurt by falling merchandise each year, saying the figures are confidential business information.

The latest figures gleaned from court records show that accidents cost Wal-Mart alone $410 million in 1994, up from $275 million in 1992.

Jeffrey Hyman, a Denver attorney who represents plaintiffs in falling-merchandise cases, said that in his nine court trials against Wal-Mart he has obtained $9 million from juries.

"These are known risks to Wal-Mart," Hyman said. "But in Wal-Mart's mind, it's simply not cost effective for their stores to install safety devices like fencing, rails, safety straps, or netting to protect merchandise from falling.

"When a jury returns with a multimillion-dollar verdict, the community is saying that Wal-Mart isn't doing things right," he said. "But they don't seem to have gotten the message."

MOUNTING EVIDENCE

No agency keeps statistics about the number of people killed or injured by falling merchandise, but the tragedies have been litigated in courts across the country:

- In 1992, a three-year-old girl was crushed to death by a falling door at a Home Depot store in San Diego. Her twin brother and her parents witnessed the accident.
- A forty-six-year-old Edmonds, Washington, woman was killed at a HomeBase in 1994, when a 3,000-pound pallet of ceramic tiles collapsed on her.
- In 1996, a wardrobe toppled and killed a child at a Sam's Club in Abilene, Texas.
- In 1997, a two-year-old girl died after a 100-pound television cabinet fell on her in a Wal-Mart store in Virginia Beach, Virginia.

For each fatality, scores of other shoppers are hurt by items tumbling off shelves. Copeland, the Wal-Mart spokesman, said the majority of claims against the company involved small cuts, bruises, and minor cases in which shoppers hurt themselves while pulling down merchandise.

But many involve serious head injuries which forever change the lives of some shoppers.

Take Todd Carranto, for example. Just twenty-three years old, the U.S. Air Force enlistee hoped to become a medical doctor after his military service. But those aspirations evaporated a few years ago when Carranto entered a Wal-Mart store in Las Vegas. Falling boxes of merchandise struck Carranto, slamming his head to the store's concrete floor.

Carranto became "totally and permanently disabled," according to court records. He has "no reasonable expectation of engaging in gainful employment" and "will require treatment and medication for the reminder of his life" to cope with the seizure and mental disorders caused by the accident.

A federal judge in Las Vegas awarded Carranto and his family $4 million. Wal-Mart has appealed the amount, saying it's unduly generous—even though Carranto's attorneys argued that the money was not enough to pay for their client's around-the-clock nursing care.

"SKY SHELVING" UNDER SCRUTINY

High stacking of goods, or "sky shelving," as it is known, was introduced in the retail industry some two decades ago by retail giants Wal-Mart, Home Depot, and Kmart, among others.

"They like the store to look full," said David Bell, a professor at Harvard Business School. "By creating this visual impact, they want customers to say, 'These guys are never going to be out of stock.'"

But the main reason these merchandisers stack goods from floor to ceiling is pure economics. Warehousing goods is expensive, so some retailers save millions of dollars by turning their stores into working warehouses, according to Bob Blattberg, director of the Center for Retail Management at Northwestern University's Kellogg Graduate School of Management.

"It's a lot easier and cheaper to stack the goods on top of the shelf than in a back room or in a warehouse," he said.

Former Wal-Mart president David Glass explained the concept this way: "The thing that sets it apart, it's a working distribution center where you deal with the movements of very, very large amounts of merchandise in very efficient methods."

Glass's comments came during the trial of a lawsuit filed by survivors of a Briscow, Oklahoma, homeowner who was killed in one of Wal-Mart's Sam's Club stores about a month after its grand opening in 1985. The fatal accident was probably the first deadly warning to the retail industry that forklifts and sky shelving in warehouse-type stores were a combination fraught with danger.

The victim, Dolly Cain, seventy, had gone to Sam's Club to pick up cleaning supplies. Her daughter, Judith Dotson, now fifty-eight, accompanied her.

"I heard things falling and the next thing I knew boxes of Final Touch and Fresh Start [laundry detergent] were falling on her," said Dotson. "She was bleeding from a gash [that stretched] from her eyebrow to the crown of her head. After they pulled the stuff off her, she took one look at me and said, 'I'm not going to make it.'"

Dotson rode in the ambulance with Cain to a nearby hospital, but the retired postal worker was pronounced dead within an hour, according to Dotson.

Dotson said she later learned that a forklift driver moving a pallet of drinking straws in an adjacent aisle had accidentally pushed the goods from about twelve feet high onto her mother.

Dotson and other relatives sued and received a $3.9 million verdict. After Wal-Mart appealed, the parties reached a confidential settlement.

RETAILERS URGE CAUTION

In interviews and court documents, Home Depot, Wal-Mart, Kmart, and other retailers blamed customers for injuries suffered from falling merchandise. They say people should know the risks associated with shopping in a warehouse-style retail store.

"People should be aware that they are in a working warehouse," said Carol Schumacher, Home Depot's vice president of communications. "You need to be aware of what's going on around you just like when you're driving a car."

Tyrone Maho, a Santa Barbara attorney who said he has successfully defended Wal-Mart in falling merchandise suits, blamed "plaintiff attorneys who are trying to indict the entire retail industry and line their pocketbooks" for the hundreds of damage suits.

"People interact with merchandise and there's always the potential for an accident," said Maho. "This is the nature of self-service. We can't be in the business of personally guiding everyone through our stores."

But the courts don't always buy the retailers' argument that shoppers bear some responsibility to be on the lookout for falling merchandise. In a case involving a woman struck by falling toys at a Kmart store, a Colorado judge rejected the argument that shoppers need to beware.

"The consequences of placing the burden on the [shopper] in this case are such that if one took it to its logical extreme, everyone would have to take a crash course, if you pardon the expression, in taking care," said Arapahoe County district judge John P. Leopold. "You'd have to wear safety helmets indoors. And I'm not prepared to do that."

Wal-Mart and other retailers say they've adopted safety measures over the years to make their stores safer. Signs warn customers to ask for a clerk's help before reaching for high objects.

Copeland, the Wal-Mart spokesman, said the retailer has

taken several measures to ensure that its stores are safe from falling merchandise. Through a computerized program, new hires learn how to stack merchandise properly.

Employees, according to Copeland, are encouraged to use the "bump test," where they bump a stacked shelf to ensure that merchandise is stable. If items are wobbly, they must be restacked. In addition, he said, safety teams constantly roam the aisles, checking on safety.

"We make mistakes, but we do a lot of things to prevent these [accidents] from happening," he said.

Some retailers such as Home Depot have written policies requiring stores to shrink-wrap all goods stacked high on shelves. Several years ago, Home Depot and Wal-Mart began requiring spotters to prevent shoppers from entering the area—and the adjacent aisles—where forklifts are operating.

But plaintiff's lawyers allege that stores do not always follow these policies, hence the thousands of accidents each year—a charge that retailers contest.

Penturff, the Santa Monica woman, for example, would not have been killed last year had store officials followed Home Depot's policy to cordon off the aisles where forklifts are stacking or retrieving goods.

Critics say Home Depot executives know too well about the risks involved in allowing shoppers to mingle among forklifts. In one New York case that resulted in an $825,000 verdict, lawyers for a man struck by a forklift in a Home Depot store played a company's video training tape advising workers of the need to be especially careful because "one would never know what a customer will do" and that operating a forklift in the store was like "driving a tank in a public area."

Last year a federal appeals court found evidence in the Carranto case suggesting that "Wal-Mart knew its method of stacking merchandise posed a significant risk to customers."

Stacking merchandise to the ceiling is an added worry in earthquake-prone California. Home Depot officials acknowledged as much in a videotape obtained earlier this month by the *San Francisco Chronicle.*

Four of the company's Los Angeles stores suffered $2.3 million in damage during the 1994 Northridge quake. A video produced for store managers depicted the extensive damage—collapsed steel shelves and mounds of fallen boxes, tiles, and other merchandise piled high when they toppled in the aisles.

"Imagine the injuries and even deaths that would have occurred if anyone had been standing here when the first tremors hit," the video narrator said.

Home Depot says its steel racks exceed code requirements.

ALLEGATIONS OF LAX REGULATION

Hyman and other critics say mass merchandisers operate in an industry where safety inspections are lax. The federal Occupational Safety and Health Administration, which monitors workplace safety, has rules requiring that goods stored in tiers be "stacked, blocked, interlocked, and limited in height so that they are stable and secure against sliding or collapse."

But OSHA seldom fines retail superstores, according to statistics examined by the *Times,* even in cases where consumers die as a result of falling merchandise or some other accident.

For example, in the last five and a half years, state and federal OSHA inspectors have made only 100 planned workplace safety checks on the thousands of outlets operated by Home Depot and Wal-Mart and Sam's Club agreement.

"We don't want consumers hurt, but it's not in our area of coverage," said an OSHA official in Washington.

He said the agency sometimes steps in if officials learn through news reports about a death or injury of a shopper—but only if they believe that workers' safety is being jeopardized.

Rasak, the attorney for Penturff's daughters, said neither he nor the family received any inquiries from OSHA after the accident.

Last week, however, Rasak received word from Home Depot's lawyers that the firm was ready to settle the suit for $900,000. Penturff's daughters rejected Home Depot's request to keep the settlement confidential, saying they wanted to alert other shoppers to the dangers in these stores.

Experts say that barring legislation or a massive jury verdict, some retailers are unlikely to improve their safety measures so that more accidents are prevented.

"Making the changes necessary to make all the shelving safe is not an insignificant cost," said Blattberg, the Northwestern professor. "Maybe they will pay attention when a jury comes back with a $100 million verdict. That could be the wake-up call."

The death of paper was greatly exaggerated, Steve Silberman contends in this *Wired* article. If this Swedish firm is successful, a special pen put to paper will be all we need to connect directly to the digital world. The article makes us rethink the traditional relationship between the different forms of modern communication. It also explains the intricate technology behind what appears to be a straightforward concept, but which could change everything.

Steve Silberman

The Hot New Medium: Paper

THEY'RE BUILDING SOMETHING enormous at a research park outside of Lund, Sweden. Like any concept that eventually becomes the standard by which imagination is measured, it started out small and grew as its creators came to understand the scale of what they were making. Now it's half as big as the United States.

By dawn—which means midmorning in winter at this latitude—the bulldozers have already been roaring for hours, churning mountains out of the red, muddy soil, forcing drivers to improvise roads over the fresh muck. The chaos of construction is not unusual here. The wireless boom in Europe and Asia is bringing dozens of new office buildings to research parks like this one all over Scandinavia, from start-ups incubated as student projects to established firms poised to surf the wave of personal-area-network devices that will wash ashore in the next couple of years. Even more ambitious, however, is the project taking shape in a cluttered second-floor office known as the monkey cage by the engineers and programmers who work there.

As Christer Fåhraeus tries to describe the magnitude of what he and his team are designing, his fingers dance with a pen across a sheet of paper. A compact, straw-haired, thirty-five-year-old Swede, Fåhraeus gives off the aura of a tensely coiled spring. In Swedish or English, he speaks staccato, as if there were too many ideas backing up behind the frustratingly slow buffer of syntax. To relieve the pressure inside him, he sketches arrows, rectangles, and intersections that form the true arc of his thoughts. Words come secondarily to him, Fåhraeus tells me—his brain thinks in images. He holds up the paper.

"This is the most advanced digital input screen ever developed," he declares. "It has very high resolution, perfect contrast, and costs a fraction of a cent to produce. Any graphical interface can be printed on it, and you get years of full-time education, paid for by the government, to learn how to use it. It will not be beaten in our lifetime."

He puts the paper in my hands. "And I can *give* it to you, because I have hundreds more," he offers, gesturing toward a stack of blank paper on his desk. Fåhraeus isn't handing me a sketch of the input screen. The paper *is* the screen.

That's what they're building at Anoto, the company Fåhraeus launched a year and a half ago beside this muddy field near the southwestern tip of Sweden: a network that can transform millions of sheets of paper into a new front end for the Internet.

By the end of this year, Ericsson will bring to market a pudgy-looking ballpoint called the Chatpen. It will be the first of a new breed of writing instrument invented by Anoto that will allow you to send e-mail and faxes directly on paper, with no personal computer or wireless tablet in sight. You'll be able to jot these messages down on business cards, legal pads, or company letterhead. To send a message, you'll simply check a box for "Send as e-mail" or "Send as fax" that's printed in the corner of the paper. Marking other boxes will route your message to pagers or mobile phones. A single scribbled note will trigger a cascade of networked events: jotting down a lunch date in your day planner could update your laptop and fire off an e-mail to your assistant.

"There are three fundamental technologies for gathering, storing, and spreading information—voice, computer, and paper and pen," Fåhraeus declares, drawing three squares on the paper and methodically checking them off. "Now we make this one digital and wireless, like the others." By closing the gap between paper and the digital domain, Anoto is planning to put the convenience and speed of the Net behind an interface that was debugged thousands of years ago.

"If we succeed," he adds, "we will have more product coverage than any other company on Earth."

If his network rolls out as scheduled, within a year you'll be able to make a check mark beside a magazine ad to receive information about a product, or even to buy it. Visualize e-commerce without the click-and-wait: browsing through a printed catalog, you'll purchase items—software, a subwoofer, or a trip to Paris—by ticking them off with a pen. Circling your destination on a city map will display, on your PalmPilot or mobile phone, the quickest route from here to there, movie showtimes, or tonight's menu at the best bistros in the area.

To do these things, you'll need an instrument like the Chatpen that contains technology developed by Anoto. (By 2003, other Anoto-enabled pens, including Pilot rollerballs and a characteristically elegant offering from Montblanc, will be available.) You'll also need a supply of the special paper that Anoto has christened "digital paper." It won't be hard to find, and it won't cost much more than standard copy stock. Unlike Xerox PARC's electronic paper or MIT/E Ink's Immedia, Anoto's technology employs real paper and commonly available inks. By the time Chatpens appear in office-supply shops and mail-order catalogs this fall, digital paper sporting the Anoto logo will be turning up everywhere. This global rollout will be branded with the most recognizable names in the office-products industry. You'll be able to buy digital Cambridge legal pads, digital At-A-Glance organizers, digital *Financial Times* diaries, and digital Franklin planners handsomely bound in leather. This winter, expect flurries of digital 3M Post-it notes.

At Comdex 2000 last fall, the buzz was that some Swedish start-up (or Japanese; the name of the company, which does sound vaguely Pacific Rim, is taken from the Latin *annoto*, meaning "I scribble") had developed a cool "smart pen." Anoto was one of two finalists for a Best of Show award, though interestingly, it lost to the Tablet PC, Microsoft's platform that supports handwriting. Bill Gates's keynote, extolling the virtues of handwritten input, included a demo in which he beamed a hand-drawn map to an assistant—with directions to the nearest Starbucks.

While the established heavyweight took home the prize, the concepts driving the Anoto network are a lot more ambitious than Microsoft's latest must-buy for the handheld sector. Pen-based interfaces are not exactly news, even if being able to write in your own handwriting is considerably easier than trying to recall the Graffiti symbol for the letter "q." While the Chatpen demo in the Ericsson booth—featuring a caricaturist whose drawings were piped to a laptop screen—was cute, it barely hinted at Anoto's potential.

Anoto's approach, in contrast to Microsoft's, doesn't require a PC. Each Anoto pen contains a Bluetooth chip that communicates with any other Bluetooth device within thirty feet, which could be your mobile phone or PDA. Ericsson will introduce the R520, the first handset to ship with Bluetooth, in the United States and Europe by the second half of this year. Nokia already sells a Bluetooth card for its 6210 phone, and Toshiba started shipping Bluetooth PC cards last fall. The penetration of these devices is expected to snowball as the cost of Bluetooth chipsets plummets to between $5 and $10 in the next three years. If the public-access Bluetooth nodes now in development at companies like Cerulic and NomadNetworks are widely installed in airports, hotels, and conference centers, eventually all you'll need to carry is an Anoto-enabled pen and a sheet of digital paper.

As nifty and convenient as the porting of handwritten text to the Net may seem, there will be even more advantages to liberation from the networked typewriter. If your native language is, say, Chinese, Arabic, or Russian, you will no longer have to translate your thoughts into an alphabet that a QWERTY keyboard understands. Once symbols and line drawings are as easy to pour into the datastream as ASCII, you won't have to depend on text at all. Storyboards, architectural sketches, fabric designs, game strategies, and comic strips will be e-mailed, faxed, or posted to the Web as quickly as they can be sketched by hand. Equations, with their special characters and sub- and superscripts, will be a breeze. If you compose a melody on sheet music, you will be able to play it instantly on your mobile phone or MIDI device. An artist will be able to zap sketches from his atelier to the Kinko's around the corner.

"Leonardo da Vinci would be our perfect customer," brags Jan Andersson, the president of Anoto.

The peerless doodler from Florence might have appreciated that the spark of genius that makes the network function does not reside in Anoto's fancy pens. It's printed on the paper.

It's a map.

The first time you see this map, you may not even notice it. Printed in a shade of carbon-based ink called Anoto Black that's more visible at the infrared end of the spectrum, the map appears as a light gray dusting of dots, forming a nearly invisible grid on the surface of the paper. Each sheet of digital paper carries only a small portion of the map. If you look at an Anoto-enabled Post-it, what you're seeing is a Post-it-sized fraction of a map that is actually 1.8 million square miles—half the area of the United States.

Here's how it works: Beside the ballpoint tip of each Anoto-enabled pen is a lens. Behind the lens is the same sort of CMOS image-sensing chip used in cash machines and digital cameras. This tiny, inexpensive eye is wired to a microprocessor in the pen. Every one-hundredth of a second, the camera takes a snapshot of whatever portion of the map is underneath the pen at any moment.

The pen doesn't actually "see" what you're writing. The CMOS chip is programmed to favor infrared, so the trail of ink is invisible to the camera. All the pen sees is the map. ("The ink is just there to make you feel comfortable," purrs a piece of Anoto documentation, with typical Swedish understatement.)

The dots that make up the map are each one-tenth of a millimeter in diameter, and they're arrayed on a grid of two-by-two-millimeter squares, thirty-six dots to a square. In a basic grid square, these dots would be arranged smoothly along x/y axes, like perfectly aligned chess pieces. All of the points on the Anoto map, however, are slightly displaced from those axes. This displacement creates a unique pattern in each square—and there are 4,722,366,482,869,645,213,696 squares in all.

To visualize this, imagine that you're writing on a huge sheet of graph paper. The pattern of dots in any particular square corresponds to an exact location on the sheet—say, B2. As you write on the paper, your pen travels over a series of locations: from B2, to B3, then over to C1 as you cross a "t," and so forth. The movement of your pen over these locations corresponds exactly to the shape of what you're writing. Using the map, the pen obtains a precise reading of its position on the vast grid, down to one-thirtieth of a millimeter. As the instrument dances across the grid, it stores a series of locations. It time-stamps this itinerary, in case later verification is needed. There's enough memory in the pen to store about 100 notebook-sized pages of writing.

Each instrument is coded with a unique identity. The pen in your pocket might be number 754348847, for example. When you check off one of the special function boxes—like "Send as fax"—in the corner of each piece of paper, the pen transmits the contents of its memory to Anoto-powered Bluetooth devices in your network. (In addition to the standard Bluetooth security layer, this information is also encrypted by the pen, using Public Key Infrastructure and 128-bit keys.) From one of those devices, such as a phone or PDA with a wireless modem, the burst of information from the pen hitches a ride to the Net.

It's important to make one thing clear: the Anoto pen does not understand language. With certain exceptions, the pen doesn't perform OCR (optical character recognition) on what you've written to translate your handwriting into standard ASCII text. The e-mail messages you send out arrive in recipients' in-boxes as small in-line graphics files displaying your words, in your handwriting, exactly the way you wrote it. (When you send e-mail to a mobile phone, it appears as a graphical SMS message.)

Certain areas on the paper will be dedicated to OCR-related functions. Letters and numbers—small addresses and subject lines, snail-mail addresses, and phone numbers—written carefully in form fields there will be converted to ASCII characters. A digital business card, for instance, might have lines on the back where you can enter contact information. Checking "Send" would e-mail that information to the person whose name is on the front of the card.

The pen doesn't know if you've just scribbled a love note, signed a pink slip, or declared war. It knows only a few things: which pen it is in the Anoto network, which locations on the map it's been seeing lately, and what time it is. This information—the pen's identity and a series of time-stamped locations on the map— is what gets transmitted to the Net.

There, the encrypted stream of bits from the pen employs standard DNS protocols, like the ones used by a Web browser, to look for the Anoto Name Server, or ANS, which is a multimillion-dollar array of Unix drives currently under construction in Stockholm. The first ANS disk array will be located there, but eventually Anoto will employ a distributed network of servers. Each transmission from the pen arrives at the ANS with a question: "Who owns the part of the map where I am now?"

This is where things really get interesting. The big map is divided into territories, with a certain number of grid squares allocated for various products and services. One area of the map, say, might be reserved for Filofax organizers. Another will be dedicated to Post-it notes. A third might belong to a software vendor who runs magazine ads printed on digital paper. By entering into a partnership with Anoto, you buy your own little chunk of real estate on the big map, which gives you the right to print that portion of the map on your products—whether your business is manufacturing legal pads, booking vacations on cruise ships, or selling DVDs from a catalog.

By tracking where each Anoto pen is on the map, the ANS knows, for instance, that pen number 754348847 made a check mark at 12:03 P.M. in an area of the grid that belongs to an on-line florist. The instrument then transmits a message to the florist's own servers to fulfill the purchase order, dispatching a dozen roses to the mailing address written at the bottom of the paper. Because OCR is dodgy business—as anyone who uses one of the fax-to-e-mail services knows—the shipping address might appear on the sender's mobile phone for verification before the bouquet leaves the warehouse.

Anoto isn't in this game to make a branded splash in the paper business, or to steal market share from Bic. Ericsson's Chatpen will be used to establish the standard, and the business of designing later versions of the pen will fall to established players like Pilot and Montblanc. Anoto won't be making paper, either.

Anoto's business model resides in the ANS—in selling off chunks of the big map and tracking every transaction scribbled on digital paper. If a purchase is made on Mead paper, with a Montblanc pen, and the product or service is delivered to the customer by an on-line merchant, then Mead, Montblanc, the merchant, and Anoto each get a cut. Anoto is betting that it will be able to tap into revenue streams created by a breed of paper-based e-commerce services that hasn't even been imagined yet.

Such streams, however, can run only in courses laid by a widely accepted standard. In that sense, Anoto is a thoroughly twenty-first-century business: it's not about making widgets and shipping them to the consumer, or about building a brand. It's about advocating a standard and then insinuating a new enterprise into the global infrastructure created by that standard.

Anoto isn't locked in to Bluetooth. If that technology confounds expectations and is not widely adopted, Anoto could swap the transceiver out of its pens for anything else that can do the job. However, the chip inside the pen gives the thousands of companies committed to Bluetooth—like Ericsson, which is keen on extending its market after facing unexpected losses early this year—an incentive to adopt Anoto's own standard for digital paper. Ericsson has picked up 15 percent of Anoto—a subsidiary of C Technologies, a publicly traded company that is another of Fåhraeus's ventures—with an option to pick up another 15 percent.

Whether or not Anoto and its partners are able to make every application come off smoothly—and more broadly, whether the entire project thrives or stumbles—the network concept offers a preview of the world to come. At one end of the digital spectrum, Moore's law and fat-pipe upgrades will deliver heart-stopping clock speeds and insane amounts of bandwidth in the next few years. But creative innovation is starting to flourish at the other end, too, where swarms of highly networked and practically disposable eyes and ears—like Anoto's pens—will be let loose on the world to swarm around us, listening and testing, and buzzing with the news of what they find.

A poet once told me that a writer must write with "the mind of God and the eyes of a spider." Before the Net came along, there was a lot of speculation that the ultimate product of technology, when we finally had the hardware to build it, would be something approximating the mind of God—a centralized superbrain. As we extend our networks into every available niche of our lives, the ultimate product of technology is turning out to be more like the sum of the sparks of intelligence in the eyes of billions of ephemeral spiders, weaving webs in all the corners of creation.

It's at this end of the spectrum that a start-up like Anoto could blow everyone's mind by establishing a standard that is widely adopted and scaling upward toward infinity.

With its labyrinth of cobblestone streets, Romanesque cathedral, and brooding medieval buildings housing bohemian cafés, Lund is the darkly enchanted European college town of your dreams. An extraordinary number of shops in Lund bear the sign ANTIK-VARIAT, meaning "a seller of old books and antique maps." So it's only fitting that a new kind of map is being conceived not far from here. The town's fascination with cartography goes back at least as far as the fourteenth century, when a fantastically painted astronomical clock was installed in the Lund cathedral to track the sun and the moon through the zodiac, marking noon and 3 P.M. with a blast of trumpets and a procession of mechanical Wise Men toward the Virgin Mary. It still keeps good time.

The town, which is much closer to Copenhagen than it is to Stockholm, lies off the beaten path of the tourist trade, in part because many local merchants shutter their windows after the students leave for the summer. Swedes celebrate Lund for the climate of philosophical ferment surrounding the university, which is balanced by an attitude that Swedish essayist Jan Mårtensson called the Lund spirit: "an ironic distance to everything [and] a barb to deflate pompous self-importance."

In 1983, faced with a decline in Sweden's traditional industrial mainstays—shipbuilding and textile manufacturing—the town broke ground for the first science park in Sweden: Ideon, where Anoto is located. Ideon's first tenant was the Ericsson Mobile Telephony Laboratory. The cross-fertilization of academic research and commercial development—inspired by U.S. models—proved fruitful. Ericsson's first portable mobile phone, the C900, was designed at Ideon and brought to market in 1987.

Fåhraeus grew up in Linköping and came to Lund as an undergraduate in 1986. His interests roamed broadly among the sciences, encompassing medical biophysics, bioengineering, and the mathematical modeling of neurons. As a teenager, he displayed a knack for making things happen. When he was fifteen, he launched the local chapter of a conservative student organization (the second largest in the country) and founded a reading circle that received funds from the government. Though Fåhraeus currently holds seven patents and has filed applications for fifty more, he says, "I never thought of myself as an inventor. I never thought of myself as an entrepreneur. But I was good at taking initiative, inventing games—or reinventing them if I was losing."

In December 1994, Fåhraeus launched his first company, Cella-Vision, which specializes in building microscopy systems that partially automate cell analysis. It wasn't easy. In the early nineties, the chill winds of a global recession, stirred up by currency speculation, blew over the Swedish krona. The Swedish National Bank boosted its lending rate fivefold while executives from companies like Volvo floated down on golden parachutes to countries with lower tax burdens, such as the United Kingdom.

Just as the telecom revolution was getting under way, young Swedish entrepreneurs scrabbled for sources of venture capital. Fåhraeus persisted. In June 1996, he founded C Technologies, which produced his most successful product to date, a handheld scanner called the C Pen. (Despite its name, the C Pen, which saw a modest $5 million in sales last year, is *not* primarily a writing instrument.) Other products created at C Tech include intelligent surveillance cameras (spun off to form a company called WeSpot) and an optical mouse. A year after starting C Tech, Fåhraeus launched Precise Biometrics, which specializes in fingerprint recognition.

The common thread running through Fåhraeus's product line is real-time image processing. What the optical mouse, scanner, and Anoto pen have in common is that they take digital snapshots of what they see to determine their whereabouts. The camera in an optical mouse (such as the Apple Pro Mouse) scrutinizes irregularities on the scrolling surface to gauge what is called the mouse's relative position. The mouse judges movement, not location. If you pick up the mouse and set it down, it forgets where it was and starts tracking from zero again.

The C Pen does let you add your own words to scanned text by tracing letters on any irregular surface, like a page in a book. But because the C Pen contains no ink, you don't see the letters you're writing. They're preserved in the scanner's memory, and you can edit or transmit them like regular scanned text. As with an optical mouse, however, lifting the C Pen from its tracking surface cancels out its relative position. To write an "x," you have to use what's called a unistroke—you must cross a single line over itself without lifting the pen, as you do with a palmtop stylus.

Understandably, this annoyed Petter Ericson, a graduate student at Lund University who began working for C Tech in March 1997. In a country of reserved, fair-skinned blonds, Ericson has the swarthy good looks of an Italian bad-boy film star. Fåhraeus also hired Ericson's high school friend Ola Hugosson. While Ericson's vitality seems barely contained under a thicket of cowlicks, Hugosson is clearly focused inward. A musician from a family of musicians, Hugosson plays Bach at home on the piano. He met Ericson when they both enrolled in a national contest for student programmers. Hugosson was impressed by the lightning rapidity of Ericson's mind, while Ericson was awed by Hugosson's intensity as he bore down on a problem. They made a powerful team. Ericson then encouraged another old friend, Linus Wiebe, to take a job at Precise Biometrics.

All three first learned how to program in the hacker subculture that sprang up around an illustrious generation of home computers whose names are legendary among programmers of a certain age: the Apple II, the Commodore 64, the Atari 800, the Amiga 1000, and the Sinclair ZX Spectrum. There was a narrow window where thirteen-year-old geeks-in-training could sharpen their chops—and make friends all over the world—by writing algorithms and hacking serious code. Before that, computers were too expensive. After the introduction of so-called user-friendly Interfaces from Apple and IBM, the good stuff was all hidden under the hood.

Ericson and Hugosson brought the old hacker brio with them to C Tech, where they were paid to explore answers to essential questions and even write their own operating system. "I used to think, 'Later in our careers, no one will ever let us do this,'" Ericson recalls. By fall 1997, there was a stew of applications for real-time image processing simmering there. One of Fåhraeus's brainstorms involved printing a pattern on a mousepad that a mouse could then read like a map. It would judge its position *absolutely,* without reference to any prior location.

One day in February 1999, after C Tech team members had been mulling over concepts like this for months, Ericson decided to go home to nearby Malmö and take a bath.

Like any good citizen in a region of the planet where baking in a cedar-planked room is considered the acme of relaxation, Ericson jumped into the tub to clear his mind. "A lot of this work is trying to solve a problem while you're continuously interrupted by ringing phones and ICQs. Your mind becomes like a bad Windows system running too many background processes," he told me geekishly. He's convinced that hot baths, like saunas, elevate the temperature of the brain, increasing the flow of uncensored creative thinking.

What came to him in the tub was dots.

Coincidentally, one of the first methods ever proposed for marrying the ease of writing by hand to the data-crunching velocity of computers also employed dots. In the fifties, Bell System switchboard operators kept records of the long-distance calls they handled on two-and-a-half-by-five-inch scraps of paper called toll tickets. Operators were scribbling 2 billion tickets a year, but paying keypunch operators to transfer a year's worth of call records to punch cards would have cost Bell $32 million. At the Eastern Joint Computer Conference in 1957, T. L. Dimond of Bell Labs outlined a method for capturing handwritten data directly. He proposed replacing the tickets with a plastic tablet energized by a flow of current through the writing stylus. To standardize the shapes of the handwritten characters so that a computer could read them, Dimond suggested training the operators to construct letters and numbers around pairs of dots, a method he called "dot constraint." Dimond named his device the Stylator.

Most of the pen-based input devices available today use variations on Dimond's strategy of embedding processing power in the writing surface. Wacom tablets run magnetic pulses through a grid of embedded wires to get a fix on the cursor's position. Many digital whiteboards employ ultrasonic triangulation to do the same thing. Palmtops, of course, allow users to write on the computer itself.

This was Ericson's flash in the bathtub: a complex pattern of dots would make an excellent map for absolute positioning. Dots are good "primaries" for low-overhead image processing because they look the same no matter which way you rotate them. Even if the organization of the dots is random, the device could consult a lookup table to determine which location in the pattern it is seeing and thus determine its position. Using such a table, however, squandered processing time and memory. "This problem," Ericson concluded, "has Ola written all over it."

After Ericson told Hugosson about his idea one Friday afternoon, Hugosson was, indeed, all over the problem. With the many constraints posed by a system that has to run superefficiently on a handheld device, it was a perfect puzzle for a mathematician who could appreciate the beauty that Bach coaxed out of rigorous symmetries. When Ericson returned to his desk on Monday morning, he found a sheet of paper, with a pattern printed on it, waiting for him.

Hugosson had spent the entire weekend pounding out the math, incubating clouds of dots in C and PostScript. His solution was to generate the pattern by using an algorithm, rather than depending on brute processing power to sort through random messes of dots. That way, the mouse wouldn't have to store the entire pattern in its memory. It could merely store the algorithm.

The pattern he presented to Ericson consisted of dots in two sizes, spaced a millimeter apart. With the number of possible permutations of small and large dots, the size of Hugosson's map was four by four meters. This seemed like more than enough area to play with because the men were thinking only in terms of a device that would track across a mousepad or a book.

Then Tomas Edso and Mats-Petter Petterson, two student

interns at C Tech, suggested using dot displacement, rather than dot size, to determine the unique pattern of locations on the grid. Each dot would then yield two bits of information, corresponding to the degree of displacement along the x and y axes, rather than one. Edso and Petterson's strategy—which employed smaller dots, with thirty-six per square instead of twenty-five—resulted in 272 possible arrangements of dots, rather than 225. Even printing the dots only .3 millimeters apart—rather than 1 millimeter—and allowing for redundancy to correct for scanning errors, the size of the grid became much larger. "How big is the pattern *today*?" members of the C Tech team would tease one another.

From an area that would have covered ten letter-sized sheets of paper, and then several football fields, the pattern eventually grew as big as Belgium, and finally to its current dimensions: the equivalent of 73 billion letter-sized sheets, or the area from the Pacific Ocean to the Mississippi, and from the Rio Grande to the Canadian border.

Clearly, there was a lot of *there* there. But what to do with it?

One day in the lab, Ericson smashed open a Bic pen, extracted the tip and ink supply, and taped it to a C Pen. Suddenly the "interface" was no longer the device itself but any surface that you could print the pattern on.

"We realized we were sitting on something fundamental," Fåhraeus told me. "We were on a clean sheet of paper."

It was Fåhraeus who had the bold notion of seeing that virtual territory as marketable real estate in an enormous network of partnerships. For the last six months, Örjan Johansson, chair of the Anoto board, has been pounding the pavement, negotiating partnerships with 3M, Mead, Ashford, At-A-Glance, Charles Letts, Time Manager International, Filofax, and Time/System International in the United States, as well as Esselte, Unipapel, and Hermelin in Europe and Kokuyo in Japan—each a market leader in its region. These companies have everything to gain: the technical demands and costs of printing the Anoto pattern on their products are trivial. (You can do it with any printing system that has 1,000 dpi resolution, and Anoto is developing plug-ins for Quark and PageMaker as part of its developer's kit, which should be available by the time you read this.)

"When you tell these companies that they can go from manu-facturing plain paper to becoming a service provider with paper as the portal, they realize they're in a whole new ball game," Johans-son told me. By convincing the largest manufacturers in every paper market to print its dots on their products, Anoto is estab-lishing a de facto global standard before consumers have even heard of the company.

At Ideon, Fåhraeus sketched out Anoto's three-year plan for world domination. First, license the pattern and pen technology to Anoto's initial partners for a song—in some cases for free—to establish and disseminate the standard. Then, in year one, sign partnerships with mobile phone companies and telcos, who see the technology as a way to siphon a flood of e-commerce sales through their own billing channels. A Chatpen would be a natural acces-sory to sell, or give, to the owner of a Bluetooth phone; the com-pany that bills for the phone service could then take a slice of every scribbled transaction. Sonera, the second-largest telecom provider in Scandinavia, signed on in February, and announcements of other major providers are expected at this year's CeBIT. When you sign up for Sonera's mobile service, you'll be offered the option to subscribe to Anoto's paper-based services.

Year two: market the technology in consumer-electronics stores, branded with names now associated with personal computers. Year three: imagine racks of Anoto-enabled Parker pens for sale at Office Depot, beside shelves of digital paper.

In January 2000, Linus Wiebe left Precise Biometrics to join Anoto as director of new concepts. Now his job is to weigh the business potential of applications such as putting the Anoto map on standardized tests, creating real-time lotto games, transmitting prescriptions directly to pharmacies, printing active hyperlinks in books, and even laying the pattern over the floors of warehouses so that forklifts can be steered remotely.

As descriptions of Anoto's technology have started to spread around the world, the proposals that land daily in Wiebe's in-box reach farther and farther afield. One e-mail he received from a university proposed printing the pattern on a curved semitransparent plastic surface and embedding the optics, processor, and Bluetooth transceiver into a two-by-two-centimeter cube. "I still do not know the problem they were trying to address," Wiebe observes dryly.

For Hugosson, this flood of potential applications for his algorithm is immensely gratifying. "When you can invent an idea that is so basic that it leads to other ideas," he says, "an idea that seems to have many implications, an idea that leads to a completely new set of thinking . . ."

He's quiet for a moment. "I don't know how to express it in words," he concludes.

Why would a posse of hotshot Swedish coders—or, more to the point, a struggling telecom giant like Ericsson—hitch their wireless wagons to a fading star? Everyone knows the paper industry must have been hit hard by the overnight ubiquity of the Palm-Pilot and the Handspring Visor. And surely, with Bluetooth—or a couple of years out, with 3G—the 2,000-year-long Age of Paper will soon be over.

So whatever happened to the paperless office? There's actually *more* paper in the digital office—cascading out of printers and clogging up copy machines—than there was ten years ago (30 percent more, according to a report by the American Forest and Paper Association). Like the paperback novel that was supposed to be supplanted by every technical marvel from the radio to the e-book, paper solves more problems than it creates. We don't hate paper—the way we hate insipid broadcast TV, tangled telephone cords, futzing with Wite-Out, five-day waits for a letter from across town, and stores that are open only at certain times of day. It's the inert state of the data stored on paper that is a vexing anachronism, and this is precisely the problem that Anoto addresses.

Palmtops are indeed eating into the market for a specific kind of product: the kind of paper—in day planners, calendars, and little black books—that stores data that wants to communicate with our digital networks. Executives for Mead and Franklin Covey carefully acknowledge that there's been "a flattening" of the market in the last two years, specifically for formats that handle contact lists and appointment schedules.

The repeat business in this sector is still the envy of other industries. Many of the 50 million customers who buy a couple of At-A-Glance calendars every year, to say nothing of the estimated 800 million who buy diaries, will part with their tattered paper products only when they're pried from their cold, dead, pulp-loving fingers. Those buyers are so fanatically loyal to specific model numbers and form factors that John Hayek, a senior VP of marketing for Mead, calls it a "religious" market. Anoto will furnish a way for people to link their beloved paper to the flow of digitized information. For Mead, Hayek says, betting on Anoto is "an acknowledgment that a paper-based organization is looking forward in the twenty-first century."

One area of the office market that is exploding, rather than flattening, is in products that make it easier to "co-use" PDAs and paper-based media. For the past few years, the companies Anoto is courting have been struggling to find their footing in a changing landscape where critical information is segregated on both sides of the paper-versus-digital divide. "Right now, we're all trying to synchronize Palms, phones, Outlook, day planners, Web sites, and thousands of floating Post-it notes," says Jeff Anderson, VP of Franklin Covey's e-products and planner division. "It's almost seamless now, but the big glaring gap is paper-back-to-digital. Anoto is the last leg to the full solution."

Despite all the clicking on the Web, there are many areas of the paper domain where digital has barely made a dent. The annual cost of processing forms that are filled in by hand, such as tax returns, is still $700 billion in the United States alone. There are innumerable applications in which digital input could migrate happily to paper: imagine putting a check mark in the newspaper to program your VCR. Anoto pens themselves will be customized by users who check off options in manuals, the interface fine-tuned by—what else?—ticking boxes on paper. If you want to customize the color of the ink or the texture of a line in an e-mail message, for instance, you'll choose from a list of options on a printed menu. Or you could create a virtual flip book by sketching a series of drawings and selecting a box labeled "Send as GIF animation."

"From a paper-product manufacturer's perspective," says Hayek, "we're talking about a little more ink for the dots. It's an easy do."

Like the other start-ups rising out of the mud at Ideon, Anoto represents not only a new generation of aggressively innovative Swedish IT ventures but a new generation of Swedes.

At a restaurant with a sweeping view of Stockholm's Old City, I washed down eight kinds of herring with five flavors of *akavit* with Per Bill, a member of parliament who championed many of the changes in policy that have made his country a leader in the emerging wireless landscape. He articulated the changes in the Swedish psyche wrought by the economic upheavals of the last decade.

"In California, it's fun to be rich, and it's also OK to go bankrupt. In Japan, if you fail, you're supposed to commit *seppuku*," he said. "Ten years ago in Sweden, you were not allowed to be rich, and you were also not allowed to fail."

Bill used a virtually untranslatable word as the key to understanding the avoidance of both conspicuous success and humiliating failure that is deeply ingrained in the Swedish psyche: *lagom*. Meaning something like "lukewarm" and "just enough," *lagom* is the inclination among Swedes to shun ostentation, accept modest rewards, be good team players, and fly under the radar. In the past, the positive side of *lagom* caused Swedes to refuse to allow the kind of desperate poverty in their ranks that is business as usual in the United States. The negative side could be seen in the tendency for the Swedish government to expend energy twiddling with the economy from the top down, rather than seeding it from the ground up by providing incentives for entrepreneurs.

What shook up the *lagom* mind-set, he explained, was the recession. Before 1994, Swedes thought that 4 percent unemployment was a catastrophe; within a year or two, more than one in ten Swedes found themselves out of work. A precipitous change in economic status became less of a cause for loss of face. To compete in the global IT marketplace, Bill observed, "you have to embrace the possibility of failure."

Start-ups like Anoto are training grounds for a generation of Swedes who grew up watching *Dallas* and *Falcon Crest,* becoming early adopters of technology, and absorbing American notions of ambition. Now that they're launching their own companies, says Lars-Fredric Hansson of Ernst & Young ePartners, they've been getting assistance from an unexpected source. The managers who made golden-parachute exits to countries with lighter tax burdens when the recession hit are coming home to Sweden to invest in the next generation of IT entrepreneurs.

There's a fitting symbol of this convergence of old and new economies outside the Ericsson headquarters at Ideon: a stone monument to Harald Bluetooth, who was the king of Denmark in the tenth century. In one hand, he holds a phone, and in the other, a laptop. The significance of the name Bluetooth for the group that developed the wireless standard originates with the king, who threw parties for his fiercest rivals. These wild affairs would "help clear out the bad feeling," said board chair Johansson, who came to Anoto after spearheading the Bluetooth initiative at Ericsson. Many members of the original Bluetooth coalition had long been cutthroat competitors: Ericsson and Nokia, IBM and Toshiba, the United States versus Japan.

"My aunt used to hold out her closed fist and say, 'How much can you get in *this* hand? It's much easier to get something in *this* hand,'" Johansson explained, relaxing his fist. In this way, the monument stands as a symbol of the positive side of *lagom*—

knowing when to lay aside your arms, even in the presence of your rivals, to achieve a common goal.

That's why Johansson wasn't particularly disappointed that Anoto lost to Microsoft at Comdex. When the Anoto team saw the Tablet PC, he says, they immediately began thinking of ways to build bridges between the two technologies. "Maybe they're creating the back end, and we're creating the front end. Writing on glass—how fun is that?"

Not as much fun, Anoto is betting, as making it possible for the mind of the Net to reach as close as the page of the magazine you're reading right now.

"The paper companies have been feeling that the digital train had passed them by," Wiebe told me in a Stockholm coffee shop. "We're throwing out a hook, saying, 'C'mon, join us. Paper has been right all along. We're bringing you with us.'"

"Business as usual" does not evoke warm and fuzzy feelings in most Americans. Society may be fascinated with the power of the corporate world and accompanying success, but few people perceive business as responsive to their own needs and goals. That sprawling issue is handled succinctly in this *BusinessWeek* piece by Aaron Bernstein, with Michael Arndt, Wendy Zellner, and Peter Coy. It points to the red flags of anticorporate feeling that executives must acknowledge now if they want to avoid increased regulation and a loss of touch with their customers.

Aaron Bernstein, with Michael Arndt, Wendy Zellner, and Peter Coy

Too Much Corporate Power?

THE UNITED STATES HAS RARELY BEEN as buoyant as it is today. The golden economy has delivered years of plentiful jobs and soaring incomes—after decades of going sideways. From janitors to dot-com billionaires, almost everyone is feeling the flush times. Paychecks are rising, and wealth is piling up on a scale unimaginable just a few years ago, when the United States struggled through the recession of the early 1990s. Even many of America's worst ghettos are seeing an influx of investment and jobs.

Most Americans recognize that Corporate America gets much credit for the good fortunes. A solid two-thirds of the U.S. public gives companies kudos for today's prosperity, according to a *BusinessWeek*/Harris Poll released on August 31. About the same number say large corporations make good products and compete well in the global economy.

Yet amid the good times, Americans feel uneasy. *BusinessWeek*'s poll shows that nearly three-quarters of Americans think business has gained too much power over too many aspects of their lives. In a response that surprised the pundits, the public seemed to rally around the sentiment expressed at the Democratic convention, when Al Gore declared that Americans must "stand up and say no" to "Big Tobacco, Big Oil, the big polluters, the pharmaceutical companies, the HMOs." Gore sensed the frustration of many voters and their desire to blunt some of the power of business, crafting a new campaign strategy that so far is working. Indeed, 74 percent of those polled by *BusinessWeek* agreed with the veep's remarks.

Gore's neo-Populist rhetoric has tapped a vein of discontent. Consumers are seething about insensitive corporate behavior. And that is only adding to a souring of attitudes toward large companies. While Americans give companies their due for producing more wealth and higher incomes, only 47 percent think that what's good for business is good for most Americans, according to *BusinessWeek*'s poll. And 66 percent think large profits are more important to big companies than developing safe, reliable, quality products for consumers. Adding to the disenchantment is the perception that companies often buy their way into government: witness the success of Senator John McCain (R-Ariz.) in pushing for campaign-finance reform during his presidential run. "There's a widespread sense of unfairness and distrust today, where people think companies are not quite playing by the rules," says Ruy Teixeira, a polling expert at the Century Foundation, a Washington think tank.

So how is it that Corporate America is both hero and villain? Oddly enough, part of the anticorporate mood may be a consequence of the rip-roaring economy itself. Now that Americans' material needs are so well satisfied, they have the luxury of focusing on their quality of life. Just as U.S. companies claim to be the architects of the boom, so too are they held responsible for its excesses and failings. "The slippage in service—it's almost epidemic, across every aspect of our lives," fumes Anne Zenzer, an executive recruiter in Oak Brook, Illinois, who flies 100,000 miles a year, mostly on United Airlines Inc.—notorious these days for delays.

The revved-up New Economy has also left many families feeling overworked and stressed out. The sticking point in last month's strike at Verizon Communications (VZ) was workers' complaints about burnout and mandatory overtime, which management finally agreed to limit. At the same time, many Americans feel they're not getting their fair share of the riches. The reason: average wages and benefits have outpaced inflation by only 7.6 percent since the last recession ended in 1992, while productivity has jumped by 17.9 percent. The gap between the rich and the poor also grates on many middle-class people. Chief executives inflame matters by granting themselves multimillion-dollar pay packages, which 73 percent of the public sees as excessive, the poll shows.

NO REINS

Indeed, corporate leaders are perceived as insensitive and more concerned with profits than with those they're supposed to be serving. "Some companies get big, they get arrogant, and they lose touch with the community," concedes Jerry Jasinowski, head of the National Association of Manufacturers. Part of the problem is that no one's reining in business anymore. Most of the institutions that historically served as a counterweight to corporate power— Big Government and strong unions—have lost clout since Ronald Reagan came to town crusading for deregulation and local control. The conservative ascendancy that followed discredited much of the New Deal social structure, leaving corporations to fill the vacuum, says Boston College sociologist Charles K. Derber, author of a 1998 book, *Corporation Nation: How Corporations Are Taking over Our Lives and What We Can Do about It.*

It's this power imbalance that's helping to breed the current resentment against corporations. Some experts draw analogies to a previous period of unchecked corporate power—in the late 1800s—when the opening of the wide-open frontier economy and robber-baron capitalism gave rise to the Populist movement. Such raw anticorporate sentiment was on display in this summer's Big Tobacco trial in Miami. When it ended, the foreman of the jury that delivered a $144.8 billion punitive-damage judgment against the industry took the opportunity to speak out, saying the jurors' deliberate intention was to "put the companies on notice—not just the tobacco companies, all companies—concerning fraud or misrepresentation of the American public."

For Corporate America, there is danger in the new climate: in a word, renewed government regulation. For two decades, market deregulation has fostered competition and lowered many prices. But the pendulum may have swung too far for many citizens, who now take the gains for granted and want to dampen the extremes that can come with unfettered capitalism. Already, Washington is making noises about curbing megamergers, regulating health-maintenance organizations and drug prices, imposing new rules on airlines, and capping energy rates in cities such as San Diego, where costs skyrocketed after the city deregulated its utilities.

Unless companies placate critics, they may prod politicians into more government intervention. While Gore's new pitch undoubtedly involves some calculated appeal to the liberal base of the Democratic party, he also may have to deliver on some of the promises if he's elected. Certainly, the pressure to rein in companies isn't likely to let up anytime soon. Just look at longtime consumer advocate Ralph Nader, who in his presidential campaign has zeroed in on companies as the bad guys responsible for many of the nation's ills. "There's an increased readiness to believe negative things about corporations today, which makes it a dangerous time for companies," warns Daniel Yankelovich, chairman of pollster DYG Inc. "Executives haven't had to worry about social issues for a generation, but there's a yellow light flashing now, and they better pay attention."

OUT OF CONTROL

Another risk for Corporate America is weakened support for free trade. At home and abroad, citizens facing globalization worry that powerful corporations override national sovereignty and can undermine political and monetary systems. On August 25, Federal Reserve chairman Alan Greenspan warned the annual gathering of central bankers in Jackson Hole, Wyoming, that the "unease about the way markets distribute wealth" could cause the "latent forces of protectionism and state intervention" to reassert themselves, both in the United States and other countries. The French have made a hero of the farmer who lashed out at McDonald's Corp. (MCD) not so much because they hate the fast-food company but because many think multinationals crush local culture. McDonald's executives say they see few effective ways to combat this attitude, except to emphasize local franchises' neighborhood roots. "It comes with the turf," laments McDonald's vice-chairman James R. Cantalupo. "I don't know if you ever get over it as long as you are the number one brand."

Similarly, the Asian crisis drove home the loss of control many citizens feel when companies and investors upend the money supply or yank investment dollars at a moment's notice. Europe has had even more demonstrations than the United States against corporate-driven globalization. World Bank and International Monetary Fund officials are bracing for another round when their annual meetings open in Prague on September 19. "The whipping boy is the corporation because it's the leading agent of change in the new global markets being created," says Boston College's Derber.

Also at play, at least in the United States, is a shift in cultural norms. Put simply, it's becoming fashionable to be anticorporate. The sudden prevalence of the dot-com companies, with their sneakers and parrots in the office, have led many professionals to turn against the hierarchical, buttoned-down environment of Corporate America. In today's tight labor markets, even Wall Street and white-shoe law firms have ditched pinstripes for slacks and sweaters, hoping to stanch the flow of talent to the on-line world. Madison Avenue, too, sees chic in the anti-big-corporation fad. A recent ad for financial consultants Salomon Smith Barney—whose parent, Citigroup (*C*), is a monster conglomerate if ever there was one—plays off the dot-com sensibility that derides business-suited executives, saying: "Suits aren't necessarily bad. When they're working for you."

Anticorporate feelings are seeping into popular entertainment, too. Rock musicians and other artists have always identified with the counterculture, but today they are rebelling against the clout of media and retail companies. Many artists perceive their decisions not to buy "offensive" material as corporate censorship. And Hollywood has seen a spurt of movies that portray companies as sinister baddies. All the negative imagery tarnishes Corporate America's legitimacy.

To some degree, corporations are victims of their own success. In the past decade, they have created global brand names by cultivating emotional connections with consumers that go beyond products. In the process, they raise consumers' expectations about their favorite companies—making them sitting ducks. "Multinationals like Nike (*NKE*), Microsoft (*MSFT*), and Starbucks (*SBUX*) have sought to become the chief communicators of all that is good in our culture: art, sports, community, connection, equality," asserts Naomi Klein, author of *No Logo: Taking Aim at the Brand Bullies,* a book that documents youth rebellion against the pervasiveness of brand names. "But the more successful this project is, the more vulnerable these companies become" to attacks on their image.

When brands do wrong, she argues, loyal consumers feel betrayed, much as fans turn against a fallen movie star or sports hero. All those college students who show up at demonstrations against globalization see corporations such as Nike Inc. as self-serving organizations that violate human rights and pollute the earth. Even teens think it's cool to hate corporations. Suburban thirteen-year-olds accuse Starbucks Corp. of driving local coffee-houses out of business and sport T-shirts that say: "Friends don't let friends drink at Starbucks." Says Irene Krugman, an eleventh grader who in 1998 helped to start the Student Committee against Labor Exploitation at her New York high school: "I still shop at those brand-name stores, but I feel really guilty about it."

Whether they admit it or not, corporate chieftains are certain to be watching this trend closely. Citizen attacks on corporations have been surprisingly effective, and many executives have seen how stonewalling and defensiveness have boomeranged. In some cases, the criticism intensifies, with the potential to damage brand images and sales, undermine companies' standing with regulators and politicians, and, ultimately, whack a company's stock price. Yet some of the moves critics find the most egregious are the ones managers say they're forced to use to compete, from downsizing to in-your-face ad blitzes to political lobbying.

In a few cases, companies have realized that the new climate requires a response before a consumer backlash spins out of control. Last April, for example, after months of protests by human-rights and student groups, Starbucks agreed to buy coffee from importers who pay Third World farmers a premium over world market prices. In mid-May, 3M said it would voluntarily stop making Scotchgard, a forty-year-old product with $300 million in sales, after 3M tests showed that the compound didn't decompose in the environment. And in late August, McDonald's tried to head off concerns about the treatment of animals through regulations for farmers who provide it with 1.5 billion eggs a year. "Corporations have to prove themselves," says John P. Rowe, CEO of Unicom Corp., a Chicago utility that has spent $1 billion to improve service after huge blackouts last summer. "Don't promise the moon, but don't promise so little that any damn fool could deliver."

If today's anticorporate backlash is more low-key than the counterculture revolution of the 1960s, it may be even more dangerous for Corporate America. Back then, antibusiness attitudes were restricted mostly to youth and college students. And they were just one element of a broader generation gap that led baby boomers to reject the entire Establishment, from its sexual mores to the Vietnam War and the military-industrial complex. Today, those Americans angry at corporations cut across generations, geography, and even income groups. And the Net amplifies the power of the tech-savvy discontented who use it the way the colonists used Paul Revere, getting out the word about the most recent outrage or exposé. "With the Internet, information flows instantly, so even if we don't have more people concerned about companies, those who are can do more about it," says Harvard University labor economist Richard B. Freeman.

Also unlike the 1960s, students today aren't necessarily antibusiness: the e-mail that antisweatshop activists send to muster rallies flashes with ads. But that doesn't preempt protesters from targeting companies they deem offensive—no matter how benign their products seem to be. "We suffer from not enough people knowing what we do [with philanthropic causes], because we can't beat our own drum too loudly, for fear of weakening the trust that we do have," laments David Olsen, Starbucks' senior vice president for corporate responsibility.

And once activists have lost faith in a company, it can be hard to rebuild confidence. Tobacco companies have been so vilified that they may never regain the tolerance they enjoyed just a few years ago. Now HMOs have become the whipping boy for a public fed up with bureaucratic decisions and lousy health care; 43 percent of Americans give HMOs poor marks at serving customers, according to the *BusinessWeek* poll, a rating as bad as tobacco received. For several years, critics have hammered the industry with gut-wrenching stories like that of Ian Malone, the baby Gore introduced to the Democratic convention who was denied coverage for a full-time nurse he needed after he was injured at birth by a medical error.

LISTEN TO ME

Such tales have put HMOs on the defensive in Congress, where the industry has been battling furiously against a bill granting patients the right to sue health care providers. HMOs concede that more regulation is needed to give patients a way to challenge corporate health care decisions. But they want to avoid fat jury awards with a system of independent reviews. "The logical extension of the demonization of HMOs is to push the problem into the courts, but employees will lose if costs go up and their employers can't afford to cover them anymore," warns Karen M. Ignani, president of the American Association of Health Plans, the industry's trade group in Washington.

Mistrust of big companies—and a feeling that they listen to citizen complaints only when forced to do so—is a common refrain among critics. Take genetically modified foods. Initially, the industry brushed off the so-called Frankenfoods complaints, arguing that no scientific studies had validated critics' concerns about health or environmental hazards. But over the past year, hundreds of protesters have descended on Food and Drug Administration hearings. This summer, potato giant J. R. Simplot Co., a major McDonald's supplier, told its farmers to stop growing Monsanto Co.'s (*MCT*) genetically modified "NewLeaf" potato, bred to resist insects. Overall, the U.S. acreage of biotech corn and soybeans has leveled off after several years of explosive growth, according to the Agriculture Department. Biotech setbacks were one reason industry leader Monsanto saw its stock fall, leading to its acquisition by Pharmacia Corp. (*PHA*) in March.

Executives even occasionally admit their mistakes. In an extraordinary essay, "The Welcome Tension of Technology: The Need for Dialogue about Agricultural Biotechnology," published in February by Washington University in St. Louis, former Monsanto CEO Robert B. Shapiro wrote: "We've learned that there is often a very fine line between scientific confidence on the one hand, and corporate arrogance on the other." Shapiro, now the nonexecutive chairman of Pharmacia, added: "It was natural for us to see this as a scientific issue. We didn't listen very well to people who insisted that there were relevant ethical, religious, cultural, social, and economic issues as well."

LOCAL HEROES

Similarly, many residents upset about urban sprawl feel ignored by the big companies they battle. When Kmart Corp. (*KM*) set out last year to build a 100,000-square-foot superstore in south St. Louis, local citizens feared that a big box store would destroy small businesses and ruin the pedestrian scale of the neighborhood. A group of twenty neighborhood associations swung into action against the chain. The group, called the Southtown Coalition, defeated Kmart before the local zoning board earlier this year by going door-to-door with a petition and packing board hearings with 150 to 300 people. Southtown, which has been talking with smaller stores about developing the location, brought the troops out again on August 23 after Kmart reapplied to a city appeals board. "This is a multibillion-dollar corporation trying to shove a big box down our throats," charges Kerri Bonasch, a marketing manager and resident who volunteers at the coalition.

After hundreds of battles nationwide, local antisprawl groups such as the Southtown Coalition now have a sophisticated body of knowledge about how to mount zoning battles and pass referendums to restrict store size. Activists haven't stopped big stores in their tracks, but they have blocked them in more than 120 locations, estimates Al Norman, the head of Sprawl-Busters, a nonprofit group. Some forty or fifty such clashes are going on at any one time today, more than triple the number of a few years ago, he says. Perhaps three-quarters of the battles involve Wal-Mart Stores Inc. (*WMT*), followed by Home Depot Inc. (*HD*). "The citizens' movement is costing the industry millions of dollars in lost sales, and at least $200,000 to $300,000 to campaign against us in each battle," says Norman.

Wal-Mart CEO H. Lee Scott, Jr., says that "without a doubt" his company faces more challenges to new stores these days, even though it wins many battles. A company spokesman estimates that activists block at least two to three new stores a year.

Concedes retired CEO David D. Glass, now chairman of the Wal-Mart board's executive committee: "Retailers need to be more responsible to look and see if problems are being created" by big-box stores.

ANGRY MOMS

Some of the most extreme anticorporate language comes from parents opposed to advertising in schools. Many object to exclusive marketing deals signed by Coca-Cola Co. (*KO*), PepsiCo Inc. (*PEP*), and other companies that pay schools for the right to sell their products in the classroom. Channel One Network became a target of their ire as soon as it was launched a decade ago. A unit of Primedia Inc. (*PRM*), the service offers schools money, supplies, and programming in exchange for the right to beam ads to students on its classroom TVs. Some 12,000 schools have accepted the deal—but far from diminishing over time, the battles have become more intense.

When Diane Gramley, a mother of five, discovered last year that the Franklin, Pennsylvania, high school her children attend carries Channel One, she formed a group with other parents. They agitate at every school board meeting to end the arrangement, distribute flyers by the hundreds, write op-ed pieces in the local paper denouncing the company, and now plan to petition parents to get rid of it. Like other Channel One foes, the parents object to their children's exposure to commercials at school. They also argue that the company's educational programming is mostly a waste of time that diverts children from their studies. "This is a big company preying on my children," says Gramley.

Similar battles are going on in hundreds of communities, says San Francisco's Center for Commercial-Free Public Education. The group, which provides resources to grassroots groups like Gramley's, says it gets some 100 requests a month for help. Channel One network affairs executive vice president Jeffrey H. Ballabon dismisses all the attacks as the work of a small number of groups. He points out that 98 percent of schools renew their contracts to carry the station.

Assaults from citizens groups are bad enough, but for most executives, the most potentially hazardous attitudes lie with their own employees. The best economy in thirty years has brought a bounty of jobs and exuberant consumer spending. The competitive wars against Europe and Japan of the 1980s and 1990s have been won. But many employees in Corporate America think they're being worked to the breaking point by CEOs who aren't sharing the wealth. Last year, 43 percent of workers at large corporations said they "find it very difficult to balance my work and personal responsibilities," up sharply from 36 percent in 1997, according to Chicago's International Survey Research (ISR), which surveys employees at hundreds of large companies annually. Meanwhile, 44 percent said that they are "very much underpaid for the work I do," up from 38 percent two years earlier.

Such feelings reflect the stark discrepancy between the high productivity rate the U.S. economy has achieved in recent years and the slower pace of wage gains. This is one reason an astonishing 40 million employees say they would vote in a union today if given the chance, double the number of a decade ago, according to pollsters Peter D. Hart Research Associates. Organizing drives have ticked up in recent years, forcing companies to fight harder to fend off unions. But even though management still usually wins such battles, today's labor-short economy means that disgruntled employees have more options and can jump ship if companies don't respond to demands for higher pay.

Certainly, soaring profits and high CEO pay have embittered many employees who feel squeezed. Just ask Reed T. Hinchliffe, a twenty-year veteran at Raytheon Co. The fifty-eight-year-old computer engineer stood up at the company's annual meeting in April and demanded that CEO Daniel P. Burnham return his $900,000 bonus because the company lost $181 million in the first quarter and its stock was trading at 20, down from a high of 76 last year. Burnham refused. "I asked him how he justifies this, but he just said: 'I intend to keep it,' like I was a peon and should shut up and leave him alone," complains Hinchliffe. He says he has personally talked to about 300 of the 600 people at his unit, a Defense Department computer complex in northern Virginia, and "they're virtually all ticked off." A Raytheon spokesman says Burnham told Hinchliffe that he respected his point of view.

Several factors have contributed to the ascendancy of the corporation in the past decade or so. The fall of communism and the triumph of Western capitalism set the stage, as did the rollback of government in the United States. But mostly it's the incredible success of the economy that allows companies to wield enormous power in American society today. With that power, however, comes added responsibility. Corporate executives would be wise to deal with the burden—and take care to avoid the hubris that so often accompanies heady success. If they don't, a growing number of Americans stand ready to call them to account.

No one ever said farming shrimp in Nicaragua would be easy, but nothing could ever be this hard. This article by Kris Hundley of the *St. Petersburg Times* transports us to Central America, where an American executive from a family-owned company encounters political unrest, pestilence, and a very different way of doing business on the rocky road to harvesttime. It paints a vivid picture of the economic and cultural disparities in international business.

Kris Hundley

Harvesting Shrimp a Jumbo Headache

THE SANDINISTAS HAVE TAKEN over two banks in town. At the processing plant, there's too much shrimp, too few bins, and a busted gear on the sizing machine. And a virus is killing off the crop in Pond 15.

At least the volcano is quiet.

If you want to raise and process shrimp in Central America, you've got to be ready for headaches. And just when Gary Cummings, who runs operations here for Sahlman Seafoods, thinks he has things under control, a tornado slices through the shrimp farm in the middle of the night, ripping the roof off the kitchen.

Nobody was killed. Cummings went back to bed.

The joke is that to make a small fortune in shrimp farming, you start with a large fortune. It's a reality for Sahlman, the largest U.S. shrimp farmer and processor in Nicaragua.

A family-owned business now in its third generation, Tampa-based Sahlman has been pulling shrimp out of the ocean since 1936. It still has the largest privately owned shrimping fleet in the

382

Western Hemisphere, operating for the past forty-two years out of Guyana on South America's Atlantic coast.

Sahlman is vertically integrated, processing and marketing its catch under the Bee Gee label to distributors worldwide. Until eighteen months ago, the company even owned the refrigerated ship that carts its frozen product to Tampa's port once a month from Guyana.

Jack Sahlman, the seventy-three-year-old son of the founder and company president, said his boats hauled 2.3 million pounds of shrimp out of the ocean last year. At an average wholesale price of $7.50 per pound, that tallies up to more than $17 million in revenues from fishing.

The company has been profitable every year but one, said Sahlman, who remembers the date without missing a beat: 1974, when high oil prices sent the cost of diesel skyrocketing and forced consumers to forgo expensive shrimp dinners.

But the ocean harvest has been steadily declining, while shrimp farming—growing shrimp from larvae in saltwater ponds—has become increasingly popular. So four years ago, Sahlman turned to aquaculture, sinking $8 million into a processing plant and massive shrimp ponds in rural northwestern Nicaragua.

The operations stumbled from early mismanagement. Two years ago, just as the plant and ponds were poised for profit, Hurricane Mitch swept through, marooning the farm and wiping out roads. Then a virus that had never been seen in this part of the world decimated shrimp farms throughout Central America.

Marty Williams, who oversees the Nicaraguan operation from Sahlman's Tampa headquarters, said the company had hoped to harvest 675,000 pounds of shrimp from its twenty-eight ponds last year. Instead, the total harvest was 163,000 pounds, less than one-quarter of projections.

"It's been very discouraging," said Williams, Jack Sahlman's son-in-law, who travels to Nicaragua about once a month to check on operations. "But there's no question shrimp farming is the future. We just happened to go down there at a bad time."

GLOBAL BUSINESS, GLOBAL CONCERNS

Shrimp farming, a $5 billion global business, is as much an art as a science. For well over twenty years, farmers and multinational conglomerates have grown shrimp on everything from tiny family plots to 100-acre ponds from Thailand to Texas.

Traditionally these farms have been built in low-lying areas or swampy wetlands to allow for tidal water exchange. Bulldozers excavate an area up to ten feet deep, pushing up earthen dikes to form a perimeter. The bottoms are sloped, so water can enter at the shallow end and flush out with the tides at the deeper end.

The word on shrimp farming was that you could simply flow water through a pond and take money out.

But as the popularity of shrimp farming grew, so did environmental problems. Developers ripped out mangroves and displaced local people to build farms. The constant effluent from ponds polluted the estuaries. And when the shrimp farms failed, companies simply abandoned the property, leaving depleted resources behind.

Cummings, the forty-four-year-old expatriate who runs Sahlman's Nicaraguan business, said he has seen damage done by shrimp farmers in the past. But he said Sahlman—and the Nicaraguan government—learned from those mistakes.

Nicaragua came late to shrimp farming, long after multinational conglomerates had parceled off the tidal flats in Honduras and Ecuador. While its neighbors were trading shrimp for international currency during the 1980s, Nicaragua was being ruled by the Sandinistas and punished by a U.S. embargo. After the Sandinistas were forced out of office in 1990, foreign investment came slowly.

In 1995, when a team of scientists visited Nicaragua under the auspices of the U.S. Department of Agriculture's Emerging Democracy Program, fewer than 5,000 acres had been developed into shrimp farms. Honduras, meanwhile, had 27,000 acres in production.

By 1999, Nicaragua was exporting 6.6 million pounds of shrimp, valued at $21 million, from ninety-four farms. Only two farms, both Nicaraguan-owned, are larger than Sahlman's operations.

David Hughes, a professor of aquaculture at Ave Maria College of the Americas in Managua, watched the development of shrimp farming in Nicaragua through the 1990s and surveyed much of the land that has been approved for government concessions.

"The government and producers have taken the stand that they only want to develop half of the potential areas," Hughes said, "and do it so the developed farms are buffered from each other."

THE WORK IS HARD AND DIRTY

Sahlman's parcel, which it leases from the government under a ten-year agreement, consists of 2,500 acres on Mangles Altos, an uninhabited island in the Estero Real, an estuary that leads into the Gulf of Fonseca. So far, the company has developed only about one-fifth of its concession; the rest remains a barren salt flat flecked with scrub.

It took Cummings and about 120 Nicaraguan workers fifteen months to carve the tract of mud-caked earth into twenty-acre rectangular ponds. Mangroves around the perimeter of the property were largely untouched.

To improve water filtration, 18,000 mangrove seedlings were planted in tidal areas abutting the ponds. From the air, the tidy rows of mangrove seedlings look like a bad hair-weave.

Everything on Mangles Altos had to be brought from the mainland down a winding river and across the mouth of the Gulf of Fonseca on an hour-long barge ride. Among the imports: rock used to reinforce the ponds' earthen banks and connecting roads; fresh water, cement, and sand to build the giant pumping station; and the five green industrial-sized pumps, which pull water in from the estuary at high tide to fill the canals that snake through Sahlman's farm.

Today, fifty-two men live on the isolated property. They sleep in hammocks under a thatched roof, listening to a staticky transistor radio that blasts Backstreet Boys in a language they don't understand. They eat tortillas, beans, and plantains at picnic tables in front of a color TV blaring Spanish-language soap operas.

Shrimp farming is hard and dirty work. First, the workers have to stock the ponds with millions of larvae, which look like miniature shrimp. They are purchased from hatcheries in Panama or Mexico or Colombia for about $5 per thousand, then released into the farm's acclimation tanks and finally the ponds. Throughout the growing cycle, which can last up to four months, the fast-growing larvae must be fed twice daily.

Though the food, a commercially milled pellet made of protein and molasses, has traditionally been sprinkled by hand from boats, Cummings recently started using feed trays in all but a few of his ponds. These round, mesh nets are attached to stakes throughout the pond and settle on the bottom when in use. By retrieving the trays, workers can look for dead shrimp and tell how much food is being eaten, avoiding waste.

The workers spend eleven days on the farm, three days off. Pay is 30 cordobas, or $2.30, per day, plus free meals and medical insurance. Men who work a harvest, which can last from seven at night until four in the morning, get an $8 bonus.

Cummings is unapologetic about the pay scale. He figures more than 500 people have been on Sahlman's payroll since the company came into Nicaragua. "That's 500 families affected by us," Cummings said. "I have no tolerance for anyone in the U.S. whining about what we pay, especially when you consider that this part of the country has over 80 percent unemployment."

Some of the men have worked at other shrimp farms in the area—there are several just down the river and dozens across the border in Honduras. Some have cut sugarcane in the fields that stretch for miles along the base of the coastal mountain range.

But in this part of the country, which is poor even by Nicaraguan standards, opportunities are few. Many families scrape a living from the land—using dugout canoes to pull fish from the river, growing bananas and beans, raising pigs and chickens. Homes are thatched huts hunched low to the ground, nearly hidden in the palms. A sign of wealth is a battered bicycle, which can carry whole families along the rutted roads.

PROBLEMS: PRODUCTION, POACHERS

One day in late August, Sahlman's workers pile into the back of the farm's pockmarked, mud-caked Toyota pickup to head out to the ponds. They are dressed in ragged shorts and T-shirts. Most are barefoot; a few wear cheap rubber flip-flops.

Nelson Penalda, twenty-seven, is at the wheel. Penalda, who wears a tan Jansport ball cap, neat polo shirt, and long pants, has been farm manager for the past year.

The farm cut back to a skeleton crew in late 1999 after the virus swept through and Sahlman decided to let the ponds dry out for the first four months of this year. Penalda was one of only seven people who survived the layoffs. He is tired, but grateful for the chance.

Penalda's mother, brother, and girlfriend live in Chinandega, twenty minutes by boat, then an hour by car. Penalda comes to the farm on Mondays and returns to town on Fridays. On Sunday morning, he attends English class.

"If there is good production, all is well," said Penalda, who earns about $800 per month plus bonuses. The night before, he had harvested a paltry 3,000 pounds of shrimp from a virus-infected pond.

Production is not Penalda's only problem. In Nicaragua, the second-poorest country in the Western Hemisphere, shrimp that wholesale for hard dollars are worth gold. About a year ago, thieves slipped onto the farm in midday, sliced a mesh drainage screen, and made off with about 1,500 pounds of shrimp before being noticed.

Cummings grabbed an AK-47, Penalda his Glock handgun, and the two men took off through the mangroves chasing the intruders. All they found were footprints in the muck as the sound of an outboard motor, speeding toward Honduras, faded into the distance.

Today men dressed in dark blue uniforms and armed with rifles patrol the property. That hasn't stopped the poaching. In September, four men with cast nets had 400 pounds of shrimp hauled out of a pond before security chased them away.

NICARAGUA'S UNEASY PROGRESS

As Nicaragua lurches toward the future, it retains vestiges of the past. Though the Sandinistas have been out of power for a decade, the party known as the FSLN still holds more than a third of the legislative seats.

In Chinandega, Sandinistas briefly occupied two banks on payday in late August before being run out by local police.

At a busy intersection in Managua, a tall bronze statue of a worker raising a gun stands as a monument to the revolution with a message from its donor: IRAN TILL THE END.

And deep in the countryside, where the roads are occupied by more pigs and horses than cars, a message from the FSLN is emblazoned on the only brick building within miles. TODO SERA MEJOR—All will be better.

The current administration of Arnoldo Aleman is fighting back with propaganda of its own. Billboards along main roads boast OBRAS, NO PALABRAS—actions, not words—as they tout the government's aggressive program of building roads, extending power lines, and providing clean water. Much of the work is being financed by U.S. and other international help after Hurricane Mitch.

People are still divided about the meaning of the ten-year Sandinista rule. Jaime Montealegre, sixty-five, manages Sahlman's landing site, a 220-acre parcel on the muddy-colored tributary that leads to the farm. For thirty-four years, he ran an Esso station in Chinandega—through Somoza, the Sandinistas, and, finally, the election of Violeta Chamorro.

Montealegre recited the indignities he endured under the Sandinista regime: gas supplies were rationed; the government set prices and operating hours. Worse yet were the Cuban cigarettes.

"They were ugly and had no filters," said Montealegre, who drives a stripped-out Russian van around the landing site's washboard roads.

Asked if he ever considered leaving during the Sandinista years, Montealegre, who lived in New Jersey in the late 1950s, scoffs. "Hell, I figured they should leave first. And they did."

About an hour down the road, in the little town of El Viejo, the FSLN is memorialized in the plaza, where there's a granite monument to one of the party's founders. Around the corner, in a store the size of a walk-in closet, sits Ignacio Bustos, a forty-six-year-old former Sandinista functionary.

Bustos sells ice cream and Pepsi whenever someone wanders into his shop, just a few steps from the main market. But business is slow, with too many underfunded shop owners in town competing for too few cordobas. Bustos said his life has not improved under the Aleman administration. People are consuming too many imports, he said, and no one can save money or own a home.

"We've lost the beautiful things of the revolution," said Bustos, as his six-year-old daughter climbed on his lap. "I think Aleman is corrupt, worse than Somoza ever was."

Bustos complained that Sahlman's processing plant, a few miles from his store, sometimes smells and should have been put farther out in the country. Then he conceded that he hasn't heard anything bad about the plant, which employs about 250 people, many from his town.

"When Mitch came through two years ago, the factory helped

us out," Bustos said, almost grudgingly. "I had 3,000 cordobas worth of ice cream here that would have melted. The plant gave me ice for free."

"THERE'S NO OTHER WORK HERE"

Workers, mostly women, start arriving at Sahlman's plant before dawn, settling like birds on the low concrete curb outside the gates, waiting to find out if there's work for the day.

One morning in late August, five women have arrived by 5:30. They've walked an hour to get there. Three fume-spewing trucks have already rumbled through the gates, bearing bins full of shrimp. There will be plenty of work today.

But the pay pales by U.S. standards. The fastest shrimp deheaders, the best-paying job on the floor, earn about $35 to $48 per week. Francesca Martinez, forty-nine, has worked at the plant for three years and said deheaders haven't had a raise since she started.

"There's no other work here, other than to be a domestic," she complained during a lull. "But food, water, and electricity are so expensive."

Jaime Garcia, a twenty-year-old who is in quality control, sees opportunity to advance with Sahlman. Garcia, a native of El Viejo, returned in June after two years at Santa Fe Community College in Gainesville, Florida, studying aquaculture and seafood processing.

"I got that scholarship hoping I'd be able to come to work here," Garcia said. "It's a good salary and a nice working environment."

Dr. Steve Otwell, a food scientist at the University of Florida, has visited more than 100 shrimp processing plants around the world. He characterizes Sahlman's plant in Chinandega as one of the best.

"It's well above average in their commitment to the handling of the product," he said. "They haven't cut corners; they pay attention to sanitation in everything from the hand-washing to clothing to personal hygiene. And they pay attention to training their employees, who understand what they're doing."

THE SHRIMP PLANT IS HIS LIFE

Tommy Guerrero runs Sahlman's plant in the shadow of San Cristobal, a volcano that occasionally carpets the countryside with ash. Guerrero is a U.S. citizen who was born in Puerto Rico and has a wife in Lakeland. He has managed shrimp plants all over Latin America, from Colombia to Honduras to Ecuador. He also once managed a Sahlman processing plant in Lakeland, which the company sold in 1997.

Two years ago, just days before Mitch hit, Guerrero moved to a comfortable ranch home right behind Sahlman's plant outside Chinandega. Now the plant is his life.

Dressed in a white lab coat and white rubber boots, a cell phone constantly to his ear, Guerrero seems to be everywhere. At the plant's reception area, where a forklift operator wheels blue bins holding 900 pounds of shrimp from trucks into the plant. On the factory floor, where workers in blue aprons line the grading machine and those in green aprons snap off shrimp heads faster than the eye can follow. On the loading dock where Nicaraguans in snowsuits and gloves are rolling 44,000 pounds of frozen shrimp, bound for Vigo, Spain, into a refrigerated truck.

On the last day of August, Guerrero, fifty-six years old and ramrod straight, moved nearly 100,000 pounds of shrimp through his plant, working two shifts. The job was complicated by the fact that the shrimp came from ten different farms.

Each farm's harvest has to be handled separately, carefully marked, and tracked from the minute the bin comes in the door to when the shrimp are packed in five-pound boxes, bound for the freezer. Guerrero charges a processing fee based on packed weight— about forty-one cents a pound for deheaded shrimp, shell on. He also buys about one-third of the product that comes through the plant. In late August he was paying $5.90 per pound for shrimp sizes averaging thirty-six to forty per pound, a size that is considerably smaller than Sahlman's ocean catch.

Guerrero guarantees his price for a week. Though shrimp prices are up over the long run, they fluctuate in the short term due to supply and demand. In late August, prices were on a downswing due to a big harvest by Mexican fleets.

Since weight is all-important—to both the shrimp processor and the producers—Guerrero insists that at least one representative from a farm must be on the factory floor while its harvest is being handled.

"I don't want them to come back to me later and tell me something is wrong," he said.

Maintaining good relations with other producers is critical as the plant strives to run at full capacity. Sahlman has developed a program to help support the local shrimp cooperatives, small family-run farms that have trouble buying feed in bulk and a hard time making it through lean years.

The company loans the farmers money to buy feed at the beginning of a growing cycle; in return, the farm commits to process its harvest at Sahlman's plant and give Sahlman first option to buy the product. About $100,000 was loaned out in the first growing cycle this year, with individual loans averaging $2,000.

"If we help raise production levels, everybody benefits," Cummings said, dismissing the suggestion that his company would be better off to let the co-ops fail, then buy up their concessions. "One outside investor did that and there was plenty of bad blood as a result. We have enough attention already as the Big Gringos. And we have plenty of work to do with the concessions we've got."

THE CHALLENGE TO TURN A PROFIT

Four years into Sahlman's money-draining Nicaraguan endeavor, Cummings is under pressure to produce. And he isn't used to losing.

For eighteen years, the six-foot-four, solidly built Cummings was in charge of logistics for high-performance auto teams on international circuits such as the Paris-to-Dakar race. His team won two world championships. Being defeated by a shrimp—or a deadly virus or a hurricane—isn't an option.

So far this year, Sahlman's plant is well on its way to a positive cash flow, as long as trucks keep pouring through the gate with shrimp, and distributors keep buying the frozen product.

Though one section of the farm has been scattershot with white-spot virus, which is harmless to humans, the other two parcels look promising. Cummings has been experimenting with smaller ponds, new larval strains, and different feeding techniques. Early results from four test ponds have been encouraging.

But things change quickly with Mother Nature.

In late August, Cummings was disgusted to see birds plucking dead shrimp out of a pond that had looked healthy just days before. Though the shrimp were only halfway through their growing cycle, they had to be harvested immediately or lost.

At dusk the next night, Cummings and a crew of fifteen were under a big spotlight, pulling shrimp out of the pond on the falling tide. Two men, waist-deep in the tidal stream, hold a fifteen-foot-long net while the harvest washes through a concrete tube draining from the pond. As the net fills, they open one end and empty it into a crate, which another worker races to an ice-filled container on the muddy bank.

Dead from the icy shock, the harvest was then sorted: blue crabs into a bucket for the workers; slippery yellow pico de oro fish flung into the mud; shrimp into a basket, then to a crudely hung scale. Next stop, a five-foot-tall bin full of ice on the back of a truck.

The men work quickly, whistling and yelling over the roar of the water, harvesting 100 pounds of shrimp in the first hour. By midnight, Cummings has seen enough to tell him the crop is healthy and surprisingly large.

A buyer had offered to buy the harvest for about $10,000 for sale to a French distributor. The pond would still be a loss, but not as big as Cummings had feared.

Leaving the farm, Cummings rousts the launch driver, shoves the boat down the rough rock bank into the fast-falling current, then hoists himself over the prow. On the shadowy dock, a security guard raises his Winchester in a halfhearted salute.

The night is overcast, the sky an inky black, the mangroves along the riverbank slightly darker, jagged against the sky. The driver guns his Mercury engine and slips effortlessly around the river's bends and into the wide opening that flows into the Gulf of Fonseca and the Pacific beyond.

Cummings stands in the bow and looks back at the farm. In the distance, the lights of the harvest glow like a beacon in the night. With luck, the farm will make money this year.

"I've learned to do what I need to do to get the job done," said Cummings, who was hospitalized with high blood pressure two years ago. "It's not as perfect as in the States, but I'd be dead if I expected perfection."

POSTSCRIPT

By mid-October, all but about four of Sahlman's shrimp ponds had been harvested and the healthy ponds outnumbered those hit by virus. Total harvest for the four-month cycle will be about 250,000 pounds, well above last year's total from two cycles.

Meanwhile, the plant has been handling record volume, packing 696,000 pounds of shrimp in September.

Experimenting on the farm with aeration pumps, new feeding techniques, and a different larval strain have paid off, said Marty Williams, Sahlman's vice president in Tampa.

"We got our direct costs back, plus some, and we learned a lot," he said. "We're committed to restocking the whole farm, plus an additional fifty or seventy-five acres, in January."

Having your name on the pants and shirts of millions of strangers must be exhilarating, especially if the phenomenon is global. But the world, alas, is a fickle place that can turn what's fashionable one day into a bad case of overkill the next. Hip-hop customers may desert you, the fashion crowd may dis you, and your marriage may break up. This detailed *New York* article by Rene Chun traces the rise and fall of Tommy Hilfiger, who suffered the consequences of embracing celebrity and mainstream popularity.

Rene Chun

Tommy's Tumble

TOMMY HILFIGER DOES NOT look like a fashion victim. The much-maligned designer—five eight in his own monogrammed sneakers—is holding court in his spacious, wood-paneled corner office. He's dressed comfortably but fastidiously in a freshly pressed blue button-down and vintage Levi's. It's exactly the type of digs you'd expect Tommy Hilfiger to have: safe, tasteful decor and a panoramic view commensurate with an eight-figure salary.

The expensive props scattered around speak to Hilfiger's eclectic tastes and pop and rock enthusiasms: a hand-carved Louis B. Mayer–sized mahogany desk; a Fender guitar autographed by Bruce Springsteen; a pair of jeans worn by Marilyn Monroe in *River of No Return.* Miles Davis, playing soft and low, wafts through the air like vapors.

Hilfiger picks up the jeans from the back of a leather wing chair and opens the fly to reveal a row of large plastic buttons, which hang from the black thread like ripe olives. "The quality is remarkable," he says. "I'm giving these to Naomi as a present." That would be Naomi Campbell, Hilfiger's friend and one of the models for his label's rock-and-rap runway extravaganzas.

In person, Hilfiger seems very different from his relentlessly cheerful public image. After all these years, the perpetual flower child finally looks his age. The goofy Beatle bangs have been replaced by a wash-and-wear brush cut. The signature toothy grin has given way to a serious mien. Tommy seems chastened. All grown up.

But it isn't his new look he wants to discuss today. It's his obituary, which he feels his peers are collectively writing at this very moment. Talk to enough industry pundits and it becomes glaringly obvious that Tommy Hilfiger is not suffering from the usual bout of designer paranoia. Indeed, the fashion jackals gathering in the Bryant Park tents this weekend have already hammered out most of Tommy's obit copy between Cosmos at Moomba.

The bullet points are certainly compelling evidence for a post-mortem: After a decade of averaging an envy-inducing 48 percent growth, Hilfiger's earnings plunged last year—as much as 75 percent in the worst quarter. The once-unstoppable stock sank from a high of 41 to a low of 6.3. His flagship stores in London and Beverly Hills were shuttered. An ambitious and widely anticipated Calvin Klein acquisition collapsed. His exuberant runway shows were canceled. A corporate housecleaning eliminated a number of Hilfiger's longtime colleagues. The hip-hop crowd that had propelled his success had deserted for younger, hipper, often blacker labels, and (horror of horrors) the company recently announced an upcoming plus-size line that may make shareholders happy but won't be seen in *Vogue* anytime soon.

"This is a $2 billion company that is disappearing day by day," says one former employee who jumped ship recently. "Just because you have Mario Testino shoot your ads doesn't make you fashionable."

As Hilfiger battled to shore up his business—and endured a ruthless satire from Spike Lee, who named a clueless Caucasian designer in his latest film "Timmi Hilnigger"—there were fires on the home front too. In the kind of when-it-rains-it-pours plot twist that drama queens relish, Tommy and his wife split up. "After twenty years of marriage, we have mutually and amicably decided to separate," announced Hilfiger in a press release issued to preempt the gossip columns. "Tommy's gay!" the fashion vultures declared gleefully, if ridiculously. *"He's pulling a Jann Wenner!"*

In the face of this barrage, Hilfiger seemed to shrink. Once a nightly presence at Moomba, he drastically lowered his profile, rarely venturing out even for lunch. "I don't love sitting in a restaurant being talked about or stared at," he says.

The gossip about his marriage and his sexuality has been particularly galling, and when, after negotiations worthy of a Mideast summit, Hilfiger recently sat for his first major interview in two years, he quickly set the record straight. "Let me assure you," he says adamantly. "I *love* women."

And he hastens to add that reports of his company's demise have been greatly exaggerated. "Suddenly our growth rate wasn't double-digit anymore," he says with a shrug. "Men's was growing at 5 percent rather than 20 percent. That's when the negative press started." He throws his hands up. "We announced for the first time ever that we weren't going to make the quarter—but we ended up doing $2 billion, and made about $170 million after taxes. That's unprecedented for any apparel company."

Probe deeper, however, and you find that Hilfiger actually agrees with some of his colleagues' criticism—he *was* a fashion victim. "At one point, I told my people, 'We *have* to be the first with trends.' So we ran out and tried to do the coolest, most advanced clothes. We didn't just do denim embroidery. We jeweled it. We studded it. We ramped it up. We really pushed the envelope because we thought our customer would respond." He takes a sip of Evian before continuing his self-flagellation.

"But the customer did not respond in a big way," he says. "And our business last year—men's, women's, juniors'—suffered as a result."

For the designer, it was both a personal and a corporate identity crisis. "When business plateaued in '99," he explains, "we thought the customer didn't want the Tommy logo anymore. So we took it off a lot of stuff. We made it tiny. We became very insecure about being a red-white-and-blue-logo brand. We thought we had to be much chic-er, more in line with the Euro houses like Gucci and Prada."

Perhaps Tommy's most telling indulgence was the now-defunct Red Label luxury line—designed to cater to the rock stars, rappers, and other celebrities Hilfiger had been dressing—which offered such items as $7,000 patchwork python trousers (he sold only four worldwide) and spent millions on fashion shows. In the process of competing with the high-flyers, he strayed from the original nouvelle-preppy vision that made his company so successful.

For a moment, Hilfiger is subdued by his confession. But he finally unveils that blinding smile. "As a result of learning from our errors, we went back to our roots: classics with a twist."

To prove his point, be holds up a colored T-shirt with the Tommy logo blown up so large as to be parodic. "This shirt is our number one seller," he announces. The Juniors Pieced Flag T-shirt he holds in his hands sold a staggering 300,000 units in the previous two months.

The story Hilfiger tells about the past year is one of soul-searching and regrouping. "Learning from our mistakes is really positive," he says. "Because we looked at the situation and said, 'These things are wrong.' We reacted immediately. The London flagship store wasn't open for a year when we realized we had made a mistake." Snobby Bond Street, observers pointed out, was the wrong address for Tommy in the first place. It looked like a matter, one noted, of "keeping up with the Laurens"—Ralph's big flagship is right down the street.

The Beverly Hills store, says Hilfiger, was also ill-conceived. "The average age on Rodeo Drive is probably fifty years old," he says. "My customers are much younger than that. We thought all the cool people in L.A. come to Rodeo. But they don't."

Buckingham Capital Management industry analyst Larry Leeds sees in the Hilfiger story a kind of fairy tale turned cautionary tale: "You have this little guy, who is a fine guy, who has a store. And he became a god, and built a business that's as big as Ralph's, you know? And he makes a fortune. And everything's great.

"But then he gets absolutely carried away with urban, ghetto youth. And he loses his preppy original niche. And the thing got very overdone, and Tommy had to get back to reality. And he did. He's a very rational guy."

Wall Street is buying this version of the story, complete with upbeat ending. By November, despite continuing declines in earnings, analysts were enthusiastic about the turnaround in the works, and the stock had climbed back to 13. By last week, when the most recent figures were released, the stock went as high as 15.

And Tommy, despite chagrin at abandoning some of his cutting-edge pretensions, has recovered his mainstream roots. "We're about color, we're about preppy, we're about classic, we're about America!" he says, reciting his mantra. "We learned the hard way that that's where we belong." He picks up a placard displaying a photo from an old Tommy ad campaign: a gaggle of meticulously art-directed models posing languidly in front of a billowing American flag. "It was my insecurity about being *this,*" he says, his eyes misting over at the sight of the iconic tableau. "I thought we could be much more than this. When in reality, just this is incredible."

If Tommy seems to have an almost corny belief in the American dream, it may be because he has lived it. Thomas Jacob Hilfiger was born on March 24, 1951, in Elmira, New York, a dreary upstate town best known as Mark Twain's summer residence. The second-oldest of nine children, Hilfiger was raised in a white clap-board Victorian house. Richard Hilfiger, a watchmaker at a local jewelry store, was an affable man of Dutch-German descent. His wife, Virginia, worked as a nurse. Even with two incomes, the Hil-figers lived from one paycheck to the next.

Tommy began working at an early age: mowing lawns at nine and pumping gas at the local Hess station at sixteen. "I worked the night shift and made $1.25 an hour, which was great money at the time," he says. "I bought all my own clothes. I helped out my brothers. I didn't depend on my parents for anything."

No one would dispute that the young Hilfiger was enterpris-ing, but nothing about him suggested that he was destined for celebrity. Small for his age, he concealed fifteen-pound weights in his pockets to make the junior-high football team. Nor was he a star pupil. In fact, he had to repeat the tenth grade. It wasn't until much later that he was diagnosed as dyslexic. "Tommy was only a C guy, and he wasn't a great athlete either," remembers Marty Herrigan, Hilfiger's football coach at Elmira Free Academy. "I guess that's why he became a businessman."

What he did possess was a precocious sartorial flair, which he inherited from a father regarded as Elmira's resident Beau Brum-mel. And he and his siblings enjoyed a certain social cachet. "Our house rocked," says Hilfiger, grinning. "My brothers practiced their music in the basement, and all the kids from the neighbor-hood came to hang out. It was a very cool spot."

Tommy's first big fashion epiphany occurred in 1969. To finance a summer away from home, Hilfiger took a sales job at a hippie clothing store on Cape Cod. The former preppy returned home from vacation decked out in sandals and bell-bottoms. His hair had grown out, rock-star-style—sort of Prince Valiant meets Brian Jones. He listened to Hendrix and Stones eight-tracks. He dropped acid. His parents were, to use Hilfiger's own words, "freaked." He was seventeen.

What happened next has become part of *garmento* folklore. Realizing that Elmira was a fashion wasteland, full of teenagers like himself who craved mod clothes but couldn't find them, Hilfiger and two high school buddies pooled their life savings ($50 apiece) and went into the jeans business. Hilfiger drove his rusted '59 VW Bug to Ithaca and scrounged up ten pairs of bell-bottoms. The initial inventory sold out in a day.

Encouraged by the enthusiastic response, Hilfiger made the 250-mile trip to New York, where he stuffed his Bug with 600 pairs of jumbo-legged jeans, which he purchased for $3.50, and flipped them in Elmira for $5.88. In a week, all 600 pairs were snapped up.

Eventually the three high school seniors decided to become retailers themselves. On December 1, 1969, they opened a store called People's Place in downtown Elmira. It conformed to the typical trippy-jean-boutique template (head shop downstairs, Day-Glo and incense all around) and became an instant hit with Elmira's high school crowd. "I couldn't wait for three to bolt from school and open the store," recalls Hilfiger. At the end of their senior year, the three partners were doing almost $1 million in volume and pulling down $60,000 salaries.

The local newspaper wrote up People's Place and Hilfiger spouted off about rebelling against "the Establishment." Larry Stemerman, one of the three original People's Place investors, says he and Hilfiger weren't nearly as rebellious as they were portrayed to be: "We laughed about it because we weren't rebelling against the Establishment—we *were* the Establishment."

In the early seventies, Hilfiger made his first trip to London. The swinging Carnaby Street scene was already winding down, but to Hilfiger "it was amazing," he says wistfully. "For the first time, I saw how music and fashion complemented each other perfectly." He came back with a rock-star wardrobe of frilly shirts and formfitting velveteen pants.

By the mid-seventies, Hilfiger and his partners had seven stores scattered around upstate New York, a six-figure income, and an automotive fleet comprising a Porsche, a Mercedes, a Jeep, and a Jaguar. People's Place was hot, with a customer list that included the J. Geils Band and Bruce Springsteen.

Hilfiger, meanwhile, was pursuing the rock-star lifestyle he had always craved. He wore monster bells so oversized that his high-heel snakeskin boots were concealed beneath the voluminous folds of fabric. He got his hair styled in a Rod Stewart rooster cut.

"I was twenty-three and chartering planes," says Hilfiger. "We were flying to rock concerts, taking dates to London and Paris." And he was spending so much time in New York that he took a pied-à-terre on East Twelfth Street near the Fillmore Theater.

In 1976, Hilfiger walked into his store in Ithaca and met a pretty teenage employee named Susie Cirona. The attraction was instantaneous and mutual. "It's no surprise they fell in love," says one friend. "Tommy and Susie were like bookends. They looked alike, they acted alike, they even talked alike. They could have passed for brother and sister."

But while Hilfiger's romantic relationship was blossoming, his business was not. Other retailers in the area finally began offering bleached bells and tie-dyed T-shirts. Making matters worse, the upstate economy was falling into a recession. Stores began folding, and the unpaid invoices piled up. In August 1977, Hilfiger and Stemerman filed for bankruptcy. "We did not tend to business," says Hilfiger sheepishly. He squirms in his chair. "It was a rude awakening."

Hilfiger and Stemerman divvied up the four remaining stores. When a buyer for Hilfiger's half surfaced, the newlyweds moved to Manhattan and waited for the checks to roll in. They never did— the buyer filed for bankruptcy after closing the deal with Hilfiger. Cash-strapped and desperate for work, the young couple began pitching themselves on Seventh Avenue as a husband-wife design team. It was the peak of the designer-jean craze, and Jordache was looking to market a full-blown collection. The Hilfigers got the nod but were fired after only a month. A job at Bonjour quickly followed; it didn't last long, either, but Hilfiger kept at it.

Despite his involvement with a string of fashion-world bottom-feeders, Hilfiger built up a reputation as a savvy and hardworking designer. He was on a shortlist to do Perry Ellis's sportswear line, and Puritan Fashions asked him to design its Calvin Klein jeans label.

When the Klein job was placed on the table in 1983, Hilfiger didn't immediately accept. Not that it wasn't tempting, especially to someone who was broke and starting a family. But what Hilfiger really wanted was his own label.

Into the breach stepped Mohan Murjani, an Indian entrepreneur with a posh Etonian accent who was looking for a young designer to launch a new line of men's sportswear. Born into a family of textile barons, Murjani was a colorful character who owned the license for Gloria Vanderbilt jeans and also for Coca-Cola clothes, which had mushroomed into a half-billion-dollar enterprise.

Hilfiger, who had always been self-conscious about his lack of design training, found a soul mate in Murjani. Far from being put off by Hilfiger's lack of atelier experience, Murjani considered it an advantage. If a design had to be altered to cut manufacturing costs, he knew Hilfiger wouldn't whine about artistic integrity.

"The plan was to be a younger Ralph Lauren," Murjani says mischievously. The contract Hilfiger signed gave Murjani ownership of both the new company and the Hilfiger name, but it gave Hilfiger financial security and the pleasure of seeing his name on backsides across the country.

Hilfiger came up with the design formula that would inform his work for years to come: classics with a twist. Like Ralph Lauren, he pillaged all the Ivy League icons, but he added quirky details. Like stitching the buttonhole with contrasting thread, or using a pastel fabric to line the collar of a sober oxford shirt. The most striking thing about the clothes was the logo. The abstract composition resembled a miniature Mondrian and made Lauren's polo figure seem stodgy in comparison.

To publicize the new line, Murjani hired legendary adman George Lois, whose hip, controversial campaigns inevitably generated media attention. For Murjani, he outdid himself, concocting a $160,000 one-shot campaign that propelled Hilfiger from relative obscurity to stardom overnight.

Lois used just a single line of ad copy: THE 4 GREAT AMERICAN DESIGNERS FOR MEN ARE: R-L, P-E, C-K, T-H. When the "initial campaign" was unveiled on a Times Square billboard in 1986, it caused a sensation.

"The whole concept was to make Tommy famous with the first ad," explains Lois. "The hubris was beyond belief. Here we were saying that somebody who hadn't sold one item of clothing yet was a great American designer." Lois stifles a laugh. It's still one of his favorite campaigns.

But the Old Guard was not amused. To this day, many designers bear a grudge against Hilfiger. Some, like Calvin Klein, because he was included in the ad copy. And some, like John Weitz, because he wasn't. Geoffrey Beene had an especially catty response: "I don't go along with the Gabor girls that any publicity is good publicity." Gleefully fanning the flames, Lois ordered a gigantic billboard right in the middle of the garment district.

Three months after the campaign was unveiled, a furious Klein confronted Lois at Mr. Chow. "Do you know it took me twenty years to get to the point where Tommy Hilfiger is today?!" the designer erupted in the crowded dining room. Lois calmly brushed aside Klein's finger and replied, "That's *my* job, schmuck. Why take twenty years if you can do it in twenty days?"

Hilfiger himself was by no means as confident as his ad campaign would suggest. "Everybody thought I was a complete jerk," he says feebly. "I considered leaving the business, because I thought I was doomed. I thought Calvin, Ralph, and Perry would somehow strong-arm Bloomies into not buying my line."

Those fears were unfounded. In only eighteen months, the nouvelle-preppy line grossed more than $11 million. With sales doubling every year, Murjani drew up an expansion plan that included opening six stores in a year, including a Rodeo Drive boutique.

Then, in 1988, the Murjani empire imploded. Hilfiger's clothes were still selling well, but his boss had overextended himself.

Coca-Cola apparel, the cash cow he had relied upon to subsidize numerous business ventures and corporate expansion, had fizzled.

Desperate not to see his label vanish, Hilfiger hired a phalanx of expensive lawyers and began hunting for a white knight. His financial savior turned out to be Silas Chou, a scion of a wealthy Hong Kong textile family. Chou insisted that he give up his ownership of the Tommy Hilfiger name, but in the end, Chou's manufacturing and financial power were difficult to turn down. Hilfiger agreed to take a 22.5 percent share of the new company.

The calculated commercialism upon which the company was based was obvious from the start and goes a long way toward explaining the fashion industry's long-standing animus. "Hilfiger is the fashion equivalent of the Monkees," said one industry analyst at the time. "They had a concept and found four guys that could play, rather than beginning with the talent."

But just as nobody cared that the Monkees were not real musicians, consumers didn't care that Hilfiger's real gift wasn't in design. In fact, the company began expanding at such a torrid pace in the early nineties—as Casual Fridays were becoming entrenched in corporate America—that the fantastic numbers *WWD* reported were initially dismissed as typos.

In 1989, Tommy Hilfiger USA leapfrogged from $28 million a year in retail sales to $50 million. The second year, from $50 million to $100 million. And then came hip-hop.

It happened thanks to a fortuitous meeting at Kennedy Airport in the early nineties between Hilfiger and rap artist Grand Puba. Returning from a business trip in Hong Kong, the designer noticed a group of hip-hop kids sauntering through the terminal wearing supersized versions of his clothes. Hilfiger's brother Andy, a former rock musician who now handles the company's celebrity-client roster, recognized the group's leader and made introductions. Hilfiger had no idea who the rapper was but was intrigued that this subculture had latched on to his label.

It was as if Carnaby Street were happening all over again. Hilfiger immediately understood the money to be made if he could align himself with popular rap stars. Andy Hilfiger began giving trunks of clothes away to any rapper with a recording contract. Soon icons in the 'hood like Raekwon and Coolio began wearing Tommy Hilfiger on their concert tours and in their videos.

Unlike other brands the rap community had embraced, like Timberland and Polo, Hilfiger went out of its way to satisfy its new urban customers. Indeed, the white-bread designer actually began to cater to their culture-specific sartorial taste: the silhouette became larger than life, the palette became brighter, and the logo blew up, in some instances so large it covered the entire garment.

But it wasn't until March 1994, when Snoop Doggy Dog wore a comically oversized Tommy Hilfiger rugby shirt on *Saturday Night Live,* that the brand really broke out. Practically overnight, every wanna-be homie from the San Fernando Valley to Valley Stream was blowing his allowance on Tommy duds. The company's stock, after an IPO in '92, soared, splitting twice and making Hilfiger rich.

By 1995, Hilfiger's salary was $6 million. He and Susie purchased a historic farm in Greenwich for almost $10 million. The twenty-two-room converted Colonial farmhouse looked like a location for a Ralph Lauren shoot. Situated next to a wildlife sanctuary (Mel Gibson and Diana Ross are also neighbors), the extensive grounds included a clay tennis court and stables. Hilfiger also acquired vacation houses in Nantucket and Mustique, the latter next door to Mick Jagger.

The rock-and-roll designer had arrived. But instead of concerts, Hilfiger's gigs were in-store public appearances. He would literally jet from one department store to the next (100 a year), promoting not albums but whatever collection or licensed product happened to be breaking at the moment. Fans, TH-logoed from head to toe, showed up en masse to catch a glimpse of their idol. At one Macy's appearance in New York, Tommy stood at the end of the runway, ripped off his jacket and sunglasses, and tossed them into the crowd.

"It was a thrill for Tommy to be recognized," says one confidant. "He got high on it." Another acquaintance confirms this. "Tommy's newfound wealth was such a hoot for him, and he had a lot of fun. He'd go into nightclubs, and if he saw people he knew, he'd send them bottles of Dom Perignon." But all that comp champagne didn't buy Hilfiger the professional respect he craved. Fashion people balked at his mainstream popularity. Not that it mattered. Hilfiger's increasing market penetration made him impossible to dismiss. Moreover, the untrained designer was compiling an enviable client list, ranging from Prince Charles to Leonardo DiCaprio.

It was hardly surprising that in 1994, Hilfiger was considered a shoo-in to win the Council of Fashion Designers of America's (CFDA) coveted Menswear Designer of the Year award, the industry's equivalent of the Oscar. Previous winners included the holy trinity of American ready-to-wear: Donna, Ralph, and Calvin. So when the CFDA chose not to hand out the prize that year, it was widely perceived as a snub of Tommy.

The CFDA did deign to give him the award the following year, but the victory was bittersweet. "I don't think there *was* another choice that year," he says. "My business was doing very well, there wasn't a new menswear designer on the horizon, and everybody else had won."

One thing that rankles fellow designers is Hilfiger's honesty about the collaborative nature of his company. He admits that being a successful designer has less to do with knowing fashion than it does with playing to one's audience. "I have a creative team," he says unabashedly. "I sit with the men's designers on a regular basis and tell them what's on my mind. I'll tell them I'd really like to see woolly fabrics or plaids and buffalo checks. I give them primitive sketches from time to time," he says, "showing them what I want to see."

When it comes to designing his women's collection, however,

Hilfiger is almost completely out of the loop. "I don't have a great instinct when it comes to women's fashion," he says with refreshing candor. "But I hire great people who do." People like Stephen Cirona, a cousin of Susie's, who is the company's de facto principal designer, responsible for the overall direction of both the women's and the men's lines.

"Stephen's great," Hilfiger says earnestly. He points to several mounted black-and-white photographs of Ali MacGraw and Ryan O'Neal. "*Love Story* is the theme for next fall," he says. "Stephen saw the movie and came in the next day so excited about adapting the clothes for the runway."

Hilfiger has also used *Vogue* fashion editor Camilla Nickerson as a consultant to help style his shows. Vogue editor in chief Anna Wintour says that since Nickerson is freelance, she has no problem with her taking outside jobs "as long as we're aware of it."

Hilfiger bristles at the notion that some of his peers see him as a mere marketer. "*Everyone* has their opinion," he says. "Look at Ralph. *He* used to be a *tie* salesman." When it's pointed out that Lauren actually designed the ties he sold, he's no longer able to contain himself. "My very first lines I designed as well. I sketched them out, stood in the sample room. I worked with the pattern makers; I did the fittings."

Now, Tommy acknowledges, he doesn't even choose the pieces that will finally make it to market. That selection process takes place at "adoption meetings," where a roomful of executives collectively decide what will sell. Hilfiger's staff seems to be genuinely fond of the designer, who moves through his headquarters jovially bantering with assistants. In fact, he has put several through college. "He spares you the diva-designer act," says one.

On a trip to his headquarters, Hilfiger ushers me to a cavernous room filled with countless pieces of clothing. Some old, some new, some designer labels, others obscure brands. A bright-red Polo jacket, crumpled on the floor, sticks out like a flair. But an ex-Lauren employee now working for Tommy dismisses its significance. "Ralph has an entire *room* devoted to Tommy's clothes," he says. Hilfiger cracks a smile.

Next, he proceeds to the juniors'-sportswear design studio, to discuss the latest collection with the department's head designer. "This is Stacy," he says happily. "She used to work for the Gap. Before she came along, we used to steal her designs." He winks. "I mean, *literally* steal her designs." Stacy starts to blush.

Designer Nicole Miller commends her colleague for his candor. "Tommy is the only designer who's come clean and said that he doesn't design everything that carries his label," she says. "Designers want you to think they do everything, but it's impossible to design everything yourself."

Timothy Gunn, the associate dean of Parsons' department of fashion design, concurs. Indeed, it is because of Tommy Hilfiger, says Gunn, that Parsons is completely changing the way it educates its design students. The new Tommified curriculum, to be introduced next fall, will stress business and marketing principles as well as pattern making and Vreeland Aphorisms 101.

"Being a designer today is much more about lifestyle than it is about clothes," says Gunn. "So we're restructuring our design curriculum. We're certainly going to accommodate the design savant, but we need to accommodate other approaches as well. Because not every student is going to be Isaac." Gunn waits a beat before delivering his punch line: "I mean, look what happened to Isaac."

The breakup of Hilfiger's twenty-year marriage, some friends say, was devastating to him, and his celebrity hasn't made it any easier. A few months ago, the *Daily News* ran a paparazzi shot of Hilfiger and Maggie Rizer, the freckle-faced blonde who appears in the current Tommy Hilfiger ad campaign. In the photograph, Hilfiger's fingers are tucked snugly beneath the waistband of Rizer's jeans. "It *did* look pretty cozy," says columnist George Rush, who ran the incriminating picture in his Sunday column. But Hilfiger denies he and Rizer had an affair. "Totally ridiculous," he says, more amused than offended.

But the designer does confirm reports linking him to Annabelle Bond, daughter of the Australian financier Sir John

Bond, and admits a more recent relationship with a paralegal from Stamford, Connecticut, named Elizabeth Somerby. He says that both relationships are casual, and takes pains to stress that his separation from Susie was amicable. "She's still my best friend," he says. He recently bought a house in Greenwich right across the street from his soon-to-be-ex-wife and their four children.

Friends of the couple speculate that a dearth of quality time was a factor in his marital problems, but some believe the real problem was Susie's aversion to the limelight. One acquaintance explains: "I remember sitting next to Susie at a dinner and she turned to me and said, 'I should be more like you. Tommy needs a wife who can hold court at a dinner table. I'm not like that.' She doesn't want to be in the spotlight."

In contrast, Tommy's relentless social life earned him weekly mentions in the columns for a while. "He became a real party animal," says one confidant. "And he's completely obsessed with celebrities." He also forged a friendship with Anna Wintour. Wintour praises Hilfiger's "easy, all-American vision" and acknowledges that he took a wrong turn when he tried to go too high-fashion. "On a personal level, I really like Tommy," she adds. "He's someone you can get on the phone right away. He calls and asks your opinion on things. You can just chat with him. He's a pleasure to have as a friend."

Interestingly enough, Hilfiger's closest circle of friends are the same ten high school classmates he grew up with in Elmira. Hilfiger keeps in touch regularly with them and is known for his unselfish support, which is frequently bestowed in the form of grand gestures. For instance, when Larry Stemerman's father was too ill to fly commercially, Hilfiger sent his private jet to pick him up so that be could see his new grandchild. "Tommy's always been generous with his money," says Stemerman. "Even in high school, if you needed ten bucks, Tommy would give it to you. "Another member of Tommy's "crew" is fellow Elmira native Michael French, now an actor living in L.A. "The degree to which Tommy has been faithful to his past amazes me," says French. "He loves to talk about the old days. We'll get together and reminisce about skipping classes and the things we did at the local pool hall."

In December 1999, Hilfiger cohosted the prestigious annual Metropolitan Museum Costume Institute gala with Wintour and Aerin Lauder, and some speculated that Wintour also used her considerable influence to help her friend gain entry to the most exclusive co-op in Manhattan—820 Fifth Avenue. "Valentino and Ron Perelman were both snubbed by that board. So when Tommy was accepted, the ladies who lunch thought it was scandalous," says one well-connected socialite. "They all thought Tommy got in because he got cozy with the queen bee of the co-op board, Jayne Wrightsman, through Anna Wintour."

Wintour blasts the gossip as "utter fabrication." In any case, after securing the $10 million co-op, Hilfiger didn't even move in, having decided that eighteen rooms was a bit grand for a bachelor pad. He did well on the deal, however, flipping the property to billionaire widow Lily Safra for $18 million.

Industry analysts see the Hilfiger company turning around, but it's likely to be without the help of the hip-hop community. The urban consumers who made Tommy a sizzling brand in the early nineties have turned their attention to lines financed by hip-hop icons like Russell Simmons (Phat Farm) and Puffy Combs (Sean Jean).

But Hilfiger doesn't care to court the rap crowd anymore. He's not ungrateful. They got him where he is today. But now it's time to win back all those free-spending boomers he alienated when he went ghetto. "Obviously, Tommy went too extreme into a narrow portion of the business," says Bloomingdale's CEO Michael Gould. "I think it may have scared off a whole lot of other customers." At the same time, Hilfiger has to keep teen customers happy. According to the 2000 back-to-school shopping survey conducted by American Express, Tommy Hilfiger is still the top-rated apparel brand overall among American teenagers, scoring an impressive 28 percent (Old Navy rates 27 percent; Nike, 26; Gap, 24; and Ralph, 17).

Wall Street is confident that Hilfiger can regain his core consumers. "It will never again be the hot, sexy, overly talked-about, flashy, zippy, fast-growing company it was, but it will be a damn nice company turning out lots of cash," one veteran analyst says. "What you've got is a company that went from an A-plus to an F-minus. And now it's going to go back to a B. And it's a hell of a business as a B."

Hilfiger knows, however, that getting back on solid footing is not going to satisfy stockholders forever. "The board of directors and the shareholders, it's like this mob that you have to keep feeding," he says. And to find that growth, he's looking overseas. Despite all the new stores he's opening Stateside—in SoHo, Dallas, Atlanta, and Miami—his main focus now is on Europe. Within the next two years, Hilfiger plans to open twenty stand-alone stores in Italy. "We're just starting in the rest of the world," he declares.

On the home front, Tommy opted out of the Bryant Park tents for this week, deciding on a smaller showroom presentation for editors. "A high-powered runway show would cost us $1.5 million," he says. "We'd rather put that into advertising." To shoot his new campaign, he hired the very hot lensman Mario Testino, who produced a series of ads as sumptuously decadent as Gucci's. Though Hilfiger praises Testino, he doesn't seem completely satisfied. "I would have liked it to be more spirited. I'd like more smiles, and for it to be more relaxed. It's beautifully photographed, but to be perfectly honest . . ."

Hilfiger doesn't finish the thought, but it's easy enough to finish it for him. The cool elitism of the fashion world, seductive as it is to a starstruck boy from Elmira, can finally seem a little empty. "People in New York and Los Angeles get a stilted image of where our brand is at. Once you get out of the precious little confine of SoHo and Seventh Avenue, you see people wearing Tommy in Kansas."

Kansas, of course, is a long way from SoHo—but it's not nearly that far from Elmira.

Our nation's leaders-in-waiting are a dutiful, goal-oriented bunch whose self-improvement and upward mobility are a way of life, according to David Brooks in this article from *The Atlantic* magazine. Such youngsters may be on the road to becoming workaholics one day, which is their own choice. But have their overprotective parents also helped purge from their minds any moral conviction and a desire to protest unfairness? Brooks talks to college students and comes up with his own take on our future.

David Brooks

The Organization Kid

A FEW MONTHS AGO I went to Princeton University to see what the young people who are going to be running our country in a few decades are like. Faculty members gave me the names of a few dozen articulate students, and I sent them e-mails, inviting them out to lunch or dinner in small groups. I would go to sleep in my hotel room at around midnight each night, and when I awoke, my mailbox would be full of replies—sent at 1:15 A.M., 2:59 A.M., 3:23 A.M.

In our conversations I would ask the students when they got around to sleeping. One senior told me that she went to bed around two and woke up each morning at seven; she could afford that much rest because she had learned to supplement her full day of work by studying in her sleep. As she was falling asleep she would recite a math problem or a paper topic to herself; she would then sometimes dream about it, and when she woke up, the problem might be solved. I asked several students to describe their daily schedules, and their replies sounded like a session of Future Workaholics of America: crew practice at dawn, classes in the morning, resident-adviser duty, lunch, study groups, classes in the afternoon, tutoring disadvantaged kids in Trenton, a cappella practice, dinner, study, science lab, prayer session, hit the Stair-Master, study a few hours more. One young man told me that he had to schedule appointment times for chatting with his friends. I mentioned this to other groups, and usually one or two people would volunteer that they did the same thing. "I just had an appointment with my best friend at seven this morning," one woman said. "Or else you lose touch."

There are a lot of things these future leaders no longer have time for. I was on campus at the height of the election season, and I saw not even one Bush or Gore poster. I asked around about this and was told that most students have no time to read newspapers, follow national politics, or get involved in crusades. One senior told me she had subscribed to *The New York Times* once, but the papers had just piled up unread in her dorm room. "It's a basic question of hours in the day," a student journalist told me. "People are too busy to get involved in larger issues. When I think of all that I have to keep up with, I'm relieved there are no bigger compelling causes." Even the biological necessities get squeezed out. I was amazed to learn how little dating goes on. Students go out in groups, and there is certainly a fair bit of partying on campus, but as one told me, "People don't have time or energy to put into real relationships." Sometimes they'll have close friendships and "friendships with privileges" (meaning with sex), but often they don't get serious until they are a few years out of college and meet again at a reunion—after their careers are on track and they can begin to spare the time.

I went to lunch with one young man in a student dining room that by 1:10 had emptied out, as students hustled back to the library and their classes. I mentioned that when I went to college, in the late 1970s and early 1980s, we often spent two or three hours around the table, shooting the breeze and arguing about things. He admitted that there was little discussion about intellectual matters outside class. "Most students don't like that that's the case," he told me, "but it is the case." So he and a bunch of his friends had formed a discussion group call Paidea, which meets regularly with a faculty guest to talk about such topics as millennialism, postmodernism, and Byzantine music. If discussion can be scheduled, it can be done.

The students were lively conversationalists on just about any topic—except moral argument and character-building, about which more below. But when I asked a group of them if they ever felt like workaholics, their faces lit up and they all started talking at once. One, a student-government officer, said, "Sometimes we feel like we're just tools for processing information. That's what we call ourselves—power tools. And we call these our tool bags." He held up his satchel. The other students laughed, and one exclaimed, "You're giving away all our secrets."

But nowhere did I find any real unhappiness with this state of affairs; nowhere did I find anybody who seriously considered living any other way. These superaccomplished kids aren't working so hard because they are compelled to. They are facing, it still appears, the sweetest job market in the nation's history. Investment banks flood the campus looking for hires. Princeton also offers a multitude of postgraduation service jobs in places like China and Africa. Everyone I spoke to felt confident that he or she could get a job after graduation. Nor do these students seem driven by some Puritan work ethic deep in their cultural memory. It's not the stick that drives them on; it's the carrot. Opportunity lures them. And at a place like Princeton, in a rich information-age country like America, promises of enjoyable work abound—at least for people as smart and ambitious as these. "I want to be this busy," one young woman insisted, after she had described a daily schedule that would count as slave driving if it were imposed on anyone.

The best overall description of the students' ethos came from a professor in the politics department and at the Woodrow Wilson School of Public and International Affairs, Jeffrey Herbst. "They are professional students," he said. "I don't say that pejoratively. Their profession for these four years is to be a student."

That doesn't mean that these leaders-in-training are money mad (though they are certainly career conscious). It means they are goal oriented. An activity—whether it is studying, hitting the treadmill, drama group, community service, or one of the student groups they found and join in great numbers—is rarely an end in itself. It is a means for self-improvement, résumé-building, and enrichment. College is just one step on the continual stairway of advancement, and they are always aware that they must get to the next step (law school, medical school, whatever) so that they can progress up the steps after that.

One day I went to lunch with Fred Hargadon, who has been the dean of admissions at Princeton for thirteen years and was the dean of admissions at Stanford before that. Like all the administrators and faculty members I spoke with, Hargadon loves these students, and he is extraordinarily grateful for the opportunity to be around them. "I would trust these kids with my life," he told me. But he, like almost all the other older people I talked to, is a little disquieted by the achievement ethos and the calm acceptance of established order that prevails among elite students today. Hargadon said he had been struck by a 1966 booklet called "College Admissions and the Public Interest," written by a retired MIT admissions director named Brainerd Alden Thresher. Thresher made a distinction between students who come to campus in a "poetic" frame of mind and those who come in a "prudential" frame of mind. "Certainly more kids are entering in a prudential frame of mind," Hargadon said. "Most kids see their education as a means to an end."

They're not trying to buck the system; they're trying to climb it, and they are streamlined for ascent. Hence they are not a disputatious group. I often heard at Princeton a verbal tic to be found in model young people these days: if someone is about to disagree with someone else in a group, he or she will apologize beforehand and will couch the disagreement in the most civil, nonconfrontational terms available. These students are also extremely respect-ful of authority, treating their professors as one might treat a CEO or a division head at a company meeting.

"Undergrads somehow got this ethos that the faculty is sacro-sanct," Dave Wilkinson, a professor of physics, told me. "You don't mess with the faculty. I cannot get the students to call me by my first name." Aaron Friedberg, who teaches international rela-tions, said, "It's very rare to get a student to challenge anything or to take a position that's counter to what the professor says." Robert Wuthnow, a sociologist, lamented, "They are disconcert-ingly comfortable with authority. That's the most common com-plaint the faculty has of Princeton students. They're eager to please, eager to jump through whatever hoops the faculty puts in front of them, eager to conform."

For the generation of runners of things that came to power in the Clinton years, at least a modest degree of participation in college-years protest was very nearly mandatory. The new elite does not protest. Young achievers vaguely know that they are supposed to feel guilty about not marching in the street for some cause. But they don't seem to feel guilty. When the controversial ethicist Peter Singer was hired by Princeton, there were protests over his views on euthanasia. But it was mostly outsiders who protested, not students. Two years ago the administration outlawed the Nude Olympics, a raucous school tradition. Many of the students were upset, but not enough to protest. "It wasn't rational to buck authority once you found out what the penalties were," one stu-dent journalist told me. "The university said they would suspend you from school for a year." A prudential ethos indeed.

Part of this is just Princeton. It has always been the preppiest of the Ivy League schools. It has earned a reputation for sending more graduates into consulting and investment banking than into academia or the arts. But this is also what life is like at other com-petitive universities today. In the months since I spoke with the Princeton students, I've been at several other top schools. Stu-dents, faculty members, and administrators at those places describe a culture that is very similar to the one I found at Princeton. This culture does not absolutely reflect or inform the lives and values of young Americans as a whole, but it does reflect and inform the lives and values of an important subset of this generation: the meritocratic elite. It is this elite that I am primarily reporting on in this article, rather than the whole range of young people across the demographic or SAT spectrum. It should also be said, though, that the young elite are not entirely unlike the other young; they are the logical extreme of America's increasingly efficient and demanding sorting-out process, which uses a complex set of incentives and conditions to channel and shape and rank our children throughout their young lives.

It will surprise no one who has kids to discover that social-science statistics support that description. Not just Princetonians lead a frenetic, tightly packed existence. Kids of all stripes lead lives that are structured, supervised, and stuffed with enrichment. Time-analysis studies done at the University of Michigan's Institute for Social Research provide the best picture of the trend: From 1981 to 1997 the amount of time that children aged three to twelve spent playing indoors declined by 16 percent. The amount of time spent watching TV declined by 23 percent. Meanwhile, the amount of time spent studying increased by 20 percent and the amount of time spent doing organized sports increased by 27 percent. Drive around your neighborhood. Remember all those parks that used to have open fields? They have been carved up into neatly trimmed soccer and baseball fields crowded with parents in folded chairs who are watching their kids perform. In 1981 the association U.S. Youth Soccer had 811,000 registered players. By 1998 it had nearly three million.

Today's elite kids are likely to spend their afternoons and weekends shuttling from one skill-enhancing activity to the next. By the time they reach college, they take this sort of pace for granted, sometimes at a cost. In 1985 only 18 percent of college freshmen told the annual University of California at Los Angeles freshman norms survey that they felt "overwhelmed." Now 28 percent of college freshman say they feel that way.

But in general they are happy with their lot. Neil Howe and William Strauss surveyed young people for their book *Millennials Rising* (2000); they found America's young to be generally a hard-working, cheerful, earnest, and deferential group. Howe and Strauss listed their respondents' traits, which accord pretty well with what I found at Princeton: "They're optimists. . . . They're rule followers." The authors paint a picture of incredibly whole-some youths who will correct the narcissism and nihilism of their boomer parents.

Not only at Princeton but also in the rest of the country young people today are more likely to defer to and admire author-ity figures. Responding to a 1997 Gallup survey, 96 percent of teenagers said they got along with their parents, and 82 percent described their home life as "wonderful" or "good." Roughly three out of four said they shared their parents' general values. When asked by Roper Starch Worldwide in 1998 to rank the major problems facing America today, students aged twelve to nineteen most frequently named as their top five concerns selfishness, people who don't respect law and the authorities, wrongdoing by politicians, lack of parental discipline, and courts that care too much about criminals' rights. It is impossible to imagine teen-agers a few decades ago calling for stricter parental discipline and more respect for authority. In 1974 a majority of teenagers re-ported that they could not "comfortably approach their parents with personal matters of concern." Forty percent believed they would be "better off not living with their parents."

Walk through any mall in America. Browse through the racks at Old Navy and Abercrombie & Fitch and the Gap. The colors are bright and chipper. The sales staff is peppy. The look is vaguely retro—upbeat 1962 preassassination innocence. The Gap's televi-sion ads don't show edgy individualists; they show perky con-formists, a bunch of happy kids all wearing the same clothes and all swing-dancing the same moves.

In short, at the top of the meritocratic ladder, we have in America a generation of students who are extraordinarily bright, morally earnest, and incredibly industrious. They like to study and socialize in groups. They create and join organizations with great enthusiasm. They are responsible, safety conscious, and mature. They feel no compelling need to rebel—not even a hint of one. They not only defer to authority; they admire it. "Alienation" is a word one almost never hears from them. They regard the universe as beneficent, orderly, and meaningful. At the schools and colleges where the next leadership class is being bred, one finds not angry revolutionaries, despondent slackers, or dark cynics but the Organization Kid.

THE ORIGINS OF THE
ORGANIZATION KID

To understand any generation, or even the elite segment of any generation, we have to keep reminding ourselves when it was born and what it has experienced. Most of today's college students were born from 1979 to 1982. That means they were under ten years old when the Berlin Wall fell and so have no real firsthand knowledge of global conflict or cold war anxieties about nuclear war. The only major American armed conflict they remember is Desert Storm, a high-tech cakewalk. Moreover, they have never known anything but incredible prosperity: low unemployment and low inflation are the normal condition; crime rates are always falling; the stock market rises. If your experience consisted entirely of being privileged, pampered, and recurringly rewarded in the greatest period of wealth creation in human history, you'd be upbeat too. You'd defer to authority. You'd think that the universe is benign and human nature is fundamentally wonderful.

But the outlook of these young people can't be explained by economics and global events alone. It must also have something to do with the way they were raised. As the University of Michigan time-analysis data show, this is a group whose members have spent the bulk of their lives in structured, adult-organized activities. They are the most honed and supervised generation in human history. If they are group oriented, deferential to authority, and achievement obsessed, we achievement-besotted adults have trained them to be. We have devoted our prodigious energies to imposing a sort of order and responsibility on our kids' lives that we never experienced ourselves. The kids have looked upon this order and have decided that it's good.

Childhood is indeed a journey, a series of stations on the way to adulthood. Snapshots of a few of the stations of contemporary childhood will show how the Organization Kid came to be.

INFANCY

We used to think that children were shaped by God, or by dark oedipal impulses, but as the twenty-first century dawns, we know better. We know that children are shaped by the interaction of their DNA and their environment. In the books and magazines that cater to parents, children are described neither as mysterious creatures, driven by the sort of subterranean passions with which Freud concerned himself, nor as divine innocents. Instead biology has displaced psychology and theology: there is a scientifically discernible structure to human life, and it is inscribed in our genetic code. If something goes wrong, it is because there was a genetic flaw, or because the synapses were not cultivated properly. In either case we may be able to supply a remedy.

"If you're a new parent," begins the introductory essay in a *Newsweek* special issue on children, "your baby had the good fortune to be born at a truly remarkable moment in human history, when science has given us extraordinary new tools for understanding what kids need to thrive physically, emotionally and intellectually." The issue is a survey of recent literature and offers an encapsulation of the ethos of contemporary child rearing. The essay continues,

At the dawn of the 21st century, we no longer have to guess about the best way to raise a child . . . researchers studying cognitive development have used sophisticated imaging technology to track the constant interplay of genetics and environment. Though they still have much to learn, they have laid down the basic building blocks of a comprehensive understanding of how experiences shape growth. It turns out to be something like the way a sculptor chips away at a block of marble; you have to work with what you've got, but skill, patience and persistence make all the difference.

Your child is the most important extra-credit arts project you will ever undertake. The *Newsweek* special issue provides information about the creature parents will be sculpting. It describes the cerebellum, the basal ganglia, and the motor cortex; accompanying diagrams show the locations of different brain activities. There are intimidating warnings: for example, although each baby develops trillions of synapses, about half of them have died off by adulthood. Even before birth, children need stimulation and feedback if they are to build a strong web of brain connections. The pressure is on.

If you walk through the parenting section of your local bookstore, you'll find such titles as *Building Healthy Minds; Baby Minds: Brain-Building Games Your Baby Will Love;* and *Right from Birth: Building Your Child's Foundation for Life.* If you go to an upscale toy store, in addition to innocent playthings you will find sophisticated development tools designed for fetus and infant cultivation. Even parents who didn't buy *WombSong Serenades,* a musical collection designed to stimulate babies' fetal brain activity, can probably still raise a perfect child if they fill the first weeks of his or her life with full doses of Mozart. My local Buy Buy Baby, the infant-oriented megastore, offers at least half a dozen selections, including *Mozart for Babies' Minds* (featuring the Violin Concerto no. 3), *Mozart Playtime* (with the Minuet in F-major), the *Parents Maga-*

zine Classical Music for Baby Mozart collection (Serenade no. 13 in G-major), and *Mozart for Toddlers* (Symphony no. 35). Parents just have to choose which one will produce the best synaptic responses in their child's cerebral cortex.

They can continue their baby's mental development with other brain-enhancement products. For example, the Tiny Love Gymini 3-D Activity Gym (a 1996 *Parenting* magazine Toy of the Year) offers high-contrast graphics to stimulate sight and pattern recognition. Car Seat Gallery flash cards can be slipped into clear-plastic pockets to stimulate brain activity during those minivan rides. Babies can move on from there to the Playskool Kick Start Busy Crib Center, which utilizes natural kicking movements to activate music, other sounds, and blinking lights, and the Lamaze Infant Development System, which features a series of devices, including stacking rings, for various phases of infant development.

Slightly older kids can move up to Sesame Street's Elmo Picture Quiz, because it's never too early to work on test-taking skills, and the Fun & Learn Phonics Bus, with interactive animals to help with letter recognition. The Skidoo 'n' Learn Solar System might be next on the curriculum, followed by either Language Little Dolls—bilingual dolls that speak English and Spanish, French, Italian, or Mandarin Chinese—or the Growing Smart "laptop computer," which improves numeric, color, and spatial-recognition skills.

All of the literature is studded with reassurances for parents whose babies are not clearing developmental hurdles ahead of the other infants in the day-care center. Childhood is a journey, not a race, the experts say. That, say the parents of the coming elite, may be fine for future Piggly Wiggly clerks of America. Moms and dads who want the best and the most for their precious children know better. They know they must construct proper environments and experiences if they are going to get the most out of their child's genetic stock. The time for molding that little burbler is now. Accomplishment begins with the first breaths of life.

ELEMENTARY SCHOOL

No one has done a meticulous scientific study of the subject, but my impression is that the big-backpack era began in the mid-1980s. Kids began carrying larger and larger backpacks to school every year; by the early 1990s I saw elementary school students lugging storage containers that were bigger than they were. I'd watch them trooping into the schoolyard and wonder what would happen to a kid who lost his balance and tipped backward onto his pack. He'd lie there like a stranded beetle, face skyward, arms and legs flailing in the air, unable to flip over again. Would he simply be stuck, pinned to the pavement by the weight of his mathematics texts, until someone came to the rescue?

Perhaps the most important event in ushering in the big-backpack era was the release of the report "A Nation at Risk," on April 26, 1983. Commissioned by Terrel Bell, Ronald Reagan's Secretary of Education, the report decried the "rising tide of mediocrity" plaguing American schools, and it caused an immediate sensation. The problem, it said, was that schools had become too loose and free-flowing. Students faced a "cafeteria-style curriculum" that gave them too many choices. They were graduating from high school having spent much of their time in elective gut classes. They didn't do enough homework. They weren't given enough "rigorous examinations" and standardized tests, nor were they forced to meet stringent college-admissions requirements.

The report represented a rejection of an era that celebrated "natural" education, student-centered diversity, and spontaneity, and that cultivated creativity over discipline and nonconformity over conformity. "A Nation at Risk" bade farewell to all that, and said it was time to reassert authority and reestablish order. Schools needed to get back to basics.

The message took, and the effect has been dramatic. During the 1960s and 1970s, schools assigned less and less homework, so that by 1981 the average six- to eight-year old was doing only fifty-two minutes of homework a week. By 1997 the amount of homework assigned to the average child of the same age had doubled, to more than two hours a week. Meanwhile, the school day, which had shortened during the sixties and seventies, has steadily lengthened since, as has the school year. Requirements have stiffened. Before 1983 the average school district required one year of math and one year of science for high school graduation. Now the average high school calls for two years of each. The culture of schools has tightened. In the 1970s, rebelling against the rigid desks-in-a-row pedagogy of the 1950s, schools experimented with open campuses and classes without walls. Now the language of education reform has changed, and the emphasis is on testing, accountability, and order.

Especially order: increasingly, and in surprising numbers, kids whose behavior subverts efficient learning are medicated so that they and their classmates can keep pace. The United States produces and uses about 90 percent of the world's Ritalin and its generic equivalents. In 1980 it was estimated that somewhere between 270,000 and 541,000 elementary school students were taking Ritalin. By 1987 around 750,000 were. And the use of the drug didn't really take off until the 1990s. In 1997 around 30,000 pounds were produced—an increase of more than 700 percent over the 1990 production level.

Far from all of that Ritalin goes to elementary school kids, but the Ritalin that does is prescribed most frequently in upper-middle-class suburban districts—where, one suspects, the achievement ethos is strongest. Some physicians believe that 10 percent of all children have the sort of conduct disorder—attention-deficit disorder, oppositional defiant disorder—that could be eased with Ritalin or some other drug. It is stunning how quickly we have moved from the idea that children should be given freedom to chart their own learning to a belief that adults have a responsibility to reshape the minds of kids whose behavior deviates from the standard. As Ken Livingston wrote in *The Public Interest* in 1997, "In late-twentieth-century America, when it is difficult or inconvenient to change the environment, we don't think twice about changing the brain of the person who has to live in it." And as Howe and Strauss wrote in *Millennials Rising*, "Ironically, where young Boomers once turned to drugs to prompt impulses and think outside the box, today they turn to drugs to suppress their kids' impulses and keep their behavior inside the box. . . . Nowadays, Dennis the Menace would be on Ritalin, Charlie Brown on Prozac."

The end result of these shifts in pedagogy and in pharmacology is that schools are much more efficient and productive places, geared more than ever toward projecting children into the stratosphere of success. Authority and accountability have replaced experimentation and flexibility.

PLAYTIME

I suspect that before long, law schools will begin sponsoring courses in the new field of play-date law. A generation ago, of course, children did not have play dates; they just went out and played. But now upscale parents fill their kids' datebooks with structured play sessions. And they want to make sure not only that the children will be occupied at somebody's house but also that the activities undertaken will be developmentally appropriate, enriching, and safe. Parental negotiations over what is permissible during these sessions can take on a numbing complexity. Americans being Americans, surely it won't be long before such negotiations end up in a court of law.

Many of the disputes in these talks revolve around what future lawyers will call VSIs (video-screen issues). Should there be a complete ban on using the computer during play dates, or should kids be restricted to didactic video games, such as the programs that enhance typing skills? What about Nintendo and PlayStation? Other disputes involve homework rituals, anxiety about pets, and sibling-control measures. But the most heated talks usually revolve around safety issues.

Will the nanny or parent transporting the children be using a cell phone while driving? Have all the child-safety seats recently been checked by a certified safety-seat professional? Are electrical outlets in the home protected by childproof covers? Do the oven controls have kid guards? Is there a foam bumper pad around the stone fireplace (such as the kind available through the Right Start catalog)? What about the toilet—has it been lid-locked so that children don't accidentally fall in and drown? And the yard—has it been aerated to make the ground softer in case of falls? Is there enough soft rubber under the outdoor play equipment?

No candy will be permitted, obviously. Sneaking chocolate into the diet in the form of a chocolate-chip granola bar is dubious. Minicarrots are usually acceptable, though they can present a choking hazard. Sugar and refined wheat should be avoided for kids with food-related hyperactivity triggers. Most organic vegetables are acceptable.

Other cultures controlled behavior by citing divine commandments. We control behavior by enacting safety rules. And we've all noticed that these rules are growing stricter and stricter by the year. Not long ago young kids bounced around in the backseat of the family sedan; nowadays any parent who allowed that would be breaking the law and would be generally viewed as close to a child abuser. Not long ago kids rode bikes unencumbered. Now a mere scooter ride requires body armor, and in many families kids aren't permitted to ride out of sight of the house.

A few years ago, while researching a magazine article, I visited the camp where I had spent summers as a camper and a counselor from 1969 to 1983. When I was a camper, roughhousing was part of life. Counselors would pound us on our chests and we'd feel privileged to have their attention. Dead arms and Indian belly rubs filled our ample free time. Now the state's health authorities have tightened the definitions of physical abuse and sexual abuse, so noogies and wedgies and all that pounding are impermissible. Every year a psychotherapist visits the camp to brief the staff on child abuse. When I was a camper, only nonswimmers wore life preservers on the lake. Now everyone does. Then there were no fences around the beaches. Now the state mandates barriers in front of the swimming areas (although the other two miles of lake-front are still open). Now camp authorities must fill out an accident report after each injury, in case of future litigation, and the director must attend risk-management seminars in the off-season. Staff life, too, is different. Two decades ago staff parties were held every Saturday night, usually with beer. Now those are outlawed: too risky.

Reading magazines published for camp directors, I found that my camp was still on the permissive side. A Florida law requires background checks on all camp counselors. The American Camping Association's magazine is full of safety advice: "For most drills, [tennis] balls should be fed across the net," writes Robert Gamble, the tennis director at a New Hampshire camp, in a typical piece of risk-reduction advice. "This protects the instructor should a camper lose control and overhit."

Presumably, parents in the past cared as much about their kids' safety as parents today do. But they took far fewer precautions than parents today and exerted far fewer controls over kids' behavior. Perhaps they thought it was important that children learn to take risks in order to develop courage. Or perhaps they thought that getting into scrapes is part of childhood and that parents have no right to let their own worries dominate their children's growth.

ADOLESCENCE

Adolescence is a complicated time, and maybe no single snapshot can sum it up. But reading through some of the best recent literature on the subject—Patricia Hersch's *A Tribe Apart,* Kay Hymowitz's *Ready or Not,* Thomas Hine's *The Rise and Fall of the American Teenager*—one is struck by how many people are grappling in different ways with a common quandary: too much space. At some point in the past sophisticated parents cottoned on to the idea that rebellion and experimentation are part of the natural order of growing up and that parents of teenagers should there-fore give their kids enough freedom and space to explore and define themselves. But these new books and a shelf's worth of foundation reports now assert that kids today do not seem to want as much freedom and space as they have been granted. So the task for parents is to define boundaries for their adolescents, to offer continual guidance and discipline. Two decades ago parents were advised to withdraw from their teens' lives as those teens flew off to adulthood. Now they are advised to serve as chaperones at all-night graduation parties.

The U-turn is dramatic. In 1967 the U.S. Supreme Court her-alded the liberationist age with its decision in the Gault case. The Court held that students have the same due-process rights as adults. That decision restricted the ways in which schools could assert paternalistic authority, but it was also a sign of the times. Children and teens should be left free to be themselves. As the legal scholar Martha Minow summarized it in an essay in *From Children to Citizens* (1987), the decision was part of a cultural and "legal march away from the conception of the child as a dependent person." Many high schools in the seventies and eighties adopted open-campus policies. Students had to show up for class, but beyond that they were free to come and go as they pleased; the high school was essentially turned into a college campus. The Emancipation of Minors Act, passed by the California legislature in 1982, enabled teenagers to sign contracts, own property, and keep their earnings. It transformed them into quasi-adults.

The prevailing view today couldn't be more different. The 1997 National Longitudinal Study of Adolescent Health empha-sized that the most powerful factor in determining the well-being of young people is the presence of parents and adults who are actively engaged in supervising and setting goals for teenagers' lives. A 1993 study, "Talented Teenagers," found that teens need security and support if they are going to explore. Hersch's highly acclaimed *A Tribe Apart* is an angry rebuke to parents who have given their teens too much space. Hersch writes,

The lives of the kids in this book illustrate in subtle and not so subtle ways the need for adult presence to help them learn the new lessons of growing up. Kids need adults who bear witness to the details of their lives and count them as something. They require the watchful eyes and the community standards that provide greater stability. . . . The kids in the book who do best are those who have a strong interactive family and a web of relationships and activities that surround them consistently.

So when we survey American childhood today, we see that a quiet revolution has taken place. The Romantics—and the neo-Romantics of the 1960s and 1970s—thought that children were born with an innate wisdom and purity. They were natural beings, as yet uncontaminated by the soul-crushing conventions of adult society. Hence, they should be left free to explore, to develop their own creative tendencies, to learn at their own pace. Now, in contrast, children are to be stimulated and honed. Parents shouldn't hesitate to impose their authority. On the contrary, it is now pretty widely believed that the killings at Columbine and similar tragedies teach us that parents have a duty to be highly involved in the lives of their kids.

Today's ramped-up parental authority rests on three pillars: science, safety, and achievement. What we ambitious parents know about the human brain tells us that children need to be placed in stimulating and productive environments if they are going to reach their full potential. What we know about the world tells us that it is a dangerous place: there are pesticides on our fruit, cigarettes in the schoolyards, rocks near the bike paths, kidnappers in the woods. Children need to be protected. And finally, what we know about life is that sorting by merit begins at birth and never ends. Books about what to expect in the first year lay out achievement markers starting in the first month, and from then on childhood is one long progression of measurements, from nursery school admissions to SATs. Parents need to be coaching at their child's side.

Imagine being a product of this regimen—one of the kids who thrived in it, the sort who winds up at elite schools. All your life you have been pleasing your elders, performing and enjoying the hundreds of enrichment tasks that dominated your early years. You are a mentor magnet. You spent your formative years excelling in school, sports, and extracurricular activities. And you have been rewarded with a place at a wonderful university filled with smart, successful, and cheerful people like yourself. Wouldn't you be just like the students I found walking around Princeton?

THE MORAL LIFE
OF THE ORGANIZATION KID

When students enter college today, they are on familiar ground. After throwing off curfews, dress codes, and dormitory supervision in the 1970s, most colleges are reimposing their authority and reasserting order, just as high schools and families are. Some universities are trying to restrict or eliminate drinking. Many are cracking down on fraternity hazing rites. Others have banned Dionysian rituals such as lascivious costume balls and Princeton's Nude Olympics. University regulations intrude far more into the personal lives of students, and the students seem to approve.

As part of an effort to cajole students into behaving responsibly, many colleges have tried to provide places where they can go to amuse themselves without alcohol or drugs. Princeton has just completed a new student facility in the Frist Campus Center, formerly Palmer Hall, an old science building. On a walk from the library to Frist one may pass Prospect House, formerly the president's residence and now the faculty club, with a sparkling, glass-walled restaurant overlooking beautifully maintained gardens. On the lawns nearby, if the weather is tolerable, a drama group might be rehearsing, and other students might be bent over heavy books or laptops. The students are casual, but they look every bit as clean-cut as students in the early 1960s did, as if the intervening forty years of collegiate scruffiness had never happened. Almost all the men shave every day. Their hair is trim and freshly shampooed. Very few students wear tattoos or have had their bodies pierced—so far as one can see—in unapproved places. Many of the women wear skirts, or sundresses when the weather is warm. "I lived an incredibly ragged life," Kathryn Taylor, class of 1974, now an administrator in alumni affairs, told me of her college days. "It never would have dawned on me to try to look nice. They seem to be much more conscious of apparel."

It was only relatively recently that Princeton went coed, but one wouldn't know it. The male students are modern, enlightened men, sensitized since the first grade to apologize for their testosterone. The women are assertive and make a show of self-confidence, especially the athletes. Members of the women's soccer team have T-shirts that read YOUNG, WILD AND READY TO SCORE. Posters advertising a weekend's races say CROSS COUNTRY! IT'S EXCITING TO WATCH SEXY WOMEN RUN!—brashness that would be socially unacceptable if the boys tried it.

The Frist Campus Center is a neo-Gothic structure, built in 1907, that once housed nuclear experiments. Coats of arms are etched in stone on the facade, from which an imposing statue of Benjamin Franklin looks down at visitors. But that is the old Princeton; the building's ground level has been turned into the up-to-date student center, where rows of computer stations allow students to check their e-mail and where modern banalities have been painted on the walls: "Only by deliberating together about moral questions will we find mutual respect and common ground.—Amy Guttman." "The locusts sang and they were singing for me.—Bob Dylan." "Race matters.—Cornel West." "If I'm not out there training, someone else is.—Lynn Jennings."

Beyond are a billiards room, a set of low chairs where students can read while watching ESPN on a big-screen TV, a kiosk selling Princeton memorabilia, and a convenience store in which you can buy Nantucket Nectars, Arizona green tea with ginseng, raspberry Snapple, and the full array of Gatorade and Powerade, in flavors such as Fierce Melon and Arctic Shatter.

Bulletin boards throughout are festooned with recruiting posters from investment firms. One, from Goldman Sachs, shows a photo of a group of wholesome-looking young people relaxing after a game of lunchtime basketball. The text reads "Wanted: Strategists, Quick Thinkers, Team Players, Achievers." Another, from the business-consulting firm KPMG, shows a picture of a pair of incredibly hip-looking middle-aged people staring warmly into the camera. The text reads "Now that you've made your parents proud, join KPMG and give them something to smile about." It's hard to imagine a recruiting poster of a few decades ago appealing to students' desire to make their parents happy.

Downstairs is a cafeteria with a variety of food stations—pasta, a grill, salads, daily specials. Except that the drinks are not free, it reminded me of the dining hall at Microsoft, in Redmond, Washington. A wall of glass looks out over a lawn. Small groups of happy-looking people—Asian-American kids here, African-American kids there—sit at the tables. They are talking mostly about their workloads, and even their conversational style is polite and slightly formal. "Hello, ladies . . ." one young woman calls out to a group of her friends. "How are you?" a young man asks a young woman in greeting. "I'm fine, thanks," she replies. "How are you?"

They're so clean, inside and out. They seem like exactly the sort of young people we older folks want them to be. Baby boomers may be tempted to utter a little prayer of gratitude: Thank God our kids aren't the royal pains in the ass that we were to our parents.

But the more I talked to them and observed them, the more I realized that the difference between this and preceding generations is not just a matter of dress and comportment. It's not just that these students work harder, are more neatly groomed, and defer to their teachers more readily. There are more-fundamental differences: they have different mental categories.

It takes a while to realize this, because unlike their predecessors, they don't shout out their differences or declare them in political or social movements. In fact, part of what makes them novel is that they don't think they are new. They don't see themselves as a lost generation or a radical generation or a beatnik generation or even a Reaganite generation. They have relatively little generational consciousness. That's because this generation is for the most part not fighting to emancipate itself from the past. The most sophisticated people in preceding generations were formed by their struggle to break free from something. The most sophisticated people in this one aren't.

"On or about December 1910 human character changed," Virginia Woolf famously declared. Gone, she wrote, were the old certainties, the old manners, the deference to nineteenth-century authority. Instead human beings—at least the ones in Woolf's circle—were starting to see the world as full of chaos and discontinuity. Einstein smashed the notion of absolute time and space. Artists from Seurat to Picasso deconstructed visual perceptions. James Joyce's *Ulysses* scrambled the narrative order of the traditional novel. Rebels upended Victorian sexual mores. And later in the century, when the modernists were exhausted, the postmodernists came along to tell us that life is even more disordered and contingent than even Virginia Woolf could have imagined. Words are detachable from their meanings. History has no grand narratives. Everything is just shifting modes of perception, a maelstrom of change and diversity.

For those growing into adulthood during most of the twentieth century, therefore, the backdrop to life was the loss of faith in coherent systems of thought and morality. Sophisticated people knew they were supposed to rebel against authority, reject old certainties, and liberate themselves from hidebound customs and prejudices. Artists rebelled against the stodgy mores of the bourgeoisie. Radicals rebelled against the commercial and capitalist order. Feminists rebelled against the patriarchal family. And in the latter half of the twentieth century a youth culture emerged, which distilled these themes. Every rock anthem, every fashion statement, every protest gesture, every novel about rebellious youth—from *The Catcher in the Rye* to *On the Road*—carried the same cultural message: it's better to be a nonconformist than a conformist, a creative individualist than a member of a group, a rebel than a traditionalist, a daring adventurer than a safe and responsible striver. "We hope for nonconformists among you," the theologian Paul Tillich preached to college audiences in 1957, "for your sake, for the sake of the nation, and for the sake of humanity."

Today's elite college students don't live in that age of rebellion and alienation. They grew up in a world in which the counterculture and the mainstream culture have merged with, and co-opted, each other. For them, it's natural that one of the top administrators at Princeton has a poster of the Beatles album *Revolver* framed on her office wall. It's natural that hippies work at ad agencies and found organic-ice-cream companies, and that hi-tech entrepreneurs quote Dylan and wear black jeans to work. For them, it's natural that parents should listen to Led Zeppelin, Jimi Hendrix, and the Doors—just like kids. They don't have the mental barriers that exist between, say, the establishment and rebels, between respectable society and the subversive underground. For them, all those categories are mushed together. "They work for Save the Children and Merrill Lynch and they don't see a contradiction," says Jeffrey Herbst, the politics professor. Moreover, nothing in their environment suggests that the world is ill constructed or that life is made meaningful only by revolt. There have been no senseless bloodbaths like World War I and Vietnam, no crushing economic depressions, no cycles of assassination and rioting to foment disillusionment. They've mostly known parental protection, prosperity, and peace.

During most of the twentieth century the basic ways of living were called into question, but now those fundamental debates are over, at least among the young elite. Democracy and dictatorship are no longer engaged in an epic struggle; victorious democracy is the beneficent and seemingly natural order. No more fundamental arguments pit capitalism against socialism; capitalism is so triumphant that we barely even contemplate an alternative. Radicals no longer assault the American family and the American home; we accept diverse family patterns but celebrate family and community togetherness. The militant feminists of the 1960s are mostly of a grandmotherly age now. Even theological conflicts have settled down; it's fashionable to be religious so long as one is not aggressively so.

Unlike their elders, in other words, these young people are not part of an insurrection against inherited order. They are not even part of the conservative reaction against the insurrection. The debates of the Reagan years are as distant as the trial of the Chicago Seven, which is as distant as the Sacco and Vanzetti case. It's not that they reject one side of that culture war or embrace the other. They've just moved on. As people in northern California would say, they're living in a different place.

The world they live in seems fundamentally just. If you work hard, behave pleasantly, explore your interests, volunteer your time, obey the codes of political correctness, and take the right pills to balance your brain chemistry, you will be rewarded with a wonderful ascent in the social hierarchy. You will get into Princeton and have all sorts of genuinely interesting experiences open to you. You will make a lot of money—but more important, you will be able to improve yourself. You will be a good friend and parent. You will be caring and conscientious. You will learn to value the really important things in life. There is a fundamental order to the universe, and it works. If you play by its rules and defer to its requirements, you will lead a pretty fantastic life.

COMPELLED BY THE KNIGHTLY SPIRIT

One has to go quite far back to find another group of sophisticated students who took for granted the idea that the universe is a just and orderly place—back to a time before World War I, before modernism, before all the chaos and disruption that Virginia

Woolf described. To find another age of such equanimity one has to go back to the Edwardian era and the years leading to World War I. Then, too, a generation of elite students accepted the established order and the life paths it laid out for them. Then, too, people had a sense that there was an underlying biological organization to life—though it had to do with Darwin rather than with DNA. Then, too, elite students idealistically committed themselves to community service, to moral and political reform, while feeling aloof from and generally disgusted by professional politics. Then, too, a pretty rigorous set of social mores regulated behavior—though it had to do with the code of the gentleman, rather than with health and safety concerns and political correctness.

Walking around Princeton, I saw the monuments to that earlier elite, and I couldn't help comparing it with the new one we are creating today. The school has buildings and developments named after some of the men who were students in that era—John Foster Dulles, James Forrestal. The old eating clubs are where the characters from F. Scott Fitzgerald's Princeton dined and drank. It is easy to imagine Professor Woodrow Wilson talking and teaching in the neo-Gothic buildings.

Of course, in obvious ways the students in those days were very different from the students now. Then they were all male, all white, almost all blue bloods. They were WASP aristocrats, not multicultural meritocrats. Today we congratulate ourselves that our code is so much more enlightened than theirs. We aren't nearly as snobbish as they were, or as anti-Semitic, or as racist, or as sexist. We aren't as closed-minded—or so we tell ourselves.

I've never met anybody who would trade our social order for theirs, who wants to go back to that old Princeton world. And yet . . . and yet there are disturbing ghosts around the campus. The old order haunts this one, and whispers that maybe something was lost as well as gained when we sacrificed all for the sake of high achievement, safety, and equal opportunity. In some of the imposing old portraits, for example, I saw a moral gravity and a sense of duty that are missing from the faces of the recent presidents, who look like those friends of your parents who encouraged you to call them by their first names—friendly, unassuming guys in tweed jackets. Those old Princetonians were not professional administrators ministering to professional students. The code of the meritocrat was not their code, and maybe in some ways theirs was the more demanding code. For the most striking contrast between that elite and this one is that its members were relatively unconcerned with academic achievement but went to enormous lengths to instill character. We, on the other hand, place enormous emphasis on achievement but are tongue-tied and hesitant when it comes to what makes for a virtuous life.

The Princeton of that day aimed to take privileged men from their prominent families and toughen them up, teach them a sense of social obligation, based on the code of the gentleman and noblesse oblige. In short, it aimed to instill in them a sense of chivalry.

"You must either discover your duty or else create it and then swear allegiance to its high behests," John Hibben, the president of Princeton, told graduating students in 1915.

> Who will prove that the spirit of peace may become the spirit of valor, and assure the solidarity and progress of our nation? Who but the choice men of our land,—the men of exceptional privilege, who by a process of natural selection have passed from one degree of excellence to another in the arduous discipline of mind and character through years of preparation for a life of service. . . . Centuries ago the knight errant rode forth on the adventure of service to champion the cause of the weak and the wronged wherever they might be found. For him there was no clear call to any definite undertaking, but compelled by the knightly spirit, he resolutely set himself to seek undiscovered duty somewhere beyond the far horizon.

Princeton did have some Bible classes as a means of teaching virtue and character, but one has the sense that the school didn't really believe these things could be taught in the classroom. Documents from those days reveal a much denser social fabric at Princeton, and it was in the social sphere that the really important lessons were learned. There were more customs, dances, processions, and bonfires; they created a setting in which students competed for glory, for the laurels of being known as a big man on campus. (I asked today's Princeton students who the BMOCs were, and many didn't even know what the term meant. Those who did said that the concept didn't apply to their Princeton.)

Students in those days passed through harrowing extracurricular challenges and ordeals. There were clubs to compete for, hazing rituals to endure, brutal combats to win. Life at Princeton was a series of tests designed to cultivate manliness and determination. Each year, for example, the freshman and sophomore classes would stage a snowball fight. The library archives contain a picture of three Princeton freshmen after one such fight. Their eyes are swollen shut, their lips are broken open, they have contusions across their cheeks and signs of broken noses and broken jaws.

The primary virtue that Princeton tried to instill, in exhortation after exhortation, was courage. "Teaching men manhood" was one of the important tasks of Harvard, a professor wrote in that school's alumni magazine in 1902. John Hibben, who was a representative figure of his age, told a Princeton alumni group in 1913,

> It would be pitiful indeed if we were constrained to confess in reference to our graduates, as Homer stated of the Trojan hero,—"He came forsooth to battle in golden attire like a girl." Homer also adds that this unprepared warrior was met by Achilles, who slew him and robbed him of his wealth. We must fit men to work and to fight for our day, and to be ready when called to devote their fighting powers to that cause of righteousness which appeals to them as their particular vocation.

Of course, one form of ordeal reigned above all others: football. When John Hibben was president and F. Scott Fitzgerald was an undergraduate, one Princeton football star personified the ideals of the age—manly courage, duty, courtesy, honor, and service. He was Hobart Amory Hare Baker, a young man who wouldn't have a prayer of being admitted to Princeton today. Hobey Baker was born into a prominent but not particularly affluent Main Line Philadelphia family on January 15, 1892. After his parents divorced, he was sent off to St. Paul's School, where he became a legendary athlete. He arrived at Princeton in 1910, preceded by his reputation. He was only five feet nine inches and 160 pounds, but he was thickly muscled. He could walk downstairs on his hands, and he entertained his friends by jiggling his back muscles in time to a song. He once won a bet that he could walk from Princeton to New York City in ten hours. He was extraordinarily handsome, from a distance looking a bit like the Duke of Windsor, though he was sturdier and more muscular, with symmetrical features and a crown of blond hair that seemed never to fall out of place. He was also a meticulous dresser.

Baker appears in Fitzgerald's novel *This Side of Paradise* as the "slim and defiant" football captain, Allenby, who is the embodiment of manly grace, casually aware that "this year the hopes of the college rested on him." Baker was the star of both the football team and the hockey team. In those days both games were different. Football was more defensive, slower but more savage. There was no passing. Teams would trade punts, hoping to get slight advantages in field position. The key play was the punt return. Baker would position himself a few yards behind where the punt was to land so that he could get a running start and catch the ball at a full spring. He didn't wear a helmet. It became a cliché to compare him to Sir Galahad, the solitary knight charging bravely into the breach.

There were no bureaucratized university sports programs or athletic scholarships or professional coaching in Baker's day. The games were more like medieval tournaments, ordeals in which the young men of the governing classes could build character and cultivate manly courage. Fatalities were relatively common in collegiate football until President Theodore Roosevelt—the epitome of the upper-class manly man—tried to instill some restraint. Speaking for the age, Charles William Eliot, the president of Harvard, declared that "effeminacy and luxury are even worse evils than brutality"; sports could transform "a stooping, weak, and sickly youth into [a] well-formed robust" one.

Hobey Baker was at least as famous for his sportsmanship as for his athletic prowess. Though opposing teams often tried to injure him, he never retaliated; he had two penalties called on him in his entire college hockey career, both hotly contested. He went to the opposing locker room after each game to thank his rivals for a good match. "Nothing was quite so characteristic as his acute modesty," his biographer, John Davies, wrote in *The Legend of Hobey Baker* (1966). "He was always polite and obliging, except when talk got around to his athletic exploits, and then he could be curt and even difficult."

Baker dominated the Princeton of his day. "The aura of Hobey Baker permeated the campus, and yet on personal contact . . . he seemed somewhat withdrawn," one of his classmates told Davies. A national celebrity, Baker was, as the Fitzgerald scholar Arthur Mizener once put it, the "nearly faultless realization of the ideal of his age." He was recognized as a model for all young boys, and he was something of a campus god.

After college Baker went off to Wall Street, following the Princeton herd. But he was bored at J. P. Morgan, somewhat at a loss in the everyday world of commerce. World War I solved his problem. He enlisted at once as an aviator—Sir Galahad of the air—and flew aerial combat in France. American newspapers followed his exploits, exaggerating them and declaring him an ace before he had shot down a single enemy plane (he ended up shooting down three). In war Baker found perfect happiness—the camaraderie of the pilots and the thrill of combat. His athletic skills served him well, and he was promoted to squadron commander, with 206 men and twenty to twenty-four planes under him. He was awarded the Croix de Guerre and showed some disappointment when the Armistice was signed.

His death was like something out of a cheap novel. Six weeks after the war was over, on December 21, 1918, his tour of duty ended. He received orders to return home. He decided he would make "one last flight." His comrades argued vehemently with him, saying that making a last flight violated a sacred tradition in aviation; it was bad luck. He insisted, and took up not his own plane but a recently repaired machine that needed to be tested. The engine stalled. There was a way to survive such a predicament, but it involved wrecking the plane. Baker tried a trickier maneuver that might have enabled him to land the plane intact; he ran out of room and crashed nose-first into the ground. He bled to death in the ambulance.

Needless to say, that romantic end transformed Baker from an ideal to a legend. And everyone seems to have understood immediately that he was symbolic of a dying ethos. It wasn't just the modesty, and the grace, and the amateur spirit—it was the chivalric world view. The alumni directory for Hobey Baker's class of 1914 twenty-five years after graduation reveals that a number of his classmates named their sons for him.

One more thing must be said about the chivalric code of that era, at least as it was articulated. It involved more than just shaking hands with one's opponents after a game and venturing acts of derring-do on the football field or the battlefield. The conflict that educators of the time talked about more than any other was internal conflict, between the good and the evil in each of us. John Hibben and others talked so much about courage and battle because they believed that a human being is half angel, half beast and that the two sides wage lifelong warfare over the soul. People who made the high-minded addresses of that era were comfortable talking about evil and sin and the devil. Here's an excerpt from Hibben's address to the graduating students in 1913.

> You, enlightened, self-sufficient, self-governed, endowed with gifts above your fellows, the world expects you to produce as well as to consume, to add to and not to subtract from its store of good, to build up and not tear

down, to ennoble and not degrade. It commands you to take your place and to fight your fight in the name of honor and of chivalry, against the powers of organized evil and of commercialized vice, against the poverty, disease, and death which follow fast in the wake of sin and ignorance, against all the innumerable forces which are working to destroy the image of God in man, and unleash the passions of the beast. There comes to you from many quarters, from many voices, the call of your kind. It is the human cry of spirits in bondage, of souls in despair, of lives debased and doomed. It is the call of man to his brother . . . such is your vocation; follow the voice that calls you in the name of God and of man. The time is short, the opportunity is great; therefore, crowd the hours with the best that is in you.

No doubt a lot of the students who were sitting in the audience that day were stuck-up country-house toffs, for whom this kind of talk merely delayed a trip in their roadsters to a New York nightclub. But many of the students raised on similar exhortations—including Teddy Roosevelt and John Reed at Harvard and Hobey Baker, Allen Dulles, Adlai Stevenson, and F. Scott Fitzgerald at Princeton—seem to have absorbed some sense that life is a noble mission and a perpetual war against sin, that the choices we make have consequences not just in getting a job or a law-school admission but in some grand battle between lightness and dark.

"LOVE AND SUCCESS AND BEING HAPPY"

This is what the comparison between the students of Hobey Baker's day and the students of today tell us: Then the leaders of Princeton were quite conscious of the fact that they were cultivating an elite. They thought it was only just and proper that these wellborn men be at the top of society. The task was to mold them into gentlemen. Now administrators at top-tier schools know they are educating an elite but they seem to feel guilty about the whole notion of elitism and elite status. Today's elite don't like to think of themselves as elite. So there is no self-conscious code of chivalry. Today's students do not inherit a concrete and articulated moral system—a set of ideals to instruct privileged men and women on how to live, how to see their duties, and how to call upon their highest efforts.

Although today's Princeton and today's parents impose all sorts of rules to reduce safety risks and encourage achievement, they do not go to great lengths to build character, the way adults and adult institutions did a century ago. They don't offer much help with the fundamental questions. "We've taken the decision that these are adults and this is not our job," Jeffrey Herbst says. "There's a pretty self-conscious attempt not to instill character." Herbst does add that students are expected to live up to the standards that apply to academic life—no plagiarism, no cheating. But in general the job of the university is to supply the knowledge that students will need to prosper and, at most, to provide a forum in which they can cultivate character on their own. "This university doesn't orchestrate students' lives outside the classroom," says Princeton's dean of undergraduate students, Kathleen Deignan. "We're very conservative about how we steer. They steer themselves." As the admissions officer Fred Hargadon puts it, "I don't know if we build character or remind them that they should be developing it."

In America today we don't tell our children they are half brutes. It's impossible to imagine a modern university president mentioning the devil or the beast in a commencement address. People don't even talk much about evil anymore, except as something that might happen far away, in Serbia or in Nazi Germany. Around us we see not evil but sickness that requires therapy. Today we speak the language of positive reinforcement.

In talking to Princeton students about character, I noticed

two things. First, they're a little nervous about the subject. When I asked if Princeton builds character, they would inevitably mention the honor code against cheating, or policies to reduce drinking. When I asked about moral questions, they would often flee such talk and start discussing legislative questions. For example, at dinner one evening a young man proposed that if we could just purge the wrongs that people do to one another over the next few generations, the human race could live in perfect harmony ever after, without much need for government or laws or prisons. I asked the other eight or nine students at the table to reflect on this, but they quickly veered off toward how long it would take to bring about this perfect world. I asked specifically if human beings were perfectible in this way. Some grunted in vague assent, and one young woman—a conservative Christian who had interned for Jesse Helms the previous summer—said that she agreed with what the young man had said. Apparently the doctrine of original sin had not left much of a mark on her.

Today's students are indeed interested in religion and good works. "In the past ten or twelve years students are no longer embarrassed about being interested in religion—or spirituality, as they call it," says Robert Wuthnow, the Princeton sociologist. "That's a huge change. People used to feel as if they had acne being raised in a religious home." I hadn't been on campus more than five minutes before I started hearing about all the students who do community service—tutoring at a charter school in Trenton, working at Habitat for Humanity–style building projects, serving food at soup kitchens. But religion tends to be more private than public with them, and the character of their faith tends to be unrelievedly upbeat. "It's an optimistic view," Wuthnow says. "You just never hear about sin and evil and judgment. It's about love and success and being happy."

When it comes to character and virtue, these young people have been left on their own. Today's go-getter parents and today's educational institutions work frantically to cultivate neural synapses, to foster good study skills, to promote musical talents.

We fly our children around the world so that they can experience different cultures. We spend huge amounts of money on safety equipment and sports coaching. We sermonize about the evils of drunk driving. We expend enormous energy guiding and regulating their lives. But when it comes to character and virtue, the most mysterious area of all, suddenly the laissez-faire ethic rules: you're on your own, Jack and Jill; go figure out what is true and just for yourselves.

We assume that each person has to solve these questions alone (though few other societies in history have made this assumption). We assume that if adults try to offer moral instruction, it will just backfire, because our children will reject our sermonizing (though they don't seem to reject any other part of our guidance and instruction). We assume that such questions have no correct answer that can be taught. Or maybe the simple truth is that adult institutions no longer try to talk about character and virtue because they simply wouldn't know what to say. John Hibben could fill books with moral instruction, but our connections to that tradition have been snapped.

One sometimes has the sense that all the frantic efforts to regulate safety, to encourage academic achievement, and to keep busy are ways to compensate for missing conceptions of character and virtue. Not having a vocabulary to discuss what is good and true, people can at least behave well. It's hard to know what eternal life means, but if you don't smoke you can have long life. It's hard to imagine what it would be like to be a saint, but it's easy to see what it is to be a success.

The compensation works, to an extent. These young people are wonderful to be around. If they are indeed running the country in a few decades, we'll be in fine shape. It will be a good country, though maybe not a great one. The Princeton of today is infinitely more pleasant than the old Princeton, infinitely more just, and certainly more intellectual and curious. But still there is a sense that something is missing. Somehow, in the world of moral combat that John Hibben described, the stakes were higher, the consequences of one's decisions were more serious, the goals were nobler. In this world hardworking students achieve self-control; in that one virtuous students achieved self-mastery.

I had lunch one day with Robert George, a professor in Princeton's politics department. Like a lot of elite colleges, Princeton has one or two faculty members who are known as the campus conservatives. They may be liked personally, and admired for their teaching and research skills, but they are regarded as a bit odd and dismissible. I don't, however, see anything specifically conservative in the message George offered that day (which I'm condensing from a thirty-minute portion of our conversation). "We would do our best if we could make sure our students had a dose of the Augustinian sense that there is a tragic dimension to life," he said. "That there is a sense in which we live in a vale of tears. We could make them aware of the reality of sin, by which I mean chosen evil, which cannot be cured by therapy or by science. We don't do enough to call into question the therapeutic model of evil: 'He has a problem. . . . He's sick.'

"I don't mean we should have a separate course on character. We don't need to give them specific answers. We could raise this awareness—through readings and discussions in history and philosophy and literature, by reading Plato's *Gorgias, Othello,* or a study of the Lincoln-Douglas debates—that the conquest of the self is part of what it means to lead a successful life. It's not enough to make a corporation succeed. It's not an external problem. It doesn't lend itself to a technical solution. Four hours spent studying in the library is not self-mastery."

George described a moment when he and a colleague were urging their students not to commit plagiarism. The honor code goes against it, George told them; the Internet makes it easier to plagiarize but also much easier for faculty members to catch plagiarists. Besides, he concluded, God will see you doing evil. Suddenly there was an awkward shifting of chairs and a demurral from his faculty colleague. The idea that it is possible to do wrong sitting alone in your room, even if you don't cause another person any harm, is hard, George said, for modern Americans to comprehend fully. The problem is that this idea is at the heart of understanding what it means to be virtuous.

George suggested that I talk to a student he had in a few of his classes, a sophomore, who came to campus with the tragic sense that George would like to impart. This young man took me to lunch in his college dining room, and when I asked him about character building, he spoke more comfortably and thoughtfully than anybody else I had met. He wasn't easy on himself, the way supercharged achievers have a tendency to be. "Egotism is the biggest challenge here," he said. "It can make you proud if you do well. It can make you self-assured and self-sufficient. You don't need help from other people. You won't need help from your wife. You won't give yourself over to her when you are married." He went on, talking calmly but faster than I could write. He was talking in a language different from that of the meritocrat—about what one is, rather than what one does. He really did stand out from the other students, who were equally smart and equally accomplished but who hadn't been raised with a vocabulary of virtue and vice.

Somebody once wrote a book called *Harvard Hates America,* about the supposedly alien Ivy League snobs who look down on the rest of the country. I don't get that sense when I visit Harvard, and I certainly didn't get that sense at Princeton. Princeton doesn't hate America. It reflects America. And in most ways it reflects the best of America. After all, as people kept reminding me, these are some of the best and brightest young people our high schools have to offer. They have woven their way through the temptations of adolescence and have benefited from all the nurturing and instruction and opportunities with which the country has provided them. They are responsible. They are generous. They are bright. They are good-natured. But they live in a country that has lost, in its frenetic seeking after happiness and success, the language of sin and character building through combat with sin. Evil is seen as something that can be cured with better education, or therapy, or Prozac. Instead of virtue we talk about accomplishment.

Maybe the lives of the meritocrats are so crammed because the stakes are so small. All this ambition and aspiration is looking for new tests to ace, new clubs to be president of, new services to perform, but finding that none of these challenges is the ultimate challenge, and none of the rewards is the ultimate reward.

The customer was supposed to be king in the new economy, yet few of us are being treated royally these days. Charles Fishman in *Fast Company* digs into the tangle of telephones, recordings, e-mail, Web sites, and people to examine the customer-service crisis first-hand. He scrutinizes the systems causing our frustration and introduces us to staffers who, like us, feel hobbled by what's passing for progress. Some solutions are also offered.

Charles Fishman

"But Wait, You Promised . . ." ". . . And You Believed Us? Welcome to the Real World, Ma'am."

I AM IN THE BELLY of the beast. I have risen early, traveled far, and overcome lines, rudeness, and indifference. Now, heedless of my chances of coming back without serious psychological or physical injury, I am journeying into a swamp that has become a source of boundless irritation, frustration, confusion—even fury—for tens of millions of Americans. I open the door and step into a customer-service call center. And not just any call center either—one that is exclusively devoted to handling problems with cell phones. It's cool inside and fairly well lit, for a swamp. I am carrying the very tool itself: a Spring PCS cell phone. I love my Spring PCS cell phone. But God help me when I have to call Sprint PCS. I have sometimes called this very building in Fort Worth, Texas. Often, I'm not even sure that the customer-care advocate I finally speak with after I've been waiting on hold for seventeen minutes even knows what a cell phone is.

I have come here at the beginning of a long journey—really, a quest of the sort that was common in antiquity—during which I will cross the continent several times and seek out both oracles and common folk. I am determined to unravel a central mystery of life in modern America: why is customer service so terrible?

At the Sprint PCS call center, I am soon teamed up with customer-care advocate Chad Ehrlich, a gracious twenty-nine-year-old with years of experience delivering service by phone. Chad takes a call from a businessman in Lubbock, Texas. The man is upset about his bill: It was running $60 to $100 a month. Suddenly, it has shot up to $1,600. "I'm not going to pay it!" the man declares.

Chad is reserved. "Let me take a look at that bill," he says. Chad whirls through screens of information. "Hold on a moment for me, sir; I'm going to get a representative from the fraud department on the line." Chad puts Lubbock on hold and dials Sprint PCS's fraud department, where he reaches a familiar recorded message and is put on hold. Lubbock is on hold for customer-service rep Chad, and customer-service rep Chad is on hold for more customer service.

A female fraud rep takes Chad's call. She can see from Lubbock's history that he's complained about this problem before. The conversation between Chad and his colleague in fraud is frisky.

Fraud: "He thought he was cloned, but he wasn't."

Chad: "His bills did go from almost nothing to sky-high. . . ."

Fraud: "We can send him to a cloning specialist and make it 'official' if you want. . . ."

Chad: "He's denying that he made or received the calls."

The impatient woman from fraud dials the Sprint PCS cloning customer-care department and . . . is put on hold.

Do you ever wonder what's going on while you're waiting on hold for customer service? Really, you couldn't even imagine.

Chad, Lubbock's customer-care advocate, is talking to a woman who is Chad's customer-care advocate. She has called *her* customer-care advocate, who is busy on another call. So now we have two customer-care advocates on hold waiting for a third customer-care advocate. Meanwhile, a fuming customer from Lubbock (who may or may not be trying to rip Sprint off for $1,600) waits. On hold.

That, right there, is customer service in the new economy. It has become a slow, dissatisfying tangle of telephones, computers, Web sites, e-mail, and people that wastes time at a prodigious rate, produces far more aggravation than service, and, most often, leaves you feeling impotent. What's even worse is that this situation is a kind of betrayal. It wasn't supposed to be this way. One of the promises of the new economy was that the customer would finally be in charge. We weren't supposed to need to call customer care—but if we did, then someone would take our call quickly. (Why not? No one else would be calling.) A customer-service rep would understand our problem practically before we mentioned it, and all would be made right. Everyone believes in delighting the customer.

Don't you spend most of your day delighted? Here's a puzzler. Why do we hear this sentence so often: "We are experiencing higher-than-usual call volumes. . . ." If you're experiencing higher-than-usual call volumes, then why aren't you experiencing higher-than-usual *staffing* volumes? How hard is *that*? What the new economy has done to customer service is exactly the opposite of what everyone predicted would happen. And as chaotic a time as it has been to be a customer, it has been a truly weird time to be delivering customer service. Consider just one example: Five years ago, discount broker Charles Schwab had 1,450 customer-service reps in call centers, and 85 percent of those reps' time was spent providing real-time quotes and basic company information, and executing trades. Those 1,450 people, sensing the Internet roaring down on them, were worried about their jobs. Rightfully so. At the end of this past year, Charles Schwab's customers did 81 percent of all of those activities without human assistance. So you would imagine that Schwab could have trimmed its costly battalion of customer-service reps to 1,000, even to 500.

In fact, the number of Schwab reps has tripled to 4,800. But they're not doing what they used to do. Customers have demanded new vistas of service. No one was more surprised than Schwab.

In short, the new economy was supposed to make service better, quicker, and more effective for customers—and easier and cheaper for companies. None of that has come to pass. What happened? I went on a journey to find out.

BOLD PROMISES, BAD RESULTS

AT&T is running television commercials for its Worldnet Internet service. One ad features a series of stand-up comics who are making jokes about the bad customer service of their Internet providers ("My on-line service is like my husband: I stare at it for hours, hoping it will move").

Cisco is running a TV commercial that opens with a regular guy on a cordless phone who hears, "Your call will be answered by the next available operator." Halfway through the commercial, the man has fallen asleep, phone to his ear.

Mockery is a great cultural barometer. Bad customer service is one of the universal—and unifying—experiences of being an American in the twenty-first century. You get it at Wal-Mart. You get it at Lord & Taylor. But is customer service really worse than it used to be? A panel of customer-service experts that I assembled couldn't agree.

Don Peppers, fifty, of the Peppers and Rogers Group, proponent of "customer-relationship management" and coauthor of the famous *One to One Future*: "I don't think that customer service sucks. I think it's bad. But I think it's better than it was five years ago."

Len Schlesinger, forty-eight, an expert in customer service, previously senior associate dean and a professor at Harvard Business School, now executive vice president of The Limited Inc.: "Let's see, we've gone from 'meeting customer expectations,' to 'exceeding customer expectations,' to 'delighting customers,' to 'customer ecstasy.' I hate to see what comes next."

Patricia Seybold, fifty-one, CEO of an e-business consulting company and author of the optimistic book *The Customer Revolution: How to Thrive When Customers Are in Control,* which is due out this month: "I agree that customer service hasn't gotten better since the Internet came along. It has gotten worse. But companies are beginning to realize that we're very angry at them. Companies that don't wake up and pay attention to this are going to be out of business."

Well, we can only hope.

Customer service is a notoriously slippery concept—hard to define, apparently impossible to quantify. But there is one guy who knows for sure what's happening to customer service, because he measures it in 65,000 interviews a year with American customers.

Claes Fornell, fifty-three, is a professor at the University of Michigan Business School and an expert on "the economics of customer satisfaction." Fornell is creator and director of the American Customer Satisfaction Index. The ACSI measures how content Americans are with the goods and services that they consume—in the aggregate, and industry by industry, company by company.

Fornell names names! His on-line data is a carnival for cranky consumers: you can click through and take glee in the lame scores of all of the companies that you love to hate.

First Union, my bank, is down 10.5 percent in satisfaction ratings since the index started in 1994.

Wal-Mart, my source for diapers, paper towels, and Tide, is down 10 percent since the index started and down 4 percent in just the past year alone.

Fornell conceived this herculean undertaking—scores are measured quarterly—because he thought that the U.S. economy was being severely mismeasured. "Eighty percent of GDP is service now," he says. "We have to behave as though we live in a service economy."

The ACSI measures the perceived quality of U.S. economic

output—the experience of being a consumer in the United States. In the past five years, the ACSI is down from 73.7 to 72.9. But that number includes everything from Whirlpool appliances to the experience of shopping on Amazon.com.

Here's the amazing thing: every measured company in the appliance, beer, car, clothing, food, personal-care, shoe, and soft-drink industries is above the national average. Even the cigarette companies have above-average customer-satisfaction ratings.

Not so for airlines, banks, department stores, fast-food outlets, hospitals, hotels, and phone companies.

It's the service that's bad.

"Oh, I think we can say that for sure," says Fornell.

THE HARD TRUTH(S)
ABOUT CUSTOMER SERVICE

I didn't begin my journey through the service jungle at Sprint PCS by accident, or because I think that the company would be a good target for mockery. Sprint PCS is a pure New Economy company. It offers nothing but service—and it's digital wireless service to boot. The company's only product is moving voices through the air. The first time that you could have made a Sprint PCS call was December 1996. From a standing start, in four years the company has grown to 28,328 employees (10,000 in customer care), 9.8 million customers, and annual revenues of roughly $6 billion. Sprint PCS signs up 10,000 new customers each day.

The company has access to every conceivable technological helper: the Net, automated phone services, and the most-sophisticated call centers. And yet my own experience dealing with Sprint PCS has been consistently aggravating. In eight years of having BellSouth provide our home service, I've had occasion to talk to them only three or four times. I've talked to Sprint PCS more than that since Halloween—always with unhappy results.

Sprint PCS knows the right thing to do. It just can't do it. Faerie Kizzire, fifty-one, senior vice president for Sprint PCS, is in charge of customer service for the company. She's a veteran: she spent nine years at Sprint managing customer service for the long-distance business, then managed customer service for a health-insurance company, and was wooed back to Sprint to create customer care for wireless.

I tell her the story of a call I have just listened to with Chad: Marlene in Ohio has had to call three times just to get a credit for charges that shouldn't have been on her bill in the first place. Before Chad, two customer-care advocates dealt with Marlene by simply telling her that she was wrong. As Chad discovers, Marlene was in fact improperly charged. So why did that happen? Why did two customer-service reps argue with Marlene, rather than credit her? Why does Marlene know more about her calling plan than customer care does?

Kizzire is disappointed. "The complexity of the product and the variations in the product can make that kind of problem very difficult," she says. "We do see some of our people falling on the side of 'I'm right' versus 'I'm going to make it right.'"

Sprint PCS looks as if it's doing all of the right things. The company's training program for reps is six to ten weeks long. Across the call center are exhortations to good service: "Did you dazzle your customers today?" Says Kizzire: "It is true that people who have a little bit of knowledge can be dangerous. We always say, Don't try to dazzle the customer with what you know. These days, many customers have years of experience."

And therein lies a clue to what's really happening to customer service—and why. The secret about customer service in the new economy isn't that it's bad—everyone *knows* it's bad. The secret is that it's harder to deliver good customer service than ever before. Why? Technology, especially in its early days, is always hard. No surprise there. Why would we expect companies that can't figure out how to run a phone center—talking to real people about problems is their own business—to be really good at using advanced technology to automate the process of taking care of us?

And customers are more demanding. We want good service,

quickly. We don't wait at gas pumps, we're antsy in ATM lines, and we pay to FedEx things to avoid standing in line at the post office. Companies have created, nursed, and benefited from this impatience. We are victims of it in our own lives. They are victims of it too. It makes providing customer service brutally unforgiving.

Technology has, in fact, made some things quicker and easier, and it has allowed us to take care of ourselves. I can plunge through the details of my on-line bank statement more thoroughly in fifty seconds than any automated voice-mail system could permit in fifty minutes, or than even the most patient phone operator would tolerate. This means that when we talk to someone in person, either things are really screwed up or we are really angry and want to share that anger with a person. Or both. Technology has made the actual person-to-person customer service of big companies much more complicated and demanding.

Despite all of the consultants, gurus, and outsource providers, customer service is hard to deliver in a mass economy. I wasn't on the phones at Sprint PCS for more than a couple of hours, and I can see that the real problem isn't customer service or even culture. No, the real problem is more fundamental: Sprint PCS offers a simple service that is really very complicated. Best tip-off? It takes someone fifteen minutes to sell me a phone and a calling plan in a Sprint PCS store. It takes Faerie Kizzire six weeks—240 hours—to teach a phone rep to handle any problems that I might have with that phone.

SOME GOOD NEWS: WHAT'S THE 411?

My favorite example of New Economy meltdown is directory assistance. Directory assistance should be the perfect New Economy product: it's just information—and simple information at that. There is an existing way to bill customers, and, given the swift accumulation of databases, directory assistance should be getting better and better all the time.

"It's gotten so much worse," says customer-service expert Patricia Seybold. "Now you get the wrong number all the time."

I've kept track during the past two months. Over several dozen calls, directory assistance delivered the wrong number about half of the time. Of course, you get charged for the wrong numbers, just as you do for the right numbers. If it's a long-distance number and it's wrong, you pay for that phone call too. As if that weren't enough, here's a moment of customer delight: call directory assistance and try to get a credit for a wrong number.

"I'm sorry, sir," says the abrupt operator. "We don't give credits."

"I beg your pardon?"

"We don't give credits, sir. You have to call your local phone company. When your phone bill comes."

"At the end of the month?"

"Correct, sir. Is there a number you need?"

So now I've paid once for the wrong number and paid again to be told that I have to call some other company, some other time, to get my $2 back.

Yet one company gives delightful directory assistance—polite, accurate, helpful. It is none other than . . . Sprint PCS. The contrast between cellular directory and landline directory is as dramatic as the contrast between Sprint PCS directory and Sprint PCS customer care. Ask Sprint PCS for a restaurant's number and they offer to make a reservation. Ask for the number of a movie theater and they offer to read you not just the number but also the movies that are playing at that theater, when they are playing, and who is starring in each movie.

Seybold was able to guess exactly what was going on immediately. "It's outsourced," she said.

And so it is. Metro One Telecommunications, a small company based in Beaverton, Oregon, handles directory assistance for Sprint PCS—and also for Nextel and many regional cellular companies. The quality of Metro One's service is no accident. As Seybold predicted, that is exactly what it is selling to cellular companies: *good* directory assistance.

The economics are great for everyone: even at what feels like an unhurried pace, Metro One's operators take fifty calls an hour (including breaks, slow periods, and training), which brings in $50 an hour. Half of that goes to Metro One; half is gravy to Sprint PCS. Of the $25 an hour that Metro One gets, operators start at some centers at $9 an hour in straight salary—before incentive pay or benefits. Me, as a customer? I get the right number, for about what BellSouth's wrong numbers cost me.

Metro One has twenty-nine deliberately small call centers: 200 operators or fewer, with 100 or fewer working at any one time. The call center in Charlotte, North Carolina, is lean—spartan compared to Sprint PCS's Fort Worth center. But you can understand the entire place in a single glance. Directory assistance, of course, is child's play compared to helping people with their cell phones. But remember: standard directory assistance is abysmal.

Heather McCuen, twenty-three, started at Metro One in March 1999, and after nine months she makes $12 an hour. Calls cascade in on her like a waterfall. "Leith Mercedes." "Larry's Plant Farm." "Start-to-Finish Tattoo Shop." "Just What the Doctor Ordered Restaurant."

"I'm amazed at what people name their businesses," Heather says.

In eleven minutes, she takes seventeen calls—38.8 seconds a call. Heather's style is efficient but deliberate. She reads the number slowly to avoid having to repeat it.

What is striking is how little it takes to make people happy, how little it takes to get it right, and how long forty seconds really is. But what is also striking is how hard it would be to automate this process. To do it right doesn't require much, but it does require a spark of human intelligence on both ends of the transaction.

Even in these brief encounters, the full range of human character is on display. "I'm looking for Shanon Pickering," says a man over a characteristically crackly connection. The Charlotte center serves mainly North Carolina and South Carolina, so the operators are familiar with local geography, but Heather and her colleagues can provide numbers nationwide. Heather patiently searches a couple of the towns that the man mentions, without luck.

"I found someone's day planner in the middle of the road," the man says. "I'm just trying to return it to her." Heather ups her intensity a notch. She broadens her search to all of North Carolina, South Carolina, and Virginia. She tries a variety of spellings for the names. Heather tells the man what she is trying. She is regretful. The man is regretful. The call spills past two minutes. No luck.

Metro One's databases are updated with fresh numbers in real time, all the time. Operators can send along complaints about wrong numbers. All kinds of searches are available. I saw one operator find a particularly elusive residential number by reading through a list of every person who lived on a street.

The Baby Bells shoot for directory calls lasting seventeen to twenty seconds, total, compared to Metro One's thirty-three-second standard. That, of course, is the difference. And as trivial as it may sound—what's fifteen seconds?—companies know how to do the multiplication. At least, they know how to do it when it's *their* fifteen seconds.

Metro One's Charlotte center handles roughly 275,000 calls a week. The math is easy. If each call lasts thirty-three seconds, as it does at Metro One, then 275,000 calls require 2,520 hours of operator time. If each call lasts twenty seconds, as it does at Bell-South, then 275,000 calls require only 1,528 hours of operator time.

It takes 50 percent more people to do it the Metro One way. To do it right.

SECRETS OF THE AMAZON:
CUSTOMER SERVICE AS R&D

For all its struggles—with its balance sheet, its stock, the union drive, and layoffs—Amazon.com has done one thing brilliantly: customer service. I placed my first order with Amazon in 1997 and have been a steady customer since. In four years of making purchases for myself and for others, I've found what I needed, ordered it, received a flurry of e-mails about my orders, and then gotten either thank-you notes or what I ordered. I've never had to contact Amazon about any matter. I have had, in essence, no customer service from Amazon. Put another way, I have had such perfect customer service, the service itself has been transparent. That is exactly what Amazon wants. The goal is perfect customer service through no customer service.

In a very short time, Amazon has set a new standard for customer service, and I went to Seattle to see how. What I discovered is a place that regards customer service as an R&D lab—a way not to help customers but to help the company.

"We want to make it easier and easier for our customers to do business with us," says Bill Price, fifty, vice president of global customer service for Amazon. "We want to have everything go so right, you never have to contact us. To do that, we have to stay tuned up. We have to keep asking, What are the problems?"

Of course, every customer-service VP in America, every customer-service VP in history, would agree with those sentiments. Two things make all the difference at Amazon: the view the company takes of customer service and customers, and the way the company is organized to drive home that view.

Amazon doesn't consider customer service to be the complaint department, or even the quality-control and customer-satisfaction department. Amazon considers Bill Price's outfit to be a research lab for discovering how to adjust and improve customer service. And Amazon considers customer service to be its core business. The company really offers nothing *but* customer service.

So every single encounter with a customer—by phone, by e-mail, even by clicking on Web pages—is considered to be the source of potentially vital information about the course of the entire company.

How does that work?

Well, to start with, the company tracks the reason for every customer contact. It keeps a list of the top ten reasons why customers contact the company—monitoring the list daily, weekly, monthly—and it is constantly working on ways to eliminate those reasons.

For years, the number one question that people asked Amazon was, Where's my stuff? Now, on every page, starting with the welcome page, there's a box labeled "Where's my stuff?"

Amazon's operations are so interwoven with customer-driven changes that employees are briefly baffled when you ask for examples.

"Two years ago," says Price, "one common problem was, 'I want to buy five books, and ship them to my five brothers, each at a separate address.' Our system was originally set up so that one order had to go to one address, forcing the customer, in a case like that, to place five separate orders. Now we have a 'ship-to-multiple-addresses' function. And you don't need to get in touch with us to figure it out."

Shortly after its consumer-electronics store debuted, Amazon was deluged with requests for a simple chart that would compare the features and prices of similar products, such as MP3 players and digital cameras. As a result, Amazon has developed a product-by-product "comparison engine" that does exactly that.

Just last year, a customer sent an e-mail pointing out something that had bugged him for years: on the main ordering page, customers are instructed to enter their e-mail address and their Amazon password. Next come two options: "Forgot your password? Click here" and "Sign in using our secure server."

Originally, the options were in that order. If someone simply tabbed from option to option, he would click "Forgot your password?"—even when what he wanted to do was sign in. Because of that single, irritated e-mail, the ordering page was changed.

Again, though, the head of customer service at any big company could tick off customer suggestions that have drifted up and changed products and operations.

But at Amazon, the notion of customer service as R&D isn't a slogan; it's a structure—an unavoidable force to be reckoned with. Price's division includes a group that does nothing but analyze and anticipate problems and cook up solutions. Indeed, representatives from customer-service project management sit on all launch teams as "the voice of the customer."

The ethic cuts deeper than it would first appear. "You can have a great overall culture," says Price, "with real empathy for the customer and passion for fixing the problems. You can have individual reps who say, 'This customer is *really* upset, and I have to deal with it.' I think we do that.

"What's missing almost everywhere else is, even if you have the empathy and the passion and you address the customer's problem, you haven't really given good customer service in total. You haven't done that until you have eliminated the problem that caused her to call in the first place." Exactly.

It is, frankly, easy to be skeptical of all of this. For such a strategy to work, the entire company has to bend to it. One incident (of many that I encountered) shows how deeply ingrained the attitude is.

The problem materialized during the 1999 Christmas season, the first Christmas that Amazon sold toys. Almost as soon as the selling season began, the company received complaints that were notable more for the level of outrage than for the actual number of problems.

Some toys were big enough to be shipped in their original packing boxes. "They were arriving on people's doorsteps, and the people called and said, 'Hey, we weren't expecting this to look like a Big Wheel. My kid came home from school and found his present! Now I gotta buy another one!'" says Janet Savage, thirty-one, who was a customer-service manager that Christmas. This quickly became known as the Big Wheel problem, and it was Savage's job to resolve it.

It was an interesting moment. One possible response—a perfectly reasonable response—would be to start warning customers about items shipped in original cartons. After all, if you buy something at Toys "R" Us, you don't complain that it comes wrapped as what it is.

That response was never considered at Amazon. Savage simply

started looking for durable, inexpensive wrapping material that would be available immediately and in large quantities. "Our customers were not happy," says Savage. "It was not acceptable to tell parents, Oh, well, too bad."

She found rolls of plastic material like the type used in big garbage bags, and Amazon started overwrapping every large toy and a selection of electronics items that were likely to be Christmas gifts. How urgent was it? "I bugged people about it on an hourly basis until we got it resolved," says Savage. "You're either Santa Claus or you're not."

GREAT SERVICE: BACK TO THE FUTURE

I have a running argument with customer-service experts that may be mostly an argument on my side. It is neatly summed up by *One to One* guru Don Peppers. He offers two key points about service. First, "Service is bad because it's hard to do." Second, "The secret to good service, really, is to treat your customer like you'd like to be treated yourself." Somewhere between point one and point two, I missed the hard part.

The hard part is not the service. The hard part is everything *but* the service. The hard part is how companies think about what they are doing and how they behave as a result. Why is the service of airlines so bad? Simple: Airlines don't think of themselves as service organizations. Airlines think of themselves as factories that manufacture revenue-seat miles. Airlines have been tuned in to the efficiency of their manufacturing operations, not to the quality of the journey that they provide.

When you spend weeks talking to people about customer service, when you visit people who do it as their livelihood, it is easy to become consumed with the challenges, the technology, and the measurements that obsess the world of customer service.

How much cheaper is it to deliver balances by automated phone menu than through a service rep? How much cheaper is it to deliver balances on the Web than over the telephone? What do people want to talk to a person about? What do they want to do themselves?

How do you create customer satisfaction, customer delight, and customer ecstasy? Most of these questions miss the larger point.

Dan Leemon, forty-seven, chief strategy officer for Charles Schwab, understands this dilemma clearly. Charles Schwab is a brokerage firm, of course. It keeps money for people, has custody of stock certificates, and functions as a bank in many ways. But like Sprint PCS or directory assistance, Schwab is really a pure customer-service organization. Its specialty is financial-services customer service—but it's service all the same. Everything else is record keeping.

"A lot of companies fall into the trap," says Leemon, "of believing that some new customer-service technology will take cost and management burden away and will eliminate the need to have very talented people on the phones and in their retail outlets.

"That has actually never been true," he says. Indeed, the complex demands of customers have increased the length of the typical call to Schwab by 75 percent during the past five years.

One Old Economy sector that is justifiably famous for service is the cruise industry. The high-end cruise lines achieve this by offering training, incentives, and quality facilities. One thing that they do particularly well is suck up customer feedback.

Royal Caribbean Cruise Lines (RCCL), for instance, has twenty-two ships. When a ship docks at home port at 7 A.M., before it clears customs, someone from RCCL has boarded to retrieve the customer-comment cards distributed to every cabin. The ratings are tabulated, the written comments are transcribed, and the results are returned to the ship's managers before the ship sails again at 5 P.M.

So before the next cruise begins, RCCL's captains, dining-room managers, housekeepers, and entertainers know how the previous cruise went—from praise to serious problems. Imagine what flying the big airlines would be like if you got a comment card at the end of each flight—and the company acted on what it learned.

But here's the really interesting piece of the RCCL story. With computers, it's easy enough to tabulate comment-card results now in a single workday. But in 1971, when RCCL had just one ship and no computers, the process was the same. Cards were tabulated by hand the day the ship came in, and the comments were typed (four carbons) and delivered back to the ship before it sailed again in the afternoon.

Ultimately, what is so striking about the customer-service revolution that we are digging our way through is how little a century of technological innovation really changes what matters.